States and

States and Illegal Practices

Edited by
Josiah McC. Heyman

BERG
Oxford • New York

First published in 1999 by
Berg
Editorial offices:
150 Cowley Road, Oxford, OX4 1JJ, UK
70 Washington Square South, New York, NY 10012, USA

Berg is the imprint of Oxford International Publishers Ltd.

Library of Congress Cataloging-in-Publication Data

A catalogue record for this book is available from the Library of Congress

British Library Cataloguing-in-Publication Data

A catalogue record for this book is available from the British Library

ISBN 1 85973 257 7 (Cloth)
1 85973 262 3 (Paper)

Typeset by JS Typesetting, Wellingborough, Northants.
Printed in the United Kingdom by WBC Book Manufacturers, Mid Glamorgan.

Dedicated to Eric R. Wolf

Acknowledgements

This book started with a conference on States and Illegal Networks held at Tarrytown, New York, on 5–8 June 1997. The conference, and the book that has come from it, were supported by the Wenner-Gren Foundation for Anthropological Research. We thank the Foundation for its generous support. Claudio Lomnitz participated in the conference, but regrettably was not able to be part of the book. We benefited greatly from his paper and his incisive comments. In making this book a reality, the editor thanks the staff of Berg Publishers and the timely assistance of James Carrier.

Contents

–1–

States and Illegal Practices: An Overview

Josiah McC. Heyman and *Alan Smart*

State law inevitably creates its counterparts, zones of ambiguity and outright illegality. Criminal underworlds, pirates and brigands, black markets, illegal migrants, smugglers, protection rackets – these topics have a certain lurid, or perhaps defiant attraction. But they do not stand apart from the state, nor the state from them. Having grown in necessary connection, state law and evasion of state law must be studied together. Often, governments tolerate ostensibly forbidden activities; even, as Jane and Peter Schneider write in Chapter 6, 'deviated pieces of the state' ally with, or 'condition' illegal networks. Certainly the state does not always conspire with crime, but it is intriguing to inquire after the conditions under which governments and illegal practices enjoy some variety of symbiosis and those which result in greater or lesser degrees of conflict. Open-minded, empirical studies of state–illegality relations enable us to transcend the stultifying assumption that states always uphold the law. Indeed, our unusual combination of inquiries, by rejecting officialism in favor of analytical complexity, gives an angle of approach to states and state-level societies that is more productive than taking governments just at their face value.

Anthropology has changed from its predominant localism toward a concern with larger contexts and histories. In this transition, anthropologists have added important ideas, but handled them in rather abstract and reified fashions: inquiries about power, transnationalism and especially states. The joining of states and illegal practices is one instance of maturation, the deepening from labeling to analysis. Looking deeply, we view the state as complex, not unitary, and the state–society relationship as processual, not static. For example, what is legitimate in formal law, in real practices done in the name of the state and in the eyes of their populations differs substantially, and also changes. A richness and depth in our view of states is thereby gained. By attending to the implications of making certain actions or relations illegal, we also consider how power relations connect to moral and conceptual orders. When formal law does not prove to be the exclusive embodiment of morality, then (as Caroline Humphrey asks in Chapter 7) what competing *mores* do state actors and illegal networks mobilize? Topics such as these will interest readers beyond those who specialize in crime and governance; our prism casts light on questions shared among contemporary cultural anthropologists, historians, sociologists and other comparative social scientists.

The intersection between government and illegality is not only fascinating, it is also urgent. For example, international debate about bribery and governmental transparency is active as we write this introduction, and in places like Sicily, is headline news. Other pressing issues addressed in these chapters include new extensions of law into the control of the environment, as nations and global regimes take increasingly regulatory approaches to the use of nature. There are also discussions of the world trade in narcotics, and more generally the criminalization of a wide variety of practices, from fights between adolescents to labor migration, which increase the extent of policing, imprisonment and low-scale warfare (under the name of interdiction and eradication) that characterize the present moment. Finding balance in societal self-regulation is extraordinarily difficult, and we do not here offer policy prescriptions. Still, the characteristic interpenetration of official law and illegal practice revealed in our case studies does caution against the purely technical and massive application of criminalization and enforcement to suppress illegal practices. It is not merely that, as anthropologists and historians, we offer complicated but insightful case studies; it is that our general perspective emphasizes the incompleteness of formal states and the unlikelihood that they will entirely master their own and people's 'illegal' maneuvers.

Approaches to Illegality

Our intentions in this volume are those of serious but humble scholars. We fully recognize the varied and venerable character of studies of both states and illegality, and do not claim to supersede this body of knowledge, only to explore some less-known directions through an emphasis on rich case studies and comparison. Humility is even more necessary in this introduction, where we attempt to position our approach in relation to prior approaches and to suggest what new contributions are offered here. Fortunately, the chapters below provide considerable reference to these traditions, in anthropology, history and other disciplines, including jurisprudence. In this section, we will briefly review some of the main approaches to the study of illegality and identify some commonalities in the approach of the authors in this volume. In the next section, we will do the same for studies of states.

The dominant themes in the study of crime have been, and still are, based on either morality or policy. Philosophers debate whether law, hence what is illegal, is simply what the sovereign commands it to be (positive law) or if there are fundamental principles and rights upon which law must be based (natural law). Legal scholars argue over whether the law of itself embodies a rational philosophy or whether it is thoroughly embedded in society and economy (legal realism). Legal practitioners, politicians and members of the public argue about both what should be done and what will work. While some of the chapters touch on these issues (for example, Vásquez-León's discussion of 'bad law' in Chapter 8), our main interests center on how such moral and practical discourses influence efforts to suppress certain types of practices, what powerful actors intend when they promulgate criminal law and what are the consequences of criminalization, particularly when the suppression efforts fail.

Beyond these moral and practical approaches, other perspectives emphasize explanation more than prescription. Classical social theorists like Toennies and Durkheim saw crime as an indicator of more general problems of malaise or *anomie* resulting from the disintegration of traditional forms of social interaction and control and the accompanying dissociation between traditional values and modern structures. The elaboration of formal structures such as bureaucratic organization was necessary in order to maintain control, as informal processes of social control lost their efficacy in urban and industrial mass societies.

The main emphasis in theories of crime that developed in this tradition concerned how to explain deviant behavior. Immigrants and the lower classes were often seen as inadequately socialized into mainstream values, sometimes producing cross-generational cycles of poverty and deviance, still current in ideas of the underclass. Critiques of this approach from symbolic interactionists made two important contributions. First, the process of labeling individuals as 'criminals' or 'delinquents' had consequences for their subsequent treatment by representatives of the state as well as encouraging self-identification with the label. This reduced the conceptual separation between state and illegal actions: the actions of state officials were seen not only to suppress crime but also to encourage it under certain circumstances. Second, informal processes of influence through subcultures and peer networks were seen as offering legitimation for practices treated by the state as deviant and illegal, and the efficacy of state suppression efforts was seen as being undermined by informal socialization and the availability of techniques of neutralization that justified illegal acts because, for example, 'everybody is doing it' (Sullivan 1989 offers a superb review and reconceptualization of the criminological literature).

Critical theorists took the next step by questioning the rationale for the criminalization of certain activities. The differential treatment of white-collar crime and street crime was seen as an indication of shared values between representatives of the judicial system and the upper classes and a way of controlling the lower classes. Furthermore, this approach shredded the assumption in mainstream analyses that criminal networks and states were formal opposites. As generations of 'muckraking' journalists had done before them, critical social scientists like Block and Chambliss (1981: 7) emphasized the ways in which organized crime is inextricably linked to capitalism and stressed that it is 'that part of the business system operative in the illicit segment of American life' (Ianni 1972: 67). They concluded that there is an 'iron law of capitalism' that 'where there is a demand there will be a supplier if the profit is high enough' (Block and Chambliss 1981: 32).

Ironically, we find the same arguments in neoclassical economics applied to illegal transactions (Reuter 1983; Fiorentini and Peltzman 1995). These authors usefully see criminals as rational agents making economic choices when illegality heightens profit opportunities, or as immigrants and visible minorities find their opportunities blocked in conventional economic spheres. Furthermore, they have developed important accounts of the operation of corruption in governmental activity through the use of public choice theory. Peter Reuter's work exemplifies the strengths and limitations of the neoclassical approach. He encourages less attention than the critical school to power and more analysis of the intersection between self-interests and technology in the shaping of illegal markets (Reuter 1983: 2). The use of violence is subject to cost–benefit analysis, where in the context of a more powerful state violence has opportunity costs. A rational agent will prefer credible threats to the actual use of force. As a result, economies of scale in producing a reputation for delivering violence encourage centralization of dispute settlement activities in the equivalent of the mafia.

Alan Smart has criticized an assumption in both critical and neoclassical analyses of illegal markets, which he labeled the 'extensionist hypothesis': illegal markets are nothing more than normal markets in which entrepreneurs have been enticed by demand to overstep the bounds of the law in search of higher profits. Conventional markets ultimately rely on state support for property ownership and contracts. With illegal economic activities, where entrepreneurs cannot turn to the law for enforcement of their claims, the mechanisms that support illicit markets become a critical issue, but one that the extensionist hypothesis largely ignores. The mechanisms that support production and distribution of illegal goods and services are diverse, including trust within networks, threats of force, linking illicit deals with legal ones, the legitimacy of the transaction, the importance of reputation for illegal entrepreneurs and reliance on corrupt officials and institutions (Smart 1988).

Even where large profits would provide sufficient reason for persistent production and distribution of illegal goods, much more is involved. As LaMond Tullis (1995: 2) says in response to the question of how people are able to produce and traffic illegal drugs:

> One might suppose that the large amount of money made in servicing consumer demand is solely responsible. Surely, money and the power that goes with it account for trafficking and much production. But other answers must be found in society. These relate to how a society is structured, how political power is accrued and wielded within it, how economic policy is applied, how the economy performs, and how resistant the cultural fabric is to the use of public office for private gain.

Although demand for illegal goods and services creates opportunities for extremely high profits, whether and how these opportunities will be exploited may vary considerably. While market analyses offer important insights, without an accompanying theory of the state and of the political and social processes that may substitute for the legal basis of conventional market relations, we inevitably miss a great deal of the dynamics of concrete situations. Anthropologists, historians and other comparative social scientists are well-placed to explore these issues, as seen in the anthropology of law.

Most of the approaches outlined above were developed and implemented in the context of North America and Europe. Until recently, however, most anthropologists have conducted their research in non-Western contexts. The result has been a rather different trajectory of development in ideas about illegality and the state, tendencies encouraged by the methodological privileging of participant observation and ethnography in anthropology. Anthropologists began by trying to understand how social control was accomplished and maintained in stateless societies, or in small-scale states without written codes of law or elaborate bureaucracies. The emphasis on dispute resolution that followed encouraged attention to informal processes and their relationship with formal rules.

Social and political changes in the period after the Second World War resulted in new research on the incorporation of non-Western peoples into, first, colonies and, later, new independent nations that in most cases adopted their formal systems of law and administration from the colonial homeland. The persistence of other sets of ideas about legitimate and illegitimate actions, and their encouragement through ideas like the colonial practice of indirect rule, resulted in considerable attention to 'legal pluralism' (where more than one system of legal norms and procedures coexist) and to local understanding and reinterpretation of formal rules (Moore 1978). As anthropologists increasingly turned to research at home, the same tendencies of studying from the bottom up and attending to multiple sets of ideas and practices characterized this research (e.g., Merry 1990).

Legal pluralism was criticized for ignoring the power differentials between the different systems, and a variety of authors turned to examining the processes involved in the 'imposition' of law on other peoples through colonialism (Burman and Harrell-Bond 1979). The claim that a law or a legal system has been imposed upon a group implies three points: (1) the source of the law is external to that group; (2) the law is not legitimate in the view of that group; and (3) the law may not be in their interests. One problem with treating colonial law as being imposed is that is obscures the many instances in which individuals and groups took advantage of the new courts and rules to pursue goals that might not have been feasible with 'traditional' rules and dispute resolution procedures. More generally, it treats imposition of law as 'a *fait accompli* rather than an interactional process affected by power differentials' (Kidder 1979: 291). While colonial states clearly illustrate how law may be seen as illegitimate, we should not assume that precolonial institutions had a monopoly on legitimacy. One way of addressing these issues is through the Gramscian notion of hegemony. Hegemony can be defined as '*the "spontaneous" consent given by the great mass of the population to the general direction imposed on social life by the dominant fundamental group*' (Gramsci, quoted in Hunt 1993: 20).

Far from denoting a strategy of domination through the inculcation of false consciousness, Gramsci's concept of hegemony recognized that any ideology is a mixture of true and false beliefs and that the domination of the ruling class involves:

> an intricate interlocking of coercion and consent embodied in a wide range of social, political, and cultural forces . . . Accordingly, hegemony does not simply correspond to a formal and coherent 'ideological' system because it submits

> largely unconscious and taken-for-granted meanings, values, and practices – that is, culture itself – to asymmetrical relations of power (Gardiner 1992: 183).

The effectiveness of hegemony depends on the skill with which people's common sense can be drawn upon to support the perception of the naturalness and inevitability of the existing state of affairs. Legitimation is an outcome of struggles in both discursive and practical arenas, and criminalizing actions and relations is often a central move in such struggles. For example, making opium illegal in Canada has been plausibly held to have been part of political efforts to exclude and marginalize Chinese immigrants and to increase conflicts between them and native-born workers (Comack 1991). The encouragement of moral panics has often been used to set the public policy agenda and to delegitimate certain activities (see Chapter 9 by Sullivan and Miller). While the making of some laws may reflect hegemonic ploys, the persistence of illegalities and moralities opposed to state law tells us that hegemony is not a settled question. It is important to remember that we should not simply tell plausible stories about what function a legal intervention serves for the state or the ruling classes, but should uncover the processes by which the intervention came about and whether the consequences are planned. States and illegal practices offers important terrain for studying the complexity of power and 'common sense'.

For the same reason, states and illegal practices make the influential, but also rather totalistic, theories of Michel Foucault more open and ambiguous. His detailed accounts of the development and implementation of disciplinary technologies (especially Foucault 1977), and the conjunction between power and knowledge that supports them, have resulted in many new insights in legal anthropology (see, for example, Starr and Collier 1989). For Foucault, the state only exists through the 'assemblage of practices, techniques, programmes and so forth that facilitate intervention in civil society' (Murdoch and Ward 1997: 310). Suppressing activities relies on prior processes of law in which 'the objects of policy are problematized and rendered amenable to administration via particular forms of expertise and knowledge practices' (Murdoch and Ward 1997: 310), as Chapter 8 by Vásquez-León indicates. On both sides of the state/illegal practice nexus, practices are of central importance, and by highlighting the practices of knowledge and cooperation we hope to open up the debate on their interaction. Emphasizing practices and processes rather than rules or structures provides a space within which indeterminacy, ambiguity and double-dealing can be analyzed more clearly.

The subject of states and illegal practices thus stands at the center of current legal anthropology. It requires the insights of the systematic theorists of power, both imposed state laws (as in colonial situations) and more subtle, embodied hegemonies and practices. But it also retains anthropological threads, the awareness of the play of law on the ground, the persistence of plural or non-legal practices, the importance of particular historical states, class arrangements and cultural landscapes. It demands a very different starting-point from legal and policy formalism: recognizing that illegality does not necessarily mean that activities are illegitimate when there are incomplete hegemonies and partial, often compromised practices of the state. It uses the insights of the labeling, repressive and economic models of crime, but requires of them wider comparative range and hence stronger contextualization in history, society and culture. We therefore continue this introduction by presenting an overall temporal framework in which to consider the chapters; it helps explain why the rise of the powerful modern state does not eliminate illegality, and often stimulates it. We go on to explore issues raised in discussing Gramsci and Foucault, the coexistence of one view of law as perfect and definitive order and knowledge with another view of law as providing social resources of illegal practices and legal proceedings. We use that complex model of law as a launching point for considering the broader topic of state theory, which is usefully informed by recognizing the persistence and role of illegality. We close by considering the dilemmas of public moral choice brought on, we think informatively and realistically, by conjoining law and illegality, rather than keeping them at imaginary arm's length.

A Historical Framework

The chapters in this book range widely over space and time. They do, however, fit in a broad historical pattern that has seen increases in both the imposition of state law and overt illegality in the modern world system (1450–present). Undoubtedly, illegal practices as much as states are older than this. Nevertheless, the gradual emergence of the modern, interventive and well-funded state causes particularly interesting counter-developments in the arena of illegality. In the early modern era, states precipitated gradually from violent networks, and predation was a frequent step in the accumulation of capital (Lane 1975: 23; Tilly 1985). In this volume, Thomas Gallant (Chapter 2) systematizes the relationship of men of violence – bandits, pirates and racketeers – to the early modern state and economy. He challenges the idea that such men of violence were antecedent to, or in opposition and contrast to, nascent modernity. He shows instead how 'military entrepreneurs', in his terms, switched between legal and illegal positions in an overall state-building and accumulative process. Thus, the man who was an estate guard in one role, enforcing new property rights, was at other times a bandit, preying on booming rural commerce. He adopts a world-systems framework to compare men of violence in peripheries and semi-peripheries, providing an impressive framework for ordering the varied patterns of predation before 1800.

After that date, however, core states began to change the terms of illegality, with peripheral and semi-peripheral states gradually following their example. Gallant's chapter indicates relatively little concern with systematic legality before 1800: England's licenced privateers were Spain's pirates. After 1800, increasingly sophisticated capitalism sought consistent application of the rule of law to guarantee the predictability and enforceability of contracts for goods transactions, labor and property laws, etc. This more recent era also saw the rise of the firm and nation-state as definite organizational forms. These developments underwrote elaboration of the law, an increase in the direct governance by the state through law (as opposed to indirect use of military entrepreneurs) and ideologies that extended the contrast between legal and illegal throughout society. We see these processes in their most nascent form in David Nugent's case study (Chapter 3) of Peru around 1900. In conflicts between rival political coalitions (*castas*), the victorious side used its temporary possession of the law to persecute its rivals as 'illegal', a politics that reinforced the idea of the Peruvian state – as Nugent says, embodying 'state-level organization' – even as they made a shambles of the actual rule of law. In other work, Nugent (1994; 1997) has shown how subsequent regional movements strengthened the Peruvian state using ideals taken from, but in rebellion against, this crude early politics of legality.

Although the modern, capitalist era has seen the delineation of a functioning rule of law, the presence of legal formalism has not ended the ambiguous and the flat-out illegal; there is no reason to assume that the capacity of the state to command obedience is ever-rising, or that defiance of the law is a temporary result of inefficiency and misguided tactics in law enforcement. In Chapter 4, Alan Smart offers a rigorous model of why illegality 'persists'; our less systematic observations here point to the same conclusion: the modern state is not made up of law and order alone, but a complex web of the legal and illegal that justifies our enterprise. First, when states forbid things, or set up one official way to conduct affairs, they create alternative markets and opportunities for illegal goods and services. Second, formality is far too clumsy to be the way to conduct all affairs. Actors, both inside and outside ruling groups, utilize informal, extralegal approaches, such as the system of gifts and bribery Smart describes for China (also see Lomnitz 1988). Third, states are constantly in formation and decline; rarely, if ever, do they achieve sustained legal hegemony. The historical context of Humphrey's Chapter 7 about protection rackets is the formation and decline of the Soviet state and the emergence of the fragile post-1991 Russian state. Even the massive US state goes through reformation, as Sullivan and Miller (Chapter 9) point out. Fourth, classes associated with particular patterns of rule and law likewise rise and decline. The Schneiders here (Chapter 6) and in a 1994 article discover the class roots of the anti-mafia movement in new urban, educated professional (if not well-employed) Sicilians. Finally, the world system encompassing states is unequal and processual. As Alfred McCoy (Chapter 5) shows for the rise and fall of Khun Sa, a Burmese heroin warlord, the global narcotics trade recreates the military entrepreneurs, violent predation and primitive accumulation that Gallant (Chapter 2) analyzed for an earlier epoch.

Almost this entire list of factors is on display in Marcela Vásquez-León's study (Chapter 8) of shrimp fishing in Mexico's Gulf of California. Poor inshore fishermen illegally shrimp out of season, in restricted zones, selling their catch to *guatero* shrimp smugglers. Their illegal shrimping responds to specific governmental regulations that can only be understood with reference to the changed class politics of the Mexican state – it is abandoning its populist/corporatist past in favor of global investor-oriented politics, the so-called 'neo-liberal' model. Giant new trawlers owned by Mexican and international capitalists are over-shrimping the Gulf, causing a natural resource crisis whose 'solution' rests on the back of immiserated small shrimpers. Most broadly, the context for the new shrimping laws are global models of economic reform and environmental management. Chapter 8 portends a new theme in world illegality, the illegal transaction of natural resources, to add to well-known flows of people, narcotics, arms, money, etc.

Surveying the various reasons why illegality persists, we encounter a common theme: states are not the totalities that they claim to be. Scholars recently have contended that with postmodern capitalism the modern nation-state is dissolving, with that weakening its role as a model for a unified society and culture (see, for example, Kearney 1995). In one sense, we agree – the nation-state is incomplete, disunited, fractured. But from the perspective of our studies of illegal practices, states never were perfect, bounded (internally and externally), or complete. In their laws, they pretend to be complete (a pretense that has real consequences); but they have never succeeded and probably never will. This is important in understanding illegal practices in a world of states. The line between 'legal' and 'illegal' is held to be clear and definitive inside a given state, a hegemonic claim. Yet the actual practice is ambiguous and subject to resourceful manipulation. Legality and illegality are thus simultaneously black and white, and shades of gray. From this observation, we essay a distinctive approach to our subject.

States and Illegal Practices

By combining states and illegal practices into one topic rather than contrasting them, we seek to understand certain characteristic phenomena. We seek to understand, for example, why some states enforcing certain laws launch law-enforcement crusades, while others tolerate brazen illegality and even collaborate quite closely with criminals. Heyman explicitly considers the former pattern in Chapter 10 on the escalation of US immigration policing, and it can be seen as well in the chapters by Sullivan and Miller, Vásquez-León and McCoy (Chapters 9, 8, and 5); the latter pattern is the theme of Jane and Peter Schneider's chapter (Chapter 6), and illuminates also Chapters 7, 2, 3, 4, and 5 by Humphrey, Gallant, Nugent, Smart, and McCoy (again). If we think of repression and mutuality as two ends of a continuum, in a given historical and social context, what accounts for states coming to a particular place on this continuum with respect to a specific illegal practice? Our approach to that question informs our central contention about how to study states and illegal practices on the whole.

Let us begin by taking apart the idea of 'the legal'. Critical legal theorists, and the legal realists before them, hold that the law is not a definite system of rules (as legal positivists had held) but an indeterminate system of meanings manipulated in actual social practice (see the summary in Campbell 1993). The critical legal theorists go on to contend that the law in its particular social context is reified, appearing as if it were definitive, unimpeachable and logical. This serves well as a model for the state *vis-à-vis* illegal practices: the state appears to be the very embodiment of reified legality, while varied actors inside and around states maneuver actual legality and illegality in complex ways. A parallel reading is suggested by Gramsci's ideas of hegemony and struggle, and especially by E. P. Thompson's nuanced view of the law in the conclusion to his classic *Whigs and Hunters* (1975). Our perspective also draws on Philip Abrams' (1988) important article about studying states. He proposes that states be studied in two ways, as 'the state idea', akin to the idea of perfect law, and as the 'empirical state', messy politics that often involve illicit alliances. Given these two angles on law, ideology and practice, our approach is not simply demystification; both are important. The righteousness of law, the claim to be the essence of order and morality, offers a resource for political entrepreneurs when campaigning for heightened power (see Sullivan and Miller, Chapter 9, and Heyman, Chapter 10). In turn, the duly legal appearance of the state, its pedestrian formality, disguises the ambiguous dealings of its agents, as shown by the Schneiders (Chapter 6). The two perspectives taken together map out a powerful analytical and research strategy in the study of states and illegal practices.

In Chapter 3, Nugent raises important questions about our categories of state and society. He suggests that we avoid the assumption that society has a formal, perhaps moral, core zone formed of the social groups most closely associated with the legal state and a social and moral periphery of illegal groups and activities. He likewise cautions against reversing the moral weighting of this deceptive duality, by seeing the extralegal periphery as more resistant to the state and societal domination. These points fit our analytical thrust: empirical state actors and social groups range among various legal and extralegal practices, while groups near the core of state politics make claim to the illusion of proper legality. While highly tendentious, that claim is still effective, not least because it shoves opponents out to the imagined anti-legal margins. By distinguishing the two levels analytically, we avoid the pitfalls Nugent points out, while opening up new paths of inquiry. To illustrate the first such path, the study of reified legality *vis-à-vis* illegality, we turn to the important work of Mindie Lazarus-Black (1994).

She emphasizes the power of British family law in codifying 'proper' kinship practices in contrast to informal, extralegal kinship in Antigua and Barbuda. Rather than law's being simply imposed on culture, law partly makes culture over time, struggling with popular practices because of its particular ranked position in colonial politics and society. Her study, converging with our own authors, suggests three main inquiries about ideological legality. First, when did key social and political actors crystallize a vision of 'true' legality in the polity as a whole? (This fits with a broader concern about state formation and transformation.) What was its specific content, especially *vis-à-vis* stigmatized 'illegal' margins? If indeterminate law is 'reified', what propositions concretely are reified, versus suppressed? And how does it persist over time, giving due attention to changing uses, reinterpretations, etc.? Second, which groups or political coalitions are the social bearers of ideological legality in a particular period? Are some group or another reified as the putative bearers of illegality? Third, how efficacious are the reifications of law? In Chapter 7, Caroline Humphrey outlines the very different propositions of Soviet law and criminal mores, and traces the declining legitimacy of Soviet law versus the rising legitimacy of the 'thieves' law'. As visions of law, they competed directly, even if in reality there were important alliances (major politicians, for example, are the 'roofs' that shelter various protection rackets).

Just as we view reified law and order as a contingent social claim, not an essence, we view illegal practices not as a category of abnormal behaviors, and especially not as the subculture of a stigmatized group, but rather as an option, a resource, that diverse groups use at varied times. A good illustration, much like Abrams' empirical state process, is Smart's description (Chapter 4) of various social-political moves in China involving gift-giving and bribery. (Our language does not imply that illegality is always a voluntary, conscious choice; instead, we speak of illegality as a position or stance in a typical social field within the modern state. From our point of view, intense, idealized legality and routine formality are as much contingent stances as routine informality and outright illegality.) What are the potential values of acting outside the law? Here we offer some research questions, with the understanding that particular options to go outside the law are necessarily historical and circumstantial.

First, who are the actors? Illegal practices are not the monopoly of criminal elements, but rather various kinds of illegality, such as black markets, bribery and undocumented capital flows, are options taken up by identifiable classes, regional groups, ethnic groups, etc. at distinctive times. Unlike what happens in the deviance/group subculture theories outlined above, groups involved in crimes are not isolates but act always in field of relations – class relations, relations to the state, relations to natural resources, etc. Hence the second question is: what is the significance in societal relations (including state–society relations) of taking a distinctly illegal stance? What are the advantages of illegal incomes, forms of enforcement without formal contracts, etc.? Third, to research the various stances of state agents *vis-à-vis* both legal and illegal practices – assuming now that we are not talking about a perfect state but a realistic one that tolerates some illegality – we need to inquire into the complexity within states. Finally, in keeping with the question of complexity inside states, we also need to inquire into illegal flows and transactions between states. We use Jane and Peter Schneider's Chapter 6 on the Italian state and the Sicilian mafia to illustrate these inquiries. They use an unusual period of 'transparency' to document the links between the mafia, the local landed elite and their urban relatives (including some judges), rogue financiers, the masons, 'deviated pieces of the state', and the world narcotics trade. The illegal option clearly had its advantages to all concerned, offering large amounts of liquid, unaccountable cash and a political structure suited to the repressive duties of the Cold War era. Equally illustrative is the denouement of the Schneiders' story, when new classes in urban Sicily lacking the older regional and global commitments ruptured the pact of toleration of the mafia.

Our aim, above all, is not to separate empirical legality/illegality and ideological legality; it is to understand how the two processes interlock. This is best illustrated by an example. Formality often serves transactions because contracts can be enforced, even between nations. But one value of the illegal position is that liquid flows of money and arms cannot easily be traced. In the 1980s, the US government sold arms to Iran and used the unaccountable monies to support the counter-revolutionaries in Nicaragua, for whom overt support had been restricted by Congress. Interestingly, significant proportions of the illegal money and arms were diverted by middlemen, against whom no formal sanctions could be applied since officially they did not exist. At the same time, in the ideological language of law the US government loudly proclaimed a boycott of formal transactions with Iran (for example, forbidding the purchase of oil by US firms); this position served interests of the government both domestically and in the Middle East. The contradiction between the legal façade and the illegal option was penetrated, if incompletely, after the latter was accidently exposed, evidence of the continuing importance of legality in the US polity (see Walsh 1994). The Schneiders make an important argument that applies here: in historical moments of 'transparency', it becomes possible to see the weaving together of illegality and legality within states and societies that is usually obscured by reification of the 'law'. While we accept their point that transparency occurs in specific historical circumstances (such as the end of the Cold War), we hold that a research strategy that combines awareness of empirical illegality and legality inside and between states, with an understanding of both the presence and the mystifications of ideological law, can approximate the clarity of transparent moments. This synthetic approach also responds to the concerns about, as well as potentials of, Gramscian and Foucauldian styles of legal and political anthropology; it recognizes the hegemonic character of reified law while leaving room for struggle, persistence and process in actual uses of law.

Our approach offers distinct messages for how to study states. The emphasis on the positional character of legality and illegality works against state theories 'from above', ones that see the state and the law as relatively unproblematic apparatuses to enact policies whose determination is the only really important question. Formal theories of the state often overstress their omniscience and omnipotence, particularly in instrumentalist, elitist and structuralist approaches (on schools of state theory, see Jessop 1982 and Block 1987). Such approaches tend to take the reified law for the entire reality. They also emphasize the unity of the state relative to its internal and external actors. As Smart writes in Chapter 4, 'states are internally complex and composed of many agents. It is inappropriate to refer to states doing or intending things.' Finally, how much capacity states actually have to pursue goals (as posited by various state theories) is an open question (Migdal 1988). Illegal practices are particularly helpful in probing the edges of and lacunae in state capacities, as in the question of how state capacities are heightened or constrained by the illegal collusion of state agents and subjects (see Lees 1986). It is evident that acts such as tax avoidance and draft evasion (Adas 1981; Scott 1985: 30–31, 272) weaken state capacities, but a more interesting feature of this volume are the instances when the revenue from and control of illegality strengthens states (a point emphasized in Chapter 2 by Gallant, for example).

The approach that we sketch here requires that states be viewed 'from below' and 'from within' as much as 'from above'. Viewing states and illegal practices from below and within emphasizes the complicated processes of enacting actual laws, policies, justice systems, etc. in relation to stubborn social and regional groups. (For an extended discussion of these approaches to the state, see Heyman 1998.) One point merits particular emphasis. The empirical state consists not only of rulers and major policies or 'styles', but also various posts, bureaucracies, regions, etc. In the day-to-day engagement with illegal practices, state workers (Heyman 1995) are particularly important. They make the arrests, receive the bribes, and bend the formal law to fit the actual decisions and conditions imposed from on high. Sullivan and Miller (Chapter 9) describe the differing (but mutually reinforcing) ways that school bureaucrats, police and local politicians criminalize urban US teenagers. Heyman (Chapter 10) draws analogies between the work of soldiers in Vietnam and the armed law enforcement officers in drug and immigration 'wars', seeking to characterize an important US experience, the alienated, militarized bureaucrat thrown into unwelcoming terrain. Vásquez-León (Chapter 8) poignantly describes the dilemmas of a Mexican government scientist, squeezed by the alliance of the central government and powerful capitalist fisheries either to violate his science or quit his job.

In making these points, we do not dismiss the value of state theory as it has developed in the recent social sciences. Indeed, the authors here constantly draw on it, implicitly or explicitly. Different state theories at various times describe the phenomena we encounter, so that we do not insist on any one approach. Because of our subject-matter, however, we tend to encounter state actors involved 'where they should not be', in illegal or quasi-illegal relationships, and we find that instrumentalist theories often help us understand such situations. Instrumentalist approaches see state institutions as tools utilized by elites or representatives of the ruling classes (see Domhoff 1990). Such approaches have been too casually dismissed as explanations based on conspiracies. As many cases in this volume attest (the Schneiders on Sicily, Humphrey on Russia, Nugent on Peru, McCoy on the heroin trade, Vásquez-León on Mexico, etc.), conspiracies exist; and some have substantial impact. In Chapter 4, Smart formalizes these insights about state rulers. Using Margaret Levi's (1988) theory of predatory rule, he models how state rulers conspire with, tolerate, or turn against illegal practices. While his model has some limitations in its treatment of ideology, it focuses attention simultaneously on the divisions between rulers and agents and on the limitations constantly besetting empirical state action. His model offers a way to make sense of otherwise confusing situations, and will certainly stimulate new research into states and illegal practices.

Heyman's Chapter 10 also uses a fairly instrumental version of state theory, emphasizing the actions (and responsibilities) of US state elites in Vietnam and on the current US–Mexico border. Yet his concern is not conspiracy with illegal actors, but its opposite: massive crusades of force. He diagnoses a characteristic US pattern of escalation, once seen in the Vietnam War and now in militarized border interdiction of immigrants and narcotics. His explanatory model is complex and illustrates many of the angles we outline above. It involves the political role of contradictions between idealized law and illegal realities (for instance, political embarrassment leading to moral crusades), the interests and understandings of state workers (as contrasted to, but in coordination with, state elites), and the ability of defiant actors to frustrate states, even the most powerful ones.

Our approach to the state is, finally, geopolitical and transnational. Many chapters involve multiple states or global processes (Gallant, Schneider and Schneider, Humphrey, Vásquez-León); here we focus on McCoy's narrative history of Khun Sa, the king of heroin (Chapter 5). Obviously profiting from international illegal commerce, Khun Sa built his career on the internal ethnic fractures of the Burmese state. More importantly, Khun Sa was allowed to rise to power because of the Thai military. Thailand supported small armed client states on its borders to increase its own power and security. Khun Sa took the opportunity to build a Shan state with over 20,000 armed men, missiles, a capital city, etc. However, needing a new supply of water that lay in his unofficial territory, the Thai government turned against the warlord, allowing the Burmese military to force his surrender. The episode had global impacts, reviving the world trade in heroin in the late 1980s and the 1990s; though Khun Sa fell, other regions and ethnic lords rose to replace him (on the earlier geopolitics of heroin, see McCoy 1991). The southeast Asian history also demonstrates, as do other chapters, that states are fractured internally by regionalism and sectionalism, as well as diverse externally. The particularly complex geography of highland southeast Asia shaped a variety of opportunities for illegal networks to grow. The question then presents itself: what shapes, what social organizations do illegal practices take in their particular political and geographic environments?

Inquiring about Illegal Practices

The conference from which this book grew was titled 'States and Illegal Networks'. The designation 'illegal networks' has been useful to several authors, and some retain it, though for the book as a whole we replaced it with 'illegal practices' to provide a more general and encompassing term. Illegal networks specifically indicates an ordered web of people centered on an illegal activity, and implies (though it does not necessarily require – see Nugent in Chapter 3) an alternative social world to the formal, legal state. Illegal practices are wider; they may include illegal conduct in everyday life, such as proscribed sexual or religious orientations, or tax avoidance, which may be widespread in a population that is otherwise relatively aligned with a state. Nevertheless, there is a kernel of insight in the phrasing 'illegal networks' that is missing from the looser 'illegal practices'. Networks rest on the human capacity for mutuality, trust and exchange in relationships. Illegal practices, because they are require some discretion and cannot be enforced contractually, emphasize the very qualities mobilized in networks (Smart 1988). Therefore, illegality, along with secrecy, tends to form itself into network types of organization.

This observation led us to one of the major questions of the conference: what are the characteristic social organizations of illegality? In particular, we ask how the political economies and geographies of states shape the social organization of illegal practices, rather than trying to systematize types of illegal organization in themselves (a comparative exercise that would be very helpful). For example, in interstices between strong state areas, but with connections to the world economy and perhaps to sponsoring states, we expect to see warlords such as Khun Sa (McCoy in Chapter 5). The peripheral regions that Gallant analyzes gave rise to similar 'military entrepreneurs' and the weak, formative Peruvian state permitted state-like *castas* (Nugent in Chapter 3). Inside effective states, however, such rival political domains are quashed; in fact, this was an important step in Gallant's story of state formation. In that situation, one form of illegality is described by Humphrey in Chapter 7 as 'alternative foci of predation' – alternative to the taxation cum violence capacity of the state, that is.

Alternative foci deliver violence and protection from violence (better than the state in some arenas and regions) as their key tactic (i.e., even when their direct enterprise is something else, such as narcotics smuggling). In some places and times, alternative foci are hierarchical and tightly-organized, such as the Sicilian mafia (Schneider and Schneider in Chapter 6) and Russian protection rackets (Humphrey in Chapter 7). In other cases, these illegal networks are hierarchical but have a smaller and more fragmented form, such as the shrimp black marketeers (Vásquez-León in Chapter 8) and the US–Mexican border smugglers of immigrants (Heyman in Chapter 10). Perhaps we can think of these as resembling firms, oligopolistic versus fractured, as opposed to the near-state forms of warlords and *castas*. But unlike overt firms, which can rely on the force of law, these groupings require violence independent of the government's. In these cases, illegality has (at most) incomplete legitimacy in society, so that specialized groups and quasi-groups are required to insulate and conduct the practices.

Such is not the case for the sets of activities that Smart diagnoses as having widespread legitimacy, even when illegal. One such organization, archetypical in the literature, is the informal sector, which often involves illegal practices required for the livelihood, housing, etc. of large populations. The specifically illegal character of some cases of the informal sector is highlighted by Vásquez-León in Chapter 8 and in her 1994 article, as well as by Smart's (1988) analysis of Hong Kong housing markets. The loose boundaries between legality and illegality do not just exist for the poor and marginal, however, as Smart's Chapter 4 demonstrates; middle classes and the rich dabble in illegal practices also.

The more formal and the more informal social organizations of illegality do not stand apart from each other, but rather illegality mutates between them according to opportunity and temporal development. Sullivan and Miller (Chapter 9) describe young teen violence channeled in disorderly and predatory ways by institutional spaces, such as schools. Various state actors with diverse interests, including school officials, police, juvenile justice officials and local politicians, label young teens in ways that affect their further development. Some, as they get older, join more organized foci of theft and predation. This adolescent transition to criminal careers varies according to the particular geography of labor and goods markets, legitimate networks (or their absence) and government jobs, as demonstrated by Sullivan's powerful comparative anthropology of Brooklyn neighborhoods (Chapter 9 here and Sullivan 1989). The broadest context is the overall US pattern of removing social redistribution and criminalizing the response. In delineating this particular case, Sullivan and Miller offer a strong demonstration of how states and political economy shape the social organization of illegal actors who appear, on the surface, to be dropping out of official control.

Hence, what is distinctive about our approach is that we do not isolate ethnography of the 'illegal' as a deviant subculture in the anthropological tradition of studying the strange and marginal, but rather we offer, as both agenda and specific examples, ethnography of illegal networks contextualized in arenas like pieces of the state, legal and illegal positions in society as a whole and the ideology of the law. As we have noted, the very fact of having to operate outside the predictability and enforceability of the law leads to specific social and cultural patterns in illegal markets (Smart 1988). Lazarus-Black (1994) also demonstrates how 'illegal' culture emerges precisely as an alternative to legally-mandated culture. Our authors are very interested in viewing cultural practices in the context of state law, two examples being legitimacy and secrecy/openness.

We broached the topic of legitimacy above. As we pointed out, in the reified view, legitimacy always rests with the law and never with crime or illegality. Yet black markets, bribery, illegal migration, protection by racketeers, etc. are accorded considerable real legitimacy, sometimes by segments of society and sometimes by society as a whole. Elizabeth Leeds (1996) offers a penetrating study of how drug traffickers gain more legitimacy than the Brazilian government in the poor neighborhoods of Rio de Janeiro. In this book, Humphrey (Chapter 7) shows how criminals in the Soviet Union, and later Russia, constructed alternative moral codes, quite deliberately contrasting them with those of the Soviet state. Her rich account details how specific criminal *mores* emerged in Soviet prisons, and how they were then elaborated and applied as criminal networks spread through Soviet and post-Soviet society. At the end, she considers whether criminal *mores* are a source of new legitimacies in post-Soviet Russia. The chapter deftly balances two perspectives on illegality, the market logic of illegal opportunities that de-emphasizes context in favor of rational calculations, and the historical and cultural history of Russian criminals that emphasizes particular contexts and patterns; combining the two is more promising than using either analytical angle alone.

Like legitimacy and illegitimacy, the authors identify secrecy and openness as important points of inquiry. It is normal to expect secrecy of illegal practices and openness of governance and the state; we find it especially interesting to note zones of secrecy in the state and openness in illegality. In general, this inversion is a case of the opening up of illegality to rational analysis (not neo-classical economic analysis *per se*, however). Social scientists, as with people at large, use relatively unloaded terms in the legal sphere, but take up a moral discourse as soon as they enter the topic of illegal activities. Morality is important; but jumping right to morality prevents us from using strong analytical terms, such as firm, entrepreneur, government intervention, etc., to understand more about illegal practices and the people associated with them. In general, the order and balance of moral and amoral analyses has not been well defined for the social sciences, and the case of states and illegal practices makes this glaringly obvious.

A Moral of the Story?

The authors in this book generally approach their material in a descriptive and analytical fashion, rather than advocating public positions. In several cases, however, the public arguments are clear. Vásquez-León in Chapter 8 proposes the idea of a bad law, a law that does not effectively guide behavior, but rather creates illegality by forcing desperately poor small fishermen to break regulations and to sell on the black market. She likewise posits the concept of bad science, implying that relatively objective science is distorted by powerful greed to legitimize bad laws. Heyman's arguments about escalation (Chapter 10) likewise suggest that adding enforcement in certain situations causes more violence and harm than it prevents, and he criticizes the tendency of the US government to use this approach. A number of other chapters also imply this criticism: laws that lack effective legitimacy and demand force without societal support simply increase illegality, with all the negative effects that come after it, including internal violence, predation, covert worlds, rogue finance, etc.

It might seem, in this critical stance, that we are not distinguishing between legal and illegal, prudent and harmful, right and wrong. Indeed, we make much of the continuing social and political presence of illegality, its links into the states that seemingly banish such acts and actors, and thus we may appear to be saying that illegality is (a) normal and (b) acceptable. At times we argue the first, though that is an empirical matter; but the second implication is not our point. We find the following a better formulation. Much illegality is dangerous, and much legality is reasonable. Both financial fraud and physical violence should be prohibited, prosecuted and punished. The mere fact that illegality persists and often interweaves with the legal, formal world does not justify a purely relativist stance. Likewise, though the state is an instrument of organized force and predation (taxation), in so far as it embodies these reasonable elements of law, it is not entirely equivalent to illegal force and predation. However, we cannot sustain the converse, that everything the formal state does is morally efficacious, and that all illegal activities are immoral and should be quashed. This does not hold either in an empirical sense, as our multitude of examples shows, or in a moral sense. In the latter instance, many illegal-labeled activities have much legitimate life in society (or in particular groups), and under such circumstances the state response constitutes bad law, adding to illegality and persecution, including 'wars' of various sorts, that are morally worse than the original violation. Careful work by scholars, transcending the assumption that all formal law is good and that all illegality is a 'problem' to be eliminated, sorting out the particular balance in each case, can help inform the public moral choices we must make.

References

Abrams, Philip (1988), 'Notes on the Difficulty of Studying the State', *Journal of Historical Sociology* 1: 58–89.

Adas, Michael (1981), 'From Avoidance to Confrontation: Peasant Protest in Precolonial and Colonial Southeast Asia', *Comparative Studies in Society and History* 23: 217–47.

Block, Fred (1987), *Revising State Theory: Essays in Politics and Post-industrialism*. Philadelphia: Temple University Press.

Block, A. A., and W. J. Chambliss (1981), *Organizing Crime*. New York: Elsevier.

Burman, Sandra B., and Barbara E. Harrell-Bond, eds (1979), *The Imposition of Law.* New York: Academic Press.

Campbell, Tom D. (1993), 'Legal Studies', in Robert E. Goodin and Philip Pettit (eds), *A Companion to Contemporary Political Philosophy.* Oxford: Basil Blackwell, pp. 183–211.

Comack, Elizabeth (1991), '"We will get some good out of this riot yet": The Canadian State, Drug Legislation, and Class Conflict', in Elizabeth

Comack and Stephen Brickey (eds) *The Social Basis of Law*. Halifax: Garamond Press, pp. 48–70.

Domhoff, G. William (1990), *The Power Elite and the State: How Policy is Made in America*. Hawthorne, NY: Aldine.

Fiorentini, G., and S. Peltzman (1995), *The Economics of Organised Crime*. Cambridge, UK: Cambridge University Press.

Foucault, Michel (1977), *Discipline and Punish: The Birth of the Prison*. New York: Random House.

Gardiner, Michael (1992), *The Dialogics of Critique: M. M. Bakhtin and the Theory of Ideology*. London: Routledge.

Heyman, Josiah McC. (1995), 'Putting Power in the Anthropology of Bureaucracy: The Immigration and Naturalization Service at the Mexico–United States Border', *Current Anthropology* 36: 261–87.

—— (1998), 'Immigration Law Enforcement and the Superexploitation of Undocumented Aliens: The Mexico–United States Border Case', *Critique of Anthropology*, 18: 157–80.

Hunt, Alan (1993), *Explorations in Law and Society*. New York: Routledge.

Ianni, J. J. (1972), *A Family Business: Kinship and Social Control in Organized Crime*. Mentor: New York.

Jessop, Bob (1982), *The Capitalist State*. New York: New York University Press.

Kearney, Michael (1995), 'The Local and the Global: The Anthropology of Globalization and Transnationalism', *Annual Review of Anthropology* 24: 547–66.

Kidder, Robert L. (1979), 'Toward an Integrated Theory of Imposed Law', in Sandra B. Burman and Barbara Harrell-Bond (eds), *The Imposition of Law*. New York: Academic Press, pp. 289–306.

Lane, Frederic (1975), *Venice: A Maritime Republic*. Baltimore: The Johns Hopkins University Press.

Lazarus-Black, Mindie (1994), *Legitimate Acts and Illegal Encounters: Law and Society in Antigua and Barbuda*. Washington, DC: Smithsonian Institution Press.

Leeds, Elizabeth (1996), 'Cocaine and Parallel Polities in the Brazilian Urban Periphery: Constraints on Local-Level Democratization', *Latin American Research Review* 31(3): 47–84.

Lees, Susan H. (1986), 'Coping with Bureaucracy: Survival Strategies in Irrigated Agriculture', *American Anthropologist* 88: 610–22.

Levi, Margaret (1988), *Of Rule and Revenue*. Berkeley and Los Angeles: University of California Press.

Lomnitz, Larissa Adler (1988), 'Informal Exchange Networks in Formal

Systems: A Theoretical Model', *American Anthropologist* 90: 42–55.
McCoy, Alfred W. (1991), *The Politics of Heroin: CIA Complicity in the Global Drug Trade*. Brooklyn: Lawrence and Hill.
Merry, Sally Engle (1990), *Getting Justice and Getting Even: Legal Consciousness Among Working-Class Americans*. Chicago: University of Chicago Press.
Migdal, Joel S. (1988), *Strong Societies and Weak States: State–Society Relations and State Capabilities in the Third World*. Princeton, NJ: Princeton University Press.
Moore, Sally Falk (1978), *Law as Process: An Anthropological Approach*. London: Routledge & Kegan Paul.
Murdoch, Jonathan, and Neil Ward (1997), 'Governmentality and Territoriality: The Statistical Manufacture of Britain's "National Farm"', *Political Geography* 16: 307–24.
Nugent, David (1994), 'Building the State, Making the Nation: The Bases and Limits of State Centralization in "Modern Peru"', *American Anthropologist* 96: 333–69.
—— (1997), *Modernity at the Edge of Empire: State, Individual, and Nation in the Northern Peruvian Andes, 1885–1935*. Stanford, CA: Stanford University Press.
Reuter, Peter (1983), *Disorganized Crime: The Economics of the Visible Hand*. Cambridge, MA: MIT Press.
Schneider, Jane, and Peter Schneider (1994), 'Mafia, Antimafia, and the Question of Sicilian Culture', *Politics and Society* 22: 237–58.
Scott, James C. (1985), *Weapons of the Weak: Everyday Forms of Peasant Resistance*. New Haven: Yale University Press.
Smart, Alan (1988), 'The Informal Regulation of Illegal Economic Activities: Comparisons Between the Squatter Property Market and Organized Crime', *International Journal of the Sociology of Law* 16: 91–101.
Starr, June, and Jane F. Collier, eds (1989), *History and Power in the Study of Law: New Directions in Legal Anthropology*. Ithaca, NY: Cornell University Press.
Sullivan, Mercer L. (1989), *"Getting Paid": Youth Crime and Work in the Inner City*. Ithaca, NY: Cornell University Press.
Thompson, E. P. (1975), *Whigs and Hunters: The Origin of the Black Act*. New York: Pantheon.
Tilly, Charles (1985), 'War Making and State Making as Organized Crime', in Peter Evans, Dietrich Rueschemeyer, and Theda Skocpol (eds), *Bringing the State Back In*. Cambridge, UK: Cambridge University Press, pp. 169–91.

Tullis, LaMond (1995), *Unintended Consequences: Illegal Drugs and Drug Policies in Nine Countries*. Boulder, CO: Lynne Reiner.

Vásquez-León, Marcela (1994), 'Avoidance Strategies and Governmental Rigidity: The Case of the Small-Scale Shrimp Fishery in Two Mexican Communities', *Journal of Political Ecology* 1: 67–83.

Walsh, Lawrence E. (1994), *Iran–Contra: The Final Report*. New York: Times Books.

–2–

Brigandage, Piracy, Capitalism, and State-Formation: Transnational Crime from a Historical World-Systems Perspective

Thomas W. Gallant

Depictions of the archetypal bandit resplendently adorned with gold and silver and accessorized with an outrageous array of weapons or the black eye-patched visage of a ruthless buccaneer are images that seemingly evoke earlier times and exotic places. Folklore and popular media have preserved those images for us as romantic figures whose actions and attitudes stand as the antithesis to the modern world with its developed capitalist economies and powerful, bureaucratized nation-states. Many scholars have followed suit in seeing brigands and pirates as products of preindustrial peasant societies; they appear in these accounts as archaic warriors fighting a rearguard action against the encroachment of the modern world. Rather than being antithetical to a world organized into nation-states and dominated by capitalist economic relations, however, military entrepreneurs, bandits and pirates are integral parts of it, and have been since the sixteenth century. Through an examination of brigandage and piracy from around the globe over the last three hundred years I demonstrate that illegal networks of armed predators played a crucial role in the spread and global triumph of capitalism. Furthermore, I show that bandits and pirates were deeply insinuated in the processes of state formation and state consolidation of power; in addition, these groups have continued to play extremely important roles in the ongoing process of state centralization. Put simply, bandits helped make states, and states made bandits. The history of brigands and buccaneers demonstrates the complexity of the relationships between states and society's men of arms over which of them wields coercive violence legitimately. Inlaw or outlaw, border guard or bandit, privateer or pirate were labels applied by the state, and depending on the designation chosen, the activities of those groups were thus deemed either legal or illegal. If the former was chosen, these men were patriots and defenders of the state; if the latter, then they became the scourges of the nation, whose eradication became a national priority. Since banditry and piracy are directly related to the processes that created the modern world-system, it should occasion no surprise that they appeared at various times and in different places in the past and that they will continue to reappear wherever the conditions, to be discussed in detail, that allow them to flourish develop (Faison 1997).

Bandit studies has two founding fathers: Fernand Braudel, whose 1947 article and magnum opus on the Mediterranean defined brigandage and piracy as crucial elements of the Mediterranean during the early modern period (Braudel 1947; 1972), and Eric Hobsbawm, whose *Bandits* (Hobsbawm 1981) set the study of bandits on a new and exciting course. His provocative thesis regarding the social bandit and his relationship to pre-modern forms of protest and rebellion provoked much comment. The field has grown immensely over the last two decades, but unfortunately too much time has been spent debating the pros and cons of Hobsbawm's social bandit model and too little on analyzing the wider phenomenon of brigandage and piracy both cross-culturally and within specific cultures. I share in this regard Gilbert Joseph's main line of attack in his recent assessment of bandit studies in Latin America (Joseph 1990; see, however, the comments by Slatta 1990, Birbeck 1990 and Singleman 1990); the social versus anti-social bandit debate generated more heat than light and has now grown even more intellectually stale. As Hobsbawm himself noted in his last discussion of the topic, the time has come to move on to more detailed comparative studies of banditry (Hobsbawm 1986).

Such a shift, however, is insufficient. Other, more significant limitations were at play. So long as the target of inquiry was banditry historians and anthropologists limited themselves to exploring only one facet of a much more complex process. As soon as the term "bandit" was applied, inquiry was restricted only to those armed predators who operated outside the law. The word 'bandit' itself is derived from the Italian verb 'bandire', meaning to exile or banish, and thus at its root a bandit is a man who has been barred from normal society. Yet, as this chapter and most of the studies cited in it show, the same men who at some points in their lives were bandits often operated at times inside the law as well. But a legal bandit is an oxymoron. By definition a bandit stands outside the law. In order to better understand the historical importance of these men, usually labeled only as 'bandits', we require a new conceptual framework that captures the ambiguity of their relationship to the law. I suggest that the term *military entrepreneur* can satisfy this need. By 'military entrepreneur'

I refer to a category of men who take up arms and who wield violence or the threat of violence as their stock in trade. I use 'military' here not in its contemporary common connotation of a national army, but in an older, more ambiguous form referring only to the use of arms and weapons. They are entrepreneurs in the sense that they are purveyors of a commodity – violence. They may act in the employ of others or as agents in their own right. The value of the concept is that it delineates a discrete set of historical actors while not restricting inquiry to only limited aspects of their activities. All bandits were military entrepreneurs, but not all military entrepreneurs were bandits. Moreover, the historical significance of the activities of the armed predators discussed in this article was probably greater when they operated in the interstice between legality and illegality. By conceptualizing them as military entrepreneurs we can better grasp the ambiguity of their actions.

A couple of other preliminary comments seem in order. First, as in any study that attempts to discuss a phenomenon over three hundred years of history, and that draws on examples from every corner of the globe, my analysis of any single case can be superficial at best. But what is lost in the details is compensated for by the clarity evident in the larger picture. Patterns of relationship that recur over time and space are undoubtedly the ones likely to reveal to us the most significant and important social, political and economic factors behind endemic and epidemic banditry and piracy. Second, I have separated an examination of the economic aspects of banditry from a discussion of its political context. This distinction is artificial. The political, the economic, and the socio-cultural aspects are closely intertwined, and elements from all contribute to the formation of the conditions that allow brigandage and piracy to flourish. I have focused on the first two and not so much the third of these aspects, not because I consider the political and the economic more important than the socio-cultural, but because at the scale at which this analysis is pitched, recurring patterns of relationship are more easily discerned between them and the range of variation is less than with culture.

Military Entrepreneurs and the World Economy

Bandits and pirates stole. By definition, they expropriated goods and commodities illegally. Nevertheless, even this seemingly straightforward proposition is not without its difficulties once we move beyond the labels. Depending on the context and on which historical actor's viewpoint we adopt, the identical depredations by the same men could be and were considered legitimate by some and illegitimate by others. One state's pirate was another state's privateer. And when it came to opening their household larders to outsiders, it made little difference to peasants and rural laborers whether the open-palmed claimant was the taxman or an extortionist brigand. Both made questionable claims on scarce resources. The discussion of the economics of military entrepreneurship has not proceeded far. Other than the rather obvious point made above, the main focus of attention has been on the stage of economic development at which endemic and epidemic banditry appear. In his initial formulation, Hobsbawm argued that banditry developed in social systems constituted by a traditional peasantry and in a precapitalist, preindustrial economic environment. He noted further that it was at the point of transition from the old to the new that banditry often became most prominent (Hobsbawm 1972; Hobsbawm 1981; Hobsbawm 1986). Pat O'Malley has been Hobsbawm's most vocal critic on this point. In a series of articles focusing on nineteenth-century Australia, eighteenth-century England, and the United States in the post-Civil War era, he showed that banditry became a feature of socio-economic systems that were neither precapitalist nor based on a traditional peasantry (O'Malley 1979a, b, 1980, 1983). Others have leveled a similar charge.

Military Entrepreneurs and the Economic World System

The 'social bandit debate' provides little insight into economic importance of military entrepreneurs because of the crudeness of the categories both sides employ. Precapitalist versus capitalist, or preindustrial versus industrial are simply too broad and encompass too much variation to reconstruct meaningfully the economic contexts that enable military entrepreneurs to develop and flourish, and they suggest a historical periodization that is incapable of explaining why this phenomenon recurs after the ascendancy of capitalism and industrialization. The application of a world-system framework is more useful. First, it proposes more precise categories of development, rather than just a simple dichotomy; it offers a number of different levels of economic development – core, semi-periphery, and periphery. Second, the model suggests that there are variant forms of labor exploitation, surplus extraction, and capital accumulation that correspond to each level. These elements combined enable us to probe more deeply into the precise nature of the relationship between an economic system and its social consequences, including the propensity to encourage military entrepreneurship. Third, since the three categories of economy in the world-system model and the relationship between them are *processual* rather than being discrete, they allow us to explain why the phenomenon recurs over time and across space (Wallerstein 1974,

1979, 1980). Recent studies have breathed new life into Wallerstein's world systems model and demonstrated the relevance of his three analytical categories (Chase-Dunn 1989; Chase-Dunn and Hall 1991; Shannon 1996).[1] These works suggest that is not only possible but very fruitful to categorize broad economic systems at specific moments in the past in the way that I do in this chapter on the basis of capital accumulation, labor appropriation, and mode of exchange. For these reasons, it seems to me that by utilizing a world-system perspective we can escape the conceptual deficiency that lay behind much of the Hobsbawm and O'Malley debate, and we can better understand the persistence and ubiquity of brigandage and piracy and their related manifestations.

The following passage from Shannon's synthetic account of world-system theory indicates some of the salient features of peripheralization and semi-peripheralization that may account for the development of endemic and epidemic banditry and piracy.

> The result [of peripheralization] was a class system composed of a tiny group of wealthy landowners and a great mass of impoverished peasants bound to the land by law and custom. The failure of domestic manufactures to develop (because of foreign imports and the lack of a large domestic market), the political dominance of the landed aristocracy (at the expense of the towns), and foreign control of international trade all kept the merchant class and urban artisan class small and relatively impoverished.
>
> Class relationships in the semi-periphery were rendered more complex than in the periphery by that zone's intermediate position in the world-system. . . . The capitalist merchant class was larger and wealthier than that of the periphery. Core-like craft manufactures supported a small class of urban artisans and workers who were still organized more as feudal guilds than those in the core (Shannon 1996:59).

A cross-culturally comparative assessment of military entrepreneurship conducted with an eye to world-system theory shows that it occurs in variant forms in the periphery and the semi-periphery. This observation alone allows us to set aside the Hobsbawm–O'Malley controversy; one focused mainly on developments on the periphery, while the other refuted the work of the former by showing that banditry also occurred in the semi-periphery. The empirical evidence shows that military entrepreneurs flourished in both. What are the elements of peripheralization and semi-peripheralization that encourage the development and expansion of predatory activities? Just as specific modes of labor extraction and capital accumulation characterize and distinguish the periphery from the semi-periphery, so too may predation take on different forms in each situation.

In peripheral areas, capital accumulation occurred in the form of large landed estates that were usually created through the extirpation of small, subsistence-orientated peasant forms of agriculture and their replacement by more commercialized agrarian regimes. We find, furthermore, that wherever this transformation occurred, be it in southern Europe, India, Latin America, or Asia, banditry developed. Estate formation set up a double dynamic that generated the conditions conducive to rural brigandage and violence. One dynamic created situations in which men were pushed off the land. Wherever estates formed, they did so through expropriation of smallholders. This alone would have initiated a radical transformation of rural society, especially through the introduction of new forces of labor extraction in the form of sharecropping or even more direct forms such as servitude. In any event, the results were much the same. In the wake of the intrusion of estates and capitalist agriculture, poverty and unrest increased. Disgruntled and displaced young men provided a fertile breeding ground for violence. Because this type of agrarian system was predicated on coercion, generated a potentially hostile social environment, and, as we shall see shortly, developed in political climates characterized by weak states, large landowners and estate managers created private armed bands to control their labor force and to protect their property. This paramilitarization of one sector of the rural population, however, created a sword that cut two ways. Bandits and estate guards were drawn from this same manpower pool of military entrepreneurs.

This contributed to a second social dynamic. Being an estate guard offered a way out of rural poverty. Wages, perquisites, prestige, and authority all came with the job, along with the guns and distinctive garb. The slide over to banditry was an easy one, and accordingly wherever we find estate guards we find brigands as well. Landowners used their private gangs in political disputes and struggles for power. The ambiguity of labeling appears again. Bandit or guard? The answer depended on who was asked. That both were drawn from the same generic category of military entrepreneurs is clear.

In addition, the economics of plantation agriculture generated novel and abundant opportunities for predation. An integral characteristic of peripheral and semi-peripheral systems was the linking of agrarian commodity production to international markets. Because of the rudimentary transportation technology usually found in the periphery, a very vulnerable form of economic geography developed. Goods had to be transported long distances along narrow linear trade routes, which traversed sizeable tracks of difficult terrain or crossed open seas (Hoekveld 1993). Consequently, they were open to attack by predatory armed bands.

This was the pull factor. Men who took to the highway or the open seas to attack caravans and merchantmen sought material gain and wealth, even if, as was often the case, they sought to transform those ill-gotten gains into power and influence in their natal villages (Brögger 1968; Gallant 1988). Some case studies of the actions of these armed cadres exemplify my argument.

Dacoity in rural India during the nineteenth century, for example, was closely connected to the advent of agricultural commercialization and the practice by holders of *zamindari* estates of hiring armed guards. Arnold cites a number of examples where *zamindari* holders actually employed the very same dacoits who had been harassing them (Arnold 1979: 142–3; see also Adas 1982; Ahmad 1992). In Egypt as well, 'notables also tried to stay on the good side of the bandits in order to avoid being their targets. (For this reason large landowners often hired those reputed to be bandits as guards.)' (N. Brown 1990: 261–3) The pattern holds for other parts of Africa (Crummey 1986: 133; Fernyhough 1986; Cooper 1993; Isaacman 1993). In the Huaibei region of north China, Elizabeth Perry observed that large farm-owners hired gangs of armed men to guard their fields during the harvest, and that these were the same men who were often bandits. As she noted 'wealthy households hired vigilantes – usually the local rifraff – to provide protection' (Perry 1980: 84; this pattern was found in many other areas of China: Billingsley 1988; see also Cheah Boon 1988).

Moving over to the Western Hemisphere, the Latin American bandit literature is replete with examples showing the close connection between capitalist accumulation, estate formation, and endemic banditry. Numerous studies examine the agrarian question in Latin America (for a recent summary of this literature see, Stern 1993 a, b; Roseberry 1993), and many explicitly discuss the linkage between estates and banditry. For Brazil, both Billy Jaynes Chandler and Linda Lewin have shown that there were intimate ties between large landowners and military entrepreneurs (Chandler 1978, 1987; Lewin 1979). Almost every study that discusses banditry or the hacienda system of agriculture in Mexico notes the presence and ambiguous role of the guards (Brunk 1996; Vanderwood 1981, 1987; Knight 1986: vol. 1, 123–6; Katz 1988). In the Dominican Republic, Julie Franks has observed that plantation workers joined armed gangs on the promise of 'a pair of pants and cigar' and that the estate guards on sugar plantations were usually hired from the same *gavillero* (outlaw) bands whose depredations made the countryside unquiet (Franks 1995: 165).

The same pattern is evident in southern Europe and the Mediterranean. During the seventeenth and especially during the eighteenth century, the economy of the Ottoman Empire became more closely articulated to the burgeoning Eurocentric world system as part of the periphery (Wagstaff 1993; Hütteroth 1993; McGowan 1981). This transition initiated some changes in the ways that estates were organized and operated. One result was a dramatic increase in the employment of private military men as protectors and enforcers. In Greece, for example, it was customary for large landowners to have their own armed gangs (Gallant 1988; Koliopoulos 1987; Sotiropulos 1868). The use of informal cadres of armed warriors was common throughout the Balkan provinces of the Ottoman Empire (Alexander 1974–5, 1985; Asdrahas 1972; Cassia 1993). Karen Barkey found that in Anatolia during the eighteenth century for large landowners 'having a retinue became a matter of prestige and honor and an indicator of local power. The need for more and more men drove power holders to enlist peasants, shifting the source of retinues from traditional slaves to peasants' (Barkey 1994: 166).

In Andalusia, Spain, 'with the introduction of capitalist property and production relations in the countryside a new figure appeared on the local scene, the private estate guard (*guarda jurado*) . . . These private guards, the strong arms of big landowners, were registered by local and provincial authorities. They could be sworn in only after having been screened by the local authorities who gathered information about their background from the parish priest and mayor of their place of birth. They usually went mounted in a grey uniform and were armed with a rifle. They were hated by the agricultural proletariat, for it was their duty to prevent thefts of crops and poaching, a means of survival for the landless in times of unemployment' (Driessen 1983: 100). Furthermore, after examining the careers of a number of prominent military entrepreneurs, Driessen concluded that the distinction between estate guard and bandit was vague (1983:100–1).

The literature from Italy and Sicily is particularly rich on this topic. The works by Jane and Peter Schneider and Anton Blok show how the Sicilian Mafia arose out of the interstitial power vacuum that developed on the island alongside the formation of great landed estates. Without a strong state and in the economic context of severe deprivation and hardship, absentee landlords hired armed 'men of respect' to oversee and protect their interests (Schneider and Schneider 1976; Blok 1974; Catanzaro 1992). A similar pattern has been identified and widely studied in other areas of Italy as well (Snowden 1986; Arlacchi 1983; Arrighi and Piselli 1987; Davis 1988: 88, 90; Petrusewicz 1996).

From this brief global survey, it appears that there were very strong structural and causal linkages between certain key aspects of economic peripheralization relating specifically to capital accumulation and labor extraction that created constraints, pressures, and opportunities for the formation of military entrepreneurs. When they operated with the consent of the state or rulers, their depredations and activities were legitimate, as when they operated as guards on landed estates and plantations; but when they fell from political favor, they became literally outlaws – bandits. There are undoubtedly a wide variety of political, social, and cultural factors as well that shaped the precise ways that brigandage was manifested in those areas characterized as peripheral. Nonetheless, what is striking are the general and recurrent features highlighted above from cultures spanning the globe over the last three hundred years.

The examples of banditry analyzed to this point have all come from areas that fit best the characterization of peripheral regions. I want to examine now some cases drawn from the semi-periphery. Just as the areas categorized as semi-peripheral manifest aspects of capital accumulation, labor exploitation, and modes of exchange that resemble those of both core and peripheral regions, so too there are some similarities and differences in the manifestations of brigandage and banditry. According to world system theory, some of the salient differences of semi-peripheral areas are: (1) There developed some form of industrialization or protoindustrialization; (2) This increased the size, coherence, and importance of the capitalist merchant class; (3) Economic relations in the semi-periphery were more complex and variegated; (4) Capital accumulation took on slightly different forms, and when it did take the form of land, estate formation provided just one possible mode of exploitation; just as common was the development of capitalist wage-labor relations, which resulted in rural proletarianization; (5) Geographically, semi-peripheral zones developed in close proximity to their cores; and (6) An economic system characterized as semi-peripheral may embedded in a larger economic system that on a grander scale could be considered as a core region.

In terms of the opportunities or restrictions for military entrepreneurship that semi-peripheral conditions present, the most important are: (1) Different types of commodities were transported; (2) There were fewer opportunities to attack merchant capital in transit and so bandits would have to attack stationary targets like banks; (3) Because of the more restrictive physical geography in the semi-periphery, gangs could not grow as large and operate with the same levels of freedom of mobility; (4) Gangs in the semi-periphery even more than those in the periphery had to rely on the cooperation and compliance of the local population: social geography, as it were, had to take the place of the cover provided by the physical environment in the periphery; (5) Brigands in the semi-periphery much more than in the periphery were the product of the expansion of industrial capitalism. Some examples from the United States, England and Europe, and Australia illustrate these arguments.

'In the vast social and economic experiment being undertaken in nineteenth-century America, tensions and conflicts between various groups were endemic' (Seal 1996: 79). This is how folklorist Graham Seal begins his assessment of outlaw legends in the United States; legends that he directly relates to the folklore about highwaymen in England and bushrangers in Australia (both of which I discuss below). His observation, however, does not go far enough. The history of military entrepreneurs in the United States began before the nineteenth century, and it exemplifies the ways the actions of these groups took on different forms during the process of peripheralization and then through the transformation to semi-periphery. Groups that flourished during the colonial era, like Vermont's Green Mountain Boys and the South Carolina Regulators, fit well some of the patterns discussed earlier. I want to focus here on those groups that developed across America as semi-peripheralization occurred. In his excellent study of Missouri after the Civil War, David Thelen demonstrates that it fits perfectly the definition of a semi-peripheral zone and that banditry of the type epitomized by Jesse James was generated by the conditions created through the expansion into the area of industrial capitalism (Thelen 1986; see also Fellman 1989; O'Malley 1980, 1983). Alongside the processes of social and economic change, remarkably similar forms of banditry and outlawry, as well as vigilantism and other manifestations of quasi-legal violence, developed in the United States during the nineteenth century (McGrath 1984; R. M. Brown 1978, 1991). Even as seemingly archaic a practice as feuding upon closer examination can be seen as a result of economic development and semi-peripheralization.[2] In her revisionist examination of the famous Hatfield and McCoy feud, Altina Waller showed that rather than being a manifestation of time-honored but primitive custom, the feud was a manifestation of a contest for power between local folk and outside industrial capitalists. The conflict then was rooted in the context of the transformation of the region into a semi-periphery of the industrializing core of late nineteenth-century America (Waller 1988; see also Montell 1986 and Miller 1991). More recently, Blee and Billings (1996) in their study of feuding in Kentucky during the nineteenth century found that violence was most prominent among those experiencing the economic transformation of semi-peripheralization and that feuding was closely related as well to local state-building and especially to the development of clientelistic political relations – a point I turn to in the second half of this chapter. Brigandage and its related forms of violence appear in late nineteenth-century America as factors that helped to facilitate the penetration of semi-peripheralizing industrial capitalism.

Highwaymen in eighteenth-century England and the bushrangers of late nineteenth-century Australia also fit this pattern. Brigandage along the highways and byways of England achieved its zenith at precisely the moment of confluence between a number of crucial economic developments. Enclosure was accelerating the proletarianization of countryside and causing the expropriation of large numbers of rural husbandmen; poor and rootless men were thus set loose in the countryside (Snell 1985). Protoindustrialization was expanding through the 'putting out' system, and this greatly increased the flow of goods (Mendels 1972; Humphries 1990). Even with urbanization and the increased power of the eighteenth-century English State, there were still considerable tracts of land where bandits could hide (Fielding 1988 [1758]: 83). Functioning in small groups closely integrated into the local economy of the communities around which they operated, highwaymen like Dick Turpin, William Page, and James Turner were the products of English economic development, and while England as a whole constituted the core of the expanding economic world system, many parts of the island were semi-peripheral to its industrializing core. A similar argument could be proposed to explain the reasons why gangs like the Bokkerijders (Blok 1986) or the Great Dutch Band (Egmond 1986) flourished when and where they did.

The bushrangers of Australia resemble more the badmen of Missouri than the highwaymen of England. Bushranger banditry emerged during the period from 1860 to 1880 out of the conflict over capitalist penetration of the Australian countryside and the type of landholding system and economic regime that would dominate. According to Pat O'Malley, class was at the heart of the conflict. Proletarian farmers known as 'selectors' clashed with large landowners called 'squatters' and merchants and professionals, like bankers, over the distribution of land. Bandits like Ned Kelly contested how capitalist economic development would play itself out (O'Malley 1979a, b, 1980; McQuilton 1979; Seal 1996). Like the other forms of banditry in the semi-periphery, bushranging had its origins in the complex matrix of factors that the system of economic relations created.

Spreading the Wealth? The Role of Military Entrepreneurs in the Development of Capitalism

So far the discussion has focused on the economic contexts that were conducive to the development and persistence of military entrepreneurship. Nothing has been said, however, about the impact that terrestrial and maritime predation had on the expanding world economic system during the last three centuries. Other than to note that they were parasitical of commerce and trade, historians have not tried to assess either the quantitative or the qualitative impact that brigandage had on exchange and the economy. And yet, as J. L. Anderson in one of the few studies that does so shows, the impact of such activities on regional economies, local and supralocal polities, and parochial society was far more significant than has hitherto been appreciated (Anderson 1995: 179). He also follows Frederic C. Lane (1958) in seeing both direct and indirect immediate costs and longer-term dynamic costs to brigandage and other forms of organized violence. In economic terms, the depredations of both bandits and pirates became at times quantitatively significant, but over the long term they often came to be considered as the almost predictable costs of doing business in many parts of the world. Nonetheless, the magnitude of their exactions could constitute a serious threat to a region's economy and would therefore justify the costs of a concerted state-level initiative to eradicate or at least to curtail brigand activity. There is, however, another, probably even more important, economic aspect of military entrepreneurship that has not been discussed in the literature, and that is the ways that banditry facilitated capitalist penetration of the peasant economy.

The following passage from Joel Migdal's excellent synthetic article on capitalist penetration into the countryside during the nineteenth century frames well the argument I wish to make here.

> Capitalism was not some inexorable force that simply swept away existing institutions through the very force of the market mechanism. In many societies, social organization had been a means to insulate peasants from direct or sustained contact with the international market. For peasants to produce what the market demanded they produce, there had to be an additional force insuring compliance with the market's demands. That force was the state. Backed by the coercion of armies and police, the state adopted a set of policies – on land, taxation, transportation – that greatly enhanced the force of the new market. Along with its violent forces, the state brought an array of techniques capable of undoing the existing ways of organizing peasants. These techniques included tax rolls, land registers, land surveys, accounting procedures,

standardized currencies, guaranteed state bonds for railroad investment, and much more. (Migdal 1982: 73).

While I agree with much of what Migdal says, I think that he misses two vital steps in the process of capitalist penetration, and both have to do with the activities of bandits and other military entrepreneurs. An examination of the physical geography of brigandage and piracy shows that they flourished in areas where there were closely juxtaposed major trade routes and remote, inaccessible terrain like mountains or deserts. In Guangdong, China, bandits operated out of the mountainous areas of the province, but also preyed frequently on riverine traffic (Antony 1990: 32; for Huai-pei region see Perry 1980: 64–5; Billingsley 1988). Bandits in Morocco dwelt in the rugged Atlas and Jbala mountains (Hart 1987: 4–5; Lewis 1961). In the Balkans and Anatolia, brigands moved between the precious passes through the otherwise impenetrable uplands and lowland trunk routes leading up to them (see, for example, Barkey 1994: 145; Koliopoulos 1979, 1987; Vasdravellis 1975: 40). At sea, groups like the *uskoks* of Senj (Bracewell 1992: 94–5) and the Guelayi of Morocco (C. R. Pennell 1994: 176) used the treacherous currents, narrows passes, and rugged coastlines of the Adriatic and the Straits of Gibraltar as cover for their assaults on maritime commercial traffic. In both cases, they could easily have retreated into the nearby, inaccessible terrain of the Croatian Dinars or the Moroccan Rif Mountains. Numerous other examples could be cited from around the globe but these should suffice to make the point. Military entrepreneurs like bandits and pirates provided the connecting tissue that articulated rural hinterlands to developing economic zones. Their activities facilitated capitalist penetration in two ways.

First, bandits elevated the level of marketization in the countryside. In most cases, brigands stole portable commodities of value: gold or bullion, spices, jewels, opium, and the like, depending on which part of the world we are talking about. In any event, with the exception of livestock, we can generally accept that bandits stole non-consumables. But even with livestock, it was frequently the case that the stolen meat and the hides in particular were destined for the market-place (Langer 1987: 117 and 122; Alexander 1985: 151). Perforce, therefore, they had to purchase the basic foodstuffs they required for their subsistence, and they had to acquire these from the peasants and rural husbandmen among whom they lived and to whom they were often related (Hobsbawm 1981: 83–5). Granted, there are well-documented cases where armed gangs simply extorted food from villagers, but more often it appears that they purchased their supplies. After all, the gang's survival depended on the acquiescence or compliance of the peasants. Moreover, since most bandits were peasants or rural dwellers themselves, they were connected in a variety of ways with the local communities (Gallant 1988). Their relationship to rural society was more symbiotic than parasitic. As an old Chinese proverb expressed it: 'the rabbit never eats the grass around its own hole' (Perry 1980: 74). The market mechanism of exchange linked the brigand to the agriculturalist, and this led to the increased monetization of the rural economy.

Second, bandits also connected rural villages to outside markets. The stolen commodities injected into the local economy only had real value if they could be translated into other forms of wealth. In some cases, brigand gangs developed close working relationships with specific merchants. In Morocco, for example, each gang had attached to it a specific trader or *kamman* whose job it was to sell their booty (Hart 1987: 14–15). This type of arrangement is documented in India (Arnold 1979: 151), China (Antony 1990: 31; Perry 1980: 35), Africa (Kea 1986: 111), Mexico (Slatta 1987: 191–4), the Netherlands (Egmond 1986: 168–74), and the Balkans. The memoirs of the notorious thug Amir Ali in India are full of episodes in which he or members of his gang undertook delicate negotiations for the sale of their ill-gotten gain (P. Taylor 1985: 185–94).

In other situations, bandits themselves took on the role of merchants. A seventeenth-century observer concluded about the *uskoks* of Senj, for example, that 'these valorous warriors have become avaricious merchants of stolen goods, devoting themselves to nothing else than the sale of their plunder in Croatia, in Carniola, in Styria, in Hungary, even across the sea in Apulia and the Marches, and even in Venice itself, so that having abandoned the military arts they are applying themselves to one that is sweeter, that is, to profit' (Bracewell 1992: 111). Matija Daniç, to cite a particularly apt example, left the life of the brigand and accumulated a vast fortune by acting as a broker for other *uskok* gangs (Bracewell 1992: 112). The literature on piracy provides us with numerous examples of predator merchants (see, for example, Bettez Gravel 1985: 211–12). In some cases, pirate enclaves grew into regional market centers and entrepôts in their own right, like a number of towns and settlements on Madagascar (Anderson 1995: 193; Parker Pearson 1997; Thomson 1994: 47–54). So vital were pirates to the trade in the Indian Ocean during the early modern period that N. K. Chaudhuri has characterized commerce in the region as 'armed trading' (Chaudhuri 1985: 14). At times during the eighteenth century, pirates operating out of and in the Caribbean became a major economic force supplying urban markets in North America (Nash 1986: 113; Anderson 1995: 193; Rediker 1987). In numerous different settings, pirates participated actively and directly in the slave trade. Such was certainly the case at times in the Atlantic during the seventeenth and eighteenth centuries (Rediker 1987: 271). The Cossacks (Tolmacheva 1991) and the Barbary Corsairs (Anderson 1995) as well grew wealthy from their direct participation in the slave trade. In sum, bandits and pirates, either by acting as merchants themselves or by introducing merchants into rural communities, hastened substantially the process of capitalist penetration of the countryside.

Finally, the consensus, as reflected in the passage from Migdal cited above, is that it was the state that played the leading role in consolidating and furthering the expansion of capitalist relations into the rural landscape. In response to peasant rebellions and unrest, the state intruded with the military and the police, and by so doing enhanced the development of capitalist market forces, and eradicated or at least diminished overt resistance to them. But as so much of the literature on peasant unrest shows, actual rebellions were relatively rare. Banditry, however, was not. It flourished ubiquitously in a political environment in which the state was largely absent and where an ethos of self-help justice held sway. The politicization of banditry through the transformation of military entrepreneurs who had previously acted as a coercive force with the blessing of the state, tacit or grudging though it may have been, into outlaws provided the pretext for the state's forcible and ultimately successful intrusion into the countrysides of Europe, Asia, Africa, and Latin America. It is on this point that we see most clearly the close articulation of the economics and politics of banditry.

Military Entrepreneurs and States

State-formation has drawn more attention from sociologists and anthropologists than from historians. Historians have been mostly interested in illuminating how a specific state came into being rather than in explicating why states develop. A renewed interest about the role of the state has led social historians to look to the sociological literature on the subject. Following a line of inquiry originated by Norbert Elias (1978; Fletcher 1997), historians are now focusing attention on thc connection between violence, the 'civilizing process', and state-making. Drawing on Elias' work and on Max Weber's definition of the 'state', Charles Tilly has chosen to place the greatest emphasis on the state's monopoly of legitimate violence (Tilly 1985, 1992; see also Giddens 1985). States, Tilly argues, arise out of war-making. 'War makes states . . . Banditry, piracy, gangland rivalry, policing, and war making all belong on the same continuum . . . For the historically limited period in which national states were becoming the dominant organization in Western countries, I shall also claim that mercantile capitalism and state making reinforced each other' (Tilly 1985: 170). Though he mentions banditry and piracy as factors in facilitating state-formation, most of his detailed historical analysis deals only with wars between states.

Military entrepreneurs operating on both sides of the law significantly contributed to the formation of states in the modern world in the following ways and contexts. In situations where a central government, imperial or otherwise, was unable to impose a monopoly of violence over the means of coercion, there was a propensity for a class of men at arms whom I have called military entrepreneurs to develop.[3] The same absence of mechanisms of control that was conducive to their appearance compelled states and local elites to employ military entrepreneurs as the legitimate security forces. This created a situation where essentially the same groups of men were both the bandits and the police, or, in the case of pirates both the buccaneers and the navy. Inlaw or outlaw status was determined by the nature of the relationship of a group to the state at any specific point in time. The political environment in which military entrepreneurship prospered was also often subject to profound instability. The inability of weakly and imperfectly centralized states, especially in peripheral zones, to exert effective control encouraged challenges from rivals or, in imperial settings, from insurgent, sometimes nationalist or ethnic groups. In either case, military entrepreneurs provided the armed muscle for these movements. This process of politicization greatly increased the number of men at arms. When the conflict was resolved, those on the winning side often became irregular members of the legitimate security forces, while the losers became labeled as outlaws once more. Bandits contributed to the demarcation of territorial states and were partly responsible for the consolidation of state power in rural backwaters by what I have called the 'border effect'. Boundaries took on concrete form in space through the interactions between border guards and bandits who seized upon the jurisdictional ambiguity of these liminal zones as cover for their depredations. Brigandage along the frontier challenged the authority of the central state, could potentially embroil the state in an international conflict, and prevented full articulation of numerous rural areas into the national polity. Consequently, military entrepreneurs who could not be tamed by accommodation – usually by becoming members of the regular army or security forces – had to be eradicated. The writ of the state often became the law of the land as a result of the state's military and political campaigns against bandits in the hinterland and frontier areas. Just as banditry acted as a conduit that facilitated capitalist penetration into the countryside, so too did it foster the consolidation of state control in much the same way. An examination of examples from various parts of the globe over the last three hundred years supports these generalizations.

Inlaws and Outlaws: Military Entrepreneurs and the Development of States

Military entrepreneurship required certain configurations of social, political, and economic conditions in order to develop and flourish. I have already discussed some of the most important economic variables. In terms of political factors, recurrently the most important one appears to be weak centralized state control. In the absence of a monopoly of violence by the state and its inability to impose order throughout its domain, states and local powerbrokers had to turn to the men at arms who appeared in this vacuum of control. As a consequence, the activities of these military entrepreneurs were always polyvalent, ambiguous, and volatile. Both the security forces and the outlaws would be drawn from the same pool of men. But regardless of which side of the law they stood on, because the formation and development of states had at its heart a struggle over control of the means of violent coercion, they would inevitably be drawn into the political arena. Bandit-enforcers (including pirates) recurrently played critical roles in the formation and consolidation of states around the world over the last three hundred years, and they continue to reappear wherever the conditions set forth above arise.[4]

The literature on banditry and states has focused mostly on the roles that military entrepreneurs played in peasant revolutions. At the heart of Hobsbawm's notion of the social bandit was the idea that for brigands of this stripe their depredations constituted a political act of social protest (Hobsbawm 1981: 26–7). Indeed, his initial formulation of it appeared in a book devoted to the study of 'primitive rebels' (Hobsbawm 1965). Much of the debate over the ideal type of the social bandit has revolved around the question of the extent to which brigandage was or was not an act of protest against states and elites. I would argue that military entrepreneurship by its very nature was political. This is not, however, an argument I wish to develop in this chapter. What I do want to dwell on is the idea, amply supported by the historical record, that there are times and places when men of violence, as either inlaws or outlaws, become deeply implicated and participants in state formation. There are essentially two predominant types of situations where this occurs, though I would not insist upon maintaining a rigid categorical distinction between them

– historically there are well-documented episodes in which there was a clear overlap between them. The first is when military cntrepreneurship becomes politicized in the context of insurrections that sometimes become peasant rebellions. The second category refers to situations where powerful chiefs or nobles utilize military entrepreneurs in their struggles for power within a weak state framework. I shall deal with the former first.

Nationalist rebellions in Greece and the Balkans vividly demonstrate the connection between peasant rebellions and military entrepreneurs (Alexander 1985; Cassia 1993; Gallant 1988; Koliopoulos 1979, 1980, 1984, 1987, 1989; Skiotis 1971; Hobsbawm 1981: 70–6; Istrati 1970; Gordon 1916). The men who had been border guards, estate patrols, and brigands before the outbreak of the Greek insurrection of 1821 became the mainstay of the rebel army. When the war was over, however, many of them found themselves once more on the wrong side of the law. The case of nearby Italy also falls into this category. From the period of the Napoleonic occupation onwards, military entrepreneurship and brigandage became politicized and tied to insurrectionary movements. This erupted first in the guerrilla resistance to French rule (Finley 1994). During the decades of Austrian reoccupation of parts of the north and the continued political fragmentation in the south up to the onset of the rebellion of the *Risorgimento*, military entrepreneurs operating on both sides of the law flourished (Davis 1988; Ginsborg 1991). They provided many of the men at arms in the War of the *Risorgimento*. In its aftermath, however, as was often the case, those warriors who could not or would not find a *modus vivendi* with the new polity that they helped to establish found themselves outcasts and labeled as bandits once again. And in Italy as elsewhere, the fledgling state sought to establish its legitimacy and to consolidate its power through waging war against the brigands without a cause (Petrusewicz 1987). John Dickie's work in particular dissects the ways by which the state anathematized banditry by culturally constructing brigands as the antithesis of civilized society and the nation. 'In the anti-brigand campaign army officers and the government understood their opponent predominantly by means of a series of hierarchical binary oppositions, such as between civilization and barbarism, reason and violence, social order and crime' (Dickie 1992:5). In Italy, as in Greece, state-formation and banditry were deeply intertwined.

The historical record from Latin America presents numerous cases exemplifying this mode of state-formation. The history of rebellions in Mexico, for instance, contains numerous examples where state-building and the politicization of banditry went hand-in-hand. Probably the best example is Zapatismo and the Mexican Revolution. Alan Knight has noted that at times 'the kinship between social banditry and popular rebellion was . . . so close that the two can scarcely be differentiated' (Knight 1986: vol. 1: 122–3). His use of the category of the social bandit has caused comment both in support of and in opposition to his conclusion (Joseph 1990: 16–18; Brunk 1996:332). If one adopts, initially at least, the more neutral appellation of 'military entrepreneurs', then much of the contention becomes irrelevant. Viewed in this way, Brunk's (1996) revisionist argument that banditry persisted even when Zapatismo became ascendant seems far less radical than he would have it. Moreover, it would enable us to observe that the majority of the over 400 rebellions or riots discussed by John Coatsworth in his sweeping survey of rural rebellions in Latin America directly involved military entrepreneurs operating in the gray area of legal ambiguity (Coatsworth 1988). Indeed, the pattern in Latin America corresponds well to my model. A summary of the historical accounts of rebellions in Mexico, parts of Central America, Peru, Venezuela, and Brazil leads to the following conclusion.[5] In the absence of strong centralized control, various forms of nonstate armed forces developed. These military entrepreneurs formed a class of violent men who at times established informal relationships with state authorities; but more frequently, they were cultivated by local elites, powerbrokers, and large landowners. An excellent case in point are the *castas* discussed by David Nugent elsewhere in this volume (Chapter 3). Since these groups' success in obtaining an entry into the legitimate side of extortion and protection was predicated upon their demonstrable prowess as warriors, those standing outside the system had to prey upon it. Inlaws and outlaws came from the same pool of manpower. Frequently, however, these men would become embroiled in more widespread rural unrest. When, for whatever specific localized reasons, peasants rose in rebellion, military entrepreneurs, as professional men of violence, became directly involved. If they fought on the winning side, then they gained legitimacy, often becoming irregular troops for the new state. If they were on the losing side, then they either would be accommodated selectively or, as in the European examples, declared enemies of the nation who needed to be destroyed. In either case, military entrepreneurs were deeply implicated and involved in state-building in Latin America.

The second type of situation I have labeled 'warlordism'. In this mode, the issue is less about forming a new state or in leading a mass insurrection than it is about who controls an existing polity. In these cases, military entrepreneurs provide the forces employed in fighting among members of the elite who are competing for power. In their struggles for power amongst themselves these men called on the armed retinues who guarded their property and the men of violence who controlled the surrounding territory either with or without the consent of the legitimate authorities. Big men who challenged the state were considered bandit chieftains, and so in this respect banditry could provide a springboard to national power. In other words, these men sought a way into the system through their actions as bandit leaders.

Take the case of Lej Kâssâ Têwodros, emperor of Ethiopia during the 1850s and 1860s. He was sired a bastard by a noble father and reared in poverty by a common street peddler. He got into a life of crime and through his prowess rose to be the head of his own bandit gang. He preyed along the lowland trade routes. As he became more prominent as a bandit chieftain so rose his political fortunes. He married the daughter of another notorious and powerful bandit leader and nobleman. By 1846, when he entered the mainstream of political life, he had already been appointed governor. From that position he launched raids against neighboring provinces. By 1848 he was considered a 'rebel' by the monarchy. In 1852 he commenced a war against the sitting ruler, and by 1855 he had seized the throne itself (Crummey 1986).

Two cases from the Ottoman Empire demonstrate certain variations on this theme. The case of Ilyas Pasha, an Ottoman chieftain active in the early seventeenth century, is indicative of the practice of power formation. Ilyas Pasha was considered a loyal official of the government who was often assigned to provinces in Anatolia or Rumelia. He had gained notoriety for his courageous defense of the state against Kalenderoglu and various smaller rebellious groups. When in financial trouble, he had been bailed out by the state and had been assigned *sanjaks* as *arpalik* many times. Despite this, around 1620 Ilyas Pasha started to gather a large retinue in the region of Balikesir. Fearful of his growing power, state officials accorded him the title of vizier. Emboldened by this legitimization, Ilyas Pasha expanded his area of activities and even attacked the city of Manisa and its surrounding villages. Ilyas Pasha's strength, however, was temporary. It appears that, as often was the case, so long as Ilyas Pasha had allies in the government, he acted to increase his power, using his allies as well as his retinue. When his patrons in powerful positions in the government were murdered, he was quickly defeated by opposing forces (Barkey 1994: 167. Note 59).

Prince Beyazid provides another good example. He was determined to challenge for the throne, and, after having formed a large gang by arming displaced peasants and other assorted rural adventurers, he rose in rebellion in 1559. If he had been victorious, then his henchmen would have been accorded places in his now legitimate army – and this was explicitly what he had promised them; but since he lost, they became bandits. They did very much the same sorts of things after his defeat that they would have done had he prevailed – extorting levies from the peasantry, collecting tolls from passing merchant caravans, etc., except that instead of being legitimate they were outlaws, bandits (Barkey 1994: 168).

Ali l-Bu Frahi, better known as Ali the Six-fingered, rose to prominence during the late nineteenth century as a bandit chieftain in Morocco. His gang indiscriminately preyed on Muslim and European traders, and politically he played the Sultan off against the Spanish. According to Hart, Ali's goal was quite simple: he wanted the Sultan to make him governor of a large province in eastern Morocco. He soon achieved his goal. As an insider, he undertook the task of eradicating brigandage from the area, an endeavor in which he was largely successful. He soon tried to challenge for an even more elevated position in government. When asked to swear allegiance to the Sultan's head of government, he saucily replied 'my Prime Minister is my good gun and unerring aim' (Hart 1987: 7). His prowess did not match his braggadocio, and he paid with his life in his unsuccessful bid for national power. Nonetheless, for Ali, as for numerous bandit chiefs around the world, brigandage was perceived as a way into the state system.

Alfred McCoy's contribution to this volume in Chapter 5 provides an excellent contemporary variation on this theme. Khun Sa's long and varied career aptly captures many of the points made in this section about the relationship between military entrepreneurs and the state, but also exemplifies well the arguments made in the first section about their economic role. Khun Sa manipulated a variety of social, ethnic, economic, political and geographical situations in order to create a shadow state that on occasion threatened to emerge as a viable national polity in its own right.

The relationship between piracy and state formation resembles that of terrestrial brigandage. Frequently when states were unable to bear the considerable expense of mounting maritime naval expeditions against their foes, they would turn to private maritime military entrepreneurs. Privateers acting under commissions provided by a state carried out thousands of raids during the early modern period. Thomson (1994) shows how these depredations were part of proxy wars between the emerging European states. But as with those of their brethren on land, privateers' activities were always subject to definitional ambiguity. Sea dogs proved undiscriminating in their choice of prey and, even when they attacked vessels belonging to the states of their opponents, from somebody's perspective they were pirates. Because, like brigands on land, they presented authorities with a challenge to the state's claim to monopolize the legitimate means of violence, state consolidation of power had to come at the expense of maritime freebooters. In early modern Europe, state sovereignty was achieved partly through the curbing of maritime brigands' activities.

Like other military entrepreneurs, pirates could also become key players in the internal process of state formation or state consolidation. The best example comes from China during the late eighteenth century. Dian Murray (1987) in her examination of piracy in the South China Sea found that there was a close relationship between it and the Tay-san Rebellion. In their attempt to wrest power from the Emperor the Tay-san encouraged maritime predation. This politicization of piracy led to a dramatic increase in the numbers of men at arms. When the rebellion was put down, the seafaring warriors persisted in their piratical ways. If the Tay-san had been victorious then they would have been transformed into inlaws, and probably would have become the fleet of the new government. Since, however, they were clients of the losers, they stood once more outside the law, except that now their numbers were far greater than before. Unable to conquer them, the Chinese Emperor did what so many other rulers before and after him had done: he bestowed legitimate authority on some of the pirates, and ordered them to eradicate those who could not be accommodated. As we saw before, the politicization of brigandage led to an inflation of its magnitude.

Pirates acted both as economic agents and as informal warriors in facilitating European imperial expansion. V. G. Scammell has argued that European pirates and outlaws operating in Asia and Africa played an important role in the Asian maritime economy of the early modern period by sending goods and slaves to the American and Caribbean colonies. They also facilitated the extension of European power in Asia and Africa by keeping their countrymen informed of the local situation, by discovering new and important trade routes, and by enabling Westerners to enter new markets. Their activities in Asia and Africa only ended when European states institutionalized their military power over far-flung areas (Scammell 1992).

Bad Men on the Edge: Bandits, Borders, and the Consolidation of State Power

Military entrepreneurs literally and figuratively lived on the edge of society. When they operated without the sanction of the law as brigands rather than as enforcers, they often found themselves drawn and pushed into remote, inaccessible areas and frontier zones. Attracting them was the peculiar economic geography I discussed earlier and the fact that most of these men had their roots in rural society and, quite frequently, in that world's most marginal quarters. Compelling them to move to the margins was the need to seek protection from their pursuers in areas with rugged, difficult topographies and social environments open to them but inhospitable to outsiders. Another dynamic was at work as well. Newly emergent or developing nation-states and distant domains under the control of foreign empires were often forced to or found it cost-expedient to employ irregulars as the guardians of their frontiers. Almost invariably these border patrols were drawn from the same class of men who constituted brigand gangs. The dilemma of setting a thief to catch a thief arose again, and the interaction between outlaws and border patrols took on predictable forms. Brigandage flourished in the frontier zones and the security forces sent to control their depredations and guard the border were often indistinguishable from the outlaws. Nowhere, then, was the contest over control of the monopoly of coercive force more starkly evident than in the frontier zone.

The fledgling Kingdom of Greece after 1832, for example, proved incapable of controlling its hinter- and borderlands. In the absence of an effective rural police force, in the presence of a rural economy in flux, and in the midst of a crisis of national authority, military entrepreneurs flourished. Acting as estate guards and employed by the state to chase unauthorized brigands, men at arms operated pretty much as they had before independence. There was, however, a new dimension added: the border. The newly demarcated territorial boundary between Greece and Turkey needed to be guarded; and who better than the local bad men? But as before, they preyed on cross-border traffic. Moreover, since the border guards were drawn from the same class of military entrepreneurs, they would venture on bandit raids across the border. When they did this, they often had the unacknowledged approval of their government. The dilemma of labeling appears again. One side's border patrol was the other's bandit menace. It was, however, the activity of these men on the edges that elevated the role of the border zone to one of importance. Indeed it was through the activities of these men that the border actually took on real meaning and concrete form (Gallant 1997).

In a recent study of national identity formation in southwestern Europe, Peter Sahlins has argued that rather than emanating from the center outwards, national identities may take on their sharpest delineation in the border areas (Sahlins 1989). He demonstrated that in the case of France and Spain notions of being Spanish or French emerged in contradistinction to those on the other side of an imaginary line in the mountains between the two states. Unlike previous studies, especially the seminal *Peasants into Frenchmen* by Eugen Weber (Weber 1976), which postulated that the cultural dynamics of nation-state building flowed from the center to the margins, Sahlins argued that most of the real action was taking place on the boundaries, and that the center, with its national institutions, was drawn to the edges. Since no state could allow military entrepreneurs to operate outside the law and remain stable for long, I suggest that the activities of brigands in the frontier zones compelled states to intervene in marginal areas, and by so doing facilitated these areas' incorporation into the national polity. An examination of some other cases shows that this 'border effect' connecting banditry and state consolidation was widespread.

Two examples from early modern Europe demonstrate this process well. Jan Sundin (1986) has shown how armed bands operating along the frontier zone between Sweden and Denmark facilitated the process of nation-state building in northern Europe. During the sixteenth and seventeenth centuries, military entrepreneurs practiced their craft in the fluid border region. At times they operated as irregulars launching raids across the frontier with the tacit approval of their governments. At other times, they did so without such approval. At all times, bandits, or *snapphanars* as they were called, on both sides of the border robbed, pillaged, and preyed upon villages and merchants regardless of which side of the line they were on. The activities of these bands over time proved troublesome to both states, and increasingly drew the national armies into the frontier zone both to contest the actual border itself and then also to eradicate the bandits who dwelt there. The Swedish–Danish War of 1675–9 not only determined the final territorial demarcation between the two states, but also allowed each state to incorporate definitively the previously untamed frontier. Uwe Danker (1988) has argued that the German Holy Roman Empire developed into an absolutist empire largely through its endeavors to abolish banditry. German bandits, operating on the margins of society in remote forests and utilizing the boundaries between jurisdictions, posed a direct threat to the ambitions of the monarchy. By launching military campaigns and police attacks against brigands, the Empire brought law and order to the backwaters of rural Germany. In this case, the internal consolidation of the state was facilitated by the need to eradicate rural banditry.

Two examples from Africa show this process operating in imperial contexts. In late nineteenth-century Egypt 'banditry as a national problem was invented as a political weapon by Egypt's rulers as a part of the process of creating a stronger, centralized state apparatus and as an effort to keep that apparatus out of British hands' (N. Brown 1990: 260). In Brown's view, the state manufactured banditry as a widespread phenomenon as a pretext for launching campaigns aimed at incorporating rural, marginal areas and thereby exerting the state's monopoly of violence. But the campaign was more than a military venture. 'In the last quarter of the nineteenth century, a national system of criminal courts, a centralized police force, and a national law code were all developed. The need for such institutions was frequently understood in terms of banditry' (269). The twist to Brown's Egyptian tale was that the Egyptian authorities proved unable to eradicate banditry in some areas; in others, the heavy-handed tactics they adopted created a political furor. The results of their actions had severe, unintended consequences. When it became clear that the efforts to curb banditry by the Egyptians were not working, the British Colonial Office used this failure as a pretext to take over in order to ensure that this plague on the nation was cured (N. Brown 1990: 274–8). Further south in Africa, George Simpson found that, even though the British policy for the Northern Frontier District of the East Africa Protectorate was to avoid taking financial responsibility for the region, while extending their authority over it, their policy had to be reconsidered after Ethiopian runaways and bandits crossed over to the District in 1913, following a breakdown of law and order in Ethiopia (Simpson 1996). Clashes between Ethiopian outlaws and British patrols led to the death of a British officer, which forced the British authorities to exert far greater energy and to expend considerably more resources and manpower in controlling the region. Closer articulation of the margins to the center followed in the wake of campaigns to control banditry.

There are numerous other examples, but I want to end this section with a discussion of the *uskoks* of Senj because they show us a slightly different variation on this theme. The *uskoks* were Christians who had fled northward in advance of the conquering Ottoman armies. They settled at Senj in Croatia, which was at the time part of the Austrian Empire. From their base of operations at the borders of the Habsburg, Ottoman, and Venetian empires, they became irregular soldiers of the Habsburg Military Frontier in the sixteenth century and lived by warfare, piracy, or banditry, depending on the occasion and the perspective (Bracewell 1992). The perpetual warfare of the frontier, the lack of effective control by the central governments in Vienna, Venice and Istanbul, the irrelevance of political boundaries to the social, ethnic, and religious divisions in the border population and the resulting difficulty in identifying differences between raider and victims made this area a fertile zone for the *uskoks*' predatory activities. Bracewell has observed that 'the *uskok* phenomenon derived from the complex reality of border life, acted on by social, religious, national, economic, political, and military forces, each modifying the others' (1992: 17). Ideally they were to prey on Muslim merchants on land and at sea; but actually they robbed indiscriminately. Their activities eventually led to an outbreak of war between Venice, the Ottomans, and the Austrians in the early eighteenth century. As part of the settlement, the *uskok* menace was to be removed, and this was only accomplished by the Austrian Empire's stepping in and taking control of the frontier. Once again bandits helped to bring the control mechanisms of the state from the center to the margins.

Richard Pennell's work on the Spanish coastguard provides a maritime example of the border effect (R. Pennell 1995). During the 1810s and 1820s, regardless of which side was in control, the liberals or the absolutists, neither proved capable of outfitting naval forces that could protect Spain's extensive coastline from the depredations of Moroccan pirates and assorted Christian and Muslim smugglers. The state's coffers simply could not the bear the burden. But the problem was a very serious one. Smuggling was robbing the state of one of its important sources of revenue. The response by various Spanish governments was one with which we are now familiar: they employed one group of maritime predators to catch others. The coastguard, then, consisted of private corsairs who were given legal rights to patrol a specified area. They were to attack pirates, capture smugglers, levy import duties, and generally to provide protection to maritime commerce. As with brigandage on land, this method was fraught with difficulties. 'The boundary between coastguard and pirate, and even between coastguard and smuggler, was blurred by the need to make ends meet. Entrepreneurial captains could change sides and move between criminality and law-enforcement with ease' (R. Pennell: 1995: 373). The result of this was that the Spanish State marshaled at great cost a national navy that it then employed to eradicate its own coastguard. Many remote coastal communities felt for the first time the heavy hand of Madrid. Centralized state control followed the fleet.

Conclusion

The major conclusions of this global examination of military entrepreneurs are these. First, rather than being archaic remnants of the pre-modern world, bandits and pirates were directly related to the development of a capitalist world system and the formation of modern states. They were both the products of and contributors to the advancement and consolidation of capitalism and modern states. Much the literature about these groups has been marred by a too narrow a focus on the 'social bandit' debate. Rather than employing the term 'bandit', which defines or labels only one element of the phenomenon under investigation, I opt for the term 'military entrepreneur'. By this I refer to the class of men at arms who operated in the netherworld between legality and illegality, formal and informal authority, but invariably as nonstate entities.

Second, their activities were polyvalent and shrouded in ambiguity. There was a fine line between their predatory actions as protectors rather than extortionists, robbers rather than tax collectors, murderers rather than enforcers. They articulated the world of the peasant and the underclasses to the domain of the elite and the powerful. They were of the peasant world, but not totally in it. Third, they flourished in the capitalist world. But the manifestations of their activities took on slightly different forms in peripheral and semi-peripheral areas because of the variant mechanisms of capital accumulation and labor extraction characteristic of each of them. Fourth, military entrepreneurs, especially when they operated as outlaws, facilitated capitalist penetration of the countryside by increasing monetization, encouraging marketization, and by providing a venue for upward economic mobility. Fifth, military entrepreneurs were deeply implicated and involved the processes of state formation and state consolidation. The political environments in which they flourished were characterized by weak and imperfectly centralized states incapable of exerting effective control. I identified two variations on the state-building theme. In one, military entrepreneurs became embroiled in peasant mass movements, rebellions, and even revolutions against governments and the authorities. In the second, they participated in power struggles between big men. In either case, they provided the armed forces, or at least some of them. When the conflict was resolved, those on the winning side often became irregular members of the legitimate security forces, while the losers became labeled as outlaws once more. Frequently the consolidation of state power entailed the construction of brigandage by land or sea as a threat to the state, which therefore needed to be eradicated. Through this endeavor the institutions of state control were spread and its monopolization of the means of coercive violence achieved. Finally, military entrepreneurs contributed to the demarcation of territorial states and were partly responsible for the consolidation of state power in rural areas because of the 'border effect'. Brigandage in frontier zones challenged the authority of the central state and prevented full articulation of numerous rural areas into the national polity. Consequently, those who could not be tamed by accommodation had to be eradicated. The writ of the state often became the law of the land as a result of the state's military and political campaigns against bandits in the hinterland and frontier areas.

Notes

1. Many of the criticisms leveled at world systems generally, such as its supposed overemphasis on economic variables, its tendency toward teleological theorizing, its neglect of politics, and its categorical rigidity, whether they are valid or not, do not apply here. First, I use the tripartite categories of world systems theory primarily as a way of defining and categorizing economic systems over long periods of time and vast spaces; for my argument, the developmental sequence proposed by the theory is a minor concern. Second, I do not ignore politics, as this domain occupies the second half of the chapter. In sum, for the purposes of this discussion, world-systems theory provides a very useful tool for drawing out the connections between economic development, the global spread of capitalism, and the occurrence of brigandage and piracy.
2. Feuding, banditry, and a cultural ethos of blood vengeance appear in the historical record as a closely related trinity. In almost all of the thirty-five cultures that I examined where banditry occurred, feuding and a belief in blood vengeance were also present. I intend to examine why this was so in another article.
3. There are a number of other aspects that recur frequently in this situation that contribute to development of military entrepreneurs. As I suggested in Note 2, two of these are a propensity to feuding and the appearance of an ethos of blood vengeance. In the absence of a state-sanctioned form of dispute resolution, men opted for self-help justice, and frequently this included a readiness to employ violence. Culturally, aggressive behavior would be encouraged and linked to notions of proper masculine behavior. In this situation men who excelled at violence would rise in stature and reputation.
4. A perfect example of this would be Cambodia in the early 1990s. Nate Thayer has recently shown how the Cambodian government's security forces, including soldiers and police, are often robbing and assaulting Cambodian civilians and foreign aid workers, including UN personnel. Corrupt military commanders are believed responsible for ordering some of these crimes, such as the theft of over 300 UN vehicles. Soldiers say that the government's refusal or inability to pay, feed and equip them properly has forced them to practice banditry. The resulting

attacks are causing the Cambodian people to dread the very forces that are supposed to protect them against the Khmers Rouges (Thayer 1994).

5. See, for examples supporting this account: Knight (1986), Brunk (1996), Joseph (1990), numerous of the essays in Katz (1988), especially Coatsworth (1988) and J. H. Taylor (1988), and the papers collected in Slatta (1987).

References

Adas, M. L. (1982), 'Bandits, Monks, and Pretender Kings: Patterns of Peasant Resistance and Protest in Colonial Burma, 1826–1941', in R. P. Weller, and S. E. Guggenehim (eds), *Power and Protest in the Countryside*. Durham, NC: Duke University Press.

Ahmad, I. (1992), 'Thugs, Dacoits, and the Modern World-System in Nineteenth Century India', Ph.D. Dissertation, State University of New York at Binghamton.

Alexander, J. C. (1974–5), 'Some Aspects of the Strife among Moreot Christian Notables, 1789–1816', *Epetiris Eterias Stereo Elladikon Meleton,* 5: 473–504.

—— (1985), *Brigandage and Public Order in the Morea, 1685–1806.* Athens: Paragoge.

Anderson, J. L. (1995), 'Piracy and World History: An Economic Perspective on Maritime Predation', *Journal of World History,* 6: 175–99.

Antony, R. J. (1990), 'The Problem of Banditry and Bandit Suppression in Kwangtung South China, 1780–1840', *Criminal Justice History,* 11: 31–53.

Arlacchi, P. (1983), *Mafia, Peasants, and Great Estates: Society in Traditional Calabria.* Cambridge, UK: Cambridge University Press.

Arnold, D. (1979), 'Dacoity and Rural Crime in Madras, 1860–1940', *Journal of Peasant Studies,* 6: 140–67.

Arrighi, G. and F. Piselli (1987), 'Capitalist Development in Hostile Environments: Feuds, Class Struggles, and Migrations in a Peripheral Region of Southern Italy', *Review: Journal of the Fernand Braudel Center for the Study of Economics, Historical Systems & Civilizations,* 10: 639–75.

Asdrahas, S. I. (1972), 'Quelques aspects du banditisme social en Grece au XVIIIe siècle', *Etudes Balkaniques,* 7: 97–112.

Barkey, K. (1994), *Bandits and Bureaucrats: The Ottoman Route to State Centralization.* Ithaca, NY: Cornell University Press.

Bettez Gavel, P. (1985), 'Of Bandits and Pirates: An Essay on the Vicarious Insurgency of Peasants', *Journal of Political and Military Sociology,* 13: 209–17.

Billingsley, P. (1988), *Bandits in Republican China*. Stanford, CA: Stanford University Press.

Birbeck, C. (1990), 'Latin American Banditry as Peasant Resistance: A Dead-end Trail?', *Latin American Research Review,* 25: 156–60.

Blee, K. M. and D. B. Billings (1996), 'Violence and Local State Formation: A Longitudinal Case Study of Appalachian Feuding', *Law & Society Review,* 30: 671–706.

Blok, A. (1974), *The Mafia of a Sicilian Village*, Oxford: Basil Blackwell.

—— (1986), 'The Bokkerijders: Eighteenth-century Brigandage in the Meuse Valley', in G. Ortalli (ed.), *Bande Armate, Banditi, Banditismo e repressione di giustizia negli stati europei di antico regime*. Rome: Jouvence.

Bracewell, C. W. (1992), *The Uskoks of Senj: Piracy, Banditry, & Holy War in the Sixteenth- Century Adriatic*. Ithaca, NY: Cornell University Press .

Braudel, F. (1947), 'Misère et banditisme', *Annales ESC,* 2: 129–43.

—— (1972), *The Mediterranean and the Mediterranean World in the Age of Philip II*. London: Collins.

Brögger, J. (1968), 'Conflict Resolution and the Role of the Bandit in Peasant Society', *Anthropological Quarterly,* 41: 228–40.

Brown, N. (1990), 'Brigands and State Building: The Invention of Banditry in Modern Egypt', *Comparative Studies in Society and History,* 32: 258–81.

Brown, R. M. (1991), *No Duty to Retreat: Violence and Values in American History and Society*. New York: Oxford University Press.

Brunk, S. (1996), '"The sad situation of civilians and soldiers": the Banditry of Zapatismo in the Mexican Revolution', *American Historical Review,* 101: 334–54.

Cassia, P. S. (1993), 'Banditry, Myth, and Terror in Cyprus and Other Mediterranean Societies', *Comparative Studies in Society and History,* 35: 773–96.

Catanzaro, R. (1992), *Men of Respect: A Social History of the Sicilian Mafia*. New York: The Free Press.

Chandler, B. J. (1978), *The Bandit King: Lampiao of Brazil*. College Station: Texas A & M University Press.

—— (1987), 'Brazilian Cangaceiros as Social Bandits: A Critical Appraisal', in R. W. Slatta (ed.), *Bandidos: The Varieties of Latin American Banditry*. Westport, CT: Greenwood Publishing Co.

Chase-Dunn, C. K. (1989), *Global Formation: Structures of the World-economy*. Cambridge, MA: Basil Blackwell.

Chase-Dunn, C. K. and T. D. Hall (1991), *Core/Periphery Relations in Precapitalist Worlds*. Boulder, CO: Westview Press.

Chaudhuri, K. N. (1985), *Trade and Civilization in the Indian Ocean: An Economic History from the Rise of Islam to 1750*. Cambridge: Cambridge University Press.

Cheah Boon, K. (1988), *The Peasant Robbers of Kedah, 1900–1929: Historical and Folk Perceptions*. Delhi: Oxford University Press.

Coatsworth, J. H. (1988), 'Patterns of Rebellion in Latin America: Mexico in Comparative Perspective', in F. Katz (ed.), *Riot, Rebellion, and Revolution: Rural Social Conflict in Mexico*. Princeton, NJ: Princeton University Press.

Cooper, F. (1993), 'Africa and the World Economy', in F. Cooper, A. F. Isaacman, F. E. Mallon, W. Roseberry, and S. J. Stern (eds), *Confronting Historical Paradigms: Peasants, Labor, and the Capitalist World System in Africa and Latin America*. Madison: University of Wisconsin Press.

Crummey, D. (1986), 'Banditry and Resistance: Noble and Peasant in Nineteenth-century Ethiopia', in D. Crummey (ed.), *Banditry, Rebellion and Social Protest in Africa*. Portsmouth, NH: Heinemann.

Danker, U. (1988), 'Bandits and the State: Robbers and Authorities in the Holy Roman Empire in the Late Seventeenth and Early Eighteenth Centuries', in R. J. Evans (ed.), *The German Underworld: Deviants and Outcasts in German History*. New York: Routledge.

Davis, J. A. (1988), *Conflict and Control: Law and Order in Nineteenth-century Italy*. Atlantic Highlands, NJ: Humanities Press International, Inc.

Dickie, J. (1992), 'A Word at War: The Italian Army and Brigandage 1860–1870', *History Workshop,* 33: 1–24.

Driessen, H. (1983), 'The "Noble Bandit" and the Bandits of the Nobles?: Brigandage and Local Community in Nineteenth-century Andalusia', *Archive of European Sociology,* 24: 96–114.

Egmond, F. (1986), 'The Heyday of Banditry in Western Europe: The Case of the Great Dutch Band, 1790–1799', in G. Ortalli (ed.), *Bande Armate, Banditi, Banditismo e repressione di giustizia negli stati europei di antico regime*. Rome: Jouvence.

Elias, N. (1978), *Power and Civility. The Civilizing Process*. New York: Pantheon Books.

Faison, S. (1997), 'Pirates, with Speedboats, Reign in China Sea Port', *New York Times,* 20 April 1997, sec. International, col. 1–4, p. 3.

Fellman, M. (1989), *Inside War: The Guerrilla Conflict in Missouri during the American Civil War.* Oxford: Oxford University Press.

Fernyhough, T. (1986), 'Social Mobility and Dissident Elites in Northern Ethiopia: The Role of Banditry, 1900–1960', in D. Crummey (ed.), *Banditry, Rebellion and Social Protest in Africa.* Portsmouth. NH: Heinemann.

Fielding, H. (1988 [1758]), *An Enquiry into the Causes of the Late Increase of Robbers and Related Writings.* Middletown, CT: Wesleyan University Press.

Finley, M. (1994), *The Most Monstrous of Wars: The Napoleonic Guerrilla War in Southern Italy, 1808–1811.* Columbia, SC: University of South Carolina Press.

Fletcher, J. (1997), *Violence and Civilization.* Cambridge: Polity Press.

Franks, J. (1995), 'The *Gavilleros* of the East: Social Banditry as Political Practice in The Dominican Sugar Region, 1900–1924', *Journal of Historical Sociology,* 8: 158–81.

Gallant, T. W. (1988), 'Greek Bandit Gangs: Lone Wolves or a Family Affair?', *Journal of Modern Greek Studies,* 6: 269–90.

Gallant, T. W. (1997), 'Crime, Violence, and the Reform of the Criminal Justice System during the Era of Trikoupis', in K. Koutsoukis (ed.), *Harilaos Trikoupis kai i Epochi Tou.* Athens: Panteion University.

Giddens, A. (1985), *A Contemporary Critique of Historical Materialism. Vol. 2, The Nation-State and Violence*. Berkeley, CA: University of California Press.

Ginsborg, P. (1991), 'After the Revolution: Bandits on the Plains of the Po 1848–54', in J. A. Davis and P. Ginsborg (eds), *Society and Politics in the Age of the Risorgimento: Essays in Honour of Denis Mack Smith.* New York: Cambridge University Press.

Gordon, J. (1916), *A Balkan Freebooter; being the true exploits of the Serbian outlaw and comitaj Petko Moritch, told by him to the author and set into English, by Jan Gordon . . . with a portrait and illustrations by the author*. London: Smith, Elder & Co.

Hart, D. M. (1987), *Banditry in Islam: Case Studies from Morocco, Algeria and the Pakistan North West Frontier*. Wisbech, UK: MENAS.

Hobsbawm, E. (1965), *Primitive Rebels: Studies in Archaic Forms of Social Movements in the 19th and 20th Centuries*. New York: Norton.

—— (1972), 'Social Bandits: A Reply', *Comparative Studies in Society and History,* 14: 503–5.

—— (1981), *Bandits.* New York: Pantheon.

—— (1986), 'Introduction', in G. Ortalli (ed.), *Bande Armate, Banditi, Banditismo e repressione di giustizia negli stati europei di antico*

regime. Rome: Jouvence.
Hoekveld, G. A. (1993), 'World-System Theory: Implications for Historical and Regional Geography', in H.-J. Nitz (ed.), *The Early World-System in Geographical Perspective.* Stuttgart: Franz Steiner.
Humphries, J. (1990), 'Enclosures, Common Rights, and Women: The Proletarianization of Families in the Late Eighteenth and Early Nineteenth Centuries', *Journal of Economic History,* 50: 17–43.
Hütteroth, W. (1993), 'The Role of the Ottoman Empire in the Early Modern World-System', in H.-J. Nitz (ed.), *The Early World-System in Geographical Perspective.* Stuttgart: Franz Steiner.
Isaacman, A. F. (1993), 'Peasants and Rural Social Protest in Africa', in F. Cooper, A. F. Isaacman, F. E. Mallon, W. Roseberry, and S. J. Stern (eds), *Confronting Historical Paradigms: Peasants, Labor, and the Capitalist World System in Africa and Latin America*. Madison: University of Wisconsin Press.
Istrati, P. (1970), *The Bandits,* trans, W. A. Drake. Short Story Index Reprint Series. Freeport, NY: Books for Libraries Press.
Joseph, G. M. (1990), 'On the Trail of Latin American Bandits: A Reexamination of Peasant Resistance', *Latin American Research Review,* 25: 7–53.
Katz, F. (1988), *Riot, Rebellion, and Revolution: Rural Social Conflict in Mexico*. Princeton, NJ: Princeton University Press.
Kea, R. A. (1986), '"I am here to plunder on the general road": Bandits and Banditry in the Pre-nineteenth Century Gold Coast', in D. Crummey (ed.), *Banditry, Rebellion and Social Protest in Africa*. Portsmouth, NH: Heinemann.
Knight, A. (1986), *The Mexican Revolution.* New York: Cambridge University Press.
Koliopoulos, J. S. (1979), *Listes. I Kentriki Ellada sta Mesa tou 19ou Aiona*. Athens: Ermes.
—— (1980), 'Peri "Kinonikon" kai Allon Liston sti Neoteri Ellada', *Deltion tis Istorikis kai Ethnologikis Etaireias tis Ellados* 23: 422–36.
—— (1984), 'Military Entrepreneurship in Central Greece during the Greek War of National Liberation (1821–1830)', *Journal of Modern Greek Studies,* 2: 163–87.
—— (1987), *Brigands with a Cause: Brigandage and Irredentism in Modern Greece, 1821–1912*. Oxford: Clarendon Press.
—— (1989), 'Brigandage and Irredentism in Nineteenth-century Greece', *European History Quarterly,* 19: 193–228.
Lane, F. C. (1958), 'Economic Consequences of Organized Violence', *Journal of Economic History,* xviii: 401–17.

Langer, E. D. (1987), 'Andean Banditry and Peasant Community Organization, 1882–1930', in R. W. Slatta (ed.), *Bandidos: The Varieties of Latin American Banditry*. Westport, CT: Greenwood Publishing Co.
Lewin, L. (1979), 'The Oligarchical Limitations of Social Banditry in Brazil: The Case of the "Good" Thief Antonio Silvino', *Past & Present*, 82: 116–46.
Lewis, W. H. (1961), 'Feuds and Social Change in Morocco', *Journal of Conflict Resolution*, 5: 43–54.
McGowan, B. (1981), *Economic Life in Ottoman Europe. Taxation, Trade and the Struggle for Land, 1600–1800*. Cambridge: Cambridge University Press.
McGrath, R. D. (1984), *Gunfighters, Highwaymen, & Vigilantes: Violence on the Frontier*. Berkeley: University of California Press.
McQuilton, J. (1979), *The Kelly Outbreak, 1878–1880: The Geographical Dimension of Social Banditry*. Melbourne: Melbourne University Press.
Mendels, F. F. (1972), 'Protoindustrialization: The First Phase of the Industrialization Process', *Journal of Economic History*, 32: 241–61.
Migdal, J. S. (1982), 'Capitalist Penetration in the Nineteenth Century: Creating Conditions for New Patterns of Social Control', in R. P. Weller and S. E. Guggenheim (eds), *Power and Protest in the Countryside: Studies of Rural Unrest in Asia, Europe and Latin America*. Durham, NC: Duke University Press.
Miller, W. R. (1991), *Revenuers and Moonshiners: Enforcing Federal Liquor Law in the Mountain South, 1865–1900*. Chapel Hill, NC: University of North Carolina Press.
Montell, W. L. (1986), *Killings: Folk Justice in the Upper South*. Lexington, KY: University of Kentucky Press.
Murray, D. H. (1987), *Pirates of the South China Coast, 1790–1810*. Stanford, CA: Stanford University Press.
Nash, G. B. (1986), *The Urban Crucible. The Northern Seaports and the Origins of the American Revolution*. Cambridge, MA: Harvard University Press.
O'Malley, P. (1979a), 'Class Conflict, Land and Social Banditry: Bushranging in Nineteenth Century Australia', *Social Problems*, 26: 271–83.
—— (1979b), 'Social Bandits, Modern Capitalism and the Traditional Peasantry', *Journal of Peasant Studies*, 6: 410–22.
—— (1980), 'The Class Production of Crime: Banditry and Class Strategies in England and Australia', *Research in Sociology and Law*, 3: 181–99.
—— (1983), 'The Suppression of Social Banditry: Train Robbers in the

US Border States and Bush Rangers in Australia, 1865–1905', *Crime and Social Justice,* 16: 32–9.

Parker Pearson, M. (1997), 'Close Encounters of the Worst Kind: Malagasy Resistance and Colonial Disasters in Southern Madagascar', *World Archaeology,* 28: 393–417.

Pennell, C. R. (1994), 'The Geography of Piracy: Northern Morocco in the Mid-nineteenth Century', *Journal of Historical Geography,* 20: 272–83.

Pennell, R. (1995), 'State Power in a Chronically Weak State: Spanish Coastguards as Pirates, 1814–50', *European History Quarterly,* 25: 353–80.

Perry, E. (1980), *Rebels and Revolutionaries in North China, 1845–1945*. Stanford, CA: Stanford University Press.

Petrusewicz, M. (1987), 'Society against the State: Peasant Brigandage in Southern Italy', *Criminal Justice History,* 7: 1–20.

—— (1996), *Latifundium: Moral Economy and Material Life in a European Periphery*. Ann Arbor, MI: University of Michigan Press.

Rediker, M. (1987), *Between the Devil and the Deep Blue Sea: Merchant Seamen, Pirates, and the Anglo-American Maritime World, 1700–1750*. Cambridge: Cambridge University Press.

Roseberry, W. (1993), 'Beyond the Agrarian Question in Latin America', in F. Cooper, A. F. Isaacman, F. E. Mallon, W. Roseberry, and S. J. Stern (eds), *Confronting Historical Paradigms: Peasants, Labor, and the Capitalist World System in Africa and Latin America*. Madison, WI: University of Wisconsin Press.

Sahlins, P. (1989), *Boundaries: the Making of France and Spain in the Pyrenees*. Berkeley: University of California Press.

Scammell, G. V. (1992), 'European Exiles, Renegades and Outlaws and the Maritime Economy of Asia *c.*1500–1750', *Modern Asian Studies,* 26: 641–62.

Schneider, J. and Schneider, P. (1976), *Culture and Political Economy in Western Sicily*. New York: Academic Press.

Seal, G. (1996), *The Outlaw Legend: A Cultural Tradition in Britain, America and Australia*. New York: Cambridge University Press.

Shannon, T. R. (1996), *An Introduction to the World-System Perspective*. Boulder, CO: Westview Press.

Simpson, G. L. (1996), 'Frontier Banditry and the Colonial Decision-making Process: The East Africa Protectorate's Northern Borderland Prior to the First World War', *International Journal of African Historical Studies,* 29: 279–309.

Singleman, P. (1990), 'Establishing a Trail in a Labyrinth', *Latin American Research Review,* 25: 152–5.

Skiotis, D. (1971), 'From Bandit to Pasha: First Steps in the Rise to Power of Ali of Tepelen, 1750–1784', *International Journal of Middle East Studies,* 2: 232–4.

Slatta, R. W. (1987), 'Conclusion: Banditry in Latin America', in R.W. Slatta (ed.), *Bandidos: The Varieties of Latin American Banditry*. Westport, CT: Greenwood Publishing Co.

—— (1990), 'Bandits and Rural Social History: A Comment on Joseph', *Latin American Research Review,* 25: 145–51.

Snell, K. D. M. (1985), *Annals of the Laboring Poor: Social Change and Agrarian England, 1660–1900*. Cambridge: Cambridge University Press.

Snowden, F. M. (1986), *Violence and Great Estates in the South of Italy. Apulia 1900–1922*. Cambridge: Cambridge University Press.

Sotiropulos, S. (1868), *The Brigands of the Morea,* 2nd Edition. London: Saunders, Otley, and Co.

Stern, S. J. (1993a), 'Africa, Latin America, and the Splintering of Historical Knowledge: From Fragmentation to Reverberation', in F. Cooper, A. F. Isaacman, F. E. Mallon, W. Roseberry, and S. J. Stern (eds), *Confronting Historical Paradigms: Peasants, Labor, and the Capitalist World System in Africa and Latin America*, Madison, WI: University of Wisconsin Press.

—— (1993b), 'Feudalism, Capitalism, and the World-System in the Perspective of Latin America and the Caribbean', in F. Cooper, A. F. Isaacman, F. E. Mallon, W. Roseberry, and S. J. Stern (eds), *Confronting Historical Paradigms: Peasants, Labor, and the Capitalist World System in Africa and Latin America*. Madison, WI: University of Wisconsin Press.

Sundin, J. (1986), 'Bandits and Guerrilla Soldiers: Armed Bands on the Border between Sweden and Denmark in Early Modern Times', in G. Ortalli (ed.), *Bande Armate, Banditi, Banditismo e repressione di giustizia negli stati europei di antico regime*. Rome: Jouvence.

Taylor, J. H. (1988), 'Banditry and Insurrection: Rural Unrest in Central Jalisco, 1790–1816', in F. Katz (ed.), *Riot, Rebellion, and Revolution: Rural Social Conflict in Mexico*. Princeton, NJ: Princeton University Press.

Taylor, P. M. (1985 [1839]), *Confessions of a Thug,* 2nd Edition. Oxford: Oxford University Press.

Thayer, N. (1994), 'Lawless Land: Violence by Security Forces on the Rise (Cambodia)', *Far Eastern Economic Review,* 157: 18–19.

Thelen, D. (1986), *Paths of Resistance: Tradition and Dignity in Industrializing Missouri*. Oxford: Oxford University Press.

Thomson, J. E. (1994), *Mercenaries, Pirates, and Sovereigns: State-building and Extraterritorial Violence in Early Modern Europe*. Princeton, NJ: Princeton University Press.

Tilly, C. (1985), 'War Making and State Making as Organized Crime', in P. B. Evans, D. Rueschemeyer, and T. Skocpol (eds), *Bringing the State Back In*. New York: Cambridge University Press.

—— (1992), *Coercion, Capital, and European States, AD 990–1992*. Cambridge, MA: Basil Blackwell.

Tolmacheva, M. A. (1991), 'The Cossacks at Sea: Pirate Tactics in the Frontier Environment', *East European Quarterly*, 24: 483–513.

Vanderwood, P. J. (1981), *Disorder and Progress: Bandits, Police and Mexican Development*. Lincoln, NE: University of Nebraska Press.

—— (1987), 'Nineteenth-century Mexico's Profiteering Bandits', in R. W. Slatta (ed.), *Bandidos: The Varieties of Latin American Banditry*. Westport, CT: Greenwood Publishing Co.

Vasdravellis, J. D. (1975), *Klephts, Armatoles and Pirates in Macedonia during the Rule of the Turks*. Thessaloniki: Makedoniki Bibliothiki.

Wagstaff, J. M. (1993), 'The Role of the Eastern Mediterranean for the Early Modern European World Economy 1500–1800', in H.-J. Nitz (ed.), *The Early World-System in Geographical Perspective*. Stuttgart: Franz Steiner.

Waller, A. L. (1988), *Feud: Hatfields, McCoys and Social Change in Appalachia, 1860–1900*. Chapel Hill, NC: University of North Carolina Press.

Wallerstein, I. (1974), *The Modern World-system: Capitalist Agriculture and the Origins of the European World-Economy in the Sixteenth Century*. New York: Academic Press.

—— (1979), *The Capitalist World-economy*, Cambridge: Cambridge University Press.

—— (1980), *The Modern World-system II: Mercantilism and the Consolidation of the European World-Economy*. New York: Academic Press.

Weber, E. (1976), *Peasants into Frenchmen: The Modernization of Rural France*. Stanford, CA: Stanford University Press.

–3–

State and Shadow State in Northern Peru *circa* 1900: Illegal Political Networks and the Problem of State Boundaries

David Nugent

In the late afternoon of 3 May 1908 – three weeks prior to the presidential elections – Pablo M. Pizarro, his nephew Javier M. Pizarro, Pablo's two brothers-in-law Gustavo Rubio Linch and José del Carmen Tuesta, Javier Pizarro's father's cousin José María Echaíz, and Echaíz's son Fabriciano led a group of armed men into the town of Lámud, capital of the province of Luya, in the Chachapoyas region of northern Peru. They quickly assembled at the door of the *Casa Subprefectural*, or subprefectural building, located on the town square, where they expected to find the subprefect, Felipe Rodríguez, who was also a high-ranking officer in the Guardia Civil. The interlopers broke down the door of the *Casa Subprefectural* and poured in with the intention of killing the subprefect and assuming control of the province. Finding him not at his desk, however, they immediately made their way to his residence, where he was in conversation with Manuel Chávez, governor of the neighboring district of Luya. Once they had surrounded the house, the attacking forces began their assault, firing weapons into the Rodríguez home. Rodríguez and Chávez were both unarmed, and attempted to escape by the rear balcony of the house. Once outside, however, they found a number of armed men waiting, who summarily executed them.

The seven members of the Guardia Civil quartered in the town heard the shooting, left their barracks to investigate, and immediately ran into the fire of the attacking Pizarros, Rubio and Echaíz. Thus ensued a gun battle of several hours in the streets of the town, which ended only at nightfall when the attackers withdrew. Three members of the Guardia Civil were wounded in the fracas (APA 1, decreto no. 108 [29 May 1908], no. 109 [30 May 1908], no. 110 [30 May 1908]). In the weeks that followed, the outlaw group continued to harass the towns of Lámud and Luya, forcing

Prefect Manuel Hurtado to authorize the expenditure of a considerable sum of money in order to put more men in arms. By the end of May the armed band had been driven from the region.

This outlaw group actually represented one of two *castas* – elite-led, multi-class political coalitions – that vied with each other for control of the Chachapoyas region. The year prior to the attack this same group, the Pizarro–Rubio *casta*, had been involved in similar acts of violence. The Pizarro–Rubio *casta* had attempted to ambush and murder leading members of the Burga–Hurtado *casta*, which at the time was not only the ruling *casta* but also the legally constituted representative of the central government. Thinking ahead to the upcoming Congressional and Municipal elections, the outlaw Pizarro–Rubio *casta* hoped to eliminate several of the Burga–Hurtado *casta's* leading members, Eloy Burga and Felix Ocampo, who were Congressional deputies respectively for the provinces of Chachapoyas and Luya. In this way the Pizarro–Rubio *casta* hoped to 'clear the field' for their own candidates, Gustavo Rubio Linch and José María Linch (both of whom would be involved the following year in the attack on the Guardia Civil post, and both of whom became wanted for murder and sedition as a result). The attempts on the lives of Burga and Ocampo ultimately failed, but only narrowly (APA 2: 23, 25, 26 de abril de 1907). The near-success of the Pizarro-Rubio *casta* in carrying out these assassinations undoubtedly stemmed from the careful planning that had gone into the attempts. Secret night-time meetings in which the attacks had been prepared and rehearsed took place in the district of Chachapoyas, where the two men who were to be assassinated lived. The meetings were held in the home of Eloy Torrejón, a trusted member of the Pizarro–Rubio *casta*, who oversaw matters of import for the *casta* within the district as a whole (APA 2: 8, 11, 12 de mayo de 1907).[1]

The Pizarro–Rubio *casta* employed secret meetings in the homes of trusted *casta* members to do far more, however, than plan the assassination of the leading members of the legal political apparatus. Meetings of this kind took place on a regular basis, and were actually part of an extensive but illegal structure of alternative governance that incorporated large numbers of people living throughout the entire Chachapoyas region. This 'shadow state' mirrored and replicated the state structure almost in its entirety.[2] Heading the illegal network was (at that time) Pablo M. Pizarro, an individual whose ability to make unilateral decisions regarding the affairs of his *casta* made him akin to a departmental Prefect. Pizarro had drawn on affinal and agnatic ties (see below) to form alliances with other prominent individuals (most notably, members of the powerful Rubio Linch family), several of whom acted in roles parallel to that of

'Subprefect' – in the sense that each was responsible for the affairs of one of the region's three provinces. As already indicated (see Note 1), the illegal *casta* also chose individuals who were responsible for protecting and advancing (illegal) *casta* interests in the many districts and sub-districts of the region. These individuals acted in ways that were virtually identical to the district governors and lieutenant governors of the legal state structure, and lived alongside those who occupied legal administrative posts in the outlying sections of the region. In other words, the shadow state replicated the administrative hierarchy of the Executive Branch of government almost in its entirety.

The shadow state extended beyond these individuals and posts that paralleled the Executive Branch of government to include municipal government as well, once again closely mirroring the legal state apparatus (APA 3: 5 de abril de 1907):

> On December 30th of the past year [1906] . . . the ex-Governor of this city [Lámud] Don Manuel Malaver . . . publicly boasted to the [assembled] citizenry that he had interfered in the Municipal elections . . . [and had committed] fraud in order to insure that the official list of candidates [those proposed by the ruling Burga–Hurtado *casta*] would be victorious. The people have, however, repudiated this list, leading to the most complete anarchy in public administration in this Province . . . [I]n all of the districts we have the scandal of [having] two Municipal Councils, one [Council] legal and correctly elected [the Municipal Councils of the Pizarro–Rubio *casta*!] and the other [Council] born of the crime of falsification committed by the Governors and their subalterns whom the Subprefect had visited days prior to the election in order to give them their instructions and ballots personally . . . the ballots having been printed by the press that prints 'The Official Register' [the official government newspaper printed in Chachapoyas by members of the ruling *casta*].

Additional correspondence confirms that shadow Municipal Councils were a regular part of the political process in the districts of Luya Province, one set of Councils representing the interests and constituents of the ruling Burga–Hurtado *casta*, the other set of Councils representing the opposing Pizarro–Rubio *casta* (APA 3: 6, 10, 11, 15 de abril de 1907). Revealingly, in writing protests to various political officials outside the region about the existence of the Councils of the other *casta*, members of each *casta* argued that the Councils of the opposition were 'illegal'. The fact that the Burga–Hurtado-backed Councils had the support of the central government allowed the ruling *casta* to prevail in this matter – in the sense that its Councils were able to meet in public, were able to receive government support for some of their actions, etc. This fact, however, did not stop the Councils of the Pizarro–Rubio *casta* from meeting on a regular basis (if in secret), and from reaching decisions and arriving at policies that were implemented among their constituents.

In other words, those involved in the illegal political network adopted precisely the same organizational form for their activities as did those involved in the legal state apparatus. This included individuals of varying rank who were appointed to oversee matters of import to the (illegal) *casta* in all sections of the regional space – and who replicated the posts of the Executive Branch of government. It included as well individuals (provincial and district-level mayors) and corporate bodies (Municipal Councils) chosen by means of elections[3] to oversee matters of municipal concern – who also replicated the legal Municipal structure, complete with councilors for each of the areas distinguished therein. The illegal political network even had individuals whose primary responsibility was to marshal and direct armed force in the interest of the (illegal) *casta* when called upon to do so – making them much like the head of the Gendarmes.

The vitality of this 'shadow state' was made all too apparent in 1909, when a change in the Presidency in Lima brought to power Augusto Leguía, the national patron of the Pizarro–Rubio *casta*. The ascendance of Leguía allowed the members of the 'illegal' *casta* to take control over the legal state apparatus virtually overnight, and to do so with so little difficulty that it appeared they had been long been rehearsing for the positions they assumed (which as members of the shadow state they actually had been). Indeed, it was as if the electoral politics of a parliamentary democracy were in operation, and one party had simply replaced another as the result of victory at the polls!

With the rise of the Pizarro–Rubio *casta* the very individuals who just a short time before had been the leaders of an illegal political network, who had led armed attacks on the state apparatus resulting in the deaths of several of its members, who had been sought as murderers, and who had publicly demonstrated their ability and willingness to use violence to attain illegal and seditious goals, became the representatives of the *legal* state apparatus. For example, Pablo M. Pizarro became Senator for the department of Amazonas, Gustavo Rubio Linch became Subprefect of Luya province, Salvador M. Pizarro (Pablo's half-brother) became (interim) judge of Luya Province, and José María Echaíz was awarded the lucrative post of tax collector for the province of Bongará. Furthermore, the same individuals who had formerly overseen (illegal) *casta* affairs in the region's many districts in many cases became legitimate governors of those districts. In addition, the formerly illegal Municipal Councils that had met throughout the region became legitimate, legally recognized entities. Finally, those who had been responsible for organizing and directing armed force in the interest of the illegal *casta* stepped into positions of leadership in the legally constituted *gendarmería*.

Not only did the very personnel that had formerly made up the illegal *casta* come to occupy positions of power and legitimacy within the legal state apparatus, but the people who only a short time before had been the official and legal representatives of the state rapidly became fugitives from the law, persecuted and harassed. Most notable in this regard were Eloy Burga and Felix Ocampo. Burga, formerly Congressional Deputy for the province of Chachapoyas, found himself subject to trumped-up charges of murder (the judge who brought the charges was none other than Salvador M. Pizarro), which forced him to go into hiding and then flee from the region entirely. Even so, the Pizarro–Rubio *casta*, with its control of the judicial apparatus within the region, went on to brand Burga as a dangerous criminal, and to initiate an (unsuccessful) national manhunt for him (APA 1, decreto no. 116 [1 June 1909], no. 119 [4 June 1909], no. 293 [9 Dec. 1909]). Ocampo, formerly Congressional Deputy for the province of Luya, found himself subject to severe persecution by the new Subprefect of Luya province, Gustavo Rubio Linch. Ocampo was initially forced to retreat into his fortified hacienda home (Cocochó) in order to protect himself. Ultimately, however, the attacks on his person, property, and family became so intense that he was forced to quit the region entirely (APA 1, decreto no. 99 [2 April 1910]). Lower-ranking members of the Burga–Hurtado *casta* also found themselves subject to persecution and abuse by the Pizarro–Rubio *casta*, in the form of violent attacks, torture, rape, extortion, and property damage/destruction (see Nugent 1997: Ch. 4). In other words, with the rise of the Pizarro–Rubio *casta* the former Prefect, Subprefects, deputies, and the entire *casta* they represented were declared renegades and became outcasts from justice.

The 'political transition' described above – in which the illegal political network became legal and the legal network became illegal – was anything but an unusual state of affairs. Virtually identical transitions, including the violence leading up to them, and the persecutions that followed in their wake, occurred in 1885, 1890, 1895, 1902, 1907, 1909, 1912, 1913, 1919, 1923, and 1924 (see Nugent 1997: Chs. 3–4).

As the above discussion suggests, it is difficult if not impossible to distinguish legal from illegal political networks in the Chachapoyas region during the period under consideration. As will be shown at length below, neither is it possible to distinguish state from society. Rather, boundaries were blurred in all directions. This is true despite the fact that: (1) there was a government apparatus that (in theory) enjoyed a monopoly on the legitimate use of force, administered justice, collected taxes, etc; (2) all political ritual and discourse depicted the state and society as real and unproblematic entities, with clear boundaries, each nurturing and lending legitimacy to the other in a relationship of mutual support and co-constitution; (3) the institutions of the state apparatus were designed to support the public sphere imagined in political ritual and discourse – a 'society' made up of a mass of citizens, each jurally indistinguishable from the next, all of whom were united behind the cause of promoting 'progress' and 'advancement'; and (4) illegal networks were depicted as a threat to state, society, and progress, and as beyond the boundaries of state and society.

In the pages that follow I expand on this contradictory state of affairs in order to initiate a critical examination of commonly made assumptions regarding states and illegal networks. I also seek to open a discussion about the degree to which state and society can be considered conceptual categories adequate to the complex social realities of emerging nation-states like turn-of-the-century Peru. Other writers have explored similar questions based on material concerning other spatial and temporal contexts. In a seminal article, Abrams (1988) raises the general problem of the apparent but deceptive unity of the state, and the difficulty of separating state from society. Mitchell (1991) further develops this point in his critique of the 'relative autonomy of the state' literature and its applicability to modern Western nation-states. Gupta (1995) explores the difficulties of bounding the state in postcolonial India. Álvarez, Dagnino and Escobar (1998) discuss the blurred nature of boundaries between state and society in contemporary Latin America. The present chapter is intended as a further exploration of the these issues in the context of emerging nation-states.

Implicit in the very notion of states and illegal networks is the assumption that illegal networks have arisen outside the formal boundaries of the state apparatus for one of several reasons: (1) to authorize, undertake, or endorse activities deemed morally, ethically, economically, or politically *unacceptable* by the state – because of which the state apparatus is unwilling to authorize or support these activities; or (2) to replace or fill in for more neutral activities and relationships with which the state has not, cannot, or will not concern itself (for example, grassroots organizations and their activities). In other words, illegal networks are generally seen to reflect and/or fill a *void* in state activities, to point to an absence or at the least to a 'thin-ness' in 'stateness' (Nettl 1968). As a result, illegal networks are often seen as *alternatives* to formal state organization, as expressing possibilities or tendencies found within 'society' that 'the state' would like to suppress, stamp out, or simply ignore. Indeed, there is often a certain romance surrounding illegal networks; they are at times seen as carrying the seeds of radical ways of reorganizing state and society alike.

This conceptualization of states and illegal networks, I will argue, reflects deeper, problematic assumptions regarding the state, society, and the nature of state–society relations in general. According to this view the state and society are distinct 'entities', each with its own clearly identifiable boundaries and interests. Furthermore, it is generally assumed that state and society have interests that are opposed to or in conflict with one another (Nugent 1994). The state can advance its interests only at the expense of society, and vice versa. The notion of a 'zero sum game' and inherent opposition between state and society is deeply engrained in social science thinking. Indeed, so much so is this the case that virtually all the literature on the consolidation and breakdown of states is characterized by these assumptions.[4] The limits to state integration are therefore often seen in relation to the inability of states to 'absorb', 'incorporate', 'engulf' social relations that are posited as being fundamentally prior to and/or existing outside a separate sphere called the state. Even the terms so often used to characterize state-formation, or state-'building' – absorption, incorporation, penetration – reflect what is assumed to be the oppositional nature of state and society. Analyses of 'illegal networks' might therefore be seen as a special case of what is assumed to be a more general problem or phenomenon – the 'limits' of the state (see Mitchell 1991).

There are undoubtedly many instances in which this oppositional relationship accurately reflects many aspects of state–society relations. This would especially appear to be the case during times of retrenchment or reorganization in the activities of the formal state apparatus, such as are currently taking place as a result of the crisis in the international order of nation-states (Comaroff 1993; Szanton Blanc *et al.* 1995) and in the organization of global capitalism (Mandel 1975; Jameson 1984; Harvey 1989). I would like to suggest, however, that an oppositional state–society relationship is anything but a general condition. Rather, through an examination of legal and illegal political networks in northern Peru at the turn of the twentieth century, I hope to show that: (1) far from giving expression to alternative political possibilities, illegal political networks may display the same organization, and may demonstrate the same intentions, as the formal state apparatus; (2) illegal political networks may imply, even require the formal state political apparatus as a condition of their very existence; and (3) rather than helping to define the *limits* of 'stateness', or the external boundaries of some discrete entity called the state, illegal political networks may themselves be key mechanisms by means of which state organization is brought into being and reproduced, and vice versa. One implication of the analysis is that, rather than bounding 'the state', illegal political networks can be an essential part of the field of relationships that characterize specific kinds of state-level societies – specifically, emerging nation-states like turn-of-the-century Peru.

The 'State'

In order to grasp the relationship between 'state' and 'society', and between legal and illegal political networks, we must first review the formal structure of the Peruvian state apparatus at the turn of the twentieth century. We then turn to a consideration of the relations between state and society, between legal and illegal networks.

At the turn of the twentieth century the national territory of Peru was divided into a nested hierarchy of territorial/administrative units, each of which was overseen by an official appointed by the Executive Branch of government. Within this framework the country as a whole was divided into departments or states, each with its own Prefect. Each department was further subdivided into Provinces, one appointed Subprefect being responsible for each. Provinces in turn were broken down into districts, and governors were appointed to and held responsible for these units. Finally, many districts were made up of sub-districts; lieutenant governors were the officials charged with overseeing the affairs of this smallest unit in the administrative structure.

The organization of the Judicial Branch of government was grafted on to these same territorial/administrative divisions. There was a national Supreme Court, which appointed the members of regional Courts of Appeal (which heard cases for individual departments or groups of neighboring departments). There was also an *agente fiscal*, or attorney-general, designated as the highest-ranking judicial official for each department. At the level of individual provinces, a *Juez de la Primera Instancia* (Judge of the First Instance) was responsible for all civil and criminal cases within his jurisdiction. Finally, a *juez de paz* (justice of the peace) was appointed to each district (representatives of the judicial branch of government were not provided to sub-districts).

There were also 'elected' political positions that made up an important part of the state apparatus.[5] In addition to the national President, each department had several elected officials – two Senators (who were elected by and represented the electorate of the entire department), and one Congressional Deputy for each of the department's provinces (Deputies were elected by the electorate of the Province they represented).

Finally, there was also a structure of municipal government at both the provincial and district levels. That is, a mayor and municipal council oversaw a series of local affairs within the district or province of their jurisdiction. According to law, during some periods the occupants of the positions of mayor and municipal council were supposed to be elected, while at other times they were to be appointed (by the local representatives of the Executive Branch). In practice, however, even when 'elections' were held, they were manipulated in such a way as to allow the Prefect, Subprefect, or governor to appoint to these posts individuals of their own choosing.

As emphasized above, however, there was also an illegal or 'shadow' state order lurking just behind this formal structure. The reproduction of state power and the state apparatus was critically dependent upon this shadow state, despite the fact that the latter suffered vicious persecution at the hands of the former. In order to understand this apparent contradiction we now turn to a consideration of regional political processes, power relations, and factional groupings, and then trace out their relationships to the formal apparatus of government.

State Versus Society? – Chachapoyas *circa* 1900

At the turn of the twentieth century the emerging Peruvian nation-state was rent by contradictions. Although founded in the 1820s on liberal principles of democracy, citizenship, private property, and individual rights and protections, the central government was not remotely able to make good these arrangements even a hundred years later. Although such principles were uniformly invoked in all political ritual and discourse, many parts of the country were organized according to principles diametrically opposed to these precepts of 'popular' sovereignty.

Chachapoyas was one such region. Dominating the social and political landscape of Chachapoyas was a group of aristocratic families of putatively Spanish descent who saw it as their birthright to rule over the region's multitudinous mestizo and Indian peasant population. These elite families rejected all assertions of equality between themselves and the subaltern groups over which they ruled. Indeed, the elite regarded and referred to themselves as a separate aristocratic caste – the *casta española* – that was naturally entitled by right of birth to the power and privilege due to its racial purity and cultural superiority.

Peculiarities of the Peruvian state during this period meant that the central regime in Lima was forced to ally with such aristocratic families if it was to maintain even a semblance of control in the outlying sections of its territory. Those who controlled the central state apparatus were compelled to seek out clients among rural aristocratic families who would rule in the name of the central regime. In other words, although the independent republic of Peru had been born of armed struggle against absolutist, colonial Spain, and although the central government of Peru embraced precepts that had emerged out of the Enlightenment, the actual operation of the state apparatus depended crucially on maintaining social structures of the *ancien régime*. As a result, by the turn of the twentieth century two opposed notions of legitimate political and social order – two different forms of sovereignty (Foucault 1980) – had been forced into uncomfortable juxtaposition in the Chachapoyas region: aristocratic and popular sovereignty.[6] Each of these forms of sovereignty had its own totalizing vision of the social order, based on radically different ways of classifying social persons, of distributing material and non-material rights and obligations among the social persons thus defined, and of mediating their social interactions. Each, that is, had a distinct way of controlling space, and of organizing the activities of people in time and through space. It was the cultural categories and the social relationships of aristocratic sovereignty that acted as the foundation of everyday life. Aristocratic sovereignty was based on the assertion of fundamental, inherent, and qualitative *differences* among people who occupied the various categories of society. Distinctions based predominantly on race (Indian, Mestizo, White), gender (female and male), ancestry (Spanish or indigenous) and landownership segregated the population into what were (in theory) fixed and inherited social categories that did much to prescribe the life possibilities of the people who occupied them. Roles of leadership and control in virtually all domains – economic, social, political, military, legal, and religious – were reserved for the white, male elite of Spanish descent (who likewise reaped most of the benefits of dominating the social order). These elite men were to watch over and safeguard those who occupied various 'legal minor' categories – Indian and mestizo men, and women of all social classes, as these 'minors' were not considered fully capable of looking after themselves. Those who occupied the status of legal minor were burdened with highly onerous and category-specific obligations and limitations of multiple kinds – material, social, political, and cultural. The ongoing public expression of one's relative status in the regional social order was encoded in forms of dress, in patterns of socializing and 'cultural' affectations ('European' vs. 'Indian'), in deferential patterns of behavior and speech, in forms of livelihood, and in the ability to occupy important positions in public life. The sum total of these constantly reiterated distinctions helped lend an air of naturalness and inevitability to aristocratic sovereignty.

The 'modern' or popular notion of sovereignty, on the other hand, was advanced by the central government as providing the sole and exclusive terms by which national life would be organized. It was predicated on precepts diametrically opposed to the aristocratic order – on Enlightenment principles of equality, citizenship, individual rights and protections, and the sanctity of private property and individual labor – principles written into Peruvian constitutions since Independence from Spain in 1824. The modern notion of order rejected (in theory) any form of inherent privilege as the basis of society. It posited a community of like individuals each peacefully pursuing his (!) self-interest to the greater good of all members of society. Popular sovereignty articulated notions of 'progress', the 'public good', and the community of citizens, equal in the eyes of the law, who made up 'the nation'.

One of the most important ways in which individuals were rendered alike under popular sovereignty was that, in addition to being equal in the eyes of the law, all were considered equally endowed with the right to use power. Or, more accurately, all were rendered equally powerless. It was the prerogative of *no one* to use power arbitrarily for their own purposes. Conflictual relations between 'individuals' were *never* to be settled by the individuals themselves, but rather by the mediating institutions of the state.

Under aristocratic sovereignty, on the other hand, it was not held that a separate state apparatus had the sole, legitimate right to mediate conflict, or to use force or violence. Rather, members of most privileged stratum of society – the 'aristocratic', white, male elite of Spanish descent – saw it as their unquestionable, inherited right and responsibility to occupy positions of power and influence, and to rule over their social inferiors. Furthermore, in order to exercise these rights the elite believed it was their prerogative to use force whenever necessary – either against those who sought to remove them from positions of power and influence, or against those who sought to prevent them from occupying such positions.

Those who attempted to interfere with the exercise of elite privilege, including the central government, therefore did so at their peril – as is attested to by members of elite families down to the present. In this regard consider the following anecdote, related to me by an elderly member of the Echaíz family, one of the region's elite, aristocratic families:[7]

> In August of 1930 [President] Leguía finally fell from power [in a military coup]. We received word from an ally in Lima by telegram, who told us to take the Prefecture immediately. My grandfather [José María Echaíz], father [Eleodoro Echaíz], and uncles quickly assembled a very large group of followers and attacked the Prefecture. The Prefect at that time was Sr. Távara, an ally of the Rubio [Linch family], who along with his secretary and the Military Assistant of the Prefecture quickly fled once the fighting began, so we had no difficulty in taking control . . . My family had suffered for many years at the hands of the Rubio [the eleven-year period of the rule of President Leguía and his local clients the Rubio Linch], and my grandfather and father were very anxious to avenge themselves for all the outrages they had been forced to tolerate. After they took the Prefecture, they attacked the house of Miguel Rubio [Linch], hoping to catch him and make an example of him . . . but he and [his brother] Arturo escaped to [their hacienda] *Boca Negra* [located just outside Chachapoyas]. Later, fearing my family, the Rubios left Amazonas . . . With my father [Eleodoro Echaíz] in control of the Prefecture, we sent a telegram to Lima [to the Ministry of Government] informing them of what had happened. The reply came quickly – a new Prefect had been appointed, and would soon be traveling to Chachapoyas. When my father received this telegram he became *very* angry, and immediately sent back his own reply: '*I rule in Amazonas*!' The new Prefect never arrived.

There was a sense in which elite men regarded themselves as having no true peers, and certainly no masters. Rather, each believed he had the right to use power in defense of prerogatives which were legitimately his because of the elite station in life which he enjoyed by right of birth. No one – not even the state – had the right to interfere with these privileges.

Because of peculiarities of the Peruvian political order, however, it was *inevitable* that different factions of the elite *continually* interfered with one another's ability to exercise positions of power. During this period Peru was an internally fragmented polity (Burga and Flores Galindo 1979: 88–94; Caravedo 1977, 1979; Cotler 1978: 119–84; Gorman 1979). The era as a whole was characterized by numerous coup attempts, frequent outbreaks of Civil War, and constant turnover in the central government apparatus (see Basadre 1968–9, Vols 5–12). As noted above, the central regime was unable to control its national territory directly, and thus was forced to choose select elite groups in each region to act in its name. In the process, however, the central regime of necessity denied all other elite factions access to political power (Colmenares 1985; Gorman 1979; Miller 1982, 1987). The result was endemic conflict, as elite factions struggled among themselves to control the local apparatus of state. In their efforts to prevail over their enemies all factions of the elite were in turn compelled to establish extensive clienteles among the Indian peasant and the urban, middle-class mestizo families. The multi-class factions that emerged out of this process – referred to as *castas* – fought continuously with one another for control of regional affairs.

While similar tendencies were manifest in many parts of the Andes during the nineteenth and early twentieth centuries (Basadre 1968–9, Vols 9–12; Mallon 1983, Chs. 2–3; Smith 1989, Ch. 3; Taylor 1986), competition for control of political office was especially intense in the Chachapoyas region. The sole means of attaining wealth and power in Chachapoyas came from monopolizing political office – which placed an elite faction at the top of an extensive tribute-taking apparatus that spanned the entire region. Owing to the region's unusual degree of isolation from external markets during this era commercial agrarian production was *not* an important source of wealth (Nugent 1988) – and thus landed families could not rely on their estates to provide them with the wealth necessary to live according to their aristocratic self-conceptions. Because of the poverty of agrarian pursuits influential families were forced into the public, political world, where all threatened to collide in their efforts to become the single, privileged client of the state.

At stake in inter-*casta* struggles for political control was more than just wealth and power. The outcome of these struggles determined who among Chachapoyas' privileged white class would be able to live according to the exalted station in life that all members of the elite considered their birthright. Prior to the 1930s, however, there was no institutionalized, non-violent means by which a *casta* could gain control over the political apparatus that other *castas* would accept as legitimate. Rather, each elite faction considered its own claims to power as inherently more valid than the claims of its competitors. To be forced into the private sphere – to be made socially and politically invisible – was deeply shameful for people whose self-conception was that of a hereditary elite for whom privilege and rule were natural rights. As a result, not only were the prerogatives of each *casta* openly questioned and challenged by other *castas* on an ongoing basis, but each *casta* employed any and all means necessary to claim as its own the privileges of the others. Struggles among the various *castas* were thus of a continuous, and often violent, nature. Furthermore, in that the rise of one *casta* inevitably meant persecution, emiseration, decline and even demise for the others, each *casta* fought viciously to protect and promote its own interests.

In the absence of legitimate, institutionalized mechanisms for mediating relations among the *castas*, personal displays of power became the method most commonly employed. As a result, in addition to being continuous, ongoing, and violent, inter-*casta* struggles were also intensely 'personalistic' and highly gendered. Men were given the primary responsibility for protecting and advancing the cause of their family and *casta*. A key means of establishing and maintaining position for men was to *demonstrate* the ability to rise to and crush any and all of the challenges to which *casta* members were continually subject. The more a man was perceived *publicly* as potent and dangerous, the less likely he was to be challenged, and thus the more secure was the position of his family and *casta*. The following – a complaint made by a leading member of the elite Hurtado family to the President of Peru in the context of difficulties the Hurtados had controlling their elite enemy and counterpart Pablo M. Pizarro – can be taken as a fair description of the behavior of much of the elite when dealing with their male adversaries. Indeed, similar descriptions were applied to a great many men of aristocratic families by their enemies (APA 4, 6 de setiembre de 1907):

> The uncontrollable, bad-tempered, and rebellious character of this person [Pablo M. Pizarro] is well known to the Head of State. You will remember that in 1896, [when] he was Deputy, he was captured in the port city of Pacasmayo in possession of contraband weapons, a grave crime for which he was imprisoned . . . I have begun criminal proceedings against Sr. Pizarro . . . for various crimes, especially for publicly repudiating and showing contempt for me as a legally constituted political official.

Casta members thus sought to dominate, shame and humiliate the opposition at every opportunity, to establish for themselves a reputation of such potency that all competitors (and followers!) would think very carefully before confronting them. A reputation of this kind was most effectively established either by dominating and shaming opponents *publicly*, in highly visible, face-to-face confrontations, or via violent encounters that were widely discussed in public (successful or unsuccessful assassinations, ambushes, attacks, rapes, etc.). Each such act had a kind of 'demonstration effect' concerning the power of the *casta* that committed it, and made ongoing, public statements to other *castas*, and to society at large, about each *casta*'s capacity to rule.

Needless to say, not all *castas* entered into this struggle on the same footing. As already noted, because of peculiarities of the Peruvian political order during this era, it was the central government's practice to choose one particular elite faction in each region to act in its name. This 'ruling' *casta* used the broad powers of appointment it enjoyed as the state's privileged client to name elite allies and non-elite clients to positions in the judiciary, police, and government bureaucracy throughout the entire department. Such a position of strength allowed the ruling faction to safeguard its own position, and to harass members of opposing factions in a systematic manner – removing them from public office, prosecuting them for supposed crimes, seizing their goods, and doing harm to their persons and property in whatever way possible.

State backing thus allowed people associated with the ruling *casta* to *flaunt* their ability to violate the rights of others, to belittle and humiliate their enemies in addition to simply eliminating or marginalizing them as opponents – and to do so publicly. The following protest, written to the departmental Prefect by a mestizo cultivator who was a low-ranking political appointee of a deposed faction, captures the insecurity of person and property to which all people were subject when the elite faction to which they belonged fell from power (APA 1, Decreto no. 108 [2 June 1909]):

> 'Denunciation of Criminal Acts Committed in Lonya Chico and Request that Those Who Have Been Kidnapped Be Freed':
>
> Juan Mendoza, citizen of Lonya Chico, Province of Luya, Department of Amazonas . . . swears that during the night of the 30th of the present month scandals so atrocious that they are without precedent were committed against the peaceful and defenseless inhabitants of the town of Lonya Chico. The famous Governor of Lonya Chico, author of the assassinations that took place in Luya and Lámud in May of last year, who stole weapons and ammunition of the state, appeared in our house in order to take us prisoner. During the night of the 30th the governor put the following citizens in prison: Francisco Chávez, Vicente Chávez, Juan Pio Chávez, Rufino Tuesta and José Dolores Mendoza. All were taken to prison cells while being beaten with clubs, and all at present have serious wounds. Afterward, José Dolores Mendoza was freed because he was able to produce the sum of 4 soles. The rest, being unable to pay, were taken to Lámud and I suppose that they remain there even still. *Sr. Prefecto, how is it possible that such criminal acts have been committed when we are enjoying a period of peace, and when we should be under the protection of authorities who have sworn to comply with the law?* [emphasis in original]. How is it possible that various honorable individuals have been taken prisoner, and that those who are able to pay are freed while those who are not able to pay are mistreated and taken to other towns as prisoners only because they could not satisfy the desires of abusive authorities? I believe that in the light of these facts you will order an immediate investigation and will free the honorable citizens [in question] . . . the mothers, wives and other relatives of the victims have escaped to Cajamarca . . . where we will remain until justice is done.

The response of the departmental Prefect to these rather astonishing accusations typifies the way in which those who controlled the apparatus of state used it to further their own aims and to persecute their enemies. The Prefect denies the request for an investigation because he says the way that the protest is worded casts aspersions on the honor and dignity of the authorities! Rather than investigate the charges and be sure that people are not being held against their will for ransom, and are not being physically abused by his own appointees, the Prefect instructs the Provincial Judge to begin criminal proceedings against the man who wrote the protest – Juan Mendoza – for lack of respect for the legally constituted authorities! (APA 1, Decreto no. 108 [2 June 1909]).

As this example makes clear, the ruling *casta* used its powers of appointment and its control over armed force to persecute and harass members of the opposition in as systematic and comprehensive a manner as possible. Continuous and ongoing persecution of the opposition was necessary because opposing *castas* refused to accept the position of the ruling group as legitimate – and thus constantly sought to take the place of the coalition in power.

While involved in a series of violent encounters with members of opposing factions on an ongoing basis, the ruling faction was also the official representative of the independent republic of Peru within the department of Amazonas – a republic founded on liberal, Enlightenment principles of individual rights and protections, the sanctity of person and property, and equality under the law. As a result, although committed to making constant attacks upon the life and property of the opposition, the ruling faction was equally compelled to present itself in all political ritual, and in all political discourse, as the sole and true defender of state-endorsed principles of *popular* sovereignty. In these rhetorical and ritual spaces the ruling elite elaborated a mythical social order that was the antithesis of factional politics and aristocratic hierarchy. In place of violence, insecurity, and privilege, everyday life was depicted as consensual and orderly, and individuals were portrayed as universally enjoying the protections of life, liberty, and property granted them by the Constitution. In ritual and discourse unity and harmony prevailed, and distinctions of race, gender, and class – upon which the entire aristocratic order was based – ceased to exist. In place of such distinctions the ruling faction asserted the existence of a mass of identical 'citizens', each jurally indistinguishable from the next, all of whom were united behind the cause of promoting 'progress' and 'advancement'.

The particular elite faction that controlled the apparatus of state was thus forced to offer public accounts of its deeds by invoking notions of equality, individual rights and protections, progress, and the 'common good' that were in direct contradiction with its own actions – and that also provided a critical commentary on the cultural and material logic of aristocratic privilege itself. Aristocratic 'sovereignty' could not be celebrated, or even acknowledged, in formal political spheres. Popular sovereignty had to be celebrated, on an ongoing basis, despite the fact that it had virtually no relation to any existing social reality. Indeed, there was a conspicuous silence about the very *existence* of the aristocratic order in all political ritual and discourse.

While one of the preconditions of successful rule for the reigning coalition was that it engage in consistent, systematic persecution of opposing *castas*, the ability of the ruling *casta* to do so could not be sustained. Indeed, the period of strength and solidarity that characterized its initial phase of control was followed by a period of growing weakness, during which ruling *casta* members suffered many of the same violations of person and property as did members of the opposition. As contradictions inherent in *casta* rule made themselves manifest (see below), political appointees from Lima who were not beholden to ruling *casta* leaders took on roles of growing importance in local affairs. Their presence made systematic and coordinated persecution of *casta* enemies increasingly difficult, as the Lima appointees broke the monopoly on political positions formerly enjoyed by the ruling *casta* and weakened its control over armed force. At the same time members of the ruling *casta* began to struggle among themselves for access to key political positions and for control of tributary revenue, further undermining the effectiveness with which the ruling *casta* could persecute its enemies.

In these transformed conditions, members of the opposition were able to unite against the ruling *casta*, and eventually to drive it from power. Just as the ruling *casta* was forced to demonstrate its ability to violate the 'rights' of others *in public* in order to reproduce its position of dominance, the only means by which opposing *castas* could rise to power was by *publicly* violating the 'rights' of members of the ruling *casta*. They generally began such challenges in somewhat peripheral, if still public spaces – often a district located far from the town of Chachapoyas. A common strategy was to organize a group of local people to accost the district mayor or governor – both appointees of the ruling *casta* – as he attempted to collect taxes or to force people to labor at public works projects. The appointee would be insulted and ridiculed in a highly visible public place, and would be prevented from carrying out his duties. During the encounter the 'rebels' often denigrated the ruling *casta* by name, and boasted of the power and protection of the *casta* to which they belonged.

The following case, from the community of Santo Tomas, typifies this kind of challenge (APA 5, 16 de agosto de 1887):

> *Santo Tomas. 15 August 1887. Sr. Prefect of the Department of Amazonas.* From the 9th of the present month, when the *Apoderado Fiscal* [the official who collected the Indian head tax] arrived in this pueblo, the collection of the head tax has proceeded without the least novelty, even if a little slowly; but unfortunately . . . yesterday morning José Eulogio Maycelo appeared in the [main] plaza insulting and threatening me and the *Apoderado Fiscal*, saying that the Sr. *Fiscal* was a thief who had come to steal from Maycelo's labors, at which point I approached Maycelo and struck him several times, giving the order that he be arrested, because the Sr. *Fiscal* gave me the order to send him to the Prefecture, but no one in the pueblo made any attempt to take him [prisoner] using the pretext that they were not inspectors [assistants of the governor] . . . a number of Maycelo's group continued to scream [at us].
>
> This is not the first time that Maycelo has committed such acts, [rather] he is one of the constant perturbers [of order] in this pueblo along with others who accompany him and since the [time of the revolutionary] movement of Villacorta [an out-of-power *casta* leader] they never leave this pueblo in peace, [spreading] false news of Villacorta and of Yoplac [a lieutenant of Villacorta], but I have not wanted to bother you about this until now, thinking that [his behavior] would improve, but this act [represents] contempt of my authority and that of the *Apoderado Fiscal*, and sets a bad example for the remaining people of the pueblo . . . I ask you, Sr. Prefect, to assist me by sending the police necessary to make these scoundrels understand their duty and to make them respect authority and not to act as they did yesterday, by the end of which they were very drunk and were screaming messages to Yoplac.
>
> The Sr. *Apoderado Fiscal* will inform you of my behavior yesterday in the public plaza when only he and I attempted to take the troublemakers prisoner but were not able to because the rest of the people there watched with their arms folded across their chests, condemning me to fail . . .
>
> The Sr. *Apoderado* has taken the precaution of leaving early in the morning today, carrying with him the money that he has collected and leaving me with 64 receipts to collect . . . I hope that you can assist me . . .
>
> – [signed] Jose Mori, Governor of Santo Tomas, 16 August 1887.

Appointees of the ruling *casta* responded to these challenges in large part by sending communiqués to their superiors protesting a state of affairs in which these appointees were confronted with what they called 'contempt of their authority', and by demanding that criminal charges be brought against the people responsible for the crime – a request that was usually heeded.[8] Such a response would force the ruling *casta* to expend much time and effort if it was to answer the affront to its authority. Should it fail to do so decisively the challenger's success had a 'demonstration effect' of its own – generating additional allies, leading to new challenges in other spaces of perceived weakness, and altering public discourse about the relative standing of the opposing *castas*. Indeed, an escalating number of such acts of public defiance and disrespect put growing strain on the ability of the courts and police to respond to them. Gradually, challengers would increase the scope of their transgressions, coming ever closer to the centers of power, until at moments of political transition they would publicly humiliate the highest-ranking officials of the outgoing *casta*. At this point the new ruling *casta* would begin to flaunt *its* ability to violate the rights of its competitors, and thus the whole pattern would begin anew.

As a result of this set of contradictory forces, members of *all* social classes and *all* elite-led factions suffered continual insecurity of person and property – for no one faction was able to retain control of the regional political apparatus for any sustained period of time (typically, about five to ten years). Rather, as each new faction rose to power it went in pursuit of those who had formerly been its persecutors, using its control over the police and the judiciary to do harm to its enemies in whatever way it could. Mariano Rubio Pizarro, whose elite family led one of the region's major factions, described the kinds of treatment to which members of deposed factions were subject at the hands of new ruling factions:[9]

> The Echaíz took advantage of the triumph of Sanchez Cerro [an army officer who led a coup against Augusto Leguía, patron of the Rubio-Linch, in 1930] to rise up against [us] . . . [once] they knew that Leguía had fallen they organized a group of armed men who attacked the Prefecture and took control of it . . . they wanted to capture my parents and relatives . . . [especially] Miguel Rubio [Linch] . . . head of the family . . . but he escaped . . . so the Echaíz committed a series of outrages against all of my family's friends, [whom] they put in jail and tortured . . . Inside the Prefecture of Chachapoyas . . . the Echaíz hung [these men] by their arms, with their legs behind them, tied together on a piece of wood . . . and tortured them . . . and afterward they put these men on the ground on their backs, and placed their legs in a *Barra* – a piece of wood divided lengthwise in two – and closed the [pieces of wood] and locked the men in with their feet elevated . . . and the sharp edges of the wood cut into them, and [the Echaíz] threw water on the floor . . . and left them there on their backs with their legs locked in the *barra* for the entire night . . . Sr. Beltran Vilca, who was a shoemaker and who lived opposite my house and was a good friend of my father, was tortured [in this way] along with Sr. Flores, who was tortured to death . . . the people could do nothing about this, they were afraid, everyone was afraid . . . there were more than 30 friends of my father [being held] in the Prefecture, and they heard the screams

and the blows . . . I hope that [the torture] never returns, [it was of] the kind of the Spanish Inquisition . . .

Ruling faction and opposition alike were involved in a series of violent encounters with one another that served as public spectacles and statements about the ability of each to rule. Simultaneously, rulers and ruled employed the central regime's discourse of popular sovereignty, progress, equal protection under the law, and the common good to *represent* their actions and those of their adversaries – if for different purposes (the ruling *casta* to legitimate, the opposition to delegitimate). The use of this discourse by *both* groups, however, was in open and blatant contradiction with the violent, personalistic, and competitive actions that characterized *casta* behavior in general. Despite this contradiction, however, neither group made any effort to *conceal* its violent behavior. To the contrary, the principles of aristocratic sovereignty required that those who wished to occupy positions of rule *demonstrate* their ability to dominate, shame, and impose their will on their adversaries.

Noble Castas and the Control of Space[10]

While the above account describes the surface manifestations of *casta* organization and inter-*casta* struggle, a consideration of the region's political-economic structure offers a deeper analysis of the kinds of tensions that fueled such struggles.

During the period under consideration the Chachapoyas region straddled the borders of two major political-economic zones. The first of these was the core of the Peruvian nation-state, lying to the west and south of Chachapoyas, centered on the capital city of Lima. The second of these political-economic zones was focused on the jungle city of Iquitos, center of the Peruvian rubber trade.

For reasons that do not concern us here, Chachapoyas retained considerable autonomy from both of these political-economic zones; neither the products nor the labor of the Chachapoyas region participated in any regular way in the markets of either. The 'relative autonomy' and isolation of Chachapoyas contributed to the emergence of a regional political-economic structure with a number of distinctive characteristics: (1) elite families, each highly localized within the regional space, established fragile alliances with one another via marriage in an attempt to form broad coalitions ('*castas*') that could control the region; (2) these allied families and their peasant, artisan and merchant clients formed unstable, multi-class political coalitions that competed with one another for control of the regional political apparatus; (3) such political hegemony gave the ruling coalition temporary control over the 'legitimate' use of force within the region, which it used to advance the interests of its own members and to persecute members of opposing coalitions; and (4) control of space, and the ability of people and products to move safely through different parts of the regional space, was shifting and insecure, and depended on having strong political allies – none of which could ultimately guarantee the security of person and property.

Perhaps the most serious problem facing landed elite families seeking to live according to their aristocratic self-conceptions was how to 'capture' the regional space, extract wealth from its primary producers (the peasantry), and safely move themselves and their goods through the regional space, considering the facts that: (1) elite properties were scattered piecemeal throughout the region in small, isolated fragments; (2) elite families controlled little in the way of cultivated land and peasant labor; and (3) the 'sphere of influence' of any elite family was very restricted in spatial terms.[11] The key to resolving these dilemmas was to gain control over the local machinery of state, for in this way elite families could appoint clients to bureaucratic positions involving taxation, policing, and judicial functions throughout the region. Such control ensured those of the ruling coalition a steady flow of revenue, gave them access to the armed force they needed to contain threats from other elite families intent on taking their place, and made their efforts to move themselves and their goods through the regional space considerably more secure than they otherwise would have been.

As one might guess, elite families fought fiercely among themselves to control the state apparatus, and as a single family was too 'localized' within the regional space to accomplish this alone, families of the elite sought out alliances with their peers to form as broad a coalition as possible. As mentioned above, these coalitions were known as *castas*, and were referred to by the name of the dominant families that led them.

The core of the coalition was formed by means of patriarchal strategies of marriage alliance. Senior members of the region's 15–20 most powerful landed families used the marriages of their sons and daughters to effect alliances of several different kinds in order to absorb otherwise 'free-floating' resources and spaces into the family. A primary strategy for these elite families involved allying via marriage with one of the region's other powerful families – one with distinct spheres of influence in other sections of the regional space. In that the region was relatively undifferentiated in terms of wealth-producing zones,[12] it was not *particular* sections of the regional space that were sought after. Rather, this form of marriage alliance attempted to overcome the highly localized nature of even powerful families' spheres of influence by tying them to an equally powerful ally.

This alliance – out of which the core of the coalition was formed – was in many ways the most important but also the most dangerous, for it represented the union of otherwise separate, and potentially antagonistic, power blocks. Usually several marriages were considered necessary in order to tie the interests of the two power blocks together. Less stable alliances were based on a single marital union.

A second form of marriage strategy was used to build ties with families that made up a somewhat less central part of the coalition, and involved: (1) marrying daughters into less powerful landed families scattered about the regional space (who thereby acknowledged their client status to the families whose daughters they married); and (2) marrying daughters to influential individuals who were not members of the landed class – politicians and military men stationed in Chachapoyas by the central government, and wealthy merchants and 'muleteer magnates' who moved in and out of the region on a regular basis.[13] Alliances with these additional but less influential landed families increased the geographic scope of core families' spheres of influence still further. Marriage with state appointees gave the *casta* core some control over a potentially independent and dangerous source of power. And alliances with merchants and muleteers gave the coalition access to key resources that could only be procured far outside the region (weapons, most importantly), as well as the means necessary to transport them to Chachapoyas.

Connections with individuals/families in all of these categories gave an elite family access to resources, contacts and 'spaces' that it could not develop on its own. At the same time, however, it was essential that each landed family preserve the integrity of its own landed core – which was under threat of fragmentation due to laws of partible inheritance. Therefore, a third strategy pursued by older family members involved marrying their children to second cousins with properties adjacent to those of the family in question – thus reconsolidating its landed estate.[14]

One source of the instability of elite coalitions was that the pursuit of any one of these three strategies – all of which were necessary to forming a strong coalition – often conflicted with the others. That is, there were built-in contradictions between the need to maintain strength locally, and the need to ally with and absorb into the family estate those outside the local sphere. The fact that marriage was the mechanism by which these 'externalities' were made internal, however, indicates the importance of patriarchy in the politics of regional control, in the control of space, and in the ability to control the movement of people and products through space.

At any given point in time there were generally two main opposed coalitions formed on this basis, one legal and the other illegal. The competition among these *castas* to control the machinery of state focused on the electoral process, and elected positions (Deputy and Senator). Victory at the polls put the coalition in question in the position of being able to *demand* (at least temporarily) that the central regime in Lima allow it to staff the local state bureaucracy with its own clients (see below). The most effective way of controlling elections was to gain control over the membership of the *mesas receptoras*, or voting tables, where individuals cast their votes.[15] The outcome of elections was in effect decided by which coalition controlled the *mesas*, because their members 'tallied' the voting results. As a result, in the early morning of election day each coalition assembled a group of armed retainers in the provincial capitals where most voting took place. As voting commenced the various armed groups did battle with one another for control of the *mesas* until one prevailed. Deaths were common occurrences (see Basadre 1980; Taylor 1986).

The results of elections were therefore satisfactory only to the coalition that successfully controlled the *mesas receptoras*. Those who lost out often organized competing and parallel elections where they elected their own candidates. As a result, it was common for several individuals to journey to Lima and present themselves to Congress as the 'real' Deputy or Senator from Chachapoyas.[16] Congress then declared who was the winner.[17] The loser usually returned to Chachapoyas to take up a prominent position in the illegal political network – the out-of-power *casta*.

Regardless of which was recognized by Congress, the 'victorious' candidate represented an important coalition of forces within the region – one whose desires could not be ignored if the central regime was to have any real presence in the region, and one that the government could back in maintaining itself against competing national coalitions (which usually had supporters in the form of local coalitions within the Chachapoyas region). As a result the Executive Branch of government, which in theory made appointments to the key positions that controlled the machinery of state within the region – departmental Prefect, provincial Subprefects, Judges and Chiefs of Police – in practice heeded the desires of 'elected' representatives concerning who should fill such posts. By virtue of monopolizing these positions the coalition in question was able to control coveted appointments to virtually all lower-level administrative, extractive and judicial posts for the entire department, and thus to appoint its clients to govern in every province, district and sub-district. In addition to acting as the official representatives of the central government (and thus the ruling *casta*) within their zones of jurisdiction, appointees were responsible (directly or indirectly) for collecting the taxes that were the ruling *casta*'s main source of revenue.[18]

Furthermore, because those that filled these positions were united in their opposition to other coalitions, the ruling *casta* was generally able to contain threats from and ultimately cripple the opposition, and thus was able to maintain order for the central regime (while simultaneously strengthening its own position). The ruling coalition used its nearly hegemonic position within the region to discredit, manufacture evidence against, prosecute, ignore crimes committed against the persons and property of, and even seize the property of members of opposing coalitions. Faced with such conditions, upon falling from power or failing in a bid to seize it, leading members of opposing *castas*, within both regional and local arenas, often either chose to leave the region entirely or to retreat to their haciendas – where their peasant clients would gather in considerable numbers to protect them from armed assaults by the ruling coalition.

Just as the central regime in Lima was forced to rely on 'strong' clients – in the person of Prefect, Subprefect, etc. – in order to be sure of maintaining control over its adversaries, so did the Prefect have to rely on 'strong' clients in the outlying sections of the regional space. To a certain extent the ruling *casta* could rely on its marriage alliances with less influential landed families in appointing these 'strong' clients (as governor, lieutenant governor, and justice of the peace). Ultimately, however, there were many more of these low-ranking positions to fill in outlying sections of the regional space than there were affines to fill them.[19] A final, recognizably distinct section of a coalition was therefore formed out of influential individuals with whom the ruling coalition lacked even a marriage tie, who were appointed to govern in the districts where their spheres of influence were strongest.[20] These individuals made up what might be called the 'coalition periphery'. A combination of marriage alliance and the appointment of non-affines to lower administrative posts thus allowed the ruling *casta* to extend its control over the regional space and over the movement of people and products through this space.

There were two inter-related sets of contradictions, however, that continually worked toward the breakdown and reconstitution of ruling coalitions. The first relates to the centrality of marriage in forming coalition alliances. The second concerns the difficulties of maintaining centralized political rule in tributary contexts. Each will be considered in turn.

The powerful landed families that came together in forming the *casta* core were immediately faced with a dilemma. It was their *alliance* that made regional hegemony possible, and thus each family expected that its members would be appointed to key positions of power, influence and extraction. Specifically, at the center of each of these formerly independent family power blocks was the senior male who presided over the family's landed estate, his sons, and somewhat further afield the set of relatives united around the preservation of the family's landed core via second-cousin marriage. There were no rules for how the most important positions in the state apparatus would be distributed among these individuals, either within or between the families of the *casta* core. And there were many more aspirants than there were important positions to fill.[21] Working out who would be given which positions was therefore a very delicate undertaking, for there was no way to satisfy all the concerned parties. Each family had to safeguard its own interests, but also to be sure that the other family was satisfied with the arrangement.

It was inevitable that some members of both families got less than they felt they deserved, and that some got little or nothing. With little to tie them to the coalition, these individuals often looked elsewhere for opportunities to improve their situations, which often meant an alliance with a different *casta*. Thus, in the act of being formed the ruling *casta* generated powerful opposition from within its very center.

Alliances formed by marrying daughters/sisters to somewhat less influential landed families were also fraught with weakness. As were the *casta* core families, these 'second-tier' families were highly localized within the regional space, and had their own local spheres of influence from which they extracted a limited amount of wealth. Furthermore, as were the *casta* core families, these 'second-tier' families were particularly concerned with preserving the landed core of the family estate – via marriage to relatives with adjacent properties. They had only two reasons to put their localized spheres of influence at the disposal of a broader coalition: (1) the expectation of deriving benefits that came from the ruling *casta*'s control of the machinery of state; and (2) the need to ally with a powerful coalition in order to safeguard themselves, their property and family from competing local landed families.

Should either of these two possibilities fail to become realities there was little to prevent affinal allies from cutting their ties to the *casta* core and seeking out a new alliance with a different patron. This was equally true for the 'peripheral' members of the coalition. As we will see presently, it was inevitable that many 'second-tier' and peripheral members of the ruling coalition ultimately became dissatisfied with the coalition core – for they were almost sure to be eased out of the ruling coalition as a function of the second set of contradictions in *casta* organization mentioned above.

The 'second-tier' and peripheral members of the ruling coalition, who were appointed to positions of governor, lieutenant governor and justice of the peace in the region's many districts and sub-districts, received no salary from the state – and thus they had to be allowed considerable 'latitude' in organizing local extractive activities, and in monitoring the movements of people and products within their zones of jurisdiction. As a result, while 'strong' clients in the districts were essential to the Prefect for the maintenance of 'order', because they controlled extraction, labor use and commodity movements directly, they had a tendency to use these powers to strengthen and enrich themselves at the expense of the *casta* core. Ultimately, the Prefect and the core of the ruling coalition assisted them only minimally in the daily work of managing political life. In such circumstances, these 'second-tier' and peripheral members of the coalition had a tendency to disengage from the coalition core.

In order to guard against such developments, when periods of instability passed the Prefect began to replace these 'strong' clients with 'weak' or true clients – people who had relatively little power and few clients of their own, who would be more beholden to the Prefect for their positions.[22] These individuals could not use the relatively meager resources made available to them by virtue of their positions to build up much of a clientele, because they had little to work with in this regard to begin with. They governed less effectively than a strong client, but posed less of a threat. They were also less likely to disengage from the coalition core. Actually, because they had little autonomous power of their own, and were in a certain sense 'surrounded' by people more powerful than they, they were forced to appeal to the higher authorities on a continual basis because of the difficulty they had in getting anyone to obey their commands.

The same contradictory relationship obtained between the central regime in Lima and the regional coalition headed by the Prefect. Because of the powers it had bequeathed to the Prefect and the coalition he represented – out of necessity and in periods of instability and/or crisis – the central regime had in effect provided the coalition core with powers and resources it could use to strengthen itself at the *expense* of the central state. As a result, when moments of turmoil passed, the Executive Branch gradually tried to undermine the hegemonic position of the ruling group. Such attempts often consisted of appointing a new Prefect – one who was not a member of the ruling coalition, and often was not even from the region.[23] The central regime also used the formal independence of the various branches of government (judiciary, finance, government, etc.) to make appointments to regional-level positions in the judiciary and the police force without consulting the Deputy and Senator who were the elected representatives of the ruling *casta*. These newly appointed individuals did not so much oppose, as rather attempt to contain, the unrestrained consolidation of ruling *casta* power (which was generating increasing hostility among much of the population as it ruled more and more arbitrarily).

There were thus a series of internal contradictions to this form of organization: contradictions that produced weakness out of strength, and strength out of weakness. Coalitions rose to positions of regional hegemony in conditions sufficiently unstable that the state was forced to grant them extensive powers to monitor regional affairs in an autonomous manner. Similarly, coalition cores were forced to grant their more peripheral members virtual *carte blanche* in policing their local zones of jurisdiction. In both regional and local arenas, these extensive powers allowed ruling coalition members to neutralize leading members of the opposition, and to weaken opposing coalitions. In the process of doing so, however, ruling coalition members (temporarily) transformed the very conditions of instability that made them indispensable to those higher in the coalition structure. They also increasingly threatened those in these higher positions, because strong clients tended to strengthen themselves at the expense of those higher in the coalition structure.

As steps were taken to replace strong with weak clients the ruling *casta* generated its own opposition, and undermined its own organization. For those who were eased out of positions of governance – and their numerous clients – often resented this fact considerably.[24] It was common for them to seek alliance with any of the ruling *casta*'s growing number of enemies: (1) those at one time closely associated with the *casta* core, but who had disassociated themselves because they had not been given a key appointment; (2) those (generally landed families) who had been important members of opposing *castas*, and had found themselves persecuted in the period of the ruling coalition's greatest strength; and (3) those in the towns and villages (generally artisans and peasants) who had not played a role in coalition politics, but found themselves subject to the arbitrary exactions of ruling coalition members. As new alliances formed among such displaced individuals the ruling *casta*'s task of administering the regional space became ever more difficult.

The ruling *casta*'s control over the police force and other bureaucratic positions, and its ability to impose sanctions and taxes selectively, allowed it to retain a strong following through all the vicissitudes of local politics. In the context of the growing opposition that emerged out of contradictions of *casta*-based control, however, it was forced to rule in an increasingly arbitrary and autocratic manner through time – and to do so via 'weak' clients who were obliged to rely on higher authorities in order to impose their will within their localities. The longer the regime of any particular *casta* endured, then, the more coercive it was perceived to be by growing numbers of the regional population. Ultimately, the pretensions of opposing coalitions were kept in check only by the knowledge that the ruling *casta* could count on the armed support of the central state.

Consequently, opposing coalitions chose moments when the central state had a difficult time backing its local clients to mount attacks on the ruling *casta* – times either of political transition (congressional and presidential elections) or during the frequent coup attempts and outbreaks of insurrection that characterized the period. For at these moments coalitions fought one another on terms that were relatively equal.[25]

Conclusion

With this information as background we can return to the issues introduced earlier in the chapter: (1) the problems of conceiving of illegal networks as beyond the reach of the state, and the related tendency to associate illegal networks with activities deemed morally, ethically, economically, or politically unacceptable by the state; and (2) the degree to which state and society can be considered conceptual categories adequate to the social complexities of turn-of-the-century Peru. As we have seen, this latter question is made more complicated by the fact that the model of state and society, and of the relation of legality to illegality that currently dominates social science thinking, conforms closely to the forms of state and society imagined in political ritual and discourse in Chachapoyas in the early decades of this century.

Contemporary social science and turn-of-the-century Peruvian political discourse concur on their views of the state and society, and on the relation between legality and illegality in the constitution of modern states. Both view state and society as real entities with clear boundaries, each nurturing the other in a relationship of mutual support and co-constitution. Both view the state and society thus constituted as mutually legitimating, and approach competing organizations of force or power (illegal networks) as illegitimate, and as beyond the reaches of the state.

In turn-of-the-century Chachapoyas, however, it is extremely difficult to distinguish legal from illegal network, or state from society. Particularly problematic for the state–society model posited by contemporary social science and past political discourse is the question of the *boundaries* of the state. It is to this issue that we now turn.

If the central government was to have any effective presence in Chachapoyas, it was forced to ally with the major socio-political coalition of the region – the *casta*. In this sense, then, 'the state' had no autonomy nor distance from the social order, and cannot be distinguished from that *casta*-based social order. At the same time, however, *castas* were themselves in large part creations of state power, in at least two senses: (1) the prominent families that led *castas* achieved their positions of leadership by virtue of having occupied state political positions in the past; and (2) the ruling *casta* occupied its position of dominance because the monopolization of bureaucratic positions that it enjoyed made it possible to construct a region-wide political machine intent upon extracting wealth. In other words, just as 'state' cannot be distinguished from 'society', neither can 'society' be distinguished from 'state'.

Not only was the ruling *casta* (the legal network) a creation of state power, but so too was the out-of-power *casta* (the illegal network). Out-of-power *castas* took on their particular form as individuals excluded from the exercise of state power organized in order to defend their interests. As we have seen, the specific way that they organized themselves mirrored the organization of the state apparatus. Rather than having been a separate entity that was outside or prior to the state, illegal *castas* were a direct by-product of and response to state rule.

Blurring the boundaries in question even more, however, is an additional consideration; whether a *casta* was legal or illegal at any given point in time was largely a matter of circumstance, and one that was more than likely to change quite rapidly. Thus, *castas* that enjoyed legality and rule at one point in time could quickly find themselves deposed and operating outside the bounds of the law. Similarly, opposing *castas* forced to operate in secret and hounded by the 'legal authorities' could quickly catapult themselves to a position of legality and rule. Indeed, in the absence of illegal political networks (opposing *castas*), when those temporarily in control of the state apparatus fell from power state-level society itself would have collapsed. For opposing *castas* were organizations that were prepared on a moment's notice to step in and assume control over the regional power structure, and thus reproduce state presence in the Chachapoyas region.

A second issue concerns whether state–society relations were oppositional or conflictual, requiring the state to engulf or absorb society. In this case, it makes very little sense even to ask the question. Effective state power in Chachapoyas was built upon a foundation of *casta* organization, the latter being the most important social/political form found in the region. Because the boundary between *casta* (society?) and state is so difficult to delineate, one would be hard pressed even to identify the conflicting parties. It is true that there were a series of conflicts between ruling and opposing *castas*. If one chose to identify the former with the state and the latter with society, then the question at least could be posed. Revealingly, however, the same set of conflicts and contradictions that obtained *between* ruling and opposing *castas* were also found *among* members of the ruling *casta* itself, and also between the leadership of the ruling *casta* and the central regime in Lima. In a very real sense, then, *casta* organization in general (including ruling and opposing *castas*) was *the* precondition of state-level society in Chachapoyas, even as the presence of the state apparatus was a precondition of *casta* organization.

A third issue concerns the problem of associating illegal networks with activities considered unworthy of endorsement by the state – and the related tendency to view illegal networks as alternatives to the existing state order. With regard to this problem we may observe the following. In the Chachapoyas region legal and illegal political networks encompassed, endorsed, and underwrote the same activities, and were based on identical political beliefs and ideologies. Illegal networks did not fill a void in state activities. Nor did they point to an absence or even a thin-ness in 'stateness' (Nettl 1968). To the contrary: one would be hard pressed to distinguish between legal and illegal networks on such a basis.

Despite the form of state and society imagined in state discourse, and celebrated in political ritual, it would be impossible to distinguish between legal and illegal networks, or between state and society, on the basis of any criteria: formal political organization; the social identities or class positions of leaders and followers; the values and aspirations of either; the forms of behavior expected of each *vis-à-vis* the other, and in relation to the opposition; or even the control of armed force. Indeed, it was the very fact that illegal networks were modeled so closely on formal state political organization that made for such continuity in the forms and ceremonies of rule when one *casta* did replace another – a development that occurred on a regular basis. In other words, the stability of state rule was crucially dependent on the vitality and viability of political networks deemed 'illegal' and 'illegitimate', and treated as such (and with great brutality!). For these illegal networks, even though persecuted and harassed, organized the population into categories, involved them in relationships, and accustomed them to forms of discipline and rule upon which state organization itself depended. The legitimate boundaries of the state in such circumstances are blurry indeed.[26]

Implicit in the very notion of 'states and illegal networks' is the assumption that illegal networks have arisen outside the formal boundaries of the state apparatus in order to authorize, undertake, or endorse activities that the state is either unwilling or unable to support. In other words, illegal networks are usually taken to point to the *limits* of the state. In opposition to this view, I have sought to identify a social context in which illegal political networks, far from indicating the external boundaries of the state, were creations of state power, and acted as key mechanisms by means of which state organization was brought into being and reproduced. Furthermore, I have suggested that the political processes of turn-of-the-century Peru cannot be captured by the state–society distinction. The analysis presented here thus joins the growing body of literature that approaches the apparent unity and integrity of the state, and the separation of state from society, as problems to be unraveled rather than to be given the features of social orders.

Acknowledgements

A related version of this paper was presented at a conference entitled 'States and Illegal Networks', a Wenner-Gren Sponsored Symposium held on 5–8 June 1997 in Tarrytown, New York. I would like to thank organizer Josiah Heyman for inviting me to participate. He and the other conference participants provided invaluable suggestions concerning the paper I presented. In addition, I owe a debt of gratitude to Constantine Hriskos, Catherine Besteman, Tom Biolsi, and Mary Beth Mills for their insightful comments on an earlier version of the paper. The research upon which this chapter is based was generously funded by the Henry L. and Grace Doherty Charitable Foundation, Sigma Xi, the Scientific Research Society, the MacArthur Foundation Pre-Doctoral Fellowship Program, the Fulbright–Hays Pre-Doctoral Program Abroad, the National Endowment for the Humanities, the Colby College Social Science Grants Committee, the Colby College Interdisciplinary Studies Grant Program, the Program in Agrarian Studies at Yale University, and the Wenner Gren Foundation For Anthropological Research. I gratefully acknowledge the generous support of all these institutions.

Notes

1. Men who carried out identical functions for the out-of-power, illegal *casta* were found in each district in the region.
2. An enormous quantity of archival material conforms the existence of a 'shadow state' throughout the period under consideration. See Nugent (1997) for a discussion of this material as a whole.

3. There were shadow elections for more than just municipal posts. See the discussion below of 'dualidades'.
4. The literature on the consolidation and breakdown of states is vast. See Nugent (1994) for a discussion of this work.
5. As explained below, elections were generally quite violent affairs, and bore little relation to the electoral process in advanced capitalist 'democratic' contexts.
6. Cooper and Stoler (1989: 610–11) make a related point about the ways in which the spread of Enlightenment notions of citizenship, consensus, and equality as the basis of legitimate political community during the nineteenth century created problems in European colonies, where rule was based on coercion and exclusion.
7. The following quote is taken from a taped interview with Sr. Carlos Echaíz on 13 August 1990.
8. See APA 6, 15 de junio de 1898; numerous cases of *desacato* are also listed in APA 7.
9. The following quote is taken from a taped interview with Mariano Rubio Pizarro, conducted on 10 August 1990.
10. The following section of the paper is based on Nugent (1996).
11. 'Sphere of influence' refers to the space within which a member of the elite had built up a sufficient number of clients (through distributing the 'spoils' of landed wealth and/or political office) to be able to control the movement of goods and people with some security. 'Spheres' did not have precise boundaries, and changed according to the political fortunes of members of the elite.
12. The exception was the canyon/valley of the Marañon River, which was more integrated into coastal markets than the rest of the region. Estates in this sub-region produced coca, opium, cane liquor, tobacco and coffee in small quantities for coastal markets. Even here, however, estates remained small and controlled little in the way of peasant labor. Furthermore, most families of the elite had access to land within the canyon.
13. That is, individuals with large numbers of peasant mule drivers as clients (see Nugent 1988: Ch. 3).
14. First-cousin marriage was forbidden by the Catholic Church and the Civil Code of 1852. It is clear, however, that the formal rule prohibiting first-cousin marriage was circumvented in a variety of ways (see Nugent 1997: Ch. 3).
15. In practice, voting was restricted to landowning males (excluding peasants) who were either heads of households or were 21 years of age (Basadre 1980).

16. The department of Amazonas – of which Chachapoyas is the capital – was represented by two Senators and three Deputies (one for each of its three provinces).
17. These procedures change after 1896; but elections remained subject to local, dominant-*casta* manipulation until 1931.
18. An important dimension to inter-*casta* struggles concerns the 'factional organization of force' – the manner in which elite families established ties to the commanders of the police and armed forces, and thus controlled physical force beyond their own dependants. Control of appointments to these positions was a point of constant contention between the ruling *casta* and the central regime in Lima. During periods when the central government was forced to rely on 'strong' Prefects, Subprefects, etc. (see text below) the leading members of the ruling *casta* chose the commanders of the armed forces – generally selecting prominent members of one of the kin-related families that led the ruling *casta* (often the brother or first cousin of the Prefect). He in turn would recruit the rank and file from among the *casta*'s mestizo and peasant clientele. Their loyalty was insured in part by giving them considerable latitude to use their positions to engage in 'private extraction'. When the central regime in Lima sought to 'weaken' the ruling *casta* it attempted to place people of its own choice in the position of commander of the armed forces (see Nugent 1997: Ch. 3).
19. Because *casta* organization and membership was subject to constant breakdown and reformulation, there was no large kin unit with consistent or stable membership that could be drawn upon to recruit clients via marriage (compare Lewin [1987]).
20. These individuals were responsible for the wide range of mundane activities upon which political administration depended. That is, they administered people, collected taxes, mediated disputes, organized public works, maintained 'law and order', located fugitives from justice, and decided who would be allowed to dominate commerce, within their jurisdictions. Governors, lieutenant governors and justices of the peace used these powers as sources of favoritism in recruiting clients among the peasantry (Nugent 1997: Ch. 3). Both ruling and opposing *castas* recruited peasant clients in this manner in all peasant villages, because of which villages were heavily factionalized. This fact weakened not only lateral or horizontal networks among the peasantry, but also class-based, oppositional forms of peasant political action and symbolic representation of the elite.
21. This was especially true because the extraction of wealth in this region

was based predominantly on tributary mechanisms, and was focused on a subsistence-oriented peasantry with little disposable wealth.

22. District appointees had terms of one year, which made it easy to replace strong with weak clients (and vice versa).
23. At first glance, it might appear that the ability of the central government to make such an appointment signifies the power of an autonomous state apparatus. In fact, however, it was only because the ruling *casta* had first stabilized conditions in the Chachapoyas region that the central government was able even to entertain the possibility of making such an appointment. In other words, the 'relative autonomy' of the state was granted to it by the ruling *casta*.
24. It was not uncommon for governors to refuse to step down, or to refuse to hand over the seal of office and/or the files to their would-be successors, forcing the Subprefect to send in the police in order to effect the change in office. Equally common was for a former governor to harass his successor once the latter was in office, at times with the help of former and/or new political allies.
25. For purposes of clarity, I have presented coalition organization as undergoing a cycle of centralization and decentralization. In actuality, the processes in question were not nearly so regular in character. Rather, tendencies in both directions often took place simultaneously in different parts of the regional space, or reversed themselves. This irregularity only made the ability to move people and goods through the regional space even less dependable.
26. It is important to point out that these categories, relationships, and forms of rule were anything but foreign to or imposed upon the population by 'the state', conceived of as some kind of external, outside force. To the contrary: they were primarily expressions of power relations found within the Chachapoyas region (as well as within many other regions) – a fact that lent continuity to the form of state rule during this period (see Nugent 1997).

References

Primary Sources

Archivo Prefectural de Amazonas (APA), Chachapoyas, Peru.
APA 1. Decretos [Prefectura]. 1908–1910.
APA 2. Subprefectura del Cercado al Prefecto. 1907.
APA 3. Corte Superior de Loreto, Amazonas y Cajamarca, 1907.

APA 4. Mesa de Partes, Prefectura del Departamento de Amazonas, 1907.
APA 5. Oficios Recibidos de Varios Gobernadores en el Año de 1887.
APA 6. Subprefectura del Cercado al Prefecto del Departamento de Amazonas, 1893–1898.
APA 7. Mesa de Partes, Prefectura del Departamento de Amazonas, 1897–1904.

Secondary Sources

Abrams, Philip (1988), 'Notes on the Difficulty of Studying the State', *Journal of Historical Sociology* 1: 58–89.
Alvárez, Sonia E., Evelina Dagnino and Arturo Escobar (eds) (1998), *Cultures of Politics, Politics of Culture: Revisioning Latin American Social Movements*. Boulder, CO: Westview Press.
Basadre, Jorge (1968–69), *Historia de la República del Perú 1822–1933*, 17 Vols, 6th Edn. Lima: Editorial Universitaria.
—— (1980), *Elecciones y centralismo en el Perú*. Lima: Centro de Investigación de la Universidad del Pacífico.
Burga, Manuel and Alberto Flores Galindo (1979), *Apogeo y Crisis de la República Aristocrática*. Lima: IEP (Instituto de Estudios Peruanos).
Caravedo Molinari, Baltazar (1977), *Clases, lucha política y gobierno en el Perú, 1919–1930*. Lima: Ediciones Retama.
—— (1979), 'Poder central y decentralización. Peru, 1931', *Apuntes* 5(9): 111–29.
Colmenares, German (1985), 'La nación e la historia regional en los países andinos, 1870–1930', *Revista Andina* 3(2): 311–30.
Comaroff, John L. (1993), 'Ethnicity, Nationalism, and the Politics of Difference in an Age of Revolution', Paper Presentation, Institute of Social and Economic Research, Rhodes University, Conference on Ethnicity, Identity, and Nationalism in South Africa.
Cooper, Frederick and Ann L. Stoler (1989), 'Tensions of Empire: Colonial Control and Visions of Rule', *American Ethnologist* 16(4): 609–21.
Cotler, Julio (1978), *Clases, Estado y Nación*. Lima: IEP.
Foucault, Michel (1980), *Power/Knowledge*, ed. Colin Gordon. New York: Pantheon Books.
Gorman, Stephen (1979), 'The State, Elite and Export in Nineteenth Century Peru', *Journal of Interamerican Studies and World Affairs* 21(3): 395–418.
Gupta, Akhil (1995), 'Blurred Boundaries: The Discourse of Corruption, the Culture of Politics, and the Imagined State', *American Ethnologist*

22(2): 375–402.
Harvey, David (1989), *The Condition of Postmodernity: An Enquiry into the Origins of Cultural Change*. Oxford: Basil Blackwell.
Jameson, Frederic (1984), 'Postmodernism, or The Cultural Logic of Late Capitalism', *New Left Review* 146: 53–92.
Lewin, Linda (1987), *Politics and Parentela in Paraiba: A Case Study of Family-Based Oligarchy in Brazil.* Princeton, NJ: Princeton University Press.
Mallon, Florencia E. (1983), *The Defense of Community in Peru's Central Highlands*. Princeton, NJ: Princeton University Press.
Mandel, Ernest (1975), *Late Capitalism*. London: Verso.
Miller, Rory (1982), 'The Coastal Elite and Peruvian Politics, 1895–1919', *Journal of Latin American Studies* 14(1): 97–120.
—— (1987), 'Introduction', in Rory Miller (ed.), *Region and Class in Modern Peruvian History*. University of Liverpool, Institute of Latin American Studies Monograph No. 14: 7–20.
Mitchell, Timothy (1991), 'The Limits of the State: Beyond Statist Approaches and Their Critics', *American Political Science Review* 85: 77–96.
Nettl, John (1968), 'The State as a Conceptual Variable', *World Politics* 20: 559–92.
Nugent, David (1988), 'The Mercantile Transformation of Provincial Urban Life: Labor, Value and Time in the Northern Peruvian Sierra', Ph.D. Dissertation, Columbia University.
—— (1994), 'Building the State, Making the Nation: the Bases and Limits of State Centralization in "Modern" Peru', *American Anthropologist* 96(2): 333–69.
—— (1996), 'From Devil Pacts to Drug Deals: Commerce, Unnatural Accumulation and Moral Community in Modern Peru', *American Ethnologist* 23(4): 258–90.
—— (1997), *Modernity at the Edge of Empire: State, Individual, and Nation in the Northern Peruvian Andes, 1885–1935*. Stanford, CA: Stanford University Press.
Smith, Gavin (1989), *Livelihood and Resistance. Peasants and the Politics of Land in Peru*. Berkeley: University of California Press.
Szanton Blanc, Cristina, Linda Basch, and Nina Glick Schiller (1995), 'Transnationalism, Nation-States, and Culture', *Current Anthropology* 36(4):683–6.
Taylor, Lewis (1986), *Bandits and Politics in Peru: Landlord and Peasant Violence in Hualgayoc 1900–1930*. Centre of Latin American Studies, University of Cambridge.

– 4 –

Predatory Rule and Illegal Economic Practices

Alan Smart

Illegality and the state have been constant companions. It is perhaps inherent in the nature of states that they prohibit certain types of behavior, if only the avoidance of taxes. It is less clear why they should never be able to succeed in fully suppressing all that they make illegal. Certainly we have many specific case studies of failure (including those addressed in this volume), as well as general analyses based on failures of information and rationality,[1] the costs of monitoring compliance and the problem of 'who will guard the guards' (Moore 1978). These accounts are either too specific and tied to particular cases, or too quick to generalize a particular reason for the failure of suppression. I suggest in this chapter that what is needed at present is to identify the whole range of basic reasons why practices might continue despite being illegal. A typology of basic varieties of persistence is then offered. A limitation that this approach shares with other Weberian ideal types is that real-world cases usually do not fit neatly with a single type. Instead, illegal practices often continue for a variety of reasons. When more than one reason for persistence exists, suppression would seem to be even more difficult.[2] Although trying to categorize particular situations as fitting best one type or another might be seen as an academic exercise, I believe that it has the merit of clarifying thought and focusing the analysis. In the second half of the chapter, I attempt to demonstrate this through a case study of a category of illegal practices that is implicated in almost all forms of illegal persistence: bribery.

The Introduction indicates that there is a strong need for the construction of analytical frameworks that are flexible and robust enough to encompass the diversity and complexity of the interaction between states and illegal practices. They are not yet available, despite the wealth of insightful ethnographic account and theoretical engagements with such topics. Neoclassical economic and political economy analyses offer integrative frameworks that are fascinating but limited. I argue in this chapter that we might make faster progress towards better theory by devoting at least as much attention to the state side of the equation as to the illegal practices. This is particularly necessary since many illegal networks include state officials. But the reason for attending to states is more pragmatic: the models that can be adapted are more developed in state theory than in studies of illegal economic practices. We need to work from both ends simultaneously and hope that we manage to connect up in the middle, like the Channel Tunnel, and this volume demonstrates what can be accomplished when we try to dig towards the other sides.

Given the immense variety of state theories, how do we start? First, we need to recognize that states are internally complex and composed of many agents. It is inappropriate to refer to *states* doing or intending things. This volume amply illustrates the kinds of internal conflicts and complexities that enable any state action. Still, it is impractical to start with a model that accounts for all the levels and their possible permutations in the full range of diversity. A model that is adopted as a starting-point, then, should be sensitive to internal division without threatening submersion in more complexity than is necessary. Second, we need to highlight aspects of the state that are particularly relevant to the understanding of illegal practices.

Margaret Levi's theory of predatory rule has advantages on both fronts. First, she distinguishes between rulers (central executive in whatever form: monarch, prime minister or dictator) and the agents who are needed to enact their commands (but also have their own agendas). The state at a particular time and space is the product of bargains and disputes between all relevant agents, both those within the state and those officially not its agents. Second, her approach centers on an issue crucial for illegal economic practices: state production of revenues. She proposes the hypothesis that 'rulers maximize the revenue accruing to the state subject to the constraints of their relative bargaining power, transaction costs, and discount rates' (1988: 2). One of the main features common to all illegal economic practices is that they do not provide revenue to the state through official channels, although they may do so through illicit mechanisms such as bribery.

The advantages of beginning from Levi's approach are inevitably matched with problems. Most notably, our attention may be drawn away from two difficult but important sets of issues. The first involves the ways in which states achieve, maintain and lose hegemony over their subjects. The second concerns a more nuanced examination of the specific nature of the goals of rulers, and how these vary between different types of regime and state.[3] Revenues are clearly always important, but often as means to an end, and an understanding of states requires attention to the precise nature of those ends, and how they may vary by time and place. Still, on balance, I find Levi's attempt to push relentlessly her model to its limits informative, and a useful starting-point for analytical endeavours that commonly are treated either with narrow description or ungrounded policy prescription without solid theoretical grounding.

It might be the case that my use of Levi's theory to develop the following typology of varieties of persistence of illegal practice is like Wittgenstein's ladder: once having used it to climb to my objective, it is no longer required. However, I did in fact require it to get there, and it seems only just to account for how it helped inform the development of the analytical concepts that I put to the test in the case study of bribery in the People's Republic of China. That case study shows, though, the importance of bringing the analysis of legitimation and hegemony closer to the core of the analysis than is suggested by Levi's formalizing statements.

Predatory Rule, Revenue and Individual Agency

Levi (1988: 186) suggests that Marxian approaches to the state have been fruitful but suffer from limitations generated by reluctance to examine the state 'as an institution composed of and pressured by individuals, who sometimes act as a class (or for a class) but at least as often do not'. The neoclassicists pay much more attention to the choices of individuals; but for Levi, the dominant strain of public choice theory is too narrow in its emphasis on rent-seeking, and its advocates 'obsessed with demonstrating the negative impact of government on the economy'. Political incumbents and their rivals are involved in competition for direct and indirect rents available from office (Buchanan 1980). From this view political competition leads to interventions in the economy which produce rents, and rational investment in competition for these rents dissipates most of the rents in directly unproductive activity. The problem is that this approach fails to recognize that the effects of government intervention are 'variable, sometimes reducing and sometimes stimulating social waste' (Levi 1988: 24). While rulers may strive to maximize revenues, in doing so they may produce solutions to market failures and other inefficiencies that individual efforts cannot resolve, and that may deter long-term investments. If they can increase the size of the pie, the size of their piece may increase even though their share might be trimmed.

Levi's theory of predatory rule[4] is distinct from apparently similar analyses of predatory states or kleptocracies that are dedicated to maximizing graft (Marcouiller and Young 1995; Peng 1996; Manion 1997), and in which those 'who control the state apparatus seem to plunder without any more regard for the welfare of the citizenry than a predator has for the welfare of its prey' (Evans 1989: 562). Public choice theories suggest that all governments are operated as predatory states where all agents are out to maximize their self-interest, but Evans (1989) and others have argued that this situation (which he accepts as characterizing the former Zaire) is not the only outcome. He insists that some states are developmental rather than predatory.[5] Proponents of the 'developmental state' thesis argue that an appropriate set of interventions are critical to the success of late-developing states (Amsden 1990). Evans (1996) acknowledges the constraints on successful state fostering of development, but concludes that the presence of 'embedded autonomy' increases the chances of success. Embedded autonomy involves a difficult combination of an internally cohesive state bureaucracy (a precondition for capacity to intervene effectively) and state connectedness with private sector entrepreneurs (Evans 1996: 263). By contrast, in predatory states like Zaire, coherence is restricted to a small presidential clique. Beyond this, market relations dominate administrative behavior, so that 'everything is for sale . . . And in this traffic, holding any slice of public power constitutes a veritable exchange instrument' (President Mobutu, quoted in Evans 1989: 570). Levi's assumption of revenue-maximization does not require this kind of regime; rather it tries to identify conditions where such short-term and ultimately destructive forms of rule are likely to emerge.

For a variety of reasons, revenue-maximizing rulers may accept a situation where subordinates are regularly siphoning off what they can for their own purposes. Suppressing such activities may undermine their coalition of support (see Humphrey, this volume, Chapter 7). Insecurity of rule serves to increase the 'discount rate', encouraging the sacrifice of future for present gains, a point vividly illustrated by Nugent's contribution to this volume (Chapter 3). At the same time, their relative bargaining power may be weak against subordinates, or the transaction costs of monitoring the activities may be too high. As Levi (1988: 12) suggests, for rulers, 'encouraging rent seeking could be an efficient strategy despite its promotion of social waste'.

Rulers have more bargaining power to the extent that they monopolize strategic coercive, economic, and political resources. When others control resources that the ruler needs, their bargaining power increases, and deals or contracts may be made with these groups (Levi 1988: 12). This can lead to tacit tolerance of wealthy criminal entrepreneurs in illegal arms or drugs trades who support election campaigns or guerrilla-suppression efforts. Deals, once made, do not enforce themselves, and there are transaction costs involved in bargaining, measuring, monitoring and enforcing compliance. The more decentralized activities are, the higher the transaction costs. This can encourage rulers to collude in offering tacit monopolies to certain groups in exchange for keeping the illegal trade under control. What Levi (1988: 13) refers to as 'quasi-voluntary compliance' (avoiding the methodological pitfalls of the concept of 'legitimacy')[6] can reduce the transaction costs of monitoring and enforcing forms of producing revenues. Conversely, if such compliance is eroded, as when taxpayers doubt the fairness of the system and feel justified in evading taxes, transaction costs soar. The lack of quasi-voluntary compliance with, say, excise duties can lead to very high rates of smuggling (Platt 1991: 12; MacGaffey 1991).

Levi (1988: 16) states that the main implication of her theory is that rulers 'will devise and formalize structures that increase their bargaining power, reduce their transaction costs, and lower their discount rates so as to better capture gains from exchanges of politics'. Beginning from Levi's approach, in the next section I construct a typology of basic explanations for the persistence of illegal economic activities. The typology is not dependent on agreement with Levi's theory. Potentially, a similar classification system might have been developed beginning from another starting-point – perhaps Gramscian hegemony theory; but the flavour of it clearly is influenced by where I began.

Varieties of Illegal Persistence

The following classification addresses the questions of why, when and how economic activities that are illegal nevertheless persist. I have endeavored to strip these varieties down to their most fundamental features, and a much more elaborate classification system could be developed by incorporating more features and distinguishing between subtypes within each basic variety. I do not attempt this here, partially because the varieties of causes are not mutually exclusive. Furthermore, it would seem more valuable to build from this typology by looking at the consequences of concrete cases supported by multiple reasons for continuance despite illegality.[7] This is the approach I take later in the analysis of bribery.

At least five basic varieties of persistence of illegal economic activity can be identified. Here I define them, offer brief examples, and distinguish each from the others:

1. Market persistence – This type involves cases where continued demand for a good or service creates incentives that undermine state efforts to control the market. This class of cases is the one that is best known (see the Introduction in this volume). Market persistence occurs despite more or less serious efforts to eradicate the activity. The Prohibition of alcohol in the United States is one example, and the contraband drugs trade at present is another example. Legitimacy of the activity may make control harder, but it is not a precondition for market persistence, as it is for the next type, ambiguous persistence.

2. Ambiguous persistence – I group into this category cases where an activity is illegal, but usually tolerated, or only occasionally and situationally repressed. There is a significant degree of social legitimacy of the activity, despite its formal illegality. These practices can have large costs for states in lost revenue, including income taxes, property taxes, and loss of control over government land. The large informal sector in postcolonial cities is one example, and illegal squatting is another. The response of toleration is related to the transaction costs of monitoring and controlling very large numbers of small-scale transactions. This would not account for situations like squatter settlements, though, where the illegal occupation is easily visible and physically should be easily eradicable. Another factor comes into play here: the relative bargaining powers of the two groups as represented by the capacity of the squatters to resist clearance and cause a variety of inconveniences for the state. Where squatters represent valued blocks of voters, they may also be able to bargain for some collective benefits like water and electricity supplies. Some authors have argued that governments profit from tolerating squatter communities by reducing pressure for government expenditure on housing, and by cheaply reproducing labour power (see Smart 1992 for a discussion and critique of this approach). But direct benefits are more characteristic of the third variety of persistence: managed persistence.

3. Managed persistence – This variety includes situations where, despite formal illegality, the state benefits substantially from the activity and makes at most token[8] efforts to achieve control. The leakiness of illegal migration from Mexico to the United States has been suggested as an example of this (Heyman 1995). It has also been suggested that in a variety of states, bureaucracies profit from the proliferation of costly regulations in order to extract bribes from economic agents.[9] For cases that fit this category, dominant constraints differ from the first two types, since the activity is tacitly sponsored by rulers directly in pursuit of increased revenues. Where constraints may be critical here is in conditions that make it desirable to keep these activities illegal, which may be related to ideology or to the fear of undermining quasi-voluntary compliance in other sectors. Schneider and Schneider's (1994) account of the rise of the antimafia movement in Sicily, and the way in which it transformed mafia–state relations based on political collusion, is a good example of the kinds of processes involved.

4. Rebellious persistence – This type refers to cases where internal political actors, such as guerrilla groups or rebellious localities, protect illegal practices despite opposition from the ruler. In these cases, there are political spaces within the ruler's territory where there are relatively autonomous actors who have political control over what is done, and choose to support illegal practices, usually for the production of their own revenue streams or for its value as a nuisance or threat to their alleged suzerains. It is important to distinguish this reason for the persistence of illegal practices from the accretion of means of violence by illegal entrepreneurs such as the Medellin cocaine cartel.[10] Illegal practices are a means to the political ends held by rebels, whereas achieving significant means of violence and command over local areas are a means to the end of profits in the market persistence type.

5. Subversive persistence – The final category includes cases in which support for illegal practices derives from agents outside the state for purposes of undermining political control. The support by the American government for the drug-trafficking activities of the Kuomintang in Burma is a good example of this (see McCoy, this volume, Chapter 5). This variety shares some similarities with managed persistence, except that the benefits are going to the rulers of another state, rather than the one in which the activities are taking place.

Individual cases are likely to combine characteristics of two or more of the varieties. It is also likely that I haven't yet exhausted the logical possibilities of varieties of persistence, and the identification of further alternatives would certainly be desirable. The next steps that must be taken involve more than identifying other variant categories possibilities. First, we should begin to generate hypotheses about under what conditions the different forms of persistence are likely to be found. Second, we need to know what implications the different forms of persistence have for the organization of illegal practices, including whether they take a network or a closed-group form and how they relate to state bureaucracies and politicians. Third, we should move from a static definitional effort towards a dynamic exploration of the trajectories of elaboration or transformation that might be found under the influence of different reasons for the continued existence of illegal practices. Finally, we should attempt to identify what important questions and issues are occluded or omitted by beginning from the starting-point of explaining the forms of persistence in relation to the revenue-production interests of rulers. In the remainder of this chapter, I will begin to consider these questions through a brief account of bribery in post-1978 China.

Bribery in China: A Case Study of Illegal Persistence

Introduction

David Nugent's Chapter 3 suggests the danger that a focus on states and illegal networks will proceed from the assumption that illegal networks have arisen outside the formal boundaries of the state apparatus to 'reflect and/or fill a void in state activities'.[11] He argues that the implied distinction between the state and society is analytically inadequate. This is certainly the case for situations where bribery is endemic and largely expected, if not formally condoned. In such situations, state institutions are embedded in networks of private interests in ways other than those authorized by formal regulations,[12] and the operation of those private interests cannot be understood outside the context of their interactions with government officials. Exploring these practices and interactions can give us a better understanding of the nature and effects of states. Exploring the incorporation of officials into corrupt networks is particularly critical in a situation like reform China, where formal descriptions leave out some of the most important processes of governmental and societal transformation (Manion 1997). Formal rules have often followed behind, eventually legitimizing local practices made possible originally through collusion between private and foreign interests and local officials.

The offer or solicitation of bribes persists for reasons that fit a variety of the types identified above, and thus cannot in general be unambiguously classified with any one of them. Even in particular circumstances, a variety of reasons which may be sufficient but not necessary for persistence may co-exist. For example, governments might maintain unnecessary regulations in order to provide opportunities for officials to induce bribes (which would make it possible to pay officials less than would otherwise be the case; might increase their loyalty to superiors who could transfer them out of lucrative positions; and might produce a stream of kickbacks to the rulers themselves, among other benefits). In other circumstances, as in Yunnan near the Thailand and Myanmar borders, contraband drug markets survive in part by using revenues to bribe interdiction officers, so that in these cases corruption is a side-effect of market persistence. Alternatively, payment of gratuities for services provided by officials may be seen as legitimate signals of gratitude for resolving difficulties (see, for example, Eames 1990) and thereby share some of the characteristics of ambiguous persistence. This might be particularly common where the bribes are provided by informal sector operators to officials who are sympathetic to their dilemmas and wish to help as well as to line their own pockets. Certainly the payment of bribes is involved in the ways in which alternative power-holders protect illegal networks in both subversive and rebellious persistence. Bribes, then, are commonly implicated in most situations where illegal practices persist, and cannot be clearly positioned within any one of the varieties. Where more than one of these reasons for persistence simultaneously pertain, we can consider the continuing existence of bribery to be 'overdetermined': even if we removed one condition, it might not significantly reduce the prevalence of the activity.

Another reason for studying bribery and its role in governmental corruption[13] is that it allows us to examine ways in which informal processes of revenue-extraction influence the relation between rulers, their agents and their populations. In many contexts, sovereignty can become so parcellated or divided, as in feudal states or some federal systems, that rulers do not even indirectly control all the revenue of the state. Where decentralization is taken far enough, one must identify distinct rulers at different levels who interact, not as principal and agent, but as fellow rulers connected by contractual agreements or conflictual arrangements. Formal divisions of sovereignty along these lines are not the only way in which control over subordinates' actions can be severely restricted. Corruption can be related to local 'empire-building', and the capacity of rulers to eradicate these activities (or even assure their own shares) can become extremely limited over time, as occurred in Zaire (MacGaffey 1991).

The outcome of the corrupt incorporation of officials into illegal networks cannot be taken for granted. In some circumstances, it may serve to erode control by the central authorities (Rocca 1992: 403). In other situations, regulations may be created or maintained to create opportunities for graft, and the management of systematic corruption may be a central interest of predatory states. More often, perhaps, corruption may be double-sided, with governments unable to eliminate it (owing to the potential profits for poorly paid agents – market persistence – or popular acceptance of the practice – ambiguous persistence), but then attempting to channel the activities and turn them to their own advantage (managed persistence).

An examination of all the dimensions of bribery relevant to this volume is beyond the scope of this chapter. Instead I simply suggest some directions worthy of exploration through discussion of bribery in China.

To do so, however, requires some elaboration of China's changing political economy.

Political Change in China

While it is clear that bribery and 'using the back door' were prevalent during the Cultural Revolution[14] from 1966 to 1978 (M. Yang 1994), contemporary corruption takes shape in the context of wide-ranging reforms since 1978. The opening of China to foreign investment has received most attention, but more widely important has been decentralization of decision-making from central authorities to city, county and township officials as well as to enterprise managers, especially in the collective sector.

Andrew Walder (1995) has argued that it has not been marketization or privatization but the clarification of property rights that has made possible the dynamism of township and village collective industries (the fastest-growing sector since 1978). Objecting to the description of township and village enterprises (TVEs) as 'hybrid', he asserts that the key to their performance has been that 'governments at the lower levels are able to exercise more effective control over their assets than are governments at higher levels' (Walder 1995: 270). Effective decentralization has regularly moved in advance of the promulgation of laws and guidelines to govern these practices, and new, flexible practices have been the result of local actors operating in ways that are tolerated without being officially accepted. For example, the emergence of a market for land and buildings developed without legislation and at a time when private property in land was prohibited in the Constitution (Smart 1995). The development of trust between investors and local officials, often facilitated by gift-exchange practices that could be classified as bribery, stood in for uncertain property rights (Smart 1993; Hsing 1997).

The reforms have been characterized by the center authorizing experimentation and temporarily tolerating practices that are not supported by formal rules. Experiments that work are often subsequently adopted as standard practices and supported by new laws. A clear example is the household responsibility system in agriculture. A bottom-up reform, it ended the Maoist system of collective agriculture and ushered in a system of leasehold that often resembles sharecropping,[15] with the state taking the part of the landlord. By the time that new laws are drafted to support existing practices, however, new problems have emerged that are being dealt with pragmatically by local officials, producing a continual sequence of 'situational adjustment' (Moore 1978) and modified regulations,[16] which stimulates further adaptations and adjustments. Bribery has been among the results of these changes, as well as a central mechanism for enabling the situational adjustments.

Decentralization has not necessarily meant a decrease in the center's share of resources. The state's share of national income in 1991 was near its 1952–91 average of 41.5 per cent (D. Yang 1994: 61). The share of localities (provinces and sub-provincial units) in this total has increased during the reform period, but only from 57.5 per cent in 1982 to 60.86 per cent in 1990 (D. Yang 1994: 69). The biggest change has been seen in the nearly continuous decline in state budgetary investment as a percentage of total investment from over 80 per cent in 1953 and 60 per cent in 1979 to about 10 per cent in 1991. This transformation is accounted for by the rise in extra-budgetary funds that are outside central plans and are more responsive to market incentives and constraints (D. Yang 1994: 71). At the same time, the absolute amount of state revenues has been growing dramatically as a result of China's rapid growth, suggesting that reforms have so far been consistent with Levi's hypothesis that rulers strive to maximize the revenues that they control. The increasing independence of local actors (Wang 1995) seems to be one of the prices to be paid for expanded revenues, while expansion of market mechanisms has reduced costs involved in ensuring compliance with directives. However, Solinger (1996: 33) argues persuasively that decentralization has not affected all localities in any standard manner, and that it only resulted in heightened influence at the subnational level where 'other conditions – conferred by the Center itself – were also present'. Still, some conditions cannot be conferred by the Center, especially social networks with ethnic Chinese overseas, and this would seem to limit the abilities of the Center to reassert control without serious costs in certain parts of the nation.

The reforms have also involved a shift from controlling all the revenues of state enterprises towards using taxation to produce revenue. Generating compliance with unaccustomed systems of taxation is a serious problem for Chinese authorities. Ensuring compliance with any commands has become more difficult than in the past (Walder 1995). Liu (1992) suggests that China has a 'sporadic totalitarian state': central authorities can carry out radical transformations and stop any actions they dislike – if they come to their notice – but they have much less ability to monitor what is going on and control all the instances of what is formally opposed.[17] Nor is quasi-voluntary compliance widespread, unless locals find it in their interests to comply. In such circumstances, local collusion can substantially reduce the revenues flowing to the center (Oi 1989). For example, once land leases became legal (after having been traded for some years with dubious legality), the regulations stipulated that 40 per cent of land sales income should go to the central treasury. Since localities had to foot the costs of preparing land for sale, they responded with creative 'adaptation'. One reaction was that part of the rent was paid in kind by building a street or bridge (and the transfer to the treasury is based only on the reduced rent). In another variant, accounting procedures distinguished between land requisition cost, development cost, management fee, and rent, and the transfer to the treasury was calculated on the basis of the narrowly defined rent (FBIS 3 December 1992: 44).

Where access to resources external to the party-state is relatively significant, the effective control of the center can be reduced, and access to foreign capital through social connections is a clear example of such circumstances. Josephine Smart and I have argued elsewhere (Smart and Smart 1991) that Hong Kong investors[18] have relied on social connections and the development of trust with local officials to support their investment more than they have on formal rules and contracts, which they view with considerable distrust. The result has been the proliferation of deals and interactions between local officials and foreign investors that could be construed as corrupt. However, rather than simply being a destructive and inefficient practice (as public choice theory would suggest), these relations and practices have been central to Hong Kong investors' competitive advantages and to the rapid increase in local prosperity in the locations where these investments have been concentrated.

In 1978 the obstacles to investment by capitalist enterprises were immense: only the sketchiest of regulations existed. The establishment of enterprises run on a capitalist basis within a socialist nation raises problems that must be overcome in the pursuit of profit. One strategy is to utilize ties with individuals who can facilitate investment. This strategy can dramatically speed up the process of establishing an enterprise, but at the cost of relying primarily on social support. Given the complexities of going through formal mechanisms, and the lack of security offered even when apparently tightly-drafted contracts were finally agreed, we and others argued that reliance on social connections could reduce transaction costs, and help get an enterprise up and running more quickly, so that profits would help the participants subsequently to solve any problems that might arise. In practice, this meant that Hong Kong investors regularly went beyond what was officially permitted by the regulations and even by the national constitution, although rules were sometimes subsequently altered to legitimize the ways in which investors had been 'pushing the envelope' (Smart 1995).

But decentralization can affect localities in very different ways, and the production of entrepreneurial local officials is not a universal outcome. Peng (1996: 82) argues that:

> in rural Guizhou, where there are scant opportunities to carry out industrialization or other entrepreneurial activities, the local officialdom acts in a parasitic, predatory fashion as tax maximizers. The behaviour of officials in the districts that Oi and the others have studied occupies only one portion of a repertory of bureaucratic responses that, at another extreme, encompasses Guizhou-style behaviour as well. They are all part of the same system of governance.

Situations that can be characterized as corrupt, then, can increase local prosperity or reduce it further. Generalizations about corruption's effects are futile, because its ubiquity means that they vary by situation. The economists' effort to legislate the effects by using the concept of 'directly unproductive activity' misses the whole point. If corruption is found in all states at all times, then the important task is 'analysing its forms, scope, social role and the perception of it within society' (Levy 1995: 2). The forms of corruption are as diverse as the distinct property relations emerging in reform China, and firm conclusions about its effects premature. But any understanding of what is going on cannot ignore bribery and collusion, because it is involved in important ways in all local responses to the opening in governance that the reforms occasioned.

As yet, I have said little about the actual definition and nature of bribery and corruption in China, nor about efforts to control it. I turn to these issues in the next section.

Corruption in China

The standard conception of the bribe involves legal definitions. Since law usually implies a state, this may be why massive attention to gifts in anthropology is combined with near-total neglect of the bribe, despite its theoretical importance (van Baal 1975: 55). Noonan (1984: xi) defines a bribe as 'an inducement improperly influencing the performance of a public function meant to be gratuitously exercised'. Bribery is 'a legal concept, hence the law determines what counts as bribery in a particular society' (p. xi). The legal conception of bribe or 'improper inducement' is important, but it does not exhaust the social meaning of the term. Many laws restrict bribery penalties to people serving in official roles; yet bribery in the sense of instrumental exploitation of an exchange is commonly referred to in actions by ordinary citizens. Equally, the state can define as bribes exchanges that the participants see as gifts supporting a relationship rather than as inducements to do anything improper. Thus, there are both legal and informal social aspects to the concept of the bribe. Taken out of its legal context, the conception of bribes as 'improper inducements' seems to be an adequate gloss of the meaning. The impropriety may consist in breaking the law, or in socially inappropriate practices.

The legal definition of bribery is usually ambiguous, and this is certainly the case in China. Myers (1989) demonstrates that what is acceptable reciprocity one year may be redefined as corruption the next. The processes by which transactions become censured as corrupt do not just involve 'fitting' of behavior to law, but depend on transactional or political relationships between suspected corrupt individuals and officials responsible for monitoring their actions (Lo 1993: 54). Ironically, one usually effective strategy for protection against such charges is to cultivate the right connections through *guanxi* (Meaney 1989: 205).

Guanxi can be roughly glossed as 'relationships', and getting almost any practical task accomplished in China may involve mobilizing connections at some point or other (M. Yang 1994; Yan 1996; Kipnis 1997). Giving gifts to a *guanxi* partner in order to accomplish a task is not always seen as involving bribery. Transactions are most often perceived as bribes when the instrumental end appears to be more important than building and maintaining the relationship. Where the relationship is more important than the immediate goal, the exchange of gifts and favours is not usually stigmatized as bribery, however the letter of the law may read (Smart 1993). Similarly, where the transaction is seen as being in the interests of a group rather than just an individual, it will usually be seen as involving good *guanxi* rather than a corrupt relationship (M. Yang 1994; Hao and Johnston 1995: 139).

Formally, corruption in China is encompassed by three terms. The first, *tanwu*, involves state officials who misappropriate public property by embezzlement, theft or swindling. The second, *shouhui*, refers to the use of an official position to extort or to accept bribes. The third, *tequan*, concerns the use of official position to obtain illicit privileges (Hao and Johnston 1995: 119). In addition to criminal prosecution, Chinese officials are also subject to the discipline of the Communist Party and the professional standards enforced by the Ministry of Supervision (Manion 1997: 37). All of these emphasize officials; but the increasing scope of the private economy produced a need for the 1996 Provisional Regulations on Prohibition of Commercial Bribery Activities. Commercial bribery is deemed to include business operators giving property in order 'to sell or purchase merchandise to or from their opposite units or individuals' (China Legal Developments Bulletin 1997: 2).

Bribery has been prosecuted since the establishment of the People's Republic in 1949 (in 1951–2, 6,000 cases of corruption were prosecuted – Luo 1997: 69), despite several waves of anti-corruption campaigns (Gong 1994). Despite this its scope is usually believed to have expanded since the reforms (Manion 1997: 49). Public anger with corruption that surfaced during the Tiananmen protests in 1989 seems to have increased the attention of the government to corruption at higher levels of the state. Between 1993 and 1996, 236,000 criminal cases of corruption were investigated. Of these, more than 1,700 involved funds exceeding one million yuan, and high officials involved included the vice chairman of the Guangdong Provincial People's Congress, the vice mayor of Beijing, the vice chairman of the State Science and Technology Commission, and the assistant to the general manager of the Capital Iron and Steel Corporation (the prominence of the second highest official in these and other cases seems somewhat suspicious). Funds amounting to 13.96 billion yuan were recovered through these prosecutions (Luo 1997: 70).

A common tendency in official discourse on bribery is to emphasize the sources in individuals. For example Luo (1997: 69) suggests that growth in 'wealth and consumption has greatly stimulated the desire of people for material possessions and has lured some weak-willed State employees into criminal acts to seek personal gain'. Or attention may be focused on 'spiritual pollution' brought by outside actors: the flies that come in the Open Door. Zheng (1996: 77) combines the two themes by stressing how Overseas Chinese and other foreigners bribe 'weak-minded officials and staff . . . to grant them privileges in business activities, thus gaining competitive edges and unjust interests in projects of land development and investment as well as in other economic spheres'. Ying (1996: 74) discussed the increasing involvement of criminal organizations from Hong Kong and Taiwan, who have 'roped in and corrupted government officials to use them as their umbrellas, or usurped the leaderships of the grassroots organizations, thus becoming the most serious evil forces that endangered social security'.

Official discourse about bribery has downplayed structural conditions that have made bribery and *guanxi* endemic (Gong 1994). It has frequently been suggested that socialist[19] systems 'suffer from inherent structural flaws that force their members to engage in illegal actions to survive and pursue ordinary interests' (Oi 1989: 223). Mobilizing *guanxi* and paying bribes are central parts of the responses to these structural flaws. Factory managers and others circumvent or manipulate regulations or plans as a routine part of the performance of their duties (Walder 1986).

Rocca (1992: 403) asserts that corruption is not necessarily a 'negative phenomenon as it may be a means used by groups excluded from political power' and may weaken bureaucratic monopolies. In other cases, though, it can serve the aims of those in power, so there is a need to distinguish between 'the more dynamic, creative role of corruption and the predatory form' (Rocca 1992: 404). On balance, he concludes that corruption in China is of the predatory variety. High officials, both in the provinces and in Beijing and the central ministries, can extract huge amounts of illicit revenues as a result of control over what is still often arbitrary power, with the courts nearly completely ineffective for use against administrative malfeasance. Similarly, Manion (1997: 36) argues that, through corrupt officials, 'the Chinese state supplies a "public bad": in public policy terms, there is a government failure'. Furthermore, clean government 'is itself a public good more vital to the operation of government than any other, because the delivery of other public goods depends on it' (p. 36).

I would argue that both kinds of corruption exist in China. Creative bribery can be an important resource in protecting one's activities from the predation of higher officials, as well as to 'break rigid bureaucratic monopolies and controls, facilitating the flow of goods and services in the economy' (Hao and Johnston 1995: 140). Manion's argument would imply that any reduction in corrupt activity should increase efficiency. I would suggest in contrast that eradicating certain kinds of low-level corrupt activities could potentially increase the overall costs to the society of corruption from the top down. The rapid growth of township and village enterprises has been constantly impeded through the preferential access to raw materials enjoyed by less efficient state enterprises, and working *guanxi* has been an important way of getting around these obstacles (Hao and Johnston 1995: 141). There is often sufficient mutual interest between local officials and foreign or local enterprises to limit how much they are squeezed as well as to encourage collusion over the implementation of regulations from above.

There is a danger in this line of argument of returning to a functionalist interpretation of corruption. Analysts like Samuel Huntington (1970) concluded that corruption performed required functions in Third World countries, contributing to economic growth despite governmental inadequacies, and helping to stabilize societies during periods of change. Clearly, what is functional for those who benefit from the status quo may be seen quite differently by those who must pay bribes to get government services (Lo 1993: 151). I have the same basic problem with this functionalist interpretation of corruption as a positive force as I do with the definition of it as invariably unproductive. Both views fail to recognize the ambivalent nature of bribery and corruption. Bribes take different forms, and may have different outcomes: we cannot decide in advance of looking at particular situations.

While, in many circumstances, the payment of bribes and the cultivation of *guanxi* seem to facilitate efficient responses to unreliable regulatory systems, predatory corruption from above is clearly of great importance in contemporary China as well. It is widely known that what is referred to as the 'princes' party', the sons and daughters of high-level officials, have widely used their connections to become directors of trading enterprises, banks and joint ventures, and to extract huge sums in bribes and commissions (Pye 1995: 49). The former vice mayor of Beijing was implicated in a case involving concealment or illegal transfer of funds amounting to 18.3 billion yuan (Manion 1997: 47). Farther down the hierarchy, government expenditure on banquets and food and drink was over one hundred billion yuan in 1993 (more than the central government's combined expenditures for health, education, science and welfare), despite a campaign to control these expenditures (Pye 1995: 51).

Discussion

Returning to the basic question underlying this chapter, how and why does endemic bribery persist in contemporary China? Two obvious general explanations are, first, that the top leadership is deeply implicated in these practices, and it persists because it informally increases the revenues available to the rulers, or secondly, that the central authorities would indeed like to eradicate these practices but are unable to because they have inadequate control over their subordinates.[20] We do not yet have strong evidence for the direct involvement of the top leaders in bribery, although certainly some of their close relatives and associates have been able to cash in on their connections to the central leaders. If we leave aside the possibility that illegal bribery persists simply because it increases revenues for rulers, then persistence would seem to result from a deficit in the ability of principals to control their agents within the state adequately. Such a lack of control over agents, however, is common in all of the varieties of persistence that I discussed above, so we have to push the question to another level: why can't the local officials be restrained from accepting bribes?

A major part of the answer in China would seem to involve market persistence: gaps between official prices and market prices, unclear regulations and procedures, and so on create tempting opportunities for officials to generate healthy profits, which are particularly tempting when official salaries are very low and even Deng Xiaoping proclaimed getting rich as being desirable in the drive to modernize China. But there is more to it than this. Much of the payment of bribes is not used for the benefit of individual officials, but to further collective interests, for example by collusion in the non-enforcement of health and safety regulations in order to obtain a larger share of foreign investment for the official's community, or to obtain scarce raw materials for a manager's factory. While profit opportunities are clearly involved in such situations, just as important would seem to be ideas that such activities are necessary and justified if they are not done for narrow reasons of individual self-interest, but for the collective good. This collective good may even be seen to be that of the nation as a whole, if regulations are seen as unreasonable obstacles to modernization. Where informal norms support involvement in formally illegal practices, attaching the label of anomalous persistence would seem reasonable. If the local collective interest were to be seen as diametrically opposed to the intentions of the center, that is, if local officials engaged in corrupt practices in order to build resources for eventual separation, then we would be able to talk about rebellious persistence; but there is as yet little evidence for this in China.

What does this examination tell us more generally about the relationship between the state and illegal practices? First of all, it highlights the problems of controlling state agents, and the ways in which bribery serves as a mechanism that can either increase that control (positions that control lucrative squeeze potential are allocated to strong supporters) or can decrease that control and transform the processes of implementation of policies and rules. Secondly, it raises serious doubts about the public choice argument that the rent-seeking activities of politicians and officials always lead to the dissipation of wealth. This would seem in the real world to be only one possible outcome. At one extreme, there is the predatory state, where the problem of subordinates' involvement in bribery consists simply of possible reduction in the flow of bribes to the rulers themselves. Strongly in contrast is the developmental state, where bribes are relatively unimportant in comparison to other mechanisms of cooperation, although movement of officials into the private sector after retirement can be important.[21] The situation in China would seem to differ from both, with many examples of local officials accepting bribes but at the same time effectively promoting local development. It would be possible to see this pattern as involving Schumpeterian entrepreneurial officials: rather than participating only in the dissipation of wealth, many would seem to be involved in 'creative destruction', creating new market opportunities and undermining prior organizational structures as they construct and take advantages of new profit opportunities for their locality. The result may be a different kind of developmental state, one based less on collective state- and nation-building accomplished by ideal Weberian bureaucracies, and more on an unfolding political economy of competition between different systems of property rights at the local level (Smart, in press; Grabher and Stark, in press), in which corrupt practices may have useful unintended consequences.

Burawoy (1997) has recently compared Russia's economic transformation with that of China. He argues that, whereas in China decentralization has proceeded in such a way that localities cooperate to generate growth, in Russia the result has been economic involution: 'an economy that eats away at its own foundations by funnelling resources from production to exchange' (1997: 150). Corruption and the rise of the mafia as debt-collectors and entrepreneurs selling protective services are one type of result, but this form of corruption does not seem to support accumulation and economic growth, as varieties of it have in China.

The classic solution to the problem of corruption is to perfect the bureaucracy and insulate it from clientilistic influence. In these more cynical late-capitalist days, the dominant solution is to suggest diminishing the role of the state. Both approaches assume a zero-sum relationship between state and society. Peter Evans argues instead for the possibility of synergy between state and society in which 'active government and mobilized communities can enhance each other's developmental efforts' (1997: 178). Such synergy can be based on *complementarity*, in which there is a clear division of labour between the sectors based on their contrasting properties and strengths. The other pattern is more interesting for our purposes here: synergy based on *embeddedness*, which Evans (1997: 180) defines as ties that connect citizens and public officials across the public–private divide. He asks: 'Can networks which trespass the boundary between public and private be repositories of developmentally valuable social capital rather than instruments of corruption or rent-seeking?' (p. 180).

He concludes that, in certain circumstances, connections between officials and the population can indeed be critical supports for development, among other reasons because they facilitate information transfer and trust across the public–private divide. My claim here goes even farther, suggesting that in some cases even corrupt embeddedness can generate productive outcomes. Evans (1997: 192) suggests that some of the general conditions for state–society synergy based on embeddedness include ways in which social ties can be transformed from 'engines of parochial loyalties into vehicles for more encompassing forms of organizations', and political competition that encourages politicians and bureaucrats to pay attention to their citizens. Where high levels of inequality and distrust between government and citizens exist, though, synergy can be much more difficult to accomplish. This would suggest that bribery will be a very unstable basis for continued development, unless local agents can consistently be bound into variants of it that support local goals rather than personal self-aggrandizement.

Thus, even if so far the outcome of corruption in China has been on balance positive, that may not continue. Furthermore, the ways in which localities circumvent central control is hardly likely to be as positively perceived by central authorities. Hao and Johnston (1995: 145) have argued that:

> corruption has substantially weakened the state's capacity to rule. Although this might be viewed as a positive consequence of reform, one making way for a new balance of power between state and society, the functional role of the state is being called into question. . . . In short, corruption is making it more difficult to govern China from Beijing, and in the absence of clear alternatives to party-state dominance this is a serious matter.

If corruption has indeed substantially weakened the ruler's capacity to command, then the reasons for its persistence are an important question to address.

The answer would seem to lie in at least a couple of different areas. One of these has to do with unintended consequences (Gong 1994). If there are structural conflicts between the desire to use reforms to expand rapidly the wealth and influence of the Chinese nation, and the desire to maintain the capacity to control what happens at the local level, then bribery persists because the costs of making the changes that would allow its effective suppression are too high. Corruption of state agents then would be a necessary cost of maintaining socialism with Chinese characteristics. Manion (1997: 51) asserts that the maintenance of a Leninist political system in the kind of economy that has developed means that eradication of corruption is essentially impossible, since that would require an independent agency committed to the rule of law. The alternatives would be to move back towards a command economy or expand the reforms to generate a more fully capitalist political economy. As long as an intermediate position is politically and/or ideologically desirable, the structural conditions that generate endemic bribery will be likely to persist, unless new kinds of legitimacy can be generated. Why will it persist? Because the structural conflict produces extensive profit opportunities, which would then seem to suggest that we can classify bribery in China as an example of market persistence. Clearly, reasonably serious efforts are made at various times to catch individuals involved in corrupt activities without substantially decreasing the prevalence of such activities. Would all-out efforts succeed? Perhaps they would, but as long as structural conflicts continue that produce profit opportunities as a result, it would seem likely that some individuals would take advantage of those opportunities, which would become even more profitable (when successful) if the rate of involvement were to drop. Furthermore, a uniform application of rules over politics would undermine the Leninist nature of the Communist Party, and thus endanger some of the existing mechanisms of control over subordinates.

Gong's (1994) account of corruption and anti-corruption campaigns in China suggests that these circumstances not only ensure that bribery will continue to be produced, but that it will also repeatedly generate widespread suppression efforts in the form of anti-corruption campaigns. His conclusions are compatible with my analysis here:

> while the CCP intends to establish effective control over society, it has to react at times to unintended consequences which have come along with its own policies. . . . the CCP has often fought simultaneously on two fronts: one, daily problem solving to deal with chronic socioeconomic intricacies . . . and two, political campaigning to cope with new problems . . . generated by its own problem-solving efforts (p. 157).

The structural conflict is deeply reinforced by surveillance transaction costs and the relative bargaining power of local officials *vis-à-vis* the central authorities. Leaving aside possible corrupt practices of those at the very center, the problem of eradication revolves around their ability to control the activities of their subordinates. But the reforms have increased the degree of autonomy of subordinates. This has increased economic output and served many of the interests of the center, but agents are now increasingly difficult to control in any detailed way. If this were to be taken much farther, we could talk about the situation as involving rebellious persistence; but this is not yet apparent in China. Inability to prevent agents from engaging in bribery is rather a result of the advantages presented by doing so, and thus still seems to emphasize a market persistence categorization.

But legitimacy is also involved. As long as there is divergence between the legal and the societal definitions of bribery and corruption the opportunity costs of engaging in these practices will be reduced. And as long as higher officials are believed to be involved just as much or even more than local officials and ordinary people, the credibility of anti-corruption rhetoric will be limited. So anomalous persistence plays an important supporting role in the process.

My analysis so far is clearly exploratory, and the evidence is such that leaping to strong generalizations at this point is rather dubious. However, recognizing the gaps in knowledge and theory, it is still likely that the effort to delineate some basic commonalities will be informative, even if they are later discarded as incomplete. With those caveats, I propose the following suggestions about the conditions of persistence of the different varieties of bribery, summarized in Table 4.1. In this table, I first state whether or not the five possible varieties of persistent bribery (drawing here from the basic typology) are present or not in post-1978 China. Then I identify what I see as the most important necessary condition for such persistence, following this with the second and third most important conditions of persistence. Clearly, this process could be extended to many more columns of necessary conditions. It is not clear which, if any, of these necessary conditions could be considered to be sufficient conditions. Perhaps the existence of enough effective demand to generate higher than average profits is a sufficient condition for market-based forms of bribery, as the extensionist hypothesis would suggest; but even here I would argue that forms of cooperation would be a precondition for profitable involvement in such economic activities.

The next step would be to endeavour to apply this analysis of the varieties of bribery and their conditions of persistence to other cases, to see whether or not it helps explain their patterns, or whether some of their features might require fundamental revision of the model. No space is available here for such an effort, but it represents a potentially fruitful road for future analysis.

Conclusions

A variety of kinds of illegal networks persist in the contemporary world, as they have in the past. I have concentrated in this chapter on illegal economic activities, but it is important to keep in mind the existence of other kinds of illegal networks, and their implications for the task of developing a broader theoretical framework. Illegal practices can be seen as involving two poles on a spectrum of instrumentality: (1) instrumental activities that wouldn't be conducted if they weren't possibly profitable,

Table 4.1 Types of Illegal Persistence

Variety of Bribery	*Presence in post-1978 China*	*Necessary Condition 1*	*Necessary Condition 2*	*Other Necessary Conditions*
Ambiguous	yes	Discrepancy between law and informal norms	Constraints on effective eradication	Barriers to change in law
Market	yes	Effective demand for illegal goods or services	Mechanisms enabling profitable production and distribution	Barriers to change in law
Managed	yes	Deliberate legislation or enforcement to generate squeeze	Willingness to pay tribute for prohibited practices	Low discount rates on loss of legitimacy
Rebellious	possibly	Locally-based resistance to central control	Constraints on effective eradication	Effective demands for goods/services
Subversive	no	Efforts by outside powers to destabilize	Local agents allying with outside powers	Effective demands for goods/services

such as selling contraband drugs or sexual services; and (2) prohibited non-market activities (where profit is not the primary goal) such as political subversion, religious dissidence, or repressed sexual orientations. The organization of the activities, and the impact of governmental suppression, will differ relative to the degree of instrumentality. If we assume that the activities are organized and maintained primarily for instrumental purposes, rather than for 'the cause' or out of feelings of solidarity/obligation, then it would seem obvious that a political economy perspective (including but not limited to neoclassical economics) should be able to provide insights. The only question would seem to be what theoretical approach within political economy would be most effective in describing the patterns, explaining changes, and prescribing policies for the remediation of the situation.

I have provisionally adopted Margaret Levi's theory as a promising starting-point. Rulers often attempt to increase their bargaining power, reduce transaction costs, and lower their discount rates to capture increased gains from their territory. Agents involved with illegal practices conversely wish to reduce the bargaining power of the ruler *vis-à-vis* themselves, although this may involving strengthening the ruler against others. Furthermore, they will organize their activities so as to make discovery and suppression more costly, and seek situations where government officials will either collude with them or look the other way. Agents on both sides compete with innovations in technology[22] and organization, and build coalitions to pursue their interests. These coalitions may be easier to form when legitimacy is seen to be on your side (Smart 1988), but discursive efforts can undermine as well as reinforce existing levels of legitimacy on either side (Heyman, this volume, Chapter 10; Schneider and Schneider, this volume, Chapter 6).

Bribery is frequently at the heart of these processes, and an adequate theory of states and illegal practices must deal with the role played by relationships of bribery and collusion.[23] Where the rule of law is primarily fictional, as in Nugent's account of Amazonas, payoffs may be the negotiated side of otherwise brute force. Elsewhere, gifts may merge into bribes, prioritizing effective performance and the management of relationships. In other cases, overly rigid bureaucratic systems with an unresponsive political system might even benefit from a liberal sprinkling of the lubricating effects of the more positive versions of graft.

Bribery operates in a context, and the dominant constraints that are found in that context influence the kinds of bribery that we find. As Humphrey demonstrates in Chapter 7, political reform can result in more venal patterns rather than generating more civility.

The Chinese case materials raise a variety of issues about decentralization, reform, and local situational adjustment to policies lacking local legitimacy. They also remind us that bribes can simultaneously enable citizens to cope with difficult situations, and produce the difficulties that must be coped with. Double-edges are inherent in these practices, and ambiguity and deniability represent strategic resources that must be deployed on a regular basis. That which need not be said is greatly preferably to what has to be spelled out. Hong Kong investors profit from being better at playing the game of knowing what shouldn't be made explicit, while implicitly ensuring that what needs to be understood is agreed upon. But what is swept under the carpet now, may emerge later, with dramatic consequences that the Schneiders' Chapter 6 powerfully suggests. What the eventual emergence of greater transparency in China will produce remains yet to be seen, but at least it should produce some fascinating materials from the Chinese equivalent of *pentiti* for future analyses.

Notes

1. The classic debate on the feasibility of completely planning an economy is perhaps the best source for such discussions: see for example Kornai (1986).
2. In Althusserian terms, such practices could be said to be overdetermination. Stripped of obfuscation, attention to overdetermination simply reminds us that if we remove one sufficient cause for a phenomenon, the conditions may still exist for it to be produced by other causes.
3. I have emphasized the general implications of Levi's theory here, neglecting the ways in which she has practiced better than she has preached, offering nuance in great volume in her detailed social histories.
4. It should also be pointed out that for Levi it is not the state that is the focus, but the ruler, or the executive branch, which may be a monarch, a prime minister, or a president. Legislatures and civil service bureaucracies can act as constraints on the search for increased revenue by the ruler.
5. Note that this position in no way contradicts Levi's theory.
6. Attractive though this approach may be, it leaves out too many crucial issues when the main focus is illegal practices and networks. Below I attend to some of the ways in which legitimacy may influence the persistence of illegal practices, and the Introduction to this volume offers other insights.
7. In the terminology used by Althusser, when more than one cause of persistence co-exists, continuance of the illicit practice could be said to be 'overdetermined'.
8. Or perhaps very extensive but self-defeating efforts, as suggested by Heyman's analysis in Chapter 10 of this volume as well as his Vietnam analogy.
9. For China, see Levy (1995). For a comparable case, see Eames (1990).
10. The account by McCoy in Chapter 5 of this volume of Khun Sa's career shows that in particular cases it may be difficult to distinguish between rebellious and market persistence, since his efforts to control opium production eventually led to his sponsorship of armed separatism. I would suggest that the way in which concrete cases may be intermediate between the labelled types doesn't invalidate the effort to construct Weberian ideal types.
11. I acknowledge that this tendency severely limits the generality of the arguments I make in Smart (1988), although I would continue to insist

on the relevance of the analysis of regulatory vacuums for illegal practices that approximate market formulations, such as the squatter property market.

12. Which also happens in the formal sector, of course.
13. While bribery and corruption are often used as synonymous, this is not accurate. Bribery is one form of corruption, but there are others as well, such as illegitimate actions that directly benefit officials.
14. Disturbing evidence of this can be found in the memoirs of Mao's doctor, Li (1994).
15. It is difficult to generalize about the household responsibility system, since local variations are legion.
16. In Chinese, this can be referred to as 'adaptation' (Smart 1995).
17. Social control is generally acknowledged to be tighter and more effective in the cities, where employment is concentrated in state enterprises who receive welfare benefits that can be made conditional, than in the rural areas, where most of the population receives little significant redistribution. With the dismantling of collectively run agriculture, authority has broken down in much of the countryside. An estimated 20 per cent of China's villages are what is called 'collapsed', where village leadership exists in name only, with no effective government or party organization (Kelliher 1997).
18. The argument could also be applied to other investors, particularly those who are Taiwanese or ethnic Chinese overseas, but our field research has concentrated on Hong Kong enterprises.
19. Note that the same can be said for many in capitalist systems as well.
20. Note that the two positions are not mutually exclusive and that it could be quite sensible to want both to prevent subordinates from accepting bribes and at the same time to maximize the volume of bribes available to the central leaders.
21. However, Park (1995) documents the extent of bribery in the Republic of Korea, commonly seen as an exemplar developmental state.
22. Including the 'soft-technologies' of organizational innovation (Evans 1997).
23. Bailey (1991) has made an important contribution to understanding collusion in his book *The Prevalence of Deceit*.

References

Amsden, Alice H. (1990), 'Third World Industrialization: "Global Fordism" or a New Model?', *New Left Review* 182: 5–31.

Bailey, F. G. (1991), *The Prevalence of Deceit*. Ithaca, NY: Cornell University Press.

Buchanan, J. M. (1980), 'Rent Seeking and Profit Seeking', in J.M. Buchanan *et al.* (eds), *Toward a Theory of the Rent-seeking Society*. College Station: Texas A & M University Press, pp. 3–15.

Burawoy, Michael (1997), 'The State and Economic Involution: Russia Through a China Lens'. in P. Evans (ed.), *State–Society Synergy: Government and Social Capital in Development*. Berkeley: International and Area Studies, pp. 150–77.

China Legal Developments Bulletin (1997), 'Bribery'. *China Legal Developments Bulletin* 4(1): 2–3.

Eames, Elizabeth A. (1990), 'Navigating Nigerian Bureaucracies', in James P. Spradley and David W. McCurdy (eds), *Conformity and Conflict*. Glenview, IL: Scott, Foresman, pp. 38–47.

Evans, Peter B. (1989), 'Predatory, Developmental, and Other Apparatuses: A Comparative Political Economy Perspective on the Third World State', *Sociological Forum* 4(4): 561–87.

—— (1996), 'Embedded Autonomy and Industrial Transformation', in Diane Davis (ed.), *Political Power and Social Theory*. Greenwich, CT: JAI Press, pp. 259–82.

—— (1997), 'Government Action, Social Capital, and Development: Reviewing the Evidence on Synergy', in P. Evans (ed.), *State–Society Synergy: Government and Social Capital in Development*. Berkeley: International and Area Studies, pp. 178–209.

Foreign Broadcast Information Service (FBIS), Various dates. Translations from Chinese broadcasts and periodicals.

Gong, Ting (1994), *The Politics of Corruption in Contemporary China: An Analysis of Policy Outcomes*. Westport, CT: Praeger.

Grabher, Gernot and David Stark (in press), 'Organising Diversity: Evolutionary Theory, Network Analysis and Post-Socialism', in Adrian Smith and John Pickles (eds), *Theorising Transition in Eastern Europe*. London: Routledge.

Hao, Yufan and Michael Johnston (1995), 'Reform at the Crossroads: An Analysis of Chinese Corruption', *Asian Perspective* 1(1): 117–49.

Heyman, Josiah McC. (1995), 'Putting Power in the Anthropology of Bureaucracy', *Current Anthropology* 36(2): 261–87.

Hsing, You-tien (1997), 'Building *Guanxi* across the Straits: Taiwanese Capital and Local Chinese Bureaucrats', in Aihwa Ong and Donald Nonini (eds), *Ungrounded Empires: The Cultural Politics of Modern Chinese Transnationalism*. New York: Routledge, pp. 143–64.

Huntington, Samuel P. (1970), 'Modernization and Corruption', in A. J. Heidenheimer (ed.), *Political Corruption*. New Brunswick, NJ: Transaction Books, pp. 492–500.

Kelliher, Daniel (1997), 'The Chinese Debate over Village Self-Government', *The China Journal* 37(January): 31–59.

Kipnis, Andrew B. (1997), *Producing Guanxi: Sentiment, Self and Subculture in a North China Village*. Durham, NC: Duke University Press.

Kornai, Janos (1986), *Contradictions and Dilemmas: Studies on the Socialist Economy and Society*. Cambridge, MA: MIT Press.

Levi, Margaret (1988), *Of Rule and Revenue*. Berkeley: University of California Press.

Levy, Richard (1995), 'Corruption, Economic Crime and Social Transformation since the Reforms: The Debate in China', *The Australian Journal of Chinese Affairs* 33: 1–25.

Li, Zhisui (1994), *The Private Life of Chairman Mao*. New York: Random House.

Liu, Yia-ling (1992), 'Reform from Below: The Private Economy and Local Politics in the Rural Industrialization of Wenzhou', *China Quarterly* 130(June): 293–316.

Lo, T. Wing (1993), *Corruption and Politics in Hong Kong and China*. Buckingham: Open University Press.

Luo, Ji (1997), 'Public Prosecutors: A New Force against Corruption in China', *China Law* 1997(1): 68–70.

MacGaffey, Janet (1991), *The Real Economy of Zaire*. London: James Currey.

Manion, Melanie (1997), 'Corruption and Corruption Control: More of the Same in 1996', in Maurice Brosseau *et al.* (eds), *China Review 1997*. Hong Kong: The Chinese University Press, pp. 34–56.

Marcouiller, Douglas and Leslie Young (1995), 'The Black Hole of Graft: The Predatory State and the Informal Economy', *American Economic Review* 85(3): 630–46.

Meaney, Constance S. (1989), 'Market Reform in a Leninist System', *Studies in Comparative Communism* 22: 203–20.

Moore, Sally Falk (1978), *Law as Process*. London: Routledge and Kegan Paul.

Myers, J. (1989), 'Modernization and "Unhealthy Tendencies"', *Comparative Politics* 21: 193–213.

Noonan, John Thomas (1984), *Bribes*. Berkeley: University of California Press.

Oi, Jean C. (1989), *State and Peasant in Contemporary China*. Berkeley: University of California Press.

Park, Byeong-Seog (1995), 'Political Corruption in South Korea: Concentrating on the Dynamics of Party Politics', *Asian Perspective* 19(1): 163–93.

Peng, Y. (1996), 'The Politics of Tobacco: Relations between Farmers and Local Governments in China's Southwest', *The China Journal* 36: 67–82.

Platt, Richard (1991), *Smuggler's Britain*. London: Cassell.

Pye, Lucien W. (1995), 'Factions and the Politics of *Guanxi*: Paradoxes in Chinese Administrative and Political Behaviour', *The China Journal* 34: 35–53.

Rocca, Jean-Louis (1992), 'Corruption and its Shadow: An Anthropological View of Corruption in China', *China Quarterly* 130: 402–16.

Schneider, Jane and Peter Schneider (1994), 'Mafia, Antimafia, and the Question of Sicilian Culture', *Politics and Society* 22(2): 237–58.

Smart, Alan (1988), 'The Informal Regulation of Illegal Economic Activities: Comparisons between the Squatter Property Market and Organized Crime', *International Journal of the Sociology of Law* 16: 91–101.

—— (1992), *Making Room: Squatter Clearance in Hong Kong*. Hong Kong: Centre of Asian Studies.

—— (1993), 'Gifts, Bribes and *Guanxi*: A Reconsideration of Bourdieu's Social Capital', *Cultural Anthropology* 8(3): 388–408.

—— (1995), *Local Capitalisms: Situated Social Support for Capitalist Production in China*. Department of Geography, Chinese University of Hong Kong Occasional Paper Series No. 121. Hong Kong: Chinese University of Hong Kong.

—— (in press), 'Economic Transformation in China: Property Regimes and Social Relations', in Adrian Smith and John Pickles (eds), *Theorising Transition in Eastern Europe*. London: Routledge.

Smart, Josephine and Alan Smart (1991), 'Personal Relations and Divergent Economies: A Case Study of Hong Kong Investment in South China', *International Journal of Urban and Regional Research* 15(2): 216–33.

Solinger, Dorothy J. (1996), 'Despite Decentralization: Disadvantages, Dependence and Ongoing Central Power in the Inland: The Case of Wuhan', *China Quarterly* 145(March): 1–34.

van Baal, Jan (1975), *Reciprocity and the Position of Women*. Assen: Van Gorcum.

Walder, Andrew (1986), *Communist Neo-Traditionalism: Work and Authority in Chinese Industry*. Berkeley: University of California Press.

—— (1995), 'Local Governments as Industrial Firms: An Organizational Analysis of China's Transitional Economy', *American Journal of Sociology* 101(2): 263–301.

Wang, Shaoguang (1995), 'The Rise of the Regions: Fiscal Reform and the Decline of Central State Capacity in China', in A. Walder (ed.), *The Waning of the Communist State*. Berkeley: University of California Press, pp. 87–113.

Yan, Yunxiang (1996), *The Flow of Gifts*. Stanford, CA: Stanford University Press.

Yang, Dali (1994), 'Reform and the Restructuring of Central–Local Relations', in David Goodman and Gerald Segal (eds), *China Deconstructs*. London: Routledge, pp. 59–98.

Yang, Mayfair Mei-hui (1994), *Gifts, Favors and Banquets: The Art of Social Relationships in China*. Ithaca, NY: Cornell University Press.

Ying, Tebo (1996), 'China Pays Close Attention to the Prevention and Control of Organized Crime', *China Law* 1996(1): 74–5.

Zheng, Yizheng (1996), 'On Information Exchanges and Judicial Assistance Concerning Multi-national Embezzlement and Bribery Cases', *China Law* 1996(3): 77–9.

–5–

Requiem for a Drug Lord: State and Commodity in the Career of Khun Sa

Alfred W. McCoy

The relationship between the state and its outlaws remains a riddle for both academics and authorities. During the decade past, for example, the United States has demonstrated a consistent failure of imagination when confronted with the drug lord Khun Sa and the complexities of his relationship with the Burmese state. In March 1990, the head of the US Drug Enforcement Administration (DEA) branded Khun Sa the 'king of opium'. The US Attorney-General called him the 'prince of death' and indicted him, with little effect, for smuggling over a ton of heroin into New York City (Cox 1996: 47–50). Six years later, when the Burmese military turned on Khun Sa and his heroin empire finally collapsed, Washington demanded his extradition. But Rangoon refused, prompting the State Department to offer a quixotic two-million dollar reward for the capture of the world's wealthiest drug lord.[1] A year later, with heroin exports still booming, US Secretary of State Madeline Albright, reflecting Washington's frustrations, described Burma's 'military' regime as 'drug traffickers and thugs'.[2] Her combination of these terms, in effect conflating the 'state' with its 'outlaws', indicates that her department had not grasped their deeper meaning. While both are difficult enough in isolation, their intersection, the subject of this chapter, is even more elusive. Neither are mere words, but are, in fact, paradigms, powerful lenses that can either enlighten or obscure our insight into these issues.

Khun Sa, with his 20,000-strong army and control over half the world's heroin supply, strains the terminology that the academy has coined for his kind. In his global survey of 'outlaws' in the early-modern age (Chapter 2), Thomas Gallant offers a glossary of relevant terms – pirate, privateer, bandit, brigand, highwayman, military entrepreneur, man of respect, man of violence, man of prowess, rebel, and chief. As Gallant makes clear, none are mutually exclusive and none, on its own, is entirely satisfactory. Even the underlying distinction between law and outlaw is murky, since, in the early-modern era, 'bandits helped make states, and states made bandits'. That is, through a process of either co-opting or crushing rural outlaws states experienced a 'border effect' that strengthened their capacities (Chapter 2). Indeed, Khun Sa, in his half-century rise from boy soldier to pre-eminent drug lord, has filled most of these categories. While his career contains many sudden, often stunning, changes in role, two factors have remained constant – his extraordinary qualities as a man of prowess, and the paradoxical dependence of his fate upon the action or inaction of the Burmese state. Khun Sa rose by manipulating the weakness of the Burmese state, and he fell by miscalculating its surprising strengths.

But understanding that the globe's greatest drug lord emerged as an outlaw at the margins of a weak state does not, in the end, say much. To read meaning into and out of Khun Sa's exceptional career, we need to historicize these terms 'outlaw' and 'state'. Like many historical actors, Khun Sa is a complex, multifaceted manifestation of the specific and the universal. Since his political biography, which forms the bulk of this essay, is the sum of particulars, we need, at the outset, to analyze the comparable elements encoded in these two words. When we try to reduce Khun Sa's complexity, his extraordinary career and expansive personality, to narrow analytic categories, four central elements emerge: (1) the processes of state formation; (2) the geography, physical and cultural, of outlaw zones; (3) the global economic context ; and (4) the role of outlaws as both political and economic entrepreneurs.

As states expand, they often leave peripheries that are, like Khun Sa's native Shan State, poorly integrated into a central apparatus still struggling to take form. In these mountain and maritime fringes, weak state control can provide an opening for men of prowess – pirates, bandits, warlords, or ethnic chiefs – to mediate between the center and its margins. Such a view detaches itself from an economic or developmental determinism, with its implied teleology, and argues instead that economic change is constant and state configurations are in an endless state of flux, cohering and collapsing, with peripheries and interstices thus contracting or expanding. If so, the attributes of early-modern bandits – extraordinary power, political volatility, and mutability of roles from inlaw to outlaw – are evident in Khun Sa's recent career.

Even as we subvert such linear analysis, we cannot utterly discard it. In Southeast Asia, bandits, pirates, and warlords are, in significant ways, a manifestation of an ongoing, incomplete process of state-formation (Abrams 1988: 58–9; Evans *et al.* 1985; Migdal 1988: 31–2). In the past two centuries, the rise of the modern state has created interstices, zones within and between nations, where outlaws like Khun Sa gain power by mediating between capitals and their margins. In these remote localities, history often provides a brief moment for these extralegal entrepreneurs – creating actors called, variously, bandits, pirates, smugglers, warlords, or rebels. If Khun Sa's rise was a manifestation of the Burmese state's weakness, then his ultimate downfall might be taken as an index of its increased capacities.

Applying these abstractions to opium's reality, Khun Sa's biography forces us to examine the relationship between entrepreneur, state, and market in the making of the modern drug traffic. Clearly, such broad historiographic questions, now ignored by the United States and United Nations, have profound implications for international enforcement efforts and, more theoretically, for our understanding of the relationship between the state and its outlaws. As both the creation of one state and the would-be creator of another, Khun Sa provides us with an opportunity to grasp something of these social and spatial processes.

Yet, in this analysis we cannot ignore Khun Sa himself. Indeed, outlaws are, almost by definition, extraordinary personalities. As both creation and creator of this region's drug trade, Khun Sa raises some contradictory questions about the role of the individual in history – that is, the power of one man to direct complex economic, social, and political changes. At one level, Khun Sa is just another drug lord who would, through cunning and circumstance, momentarily capture Burma's heroin supply. Viewed differently, he seems, by contrast, a 'world historical' entrepreneur who would, through sheer force of personality, recast Burma's opium trade and use it to reshape both local politics and global traffic. If for no other reason, his extraordinary longevity in the Darwinian world of Shan highland warfare draws our attention to his history and personality.

Biography of a Drug Lord

Khun Sa is a man with two names. Born in February 1934 of a Shan mother and Chinese father in the Burma borderlands facing China, he grew up within two cultures – the itinerant Muslim Chinese caravan traders, the Haw, who know him as Chan Shee-fu; and the settled Shan Buddhist farmers, who call him Khun Sa, or 'prosperous prince'. Orphaned and only semi-literate in Chinese, Khun Sa would, from adolescence, develop personal attributes that would allow him to survive, even prosper, in this remote region during a chaotic period (Lintner 1994b; Khun Sa n.d.: 43–9; McCoy 1991: 423–35; Yawnghwe 1987: 18–27, 189–90, 1995: 22–6).

History has made ethnicity the text of Shan State politics. Lying astride the trade routes between India, China, Burma, and Thailand, the Shan Plateau and its surrounding hills have long been a borderland of extraordinary ethnic diversity and political volatility. By accident of British conquest in the 1880s, the Tai-speaking Shan States and Burmese kingdom became loosely joined under a contradictory colonial policy. Through surveys at the turn of the century, Britain fixed the present borders, making the Tai-speaking Shan a minority at the periphery of a Tibeto-Burman majority. However, the British administered the Shan and Burmese separately, denying them any basis for future cooperation. Indeed, the British recognized the authority of the Shan princes and, in 1922, combined their 34 principalities in a quasi-autonomous colony called the Federated Shan States. Thus, as Burma moved to independence in 1947, its leader Aung San persuaded the Shan princes to join the Union by promising them the 'financial autonomy now vested in the Federated Shan States'. These understandings influenced Burma's original constitution, which guaranteed the Shan 'the right to secede' ten years after independence (Shan State National Congress 1994: 4-6, appendix 6, 7; Trager 1966: 82-83).

During this decade, a mix of local ethnic tensions and Cold War conflicts sparked a Shan secessionist revolt. By the early 1980s, four major groups would be battling for control of these borderlands. Most importantly, the four million 'Shan', a Tai-speaking, Buddhist ethnic group, controlled the major valleys and towns on the rolling Shan Plateau of northeastern Burma. Just as their precolonial ancestors had divided these highlands into more than 30 micro-states, each with its own prince or *saopha*, so the Shan nationalist revolt of the 1960s soon fragmented into dozens of rival armies. During much of this century, the Shan had a volatile relationship with the 'Burmans', the Tibeto-Burman ethnic majority who command the national army that has occupied the main Shan towns for the past forty years. In the northeastern border near China, the million Mon-Khmer 'Wa', the largest of the region's highland minorities, have long been regarded, by British colonials and Shan nationalists alike, as an archetypal martial tribe. In the colonial period, their head-taking raids and fortified villages, surrounded by earthen bulwarks spiked with sharpened stakes, made them formidable enemies – just as their aggressive guerrilla tactics would, a century later, make them the ultimate victors in the battle for Burma's opium (Smith 1991: 29–30, 349–50). Finally, in this ethno-historical catalogue none can equal Yunnan's Chinese Muslims for martial skills. Driven into the Shan Hills by the defeat of their Dali Sultanate in China's southeast during the 1870s, these small communities of Muslim caravan traders, known as 'Jin Haw', have long demonstrated a remarkable flair for commerce and warfare across the highlands of Southeast Asia.

Just as ethnicity writes the text of Shan State politics, so inter-state relations binds that text within a larger framework. After independence in 1948, Burma struggled to contain an eruption of ethnic insurgency along the length of its eastern frontier with China and Thailand – an instability that external powers were quick to exploit. Driven by the bipolar logic of the Cold War, the United States played Thailand against Burma, using Bangkok as a regional surrogate for its conventional and covert operations against Communist China. After 1975, Washington would apply a similar bipolar diplomacy to wage a drug war in this region, by then the source of its rising heroin supply. Thailand, practicing a statecraft that concentrated its armed forces around the royal capital at Bangkok, used Shan rebel armies to project its influence inside Burma. China, often inattentive to a region so remote from its main strategic concerns, intervened only occasionally, but with great effect, to control its remote southwestern border with Burma.

These geopolitics would be played out in a region with a distinct political economy. Over the past two centuries, opium has become a major global commodity linking the cities of Asia and the West to an opium zone that stretches for 5,000 miles across the southern mountain rim of Asia. During the first millennium AD, opium had spread from its home in the eastern Mediterranean to India and China. Stimulated by growing demand during the nineteenth century, its cultivation expanded rapidly to new areas, creating a loosely integrated opium zone from Turkey to China. Then, through an accident of history, the iron curtain came down along the southern borders of China and the Soviet Union, making this Asian opium zone a key front of Cold War confrontation.

In the late 1940s, when Khun Sa was still a teenager, Burma's northeast was, through the dynamic of global geopolitics, entering a half century of political chaos. As its empire unraveled after the Second World War, Britain granted Burma independence in 1948, only a year before the Communist Revolution drove remnants of the Nationalist Chinese forces across the border into Burma's northeast. Khun Sa came of age as his homeland was becoming a battleground between Nationalist Chinese troops, the Burmese army, Haw warlords, and Shan rebels. With his mixed Chinese–Shan descent and complex personality, Khun Sa would flourish in these troubled times.

Fleeing from Mao Zedong's Red Army in 1949, the Nationalist Chinese troops crossed into Burma and settled along the country's rugged frontier facing China. Seeking a second front against Communist China in the Korean War, President Harry Truman ordered the Central Intelligence Agency (CIA) to mobilize some 14,000 of these Nationalist Chinese remnants for a clandestine invasion of southwestern China. After their incursions were repulsed in 1950–51, the Nationalist troops occupied Burma's northeast for another decade, turning to opium to finance their operations. By forcing local hill tribes to produce the drug, these Chinese troops (called Kuo Min Tang, or KMT) presided over a massive increase of poppy cultivation on the Shan Plateau – from some 18 tons in 1958 to an estimated 400–600 tons in 1970 (Yawnghwe 1987: 57; see Map 5.1). After the Burmese Army evicted them in 1961, the KMT forces established new base camps just across the border in Thailand, and from there dominated the Shan opium trade until the mid-1980s.

The Union of Burma army, composed almost entirely of ethnic Burmans, countered the KMT invasion by occupying much of the Shan States. Badly paid and poorly disciplined, Burmese troops abused Shan villagers, who had earlier had limited contact with the new state. Under such conditions, the postcolonial integration of the Shans into this new nation became problematic and their leaders were pushed, though these events, to secessionist revolt in 1958. In its attempts to contain the revolt, the Burmese Army would create a rival local militia, backing these local allies with arms and informal authority to trade in opium.

Without Bangkok's tacit support, the Shan revolt could not have prospered as it did. Thailand's role in this region was the product of frustrated territorial ambitions and a *de facto* defense policy. Reflecting linguistic and cultural affinities, Thailand had, since the late nineteenth century, regarded the Shan States as a natural part of the Thai nation. During the Second World War, Bangkok annexed the area and an army faction, commanded by General Phin Choonawan, an influential postwar leader, occupied the southern Shan State for two years. In the late 1950s, the Thai military, reviving an earlier style of Southeast Asian statecraft, began supporting the Shan revolt by providing borderland camps to the KMT militia, Shan rebels, and Haw warlords.

By the time KMT withdrew in 1961, the Shan State had the elements that would make it a volatile, even fissiparous region – tenuous central control, ethnic insurgency, opium trafficking, and external intervention. The sum of all these influences would produce, for the next thirty years, both a constant fragmentation and a periodic concentration of paramilitary power over the Shan State and its opium trade. Compounding the Shans' localized political authority, the opium harvest fueled an incessant warfare as old armies split over its spoils and new warlords rose from its profits –

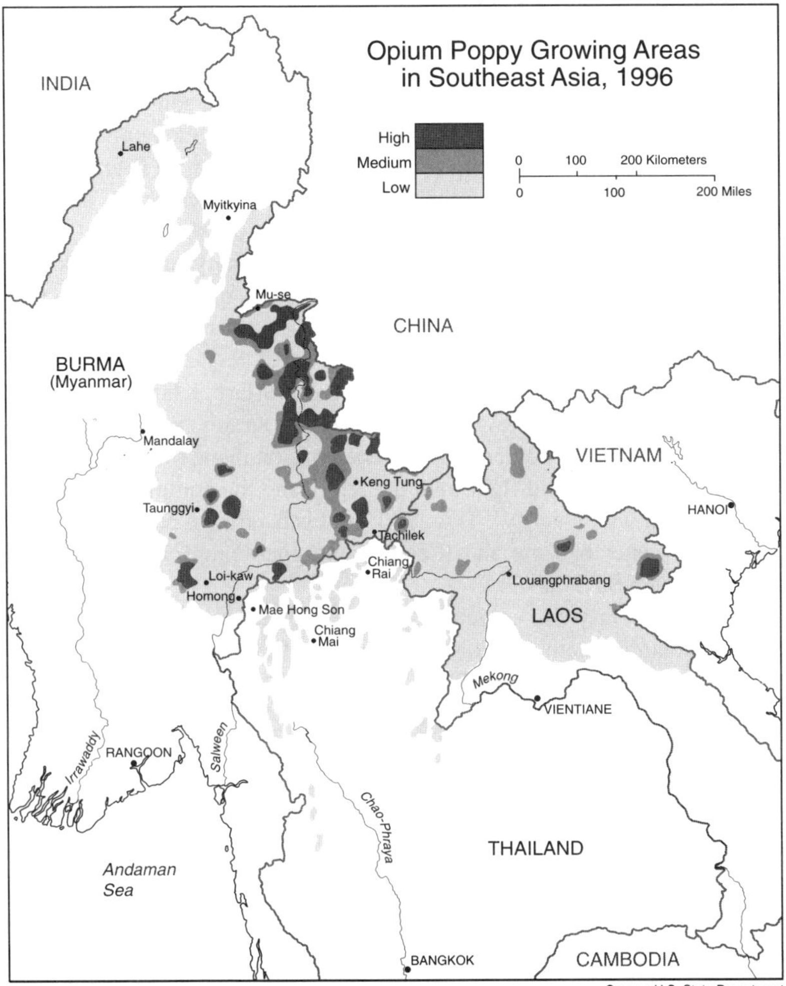

Source: U.S. State Department

ultimately, crippling the secessionist movement. With rebel forces splitting and the Burmese military promoting rival militias, there were, at any given moment, up to forty armies operating in the Shan State. Yet from this chaos, a succession of pre-eminent warlords emerged to impose some order on the opium trade – in the 1950s, the KMT generals; in the late 1960s, Khun Sa ; in the early 1970s, his rival Lo Hsing-han; in the 1980s, Khun Sa again; and, most recently, the United Wa State Army.

At the outset of this protracted chaos in 1950, Khun Sa launched his military career when, at the age of sixteen, he formed a militia band in his home area of Loi Maw – first serving the Nationalist Chinese and later, in his own account, raiding one of their outposts to seize some thirty rifles for his men (Khun Sa n.d.: 47; Yawnghwe 1995: 25). Such opportunism served him well, and the young soldier would, over the next fifteen years, maneuver among the Shan rebels, the Rangoon government, and the narrow middle ground between. With each political shift, he extracted arms, supplies, and concessions. During the first thirty years of his career, Khun Sa remained a typical Haw opium warlord – speaking Yunnanese, trusting only Chinese officers, and avoiding any lasting commitment to the Shan revolt.

After his first decade in the world of Shan warfare, Khun Sa faced an 'immediate' problem: 'How', his authorized biography asks, 'should he build up his strength?' When Burma's Eastern Command offered him state recognition if he would fight both the KMT and the communists, Khun Sa 'accepted with alacrity'. Thus, in 1960 his band won recognition and three years later became an official 'home guard' unit, or *Kwa Ka Ye* (KKY) (Khun Sa n.d.: 47).

Khun Sa's early rise coincided with developments that weakened the already tenuous state controls over this troubled region. In 1962, the Burmese military seized power and arrested senior Shan leaders to prevent them from exercising their constitutional right to secession. A year later, seeking some control over the rising insurgency, Rangoon formed the KKY militia and forged alliances with local warlords. Finally, in 1964, the military imposed socialism and demonetized the currency, effectively detaching the Shan State from Burma's economy and launching it as a satellite of overseas Chinese capital. Over the next quarter century, this cluster of policies contributed, directly and indirectly, to the periodic rise of powerful Chinese drug lords – the KMT's General Ly Wen-huan, and the Haw warlords Lo Hsing-han and Khun Sa (Yawnghwe 1995: 24–6).

Instead of fighting the enemies of the Burmese state, some official militia used their arms and opium profits to become warlords, with troops who were often better equipped than the Burma Army. Indeed, in 1964 Khun Sa broke temporarily with the Burmese and moved his troops across the Thai border to join a short-lived coalition of five Shan rebel armies under the Princess of Yawnghwe. But several of his new allies betrayed him, and the Thai military, in one account, or the KMT, in Khun Sa's own version, raided his camp. Another source reports that Khun Sa's rise had attracted the attention of the KMT's General Ly Wen-huan, who imprisoned him in a deep pit for several weeks – a humiliation that scarred the rising young warlord. Angered, Khun Sa rallied to Rangoon and used his new status as chief of all KKY in the Shan State to go on 'a rampage, shattering and scattering' the rebels who had betrayed him (Yawnghwe 1987: 18–21, 189–90; Khun Sa n.d.: 48; Shan State 1986: 81–82).[3]

In 1967, when Khun Sa was just thirty-three, he challenged General Ly's dominion over the Golden Triangle drug trade. In May, he set out from his home in Loi Maw with a sixteen-ton opium caravan whose 500 soldiers and 300 mules stretched for more than a mile along the ridges of the Shan Plateau. Ordinarily, the KMT posts along the northern Thai frontier would have welcomed such a large shipment, but Khun Sa had signaled his refusal to pay their 'opium tax'. After the convoy crossed the Mekong River into Laos in mid-July, the Nationalist Chinese forces intercepted it near a lumber mill and pinned it down with maximum firepower. In the midst of this stand-off, the commander of the Royal Lao Army, General Ouane Rattikone, himself a major opium dealer, sent in commandos and dive bombers, blasting the battlefield until both sides were forced to flee without the mules and their opium. Undeterred, Khun Sa continued his running war against the KMT control of the Shan opium trade.

By 1969, Khun Sa had rebuilt his fortunes and was again on the rise when a minor indiscretion produced a major blow to his career. Suspicious of his contacts with the Shan State Army, the most radical of the separatists, Burmese military intelligence arrested Khun Sa as hc passed through Taunggyi, capital of the Shan State. Charged with treason, he was placed in solitary confinement in Mandalay Prison for the next four years (Yawnghwe 1987: 27). Then, in April 1973, one of his Chinese commanders entered Taunggyi and, on impulse, kidnapped two Russian doctors who were on a goodwill mission to inspect a Soviet-built hospital. Although Rangoon threw an entire army division into the search, the regime was finally forced to capitulate and swap Khun Sa for the Russians in September 1974. Significantly, the mediator in these negotiations was General Kriangsak Chamanand, the Thai officer responsible for the northern frontier and Khun Sa's future patron (Smith 1991: 335). After a year under house arrest, in February 1976 Khun Sa finally escaped and rejoined his troops in northern Thailand.

Despite these reverses, the battle and its aftermath marked Khun Sa as the only Shan warlord capable of unifying the fragmented Shan and challenging the KMT grip on the opium trade. When I first surveyed the region's heroin trade in 1971, Khun Sa alone seemed to have qualities of ruthlessness, boldness, and determination that marked him as an exceptional leader among the forty-plus warlords then contending for Burma's drug trade.

During his years of incarceration, structural changes in the region's drug trade created an opening for an entrepreneur to achieve unprecedented power. In 1969–70, the KMT and other CIA assets had opened a complex of laboratories in the Golden Triangle that were, within two years, producing 70 per cent of the world's illicit heroin. As Southeast Asian narcotics entered America, Washington extended its 'war on drugs' to the Golden Triangle. In its first major operation in the region, the DEA branded the reigning drug lord, the Haw merchant Lo Hsing-han, as 'kingpin of the heroin traffic' and targeted him for elimination. By the early 1970s, Lo, a KKY militia chief in his native Kokang State, sent 20 tons of opium south to Thailand in caravans with up to 500 soldiers and a thousand mules. 'It stretched out for three miles', the drug lord reminisced in a 1998 interview with the *New York Times*. 'If it went smoothly, it took about 26 days.' By the early 1970s, Lo had seized much of Khun Sa's old territory and controlled half the Shan opium trade, emerging as a powerful political leader among the hill farmers. 'I was working for the Kokang people and the poor people who were looking for a way to sell their product. I did so much for them.' After breaking with the Burmese to ally with the Shan nationalists, Lo, desperate for state protection, proposed to eradicate the Shan opium trade by selling the entire crop directly to the United States. When he agreed, rather naively, to discuss his plan at the DEA office in Chiangmai, Thai authorities deported him to Burma where he was condemned to death for 'insurrection against the state' – a sentence later commuted to eight years in prison. By the mid-1970s, Lo's downfall and the continuing rise in heroin production created an opening for a new 'opium king' (McCoy 1991: 426–7; Cowell 1996: 14–19).[4]

After his escape, Khun Sa soon succeeded his rival Lo Hsing-han as Burma's dominant drug lord. He formed a new militia named the 'Shan United Army' – using the term 'Shan' for the first time to court support from Thai generals sympathetic to the secessionist cause. With their support, Khun Sa opened a major heroin refinery at the northern Thai village of Ban Hin Taek, near the old KMT camp at Mae Salong and astride the caravan routes that crossed the border from Burma. In the 1976–77 crop year, his new army of 3,500 troops hauled 70 tons of raw opium in twelve caravans averaging 116 mules and 335 armed guards each (US Congress 1977: 55–8). Using his heroin profits, Khun cultivated allies at the apex of the Thai military. Emerging as significant player in Thai politics of the 1970s, he made financial contributions to the election campaigns of the country's prime minister, General Kriangsak Chamanand, and allied himself with the country's powerful right wing (McCoy 1991: 420–1).

But even his powerful Thai patrons could not save Khun Sa from himself. Soon after his arrival in Thailand, the warlord, with the brash self-promotion that became his trademark, gave a series of flamboyant interviews to the Bangkok press, proclaiming himself 'King of the Golden Triangle' and producing front-page headlines reading 'I Can Stop the Drug Flow' (McCoy 1991: 419).[5] His heroin mountain of Ban Hin Taek became an international embarrassment that Thailand could not afford. In January 1982, some 1,500 Thai troops, backed by jet fighters and helicopter gunships, attacked his hilltop village, forcing Khun Sa to retreat into Burma leaving behind 15 tons of weapons and 53,000 rounds of ammunition (Tomlin 1989). Although the press described the operation as a fatal blow to his heroin empire, the attack had inadvertently positioned the warlord for a rise to unprecedented power.

Within a year, Khun Sa had rebuilt his heroin redoubt at Homong, his headquarters for the next fourteen years (see Map 5.2). In March 1983, his troops, pushing westward from their established hilltop heroin refineries, marched into the Homong valley in a demonstration of 'adroit intimidation' that forced the outgunned Shan State Army to withdraw without a fight.[6] Lying halfway between the deep Salween River gorges and the Thai border, Homong was an almost impregnable position for the future capital of his Free Shan State – a secessionist enclave that Khun Sa would carve from the forest with each successive opium harvest. Stung by his recent defeat, he now moved quickly to occupy the strategic Thai–Burma border and extend his control into the central Shan State – building his army, expanding the drug traffic, allying with Shan rebels, and attacking any commanders who resisted.

In a characteristically dramatic gesture, Khun Sa announced his dominion over the region's drug trade with a thunderclap. On 11 March 1984, a truck drove up into a walled compound in the northern Thai city of Chiangmai and stopped. The driver jumped from the cab and started running. A ton of explosives erupted, blasting a crater in the earth where General Ly's house and headquarters had been and shattering the glass in hundreds of surrounding homes. Although the Nationalist Chinese commander was away in Bangkok, his prestige died in an explosion that marked Khun Sa's ascension as the Golden Triangle's 'king of opium'. With General Ly in retreat and the other KMT army scattered by the death of its leader four years before, several Nationalist Chinese units rallied to Khun Sa and became the steel in his growing army. After thirty-five years of direct and indirect intervention, the KMT role in Shan State was finally ending (Boucaud and Boucaud 1985: 36–7; Lintner 1994a: 264–5).

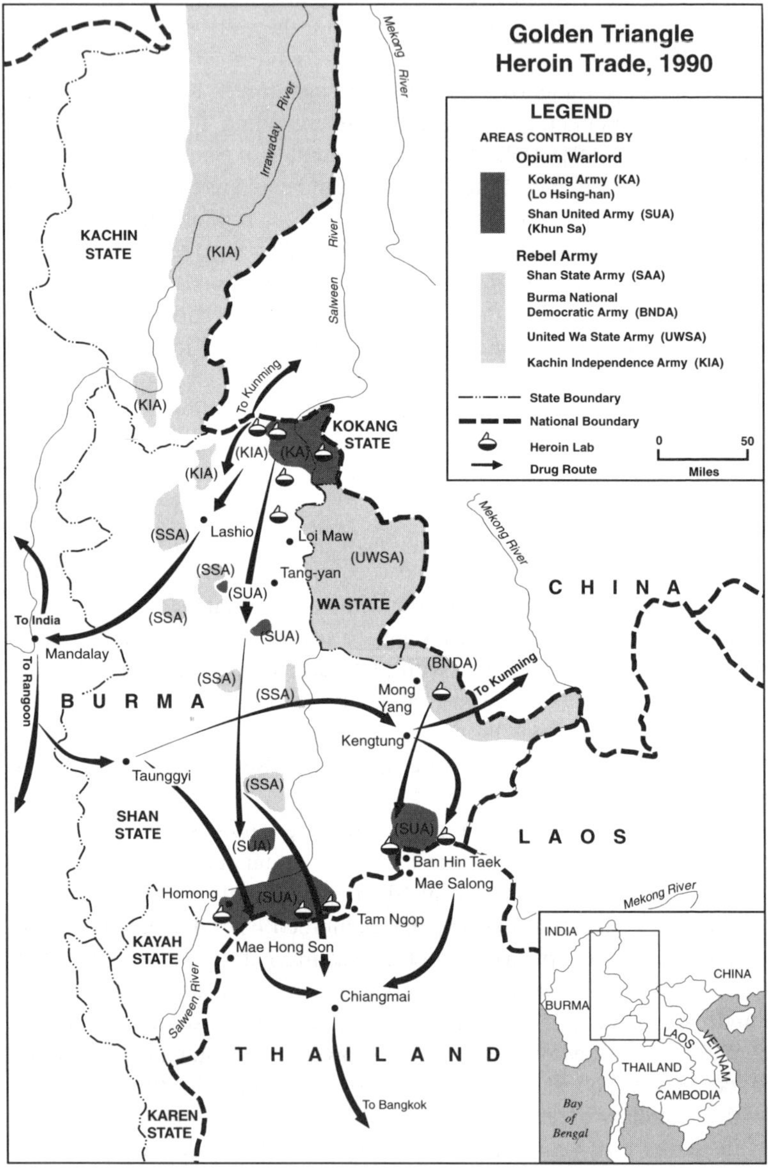
Golden Triangle
Heroin Trade, 1990
LEGEND
AREAS CONTROLLED BY
Opium Warlord
Kokang Army (KA)
(Lo Hsing-han)
Shan United Army (SUA)
(Khun Sa)
Rebel Army
Shan State Army (SAA)
Burma National
Democratic Army (BNDA)
United Wa State Army (UWSA)
Kachin Independence Army (KIA)
State Boundary
National Boundary
Heroin Lab
Drug Route
0
50
Miles
KACHIN
STATE
(KIA)
Irrawaday River
Mekong River
Salween River
To Kunming
KOKANG
STATE
(KA)
Lashio
Loi Maw
(UWSA)
(SSA)
Tang-yan
(SUA)
WA STATE
To India
Mandalay
To Rangoon
B U R M A
(BNDA)
Mong
Yang
Kengtung
Taunggyi
SHAN
STATE
C H I N A
L A O S
Ban Hin Taek
Mae Salong
Homong
Tam Ngop
Mae Hong Son
KAYAH
STATE
Chiangmai
T H A I L A N D
To Bangkok
KAREN
STATE
INDIA
CHINA
BURMA
LAOS
VEITNAM
THAILAND
CAMBODIA
Bay
of
Bengal

Map 5.2

During his first three years inside Burma, Khun Sa maneuvered cautiously among surrounding states, balancing Bangkok's opposition by courting Rangoon. With the tacit support of the Burma Army's Eastern Command, his 3,000 troops occupied 150 miles of strategic trafficking territory along the Thai–Burmese border, attacking rebels hostile to Rangoon and using this zone to take control of two-thirds of the Shan opium crop (Smith 1991: 342–3).[7] In 1987, when Thailand and Burma launched a joint military operation against these heroin refineries, Khun Sa shifted several east into Laos, forging a loose alliance with the country's communist leaders (McCoy 1991: 432–3). In effect, Khun Sa's influence did not rely upon occupation of the best opium territory, which was in fact further north in the rugged Wa hills, but instead upon his control, direct and indirect, over heroin processing and marketing along the Thai–Burmese border. In 1987, the DEA's Bangkok office estimated that Khun Sa's refineries processed some 80 per cent of the Golden Triangle's heroin.[8] A year later, he claimed, in an interview with *Newsweek* (15 May 1989: 42), an annual income of $200 million from the 40 per cent tax he imposed on the 10 to 20 laboratories operating along this frontier.

Although he committed himself to the Shan cause, Khun Sa remained a realist who knew the importance of patrons who could neutralize the power of surrounding states. Even after his expulsion from Thailand in 1981, he had continued his generous payment to senior Thai officers, winning open access to Thailand for arms, banking, and chemicals vital to his opium army. Simultaneously, he cultivated allies at the apex of Burma's military dictatorship and Laos's socialist republic. Just as he had forged a close alliance with the Thai general Kriangsak Chamanand in the 1970s, financing his rise from frontier officer to prime minister, now, with equal acumen, he cultivated a rising figure within Burma's military regime. Through payments totaling several million dollars, he transformed General Maung Aye, then Burma's Eastern commander and later a power in the SLORC regime, from enemy into protector.[9] In both cases, Khun Sa was acute in his choice of allies and judicious in use of his funds to finance their rise from the state's margins to its center.

Under Khun Sa's leadership, Burma's opium production soared from 550 to 2,500 tons during the 1980s – an extraordinary 500 per cent increase. Fueled by Burma's rising poppy harvest, Southeast Asia's share of the New York City heroin market jumped from 5 to 80 per cent between 1984 and 1990. By then, Khun Sa controlled over 80 per cent of Burma's opium production and almost half the world's heroin supply – making him history's most powerful drug lord (US State Department 1990: 271–9, 286).[10]

This flood of Burmese heroin brought lower prices and higher purity in the American drug market. Between the mid-1980s and mid-1990s, the annual US heroin supply rose from 5 to 10–15 metric tons, sustaining an expanded population of 600,000 hard-core American addicts. As Burmese heroin, known on the street as 'China White', landed in unprecedented quantities, the retail price in New York City dropped from $1.81 per milligram in 1988 to just $0.37 in 1994. Simultaneously, the national average for heroin content of 'street deals' rose from just 7 to 40 per cent, reaching 63 per cent in New York City and even higher elsewhere. On the street, unknown entrepreneurs – negotiating the variables of price, purity, supply, and market – dealt with this surge in supply by raising purity and changing the drug's demographics (US General Accounting Office 1996: 2–7; US Department of Justice 1995).

Commodity transformed culture. The new, pure heroin could be snorted or smoked, cutting the link between intravenous injection and HIV infection. Once stigmatized in the 1960s as a ghetto drug, the mark of the social marginal, American youth culture of the 1990s reinvented this cheaper, 'safe' heroin as a badge of alienated authenticity. Cult figures Kurt Cobain and River Phoenix became the celebrity heroin deaths of a young decade. In May 1996, *Rolling Stone* (30 May 1996: 15–20) ran a feature titled 'Rock & Roll Heroin', which listed dozens of mega-stars with major habits. Two months later, the glossy, life-style magazine *Allure* (July 1996: 90–5) reported that the fashion industry's 'baffling concept of heroin chic' was a reality snapshot – top models were regular users. Though few knew his name on the fashion ramps or the club floors, it was Khun Sa who had made heroin chic happen.

With these heroin profits, Khun Sa transformed his warlord militia into the Mong Tai Army (MTA), a force of 20,000 heavily-armed men, and used it to take control of the Shan nationalist movement. In 1985, he sought legitimacy by allying with the Shan State Army and General Mo Heng, the renowned, one-armed Buddhist revolutionary – proclaiming their joint army the sole vanguard of the nationalist cause and driving the last KMT forces out of the Shan State (Khun Sa n.d.: 48; Shan State National Congress 1994: 22). Rivals who resisted Khun Sa's call for unity, including a half-dozen leaders of the more idealistic Shan State Army, were tracked down by hired killers and assassinated (Lintner 1994a: 264). By the early 1990s, as other rebels rallied to its flag, the MTA became a *de facto* alliance of his old Yunnan-Chinese officers, who controlled logistics and drugs, and the Shan nationalists, who directed politics and recruitment. These separate structures within a single army were joined in the person of Khun Sa, who, through his mixed Shan–Chinese background, had the unique bicultural capacity to command both.

Through this process, Khun Sa shed his image as an opium warlord to become the head of a secessionist state. Although many Shan leaders felt reservations about his ruthlessness and Chinese background, most realized that he alone had the mix of command experience and commercial acumen needed to build the fragmented Shan revolt into a viable state (Khun Sa n.d.: 55). Thus, in December 1993, the 79 members of the Shan State National Congress convened at Homong to proclaim independence and pick Khun Sa as their leader. 'I gave you my word that I would never do anything that would compromise the nation, our territorial integrity and the Resistance', he proclaimed in his inaugural address. 'I would rather die first.' Praising him as a man 'glorified by his people', the delegates unanimously condemned the way Khun Sa was 'misportrayed to the world as a ruthless warlord' and asked the United States to 'repeal' his arrest warrant. The Congress approved an idealistic appeal to the UN that 'the world community recognize Shan independence'; but it also endorsed Khun Sa's *realpolitik* proposal for complete opium eradication 'once the Burmese withdraw from Shan soil' (Shan State Congress 1994: appendix 14, 17).[11] For, as he put it in an assessment of intra-state politics that was both bleak and flawed: 'The road to Shan independence is through the opium issue because in the strategic calculations of the superpowers our Shan State is only a small country which is better ignored, except for its opium' (Khun Sa, n.d.: 61).

It was these miscalculations about the nature of the state and the global system of states that led to Khun Sa's downfall only three years later. By investing all his resources in the Shan national cause, he sacrificed the outlaw's flexibility of maneuver among states that had served him so well. Indeed, by building this capital as a symbol of Shan independence, he created a fixed target for the inevitable Burmese attacks. Rangoon's military was tolerant of drug dealing, but secession of the Shan States, with nearly 20 per cent of the nation's population, threatened its territorial integrity. Moreover, his attempt at diplomatic blackmail by unleashing a flood of heroin until the world gave the Shan their independence aroused scorn, even outrage, in Washington. No longer just another warlord, Khun Sa had challenged the state's authority and defied the world order (Tomlin, 1989).[12]

It was at this point in his career – when Khun Sa was at the peak of power accumulated from forty years of warfare – that he invited me to visit him in his capital at Homong. In March 1994, I was in northern Thailand narrating a television documentary about opium when the Australian director asked if I could interview a cooperative Burmese drug lord. A journalist friend in Bangkok advised me to telephone Khun Sa at Homong via his satellite phone connected, illegally, into the Thai cellular system.

Two days later, I was climbing up a 5,000-foot mountain with a cameraman and two Shan guides, crossing from Thailand into the Free Shan State. After we reached Khun Sa's guard post on his side of the Burma–Thai border and were issued papers to proceed, we hitched a ride on a merchant's truck along a road that the general had cut through densely timbered hills. Emerging from a forest where overhanging boughs blocked the sun, the truck crested a hill and stopped at a sentry post. Suddenly, spreading down a valley before us, was Homong, a city of ten thousand people. Only a decade before, this contraband city had been little more than a mule track and a cluster of bamboo houses.

Homong had the bustle of a free port and the austerity of an army post. For the better part of an hour, the truck twisted its way through the city's segments along the valley floor – past the hydroelectric dam, sawmills, gem factory, Buddhist temple, schools, and training camp; to the rebel regime's cantonment, with a modern hospital, legislative buildings, and military offices. The roads were crowded with soldiers marching and heavy machinery at work. Trenches lined the valley's high points; bomb-shelter entrances protruded from the hillsides; and SAM-7 missiles, so lethal against US B-52s over Hanoi in 1972, spiked the peaks. At the center of these fortifications, sited dramatically above a manicured parade ground, was a headquarters that commanded 20,000 troops across the Shan State in an episodic war against three Burma Army divisions.

As both president and supreme military commander of the Shan State Restoration Council, General Khun Sa controlled all activity in Homong and its surrounding territory. Troops marched, caravans moved, and legislators assembled at his command. All movement through the half-dozen sentry posts on the road out of Homong required his written authority. Several aides who worked at his side, and praised him during our visit, had lost relatives and close comrades to his hired assassins. Some months before our arrival, Khun Sa had ordered his soldiers to slaughter 61 farmers in one village and over 100 residents in another, including women and children, for selling their opium and rubies to his rivals.[13] With a death sentence on the family for any desertion, he conscripted at least one son from every household in his territory, proclaiming, in an official manifesto: 'You don't dodge death by avoiding military service . . . If each family furnishes a soldier, then we will have an armed force of one million troops and the war will be won with ease' (Khun Sa n.d.: 53).[14]

With the flair of a natural showman, Khun Sa reveled in the spectacle of power, posing for press photographers and parading with his soldiers before television cameras. Visitors – whether London socialites, former White House drug advisor Peter Bourne, or Colonel James 'Bo' Gritz – were regaled with marching troops and adoring villagers (Lintner 1994a; Gritz 1988: 162–3).[15] His 1989 appearance on ABC Television's '20/20' show revealed a flamboyant Khun Sa who seemed to play to Western stereotypes of the ruthless Asiatic drug lord. With an eye on the camera, the general posed training a rearing horse, slopping hogs, outfitting boy soldiers. 'President Bush may have the button for nuclear weapons', he told ABC's reporters, 'but I have the button for opium. My opium is stronger and more potent than your nuclear bombs. I should just feed you this poison.' Then, with a throaty laugh, he asked rhetorically, 'Why should I do anything else?' After claiming an army of 15,000 men and the cunning to survive 42 assassination attempts, Khun Sa, whom the network called 'the king of heroin', made President George Bush an offer: for just $48 million dollars a year, he, Khun Sa, would destroy Burma's opium crop. To demonstrate his capacities, he marched through an opium field pulling up poppy stalks while the network camera trailed behind (Tomlin 1989).

Even our interview before a single video camera for a low-budget documentary was staged for maximum effect. After a two-hour wait in an open-air pavilion at his headquarters, Khun Sa raced up the hill in a Japanese truck, six guards with M-16 rifles braced in the back. The truck lurched to a sudden halt, the troops jumped out to form an armed cordon to our tea table, and Khun Sa marched up the aisle as everyone leapt instinctively to their feet.

The interview seemed on the surface amicable, at times even jovial. Looking at the video-tape several months later, I was struck by a certain symmetry of mutual fascination – my orientalism of the Shan warlord, his occidentalism of the American academic. Just as I am captivated by Khun Sa's capacity to expand self into an army, a state, and a commodity, so he seemed to me, as he flipped and fingered my book ceaselessly, to be taken with my capacities for compression – enfolding the three-dimensional reality of the Shan state, its armies, its drugs, and its battles into two dimensions, between two covers.

But engaging Khun Sa was still exhausting. In every encounter, no matter how insignificant, he seems determined to dominate, exhibiting the absolute will that had lifted him from boy soldier to opium king. Opening with an offer to buy my services as an author, Khun Sa took control, narrating his life and reconstructing himself as a life-long Shan nationalist. Realizing that he would, if left to talk, engulf us in platitudes of Burmese oppression and Shan liberation, I struggled to shift the ground to *realpolitik* – guns, drugs, and dollars. After what seemed endless minutes of psychological sparring, Khun Sa yielded to the authority of the camera, chafing as my questions took him into an uncomfortable terrain.

Then, when the interview ended and we stood for a photograph, the general, who is a head taller than most Shan soldiers, announced with a note of irritation, 'This man is taller than I am.' He pressed his cheek hard against mine. So close I could see the jaundice of malaria in his eyeballs, black hairs in his nostrils. Then, in schoolyard gesture of dominance, he shifted his handshake for leverage, rolling my knuckles in a painful squeeze that was surprisingly strong for a man of 60. Shouting for the guards to form their cordon, he marched between their rifles to his truck, wheels spitting dust as he raced off. Instead of photographing his departure as planned, I collapsed in my chair, arms jerking outward in a spasm of fear that sent my camera flying across the room, breaking open, spoiling the film (Hilton 1995).

This display of warlord power that seemed so dramatic, so alluring in the Shan hills, created a sordid reality in the world beyond. As the heroin shipments left Khun Sa's highland laboratories, they traced a track of mass addiction, HIV infection, corruption, and criminality.

The General in Retreat

The forces that had created Khun Sa also contributed to his downfall. Looking back on his January 1996 capitulation, we can see how his miscalculations fostered an *ad hoc* alliance of surrounding states – Rangoon, Bangkok, Beijing, and Washington – that crushed his bid for an independent Shan State.

The government of Thailand, so important in Khun Sa's rise, was instrumental in his downfall. With its best divisions concentrated in Bangkok for coup and counter-coup, Thailand had, over the preceding thirty years, defended its frontiers with outlaw allies, transforming its borderlands into zones of controlled chaos. By the late 1970s, the Thai military, in a modern variant of Southeast Asian statecraft, guarded its frontiers with a diverse collection of client armies – Pol Pot's communist Khmer Rouge, Vang Pao's rightist Hmong guerrillas, Haw drug lords, General Bo Mya's Christian Karens, and Khun Sa's Shan rebels. Among all these rebels, Khun Sa, as leader of the Tai-speaking Shans and the wealthiest of the warlords, was, for nearly twenty years, the favorite of the Thai generals.

During the 1980s, however, the Thai economy doubled its output and changed the country's political economy. The rapid expansion weakened the military–bureaucratic nexus that had dominated Thailand since the 1932 coup, creating a new middle class that fought for democracy and struggled to push the military, and its systemic corruption, to the margins. With the economy doubling each decade from industrial and financial profits, the power of the military's black money waned and their political influence declined. The Bangkok business elite began to position themselves for economic dominion over mainland Southeast Asia, creating powerful pressures to regularize diplomatic relations with Rangoon and end Thai support for the ethnic rebels who sustained a buffer zone inside Burma. In the early 1990s, seeking to place some distance between Bangkok and the rebels, Rangoon offered Thai corporations generous timber and resource concessions in its eastern borderlands.

Perhaps most importantly, Thailand's need for water and Burma's willingness to provide it epitomized the changing forces that would doom Khun Sa. With its economy growing at 10 per cent per annum, Thailand was fast outstripping its water reserves and faced the specter of serious shortages for factories, hotels, golf courses, and air-conditioned Bangkok buildings. In early 1994, Rangoon communicated its support for construction of an Upper Salween Dam Project and an 88-kilometer tunnel – from the Salween gorges, beneath Homong's hills, to Maehongson district in northwest Thailand – in effect, conceding one of its three main rivers. In March 1994, Khun Sa announced that the Salween belonged to the Shan and his army would block any construction – an act of obstruction that produced rising Thai pressures. Bangkok soon closed its highway into Homong, blocking his main transport route into Thailand and gradually building its forces to seal the border.[16]

Starting in 1989, Burma's military – ruling as the State Law and Order Council (SLORC) – tried to consolidate its power by breaking the country's ethnic insurgencies in succession, leaving Khun Sa the only threat to its territorial integrity. Significantly, in October 1995, on the eve of its final offensive in this long campaign, SLORC's Secretary One, General Khin Nyunt, told a UN diplomat that 'the unprecedented return to "the legal fold" of 15 out of 16 ethnic armed groups' meant that the 'indispensable' process of 'national reconsolidation' was almost complete (United Nations 1996: 8). When Khun Sa surrendered just two months later, the SLORC had finally ended the eruption of ethnic insurgency that had crippled the state and denied it control over the country's vast eastern borderlands for nearly forty years.

In this assertion of central authority over an outlaw frontier, the regime deployed a strategy – integrated at economic, political, and military levels – that gives new meaning to Gallant's dictum that 'bandits helped make states'. In sum, the SLORC harnessed the illicit cross-border commerce to create a rising synergy between frontier control and state capacity. Looking back, the regime pursued, from 1989 to 1996, a two-part strategy: first, the SLORC shifted the heroin trade away from the Thai frontier where Khun Sa was king to the China borderlands controlled by its new drug-lord allies ; and, then, it used these same opium armies, with their hard-currency profits and troops, for a massive assault on Khun Sa's secessionist state.

Though diplomatically isolated after its 1988 massacre of pro-democracy demonstrators, Rangoon rearmed its forces for this campaign by turning to China for a $1.4 billion arms deal signed in October 1989.[17] To earn the requisite hard currency, Burma, starting in 1990, changed its tax and exchange regulations, seeking to channel gem and drug-smuggling income into the legitimate sector. In its review of the country's trade for 1995–6, the Centre Français du Commerce Exterieur in Paris noted $400 million in unexplained inflows and $200 million in unrecorded defense imports that may have been financed by the estimated $700 million earned from heroin exports.[18] By mid-1996, the US Embassy in Rangoon would report that the 'value of Burma's opiate exports, at Burma's border, may now approximate Burma's total declared legal . . . exports receipts'. The Embassy noted an 'overt reliance on narcofinancing of physical infrastructure', such as hotel projects with 'ties to opiate-growing or opiate exporting organizations' (US Embassy 1996: 4–5, 8–9). Significantly, the US State Department stated that SLORC 'seems more intent on . . . strengthening its political position in the border areas than in countering the narcotics trade', and had 'given ethnic traffickers significant political legitimacy . . . as "leaders of national races" . . . in the government's national constitutional convention' (US State Department 1996: 249–50).

Along its eastern borderlands, Rangoon slowly curbed the myriad of highland revolts with a strategy that combined economic manipulation, ethnic diplomacy, and military pressure. As it had since the 1960s, the Burmese state, now under SLORC's control, used its control over towns and transport to reallocate the opium trade, gradually shifting the locus of the traffic north to its frontier facing China. Using a complementary tactic of ethnic division, the SLORC signed a ten-year cease-fire with the United Wa State Army in 1989, the first of 15 such pacts with rebel armies, allowing Wa syndicates to expand heroin production in exchange for fighting Khun Sa. In just a year, 17 new heroin refineries opened inside

Wa territory along the China–Burma border; and by 1996 opium production there would double (Smith 1991: 380; US General Accounting Office 1996: 24–5; Lintner 1995: 20–1).[19] On the Burma–Laos border, the SLORC backed Lin Ming-xian, a former leader of the Communist Party of Burma, who commanded an army of 4,000 soldiers and an annual heroin production of some 2,000 kilograms.[20] Similarly, the SLORC allowed Kokang's Haw syndicates under former 'heroin kingpin' Lo Hsing-han, now one of Burma's wealthiest financiers, access to government-controlled roads for opium transport and encouraged their expansion into Khun Sa's territory (Cowell 1996: 20).[21] As an unintended spin-off of these strategic alliances, the Wa and Kokang armies began shipping their heroin exports across China to Hong Kong. 'These mainland routes have already eclipsed Burmese drug warlord Khun Sa and Thai export routes', the *Wall Street Journal* reported in January 1995.[22] Significantly, Rangoon denounced his Mong Tai Army as a mere 'drug running group' and refused to negotiate with its representatives.[23] By August, the *Bangkok Post* reported that Khun Sa's heroin shipments were down by two-thirds – reducing the cash flow he needed to keep his army on the march.[24]

Starting in early 1994, Burma's Army, now re-equipped with Chinese arms, mobilized some 10,000 troops for the first of three massive dry-season offensives against Khun Sa, finally forcing his army to fight. Since thousands would die in any frontal assault across the deep Salween gorges just west of Homong, the Burmese Army had to envelop his flanks slowly. Though Khun Sa generally preferred to retreat in the face of pressure, his army would, on several occasions, use its formidable firepower to slow the advance – raking Burmese troops with lethal machine-gun fire at a Salween River crossing in January 1994 and inflicting 546 casualties on a unit that attacked one of his border posts in June.[25]

Rangoon's first offensive opened in early 1994 with attacks that forced Khun Sa's troops out of their zone in the heart of the Shan State, reducing Khun Sa's control to a narrow strip along the Thai–Burmese border. Then, the army's hard-fought operations along the border imposed a permanent blockade on his territory around Homong, diverting opium caravans and eliminating two of his largest heroin refineries. A year later, in their 1995 dry-season operations, the Burmese Army, in a giant pincers movement, struck at Homong from the north through the Shan State and from the south through the rebel territory of the Karenni National Progressive Party and Karen Christian guerrillas – a move facilitated by a cease-fire with the Karenni and ongoing successes against General Bo Mya's Karens.[26] Pressing their advantage, the Burmese troops attacked Khun Sa's secondary border enclave near Tachilek, and the MTA retaliated, with little effect, by assaulting the town itself.[27] As Burmese pressures increased, the rebels of the United Wa State Army broke off secret talks with Khun Sa and sided with the Burmese, sending troops to fight his army in August and thereby assuring continued state protection for their heroin shipments.[28] Under these pressures, Khun Sa's position began to collapse.

In July 1995, Major Karnyord, a renowned Shan rebel and deputy commander of the MTA's 16th Brigade, broke with Khun Sa – taking some 500 soldiers and denouncing him as both a Chinese who discriminated against the Shan and as a drug dealer who used the movement for personal gain.[29] On 12 August the Shan State National Congress forced Khun Sa out of the leadership and formed a new executive under a secondary Shan leader, Zao Gunjade, who moved quickly to take control of the Mong Tai Army. As Burma Army pressure on Homong increased, Khun Sa tried to shift his territory eastward but encountered fierce opposition from the Wa who responded with heavy attacks on his border posts near Tachilek.[30] On 22 November Khun Sa resigned from the Shan executive and announced that he would retire to become a chicken farmer.[31] But by cutting the ties of political allegiance, he regained the freedom to maneuver.

Khun Sa's Surrender

On 1 January 1996, in a bold move characteristic of his career, Khun Sa allowed 1,500 Burma Army troops to occupy Homong without any resistance. As command helicopters landed in the rebel redoubt, thousands of Khun Sa's soldiers were lined up at attention, their guns lying symbolically at their feet. After celebrating his so-called 'surrender' for two days with senior Burma Army officers, Khun Sa supervised the disarming of 5,000 soldiers and delivery of 9,620 'heavy weapons'.[32]

While this first surrender was kept quiet, a second on 18 January was heavily publicized. The SLORC junta sent one of its ministers, General Maung Thint, to supervise a ceremony broadcast by Rangoon's TV *Myanmar Network*. Before the cameras, Khun Sa led 1,728 Mong Tai soldiers in surrendering 1,096 weapons. 'Let us forget the undesirable deeds of the past', he told the national television audience. 'I am of the view that we will work together to ensure that the peace we obtain is enduring and that it will last in order to . . . eradicate the opium and narcotics drugs, which endanger the entire humanity of our country.' On a contrite note, the retired rebel concluded: 'I would like to beg your pardon from the national government and the people for our wrong deeds in the past and our armed opposition against the national government' (New Light of Myanmar 1996: 9). The ceremonials soon shifted to Rangoon, where the ruling SLORC junta welcomed Khun Sa and his aides as 'our own blood brethren' and installed the retired warlord in a luxurious Inle Lake villa near the regime's strongman Ne Win.[33]

Under the pressure of changing regional politics, the Thai military was forced to accept the loss of its client armies inside Burma. 'For Thailand', Bangkok's *Nation* newspaper editorialized on 5 January, 'the handover of Shan controlled territory means the collapse of the Shan buffer zone and brings Burmese troops face-to-face with Thai soldiers at the disputed northwestern border.' The paper went on to argue that Bangkok should now resolve these border issues through diplomacy, indicating the fundamental change in Thai foreign policy that had doomed Khun Sa's rebel state.[34] That same day, Thai Army commander General Pramon Phalasin 'downplayed concerns that the presence of Burmese troops in Khun Sa's old stronghold . . . would heighten military tension'. In a move indicative of this new cooperation, the general announced that Rangoon had responded to Thailand's request by withdrawing some of its forces from sensitive areas.[35]

In following weeks, the press uncovered the maneuvers that had preceded Khun Sa's surrender, demonstrating, yet again, the qualities that had allowed him to survive so many reverses in his fifty-year career. Anonymous sources in the Mong Tai Army revealed that the warlord had paid a senior SLORC general 'millions' of dollars to arrange the surrender. Foreign correspondents claimed that General Maung Aye, formerly Khun Sa's patron as Eastern Commander and now SLORC's vice-chairman, had brokered an arrangement favorable to his benefactor.[36] The most detailed report of these terms, published in an obscure Thai newspaper a year later, claimed that the regime had promised Khun Sa: (1) freedom to engage in legal business, (2) immunity from extradition to the United States, and (3) restoration of his control over Homong and its army within two years.[37]

Over time, SLORC's commitment to the economic clause in this *entente cordiale* seems to have waned. After the surrender, the regime awarded Khun Sa 44 acres of land on the Thai border for construction of a gambling casino and licenses for three lucrative bus routes. As his ties to the Mong Tai army attenuated and his capacity for threat faded, the investments soured. To service the contract for the Tachilek–Mandalay bus route, Khun Sa imported 40 vehicles from Singapore. By early 1997, however, the rival Shan United Revolutionary Army (SURA) resumed military operations against SLORC in the central Shan States by attacking all road traffic, Khun Sa's buses included. Finding rebel fees uneconomic and the Burma Army unwilling to offer protection, Khun Sa was forced to suspend operations.[38]

Similarly, Khun Sa's attempt to launder his heroin money through state-sponsored enterprise seems to have been only modestly successful. As a condition of his surrender, the general had agreed to invest much of his capital in joint ventures with SLORC-sponsored firms engaged in 'fishing, logging, gems, and the import–export business'. Once his capital was committed, SLORC discovered legal impediments, reserving these activities to the state, that made it impossible to issue the necessary permits. Among his many investments in Rangoon, only an old cemetery, an antiquated radio station, and gem exports remained potentially profitable.[39]

After the surrender, SLORC reduced, but did not eliminate, Khun Sa's role in the country's heroin trade. At the time of the surrender, his rivals in the United Wa State Army already controlled about 80 per cent of Shan opium production, but he still dominated the downstream sector through some 15 to 20 heroin laboratories and their export networks.[40] As SLORC slowly cooled towards the retired warlord, his long-time allies in the heroin trade refused to remit his share of the profits. In the following months, several of Khun Sa's Chinese partners shifted 'at least three heroin refineries' into the Wa area under the protection of his enemies.[41] By early 1997, they refused to make payments, fearing 'any money sent to him would be appropriated by the upper echelons of SLORC'.[42] Moreover, at several of the largest laboratory sites along the Burma–Thailand border, the Burmese Army blocked Khun Sa's return by assigning thousands of its own troops to protect the independent operators.[43] Two years after the surrender, Wa commander Wei Hseuh-kang with 7,000 soldiers seemed to be emerging as his successor. 'All information is that he's getting larger by the day', a Western narcotics official observed.[44]

Nonetheless, the regime permitted Khun Sa to retain a portion of his narcotics network. In the week before his surrender, the warlord had ordered his men to dismantle a dozen of his border refineries and relocate several inside Burmese Army zones west of the Salween. Even after most of his men had stacked arms, SLORC allowed him to retain 500 of his best troops to protect his trafficking operations.[45] Thus, only six months after the surrender, Bangkok's authorities attributed the quick recovery of local drug supplies to 'the Burmese government's condoning of Khun Sa's heroin trade'.[46] Around Homong, authorities were allowing Khun Sa's former soldiers to plant opium poppies 'to ease poverty in the area'; while his network was now operating a chain of amphetamine laboratories along the Thai–Burmese border. Winston Lord, the US Assistant Secretary of State, called SLORC's alliance with Khun Sa a 'defeat for the control of drugs in all our countries'.[47]

With the passage of time, the possibility that Khun Sa will revive his opium army grows remote. After the surrender, the US State Department seemed convinced that his army would survive. 'Although the details of the peace arrangement are not yet clear', the Department said in a March 1996 report, 'it seems the MTA will be allowed to operate as an ethnic militia in the same manner that the UWSA [United Wa State Army] and MNDAA [Myanmar National Democratic Alliance Army] continue to operate in other parts of the Shan state' (US State Department 1996: 251). In effect, the report seemed to argue, Khun Sa had surrendered his Shan revolutionary forces but retained his Chinese opium army. Despite Washington's pessimism, SLORC persisted in its dissolution of the Mong Tai Army, and by March 1997 had accepted the surrender of 14,606 of its estimated 20,000 soldiers.[48] While his career as a nationalist rebel had ended, Khun Sa, freed from the constraints of ideology, was, against formidable odds, trying to execute an improbable volte-face and ally with the Burma Army in ways that would, over the long term, allow recovery of his opium army and its territory.

Rangoon may be ambiguous about some aspects of the agreement, but the regime still resisted diplomatic pressures for Khun Sa's extradition. On 6 January, just days after the surrender, US State Department spokesman Nicholas Burns demanded that 'the Burmese government turn Khun Sa over to United States authorities because he is a drug lord'.[49] A month later, on 11 February, Burma's Foreign Minister Ohn Gyaw announced that Rangoon had refused Washington's request.[50] In sum, Burma had defied the world's leading power to protect a local drug lord. Even though the US Assistant Secretary of State Winston Lord announced that Burma's refusal would arouse American ire, Burma did not bend.[51] Instead, a senior SLORC official, Lieutenant General Kyaw Ba, minister for hotels and tourism, advocated forgiveness for Khun Sa. 'Let bygone be bygone, that is the motto of the Burmese people', the general said. 'He has given up all his drug refineries and is not creating any problems.' He added that Khun Sa would be free to settle in the country's capital once the remaining renegade troops of the MTA, about 2,000 soldiers, had surrendered. Though Washington responded to this rebuff by offering two million dollars for Khun Sa, such a small reward seemed, at best, quixotic.[52]

Reflecting its long-standing diplomatic posture on the Southeast Asian mainland, the US had little influence in Burma. In the bipolar politics of the Cold War, the US position in Southeast Asia had been marked by a close alliance with Bangkok and a distinct coolness towards Rangoon. While the US signed a military aid agreement with Thailand in 1950, Washington had simultaneously authorized a CIA operation to support the KMT's army inside Burma. Within a year, the US ambassador to Rangoon was firing off secret cables to Washington protesting the 'flagrant disregard for Burmese sovereignty' and, when ignored, resigned in protest (McCoy 1991: 177). While Rangoon filed a formal complaint before the UN in 1953 and won a condemnation of this covert operation, Bangkok was becoming home to the SEATO secretariat. During the coming decade, as Rangoon continued to protest, the US built closer relations to Bangkok.

After President Richard Nixon declared 'war on drugs' in 1972, the US initiated major anti-narcotics programs in both Thailand and Burma. But there were important differences. While the DEA worked closely with Thai police in Bangkok and on the border, Washington had to buy its way into Burma. Between 1974 and 1978, Rangoon accepted eighteen helicopters under the US narcotics assistance program and cooperated with Thai police in mounting sweeps against insurgent drug operations along their common frontier. In the mid-1980s, the DEA worked with the Burmese to defoliate some 60,000 acres of Shan State forest with the lethal 2,4-D chemical – a campaign that may have stimulated production as farmers expanded their poppy crop to compensate for these losses. Despite some displays of cooperation, Rangoon diverted American aid to counter-insurgency (Smith 1991: 314).[53] The regime's anti-drug operations were a façade that could not long conceal the explosive surge in heroin production that began in the early 1980s. Burma's military was willing to defoliate and destroy poppy fields that belonged to its ethnic enemies, but still protected favored drug lords like Khun Sa and, after he rebelled, his long-time rival Lo Hsing-han.[54] By the time the US suspended its aid program in 1988 to protest the massacre of Rangoon's pro-democracy demonstrators, most of the US mission, except the DEA, regarded the anti-drug effort as an expendable failure.

When Burma's share of US heroin supply shot upward towards 60 per cent in the early 1990s, Washington suddenly found its weak relations with Rangoon a liability. Since 1989, the White House has repeatedly denied Burma certification for anti-narcotics aid, reducing DEA access to training seminars and the occasional drug burn. Playing upon internal divisions inside Washington, Burma's SLORC junta offered to deliver Khun Sa in exchange for US military aid in 1994 – in effect, dangling the lure of renewed cooperation with the DEA to win better bilateral relations.[55] By mid-1996, however, Rangoon's repeated refusal to deliver Khun Sa without concessions brought US–Burmese relations to a historic low, culminating in the US sanctions against SLORC in mid-1997 for heroin trafficking and human rights abuse.[56]

A year after Khun Sa's surrender, there were contradictory reports of his political future. A northern Thai newspaper offered a Lear-like portrait – a fallen warlord, ailing, aging, and betrayed, living out his days as a prisoner of his past. The report said that Khun Sa was 'exhibiting the symptoms of a nervous condition' from his 'growing fear and suspicion that the Burmese government was going to betray him and turn him over to the American government'. Although his diabetes had worsened and he lost use of his left arm, SLORC was denying him access to hospital care and assigned a single physician to treat him at home.[57]

By contrast, the Bangkok press coverage indicated that Khun Sa, freed from the high costs of sustaining the Shan revolt, could now concentrate on rebuilding his narcotics trade and laundering his profits into legitimate enterprise.[58] In April 1998, a *New York Times* reporter in Rangoon found the regime rather sentimental about the old warlord. 'We were fighting him for years', recalled Colonel Hla Min of SLORC's Office of Strategic Studies. 'We were not gaining much ground because he was well equipped, well dug-in, and the terrain was terrible. We were sacrificing too many casualties.' But now that bloodshed was forgotten, and the colonel called Khun Sa 'a walking encyclopedia on the drug issue', adding 'everything he knows, we know'.[59] Ultimately, with his revolt broken and his militia cut down to size, he seems, like his predecessor Lo Hsing-han, destined to become a powerful financier, mixing the legal and illegal to build the nation's economy within the bounds prescribed by the Burmese state.

Requiem

At the policy level, the most remarkable aspect of Khun Sa's political demise went almost unreported: the downfall of Burma's 'opium king' had little more than a momentary impact upon the flow of heroin out of the Golden Triangle. Only three months after his surrender, the US State Department, blaming SLORC's 'woefully inadequate' counter-narcotics efforts, complained that 'drug-trafficking armies have benefited immensely from their good relationships with Rangoon regime' and 'the drug trade in the Shan State continues virtually unchecked' (US State Department 1996: 249–50). After four months of a 'critical shortage of heroin' that followed his surrender, Bangkok's Narcotics Suppression Bureau noted that there had been a 'quick recovery of the heroin business'. A year later, the Thai press reported that the region's drug problem was 'worse' and its opium production was up 10 per cent.[60]

Khun Sa's career demonstrates the complexity of relations between the state and the outlaws whom Washington calls 'drug lords'. While they are still central to the narcotics trade, major drug lords, protected by their states, remain impervious to international pressures. They can only be arrested when the political economy of the producing regions shifts in ways that renders them redundant – stripping them of their local power, drug profits, and external support. In effect, we can only capture a drug lord when he is no longer a drug lord.

At a pragmatic level, this paradox raises some real questions about the nature of the global drug trade and the appropriateness of US anti-narcotics policy. More than any other single man in this century, Khun Sa has shaped the world's narcotics traffic – increasing Burma's heroin production fivefold and changing the demographics of drug abuse in the United States. Yet even Khun Sa's capture, at the peak of his powers in 1990, would have had little effect on the traffic. Even if he had been arrested, the poppy fields and addicts would remain; and some other drug lord would soon have reaped the profit that comes from their connection. Just as the state retains the ultimate capacity to crush any outlaw, no matter how powerful, so the global drug traffic is a vast commodity trade that interpenetrates every aspect of the modern state, compromising those same capacities.

In this context, we can see Khun Sa as something of a self-taught ethnographer, a field researcher testing the nature of the modern state through a life-long exercise in participant observation. Indeed, at every turn in his fifty-year career, his fortunes have been shaped by an encounter with multifaceted manifestations of state power – superpower conflict, postcolonial nationalism, irredentism, and ethnic secession. Thus, his remarkable career allows us to reflect upon the four elements of state–outlaw interaction outlined at the outset: the limits of state power, bandit geography, global economic context, and outlaw entrepreneurship.

While most outlaws play upon the fissures in a single state, geography and geopolitics forced Khun Sa to operate in a multi-state context. Though nominally remote, his domain in northeastern Burma lay astride the fault lines of regional and international conflicts – between rival states, Thailand and Burma; and rival superpowers, China and America. Thus, from his rise as boy-soldier to his downfall as aging warlord a half-century later, Khun Sa's success was determined by his ability to maneuver within and among states. He recruited his first troops for US covert operations against China, won a small army as a militia commander for Burma, and gained the globe's greatest drug empire as an instrument of Thai irredentism. In the end, his power collapsed in an overly bold bid to create an independent Shan state that led him to defy, simultaneously, Burma, Thailand, China, and America. Not only did his revolt challenge their individual interests, but his heroin enterprise violated the norms of an emerging international community. In an age when the global anti-narcotics effort, led by the United Nations and the United States, has won wide support, Khun Sa's stigma as a drug lord delegitimated his political aspirations and denied his secessionist state any chance of diplomatic recognition. Looking back on his downfall, the rebel Shan News Agency reported that his independence effort had failed because his Mong Tai Army had been 'totally suffocated by its negative media image'.[61] In retrospect, his attempt to fuse the roles of drug lord and national revolutionary had proved unworkable. In the end, he could not overcome his outlaw status in the eyes of both Burma and the international community. Yet, even at this low ebb, his skillful manipulation of Rangoon's ruling factions allowed him to elude the reach of the world's last superpower and avoid the fate of Panama's dictator Manuel Noriega.

Outlaws with Khun Sa's mix of economic and political power can only emerge in areas that are both politically peripheral and economically significant. In Southeast Asia, simple geography has often determined those regions that remained remote from central control. While lowland plains or river basins were usually the heart of early-modern states, both mountains and seas presented a challenge to state authority. In the sixteenth to the nineteenth centuries, for example, seas remained beyond the control of most states, creating an opening for pirates and privateers to prey upon maritime commerce. Even as late as the mid-nineteenth century, British merchantmen and Spanish navy vessels were sorely pressed to contain piracy along the north coast of Borneo, making Sarawak and Sulu outlaw zones.

As colonies and kingdoms expanded on the Southeast Asian mainland in the nineteenth century, their highland peripheries came to serve as formal and informal boundaries during a period of state consolidation. There were, of course, a complex of factors that kept central authority remote from these mountains. Most importantly, the difficulty and irregularity of the terrain restrains central control and advantages the outlander, who can use superior physical conditioning, political support, and local knowledge to make mountains a refuge. In highland South and Southeast Asia, caravan routes traverse these uplands to reach remote markets, creating an essential raiding opportunity for the uplanders. Finally, across Southeast Asia, indigenous states operated with a concept of geography that had not yet adopted either the European idea of the borders as fixed, metaphysical lines to be defended or a military technology appropriate for their defense.

Such an approach often assumes that states and their peripheries are part of dynamic economy, early-modern or modern, with elaborate long-distance exchange that provides outlaws with illicit sustenance. During the nineteenth century, for example, the rapid growth of the India–China opium trade sparked an eruption of maritime and mountain banditry. As the volume of opium sailing on the Calcutta-to-Canton route started rising in the late eighteenth century, pirate fleets appeared at the entrances, the vulnerable choke points, in the uncharted vastness of the South China Sea. Malay chiefs at its southern entrance off Sarawak and Chinese villagers in northern waters near Hainan launched pirate fleets to prey upon the unarmed British and Indian merchant ships (Murray 1987, 1995: 209–12; Pringle 1970: 46–96).[62] An ancillary boom in the export of exotic Sulu Sea products for the China market strained that archipelago's labor supply and led the local Muslim sultanate to send slaving fleets into the Spanish Philippines (Warren 1982: 415–34). Moreover, in the late nineteenth century, Yunnan-Muslim merchants, Khun Sa's antecedents, smuggled cheap Chinese opium across the country's permeable south-western frontier, undercutting the inflated prices that Southeast Asia's monopolies charged addicts for Indian imports. A century later, the abolition of these same monopolies, in the context of decolonization, would spark the new burst of outlaw opium trading and ethnic insurgency that shaped Khun Sa's career.

These outlaws – whether bandit, warlord, or tribal chief – cannot long prosper in the core of any state, early-modern or modern, and must seek refuge at its margins or interstices. During the 1950s, for example, Saigon's Binh Xuyen bandits, emboldened by their control over the city's police and illicit economy, defied the authority of Prime Minister Ngo Dinh Diem. Yet even this neophyte regime proved capable of military operations that forced the bandits from the capital and into swamps at the state's margins (McCoy 1991: 146–60). Similarly, during the 1980s, Khun Sa controlled a vast territory and an army of 20,000 troops along Burma's eastern borderlands until he proclaimed a secessionist revolt. Weak though the Burmese state may be, it still has the capacity, when its territorial integrity is threatened, to mobilize a military operation sufficient to destroy the world's largest drug lord. Just as the state can, through its incompetence or inattention, foster bandits at its margins, so it can, through its unequaled capacities, assert its authority by exterminating bandits at its core and, by fits and starts, eliminating those who seek refuge in its peripheries. Future decades will tell if this is a significant instance of Gallant's 'border effect' operating in the modern age, and whether Khun Sa, like early-modern bandits, played a catalytic role in state formation by forcing Rangoon to impose control over its frontiers (Chapter 2).

Few of the actors in this volume can be styled either 'bandits', in the simple predatory sense that state officials often imply, or 'social bandits' in Eric Hobsbawm's usage, with all of his normative, teleological undertones (1969: 13–23). If we strip the term of such biases, we can deploy it to mean, simply, an armed group that engages in some form of illicit economic activity outside the law's reach – whether in slums, mountains, forests, swamp, strand, or seas. Beyond those whom we might consider simple outlaws – smugglers, pirates, thieves, and highwaymen – these interstices also provide refuge for those who mix economic and political roles. In eras and areas where central rule is weak, these more complex characters can sometimes win sufficient political power to become, depending upon the strength of the state, rebels or warlords. If central authority weakens, as it did in China during the 1920s, then outlaws can become regional warlords with *de facto* autonomy and legitimacy. If, by contrast, the state maintains even limited capacities – as it did in Indonesia during the 1960s, the Philippines in the 1970s, or Burma in the 1990s – then these outlaws become, at best, leaders of regional revolts, whether ethnic or religious. In such times, moreover, local political leaders – *datu*, *kaitong*, or *saopha* – can reverse this process by mobilizing their clientele to become, from the capital's perspective, dangerous bandits, smugglers, or pirates.

Modern fiscal management, or mis-management, has often created the economic preconditions for the appearance of these outlaws. Under the guise of collecting taxes and promoting development, Southeast Asian states, both colonial and national, have, for over two centuries, used their powers to restrict economic activity. Indeed, from the eighteenth century onward, the region's colonial regimes applied mercantilist doctrines to create lucrative monopolies in drugs that are, to a greater and lesser extent, addictive (Baysinger *et al.* 1980: 235–68). The British East India Company and allied merchants monopolized the India–China opium trade; the Dutch East Indies Company (VOC) controlled Java's opium imports and coffee exports; and Spain's Philippine revenues relied upon its Tobacco Monopoly.

As these regimes evolved into the region's modern states a century later, they preserved, and even elaborated, these economic prerogatives into a system of monopolies, tax farms, and protected enterprises. For over two hundred years, the Philippine state, for example, has manipulated tobacco in ways that fostered illegality. Under the Spanish Tobacco Monopoly (1766–1880), farmers grew illegally and bandits smuggled to undercut the high official price for an addictive drug; the US regime (1899–

1946) manipulated trade policy to make the Philippines a prime market for American cigarettes; and the postwar Republic (1946–72) protected local production in ways that stimulated smuggling and systemic corruption. By the mid-1960s, illegal Philippine tobacco imports and Indonesian coconut exports had fused at the North Borneo port of Sandakan to form an integrated illegal trade network – creating a cast of powerful rebels, pirates, and smugglers along its arc from central Sulawesi to northern Luzon (de Jesus 1980: 47–8, 60–9; Doeppers 1991: 521–5; Reed 1963: 353–6; Golay 1961: 163–6; US Department of Commerce 1965: 8; Hartendorp 1961: 273–4; McKenna 1994: 21). Similarly, mainland Southeast Asian states, by restricting opium production under colonialism and consumption since independence have, inadvertently, fostered highland warlords, overland smuggling, and extensive drug-trading networks.

If we take a page from the work of James Buchanan and others on 'rents', the region's outlaws all seemed to be responding, in some way, to such restrictive economic management – whether rigid exchange policies, protective tariffs, regulated markets, or heavy consumer taxes (1980: 3–8; Krueger 1974: 291–303; Reuter 1983). Hence, states impose a coercive control apparatus – as rents, taxes, exemptions, protections, customs duties, tax farms, and prohibitions – that creates opportunities for illicit entrepreneurs. Through smuggling, counterfeiting, and bootlegging, these outlaws are not merely rational individuals responding to illicit opportunity, but are, more broadly, actors reconciling arbitrary state policy with economic rationality.

In the case of contemporary Burma and its opium, this irrationality is the product, not just of national policy, but of an international prohibition that sustains a rising global demand for illicit narcotics. To rationalize the irrational, Burma's SLORC, in a contemporary instance of Gallant's border effect, has tried to harness its borderland bandits and their illicit trade to strengthen the state. In marked contrast to the deep contempt that the DEA and US diplomats reserve for Khun Sa and his kind, the weak Burmese state, like its early-modern antecedents, has been forced to engage the reality of such powerful outlaws as both threat and asset. To counter Khun Sa's modern army, the SLORC was forced to harness the illicit border trade for hard currency to buy arms. When this center–periphery synergy had crushed his revolt, Rangoon then transformed Khun Sa, as it had Lo Hsing-han, from highland bandit into national financier, using his illicit assets and overseas Chinese connections to promote economic growth. This tactic of co-opting outlaws, with all their violence and criminality, was a common form of state-building in the early-modern age. But in our own era, when major powers are struggling to build a world order upon shared principles, such an ambiguous state policy has become anathema. By its alliance with outlaws, Burma has become, in the eyes of the West, an outlaw state, and thus suffers diplomatic opprobrium.

Despite the end to the Cold War and its superpower rivalries, the local and regional conditions that created Khun Sa and his rival opium warlords remain. Once a manifestation of ethnic tensions, weak state-formation, geopolitical conflict, and global drug demand, Khun Sa now seems a pioneer, the prototype of a new kind of regional warlord that has emerged from the ruins of the Cold War. With the collapse of the iron curtain, there has been an eruption of ethnic insurgency along the southern frontiers of the former Soviet Union. As states fragment across this vast swath of the globe, regional rebels, armed with drug money and fighting for power, have begun producing opium and heroin in unprecedented quantities. The circumstances that created Khun Sa are now being replicated, with variations of time and place, and with unpredictable consequences for the future of its fragile states, across the vastness of Central Asia.

Notes

1. *Washington Times*, 5 January 1996; *New York Times*, 2 January 1996, 6 January 1996.
2. *New York Times*, 28 July 1997.
3. Interview with Bertil Linter, Burma correspondent for *Far Eastern Economic Review*, Bangkok, 9 April 1994.
4. *Bangkok Post*, 12 January 1997; *New York Times* 11 May 1998.
5. *Far Eastern Economic Review*, 20 January 1994.
6. *Asia Magazine*, 23 January 1985.
7. *The Geopolitical Drug Dispatch* 52, (February 1996), pp. 1, 3.
8. *Asia Magazine*, 12 July 1987.
9. *The Nation* (New York), 16 December 1996, pp. 14–15; *The Geopolitical Drug Dispatch* 52 (February 1996), pp. 3, 4.
10. Interview with General Khun Sa, Homong, Burma, 3 April 1994; *New York Times*, 11 February 1990.
11. Shan State National Congress, 'Resolutions Reached at the Third Session of the People's Representative Assembly, 1–12 December 1993'; letter from Deving, President, Shan People's Representative Assembly, to President, UN Security Council, 5 June 1993; Shan People's Representative Assembly, 'Proposal for the Termination of Opium Production in the Shan State', 1 October 1993.

12. *Asiaweek*, 15 June 1994; *Far Eastern Economic Review*, 20 January 1994.
13. *The Geopolitical Drug Dispatch* 20 (June 1993), pp. 1, 3–4; *Far Eastern Economic Review*, 20 January 1994.
14. *Asia Magazine*, 23 January 1985.
15. *Bangkok Post*, 1 May 1994.
16. *Far Eastern Economic Review*, 14 April 1994; *Bangkok Post*, 29 March 1994, 12 January 1995; *The Nation*, 13 January 1995; *The Geopolitical Drug Dispatch* 42 (April 1995), p. 4.
17. *New York Times*, 15 July 1994; *Far Eastern Economic Review*, 3 October 1991, 30 January 1992, 11 February 1993.
18. *Far Eastern Economic Review*, 5 November 1992, 8 August 1997.
19. *Asiaweek*, 9 March 1994, 15 June 1994; *Far Eastern Economic Review*, 28 March 1991.
20. *Far Eastern Economic Review*, 18 November 1993; *Straits Times*, 12 August 1995; *Bangkok Post*, 25 July 1995.
21. *Asiaweek*, 9 March 1994, 15 June 1994; *New York Times*, 15 July 1994; *Bangkok Post*, 12 January 1997.
22. *Wall Street Journal*, 11 January 1995.
23. Agence France-Presse, *Bulletin*, 3 January 1996.
24. *Bangkok Post*, 13 August 1995.
25. *Far Eastern Economic Review*, 14 April 1994, 21 July 1994.
26. *International Herald Tribune*, 3 February 1995; *The Nation*, 3 March 1995; *Far Eastern Economic Review*, 20 January 1994, 14 April 1994, 30 June 1994, 21 July 1994, 16 February 1995, 19 October 1995; *Bangkok Post*, 1 May 1994, 8 August 1995.
27. *Bangkok Post*, 16 March 1995, 21 March 1995; *The Nation*, 22 March 1995; *International Herald Tribune*, 6 April 1995.
28. Agence France-Presse, *Bulletin*, 3 January 1996; *Bangkok Post*, 13 August 1995, 26 August 1995.
29. *The Nation*, 22 July 1995.
30. *Bangkok Post*, 13 August 1995, 23 August 1995, 25 August 1995, 1 September 1995.
31. *The New York Times*, 24 November 1995; *Bangkok Post*, 1 December 1995.
32. *New York Times*, 2 January 1996, 6 January 1996; *Far Eastern Economic Review*, 25 January 1996; *International Herald Tribune*, 3 January 1996, 4 January 1996; *Washington Times*, 5 January 1996; *Chicago Tribune*, 5 January 1996.
33. *The Nation* (New York), 16 December 1996, pp. 14-15; *The Nation*, 5 March 1996.

34. *The Nation*, 5 January 1996.
35. *The Nation*, 5 January 1996.
36. *International Herald Tribune*, 13–14 January 1996; *The Nation* (New York), 16 December 1996, p. 14; *The Geopolitical Drug Dispatch* 52 (February 1996), pp. 3, 4.
37. *Chiangmai News*, 9 February 1997.
38. *The Nation* (New York), 16 December 1996, pp. 14–15; *Bangkok Post*, 21 May 1996; *Chiangmai News*, 9 February 1997.
39. *Chiangmai News*, 9 February 1997; *Bangkok Post*, 11 October 1996, 14 November 1996, 13 January 1997.
40. *Los Angeles Times*, 1 July 1996.
41. *The Nation* (Bangkok), 21 March 1997; *Bangkok Post*, 4 April 1997.
42. *Chiangmai News*, 9 February 1997.
43. *The Geopolitical Drug Dispatch* 74 (December 1997), pp. 4–5.
44. *New York Times*, 19 April 1998.
45. *The Geopolitical Drug Dispatch* 55 (May 1996), pp. 1, 3.
46. *Bangkok Post*, 3 November 1996.
47. *The Nation* (New York), 16 December 1996, pp. 14–15; *Bangkok Post*, 23 March 1997.
48. *Bangkok Post*, 19 March 1997.
49. *New York Times*, 6 January 1996.
50. *New York Times*, 11 February 1996.
51. *The New York Times*, 18 January 1996; *International Herald Tribune*, 19 January 1996.
52. *The Asian Age*, 27 April 1996.
53. *Far Eastern Economic Review*, 28 March 1991.
54. *The Nation* (New York), 16 December 1996, p. 14.
55. *Bangkok Post*, 19 March 1997; *New York Times*, 15 July 1994, 17 July 1994.
56. *New York Times*, 22 May 1997.
57. *Chiangmai News*, 9 February 1997.
58. *Bangkok Post*, 13 January 1997, 23 January 1997, 23 March 1997, 11 July 1997.
59. *New York Times*, 19 April 1998.
60. *Bangkok Post*, 5 March 1996, 3 November 1996, 13 January 1997.
61. *Burmanet News* (Internet), 6 January 1996.
62. Reflecting their training in social history, both historians of these phenomena focus on the internal ‘push’ factors that led villagers and local elites into piracy, ignoring the ‘pull’ of rising seaborne commerce.

References

Abrams, Philip (1988), 'The Difficulty of Studying the State (1977)', *Journal of Historical Sociology*, 1: 58–89.
Allure, New York.
Asia Magazine, Hong Kong.
The Asian Age.
Asiaweek, Hong Kong.
The Bangkok Post, Bangkok.
Baysinger, Barry, Robert B. Ekelund, Jr., and Robert D. Tollison (1980), 'Mercantilism as a Rent-Seeking Society', in James M. Buchanan, Robert D. Tollison, and Gordon Tullock (eds), *Toward a Theory of the Rent-Seeking Society.* College Station: Texas A&M Press.
Boucaud, Andre and Louis Boucaud (1985), *Burma's Golden Triangle.* Bangkok: Asia Books.
Buchanan, James M. (1980), 'Rent Seeking and Profit Seeking', in James M. Buchanan, Robert D. Tollison, and Gordon Tullock (eds), *Toward a Theory of the Rent-Seeking Society*. College Station: Texas A&M Press.
Burmanet News, Internet.
Chiangmai News, Chiangmai.
The Chicago Tribune, Chicago.
Cowell, Adrian (1996), 'The Silver Jubilee of the "War on Drugs"', *Burma Debate*, 3, no. 2: 12–20.
Cox, Christopher R. (1996), *Chasing the Dragon: Into the Heart of the Golden Triangle.* New York: Henry Holt.
de Jesus, Edilberto C. (1980), *The Tobacco Monopoly in the Philippines: Bureaucratic Enterprise and Social Change, 1766–1880*. Quezon City: Ateneo de Manila University Press.
Doeppers, Daniel F. (1991), 'Metropolitan Manila in the Great Depression: Crisis for Whom?' *Journal of Asian Studies*, 50, no. 3: 521–35.
Evans, Peter, Dietrich Rueschemeyer, and Theda Skocpol (eds) (1985), *Bringing the State Back In*. Cambridge: Cambridge University Press.
Far Eastern Economic Review, Hong Kong.
The Geopolitical Drug Dispatch, Paris.
Golay, Frank H. (1961), *The Philippines: Public Policy and National Economic Development*. Ithaca, NY: Cornell University Press.
Gritz, James 'Bo' (1988), *A Nation Betrayed*, by the author.
Hartendorp, A. V. H. (1961), *History of Industry and Trade of the Philippines: The Magsaysay Administration*. Manila: Philippine Education Company.

Hilton, Chris (1995), 'Episode Two – An Unholy Alliance', Dealing with the Demon. Bondi, NSW: Aspire Films.
Hobsbawm, Eric (1969) *Bandits*. New York: Delacorte Press.
The International Herald Tribune, Paris.
Khun Sa. (no date [n.d.]), *Khun Sa: His Own Story and Thoughts*, by the author.
Krueger, Anne O. (1974), 'The Political Economy of the Rent-Seeking Society', *American Economic Review*, 64, no. 3: 291–303.
Lintner, Bertil (1994a), *Burma in Revolt: Opium and Insurgency Since 1948*. Boulder, CO: Westview.
—— (1994b), 'Lord of the Golden Triangle', *Caravan* 1(4).
—— (1995),'Ethnic Insurgents and Narcotics', *Burma Debate* 2(1): 18–21.
The Los Angeles Times, Los Angeles.
McCoy, Alfred W. (1991), *The Politics of Heroin: CIA Complicity in the Global Drug Trade*. New York: Lawrence Hill Books.
McKenna, Thomas M. (1994), 'The Defiant Periphery: Routes of Iranun Resistance in the Philippines', *Social Analysis*, 35: 11–27.
Migdal, Joel S. (1988), *Strong Societies and Weak States: State–Society Relations and State Capabilities in the Third World*. Princeton, NJ: Princeton University Press.
Murray, Dian H. (1987), *Pirates of the South China Coast, 1790–1810*. Stanford, CA: Stanford University Press.
—— (1995), 'Cheng I Sao in Fact and Fiction', in Jo Stanley (ed.), *Bold in Her Breeches: Women Pirates Across the Ages*. London: Pandora.
The Nation, Bangkok.
The Nation, New York.
New Light of Myanmar (1996), 'Homong Ceremony to Forge Peace Hailed as Auspicious for Myanmar and All Mankind', *Burma Debate* 3(2): 8–10.
Newsweek, New York.
The New York Times, New York.
Pringle, Robert (1970), *Rajahs and Rebels: The Ibans of Sarawak under Brooke Rule, 1841–1941*. Ithaca, NY: Cornell University Press.
Reed, Robert R. (1963), 'The Tobacco Economy', in Robert E. Huke (ed.), *Shadows on the Land: An Economic Geography of the Philippines*. Manila: Bookmark.
Reuter, Peter (1983), *Disorganized Crime: The Economics of the Visible Hand*. Cambridge, MA: MIT Press.
Rolling Stone, New York.
Shan State, Department of Information (1986), *Historical Facts about the Shan State*.

Shan State National Congress, Foreign Affairs Sub-Committee (1994), *Historical Facts about the Shan State*. [Homong, Myanmar].

Smith, Martin (1991), *Burma: Insurgency and the Politics of Ethnicity*. London: Zed Books.

The Straits Times, Singapore.

Tomlin, Janice (1989), 'King of Heroin', 20/20. New York: ABC Television, 28 April .

Trager, Frank N. (1966), *Burma: From Kingdom to Republic: A Historical and Political Analysis*. London: Pall Mall Press.

United Nations, Economic and Social Council, Commission on Human Rights, 52nd Session. (1996), *Report on the situation of human rights in Myanmar, Prepared by Mr. Yozo Yokota, Special Rapporteur of the Commission on Human Rights, in accordance with Commission Resolution 1995/72*, [Geneva: Commission on Human Rights] 5 February.

US Congress, House Select Committee on Narcotics Abuse and Control, 95th Congress, 1st Session (1977), *Opium Production, Narcotics Financing, and Trafficking in Southeast Asia*. Washington, DC: US Government Printing Office.

US Department of Commerce, Bureau of International Commerce (1965), *Philippines: A Market for U.S. Products.* Washington, DC: US Government Printing Office.

US Department of Justice, Drug Enforcement Administration, National Narcotics Intelligence Consumers Committee (1995), 'The Supply of Illicit Drugs to the United States, August 1996', [Washington, DC]: Drug Enforcement Administration

US Embassy Rangoon (1996), 'Country Commercial Guide: Burma', *Burma Debate* 3(4): 4–16.

US General Accounting Office (1996), *Drug Control: U.S. Heroin Program Encounters Many Obstacles in Southeast Asia*. Washington, DC: US General Accounting Office.

US State Department, Bureau of International Narcotics Matters (1990), *International Narcotics Control Strategy Report, March 1990*. Washington, DC: US State Department.

US State Department, Bureau for International Narcotics and Law Enforcement Matters (1996), *International Narcotics Control Strategy Report March 1996.* Washington, DC: US Department of State.

The Wall Street Journal, New York.

The Washington Times, Washington, DC

Warren, James (1982), 'Slavery and the Impact of External Trade: The Sulu Sultanate in the 19th Century', in Alfred W. McCoy and Edilberto

C. de Jesus (eds), *Philippine Social History: Global Trade and Local Transformations*. Quezon City: Ateneo de Manila University Press.

Yawnghwe, Chao Tzang (1987), *The Shan of Burma: Memoirs of a Shan Exile*. Singapore: Institute of Southeast Asian Studies.

—— (1995), 'Shan Opium Politics: The Khun Sa Factor', *Burma Debate*, 2(1): 22–8.

– 6 –

Is Transparency Possible? The Political-Economic and Epistemological Implications of Cold War Conspiracies and Subterfuge in Italy

Jane Schneider and *Peter Schneider*

> The almost metaphysical halo of mystery and secrecy that has always surrounded this theme is connected to extremely embarrassing facts that had to be kept hidden so as to avoid endangering careers, reputations, and the bases of legitimacy for various established powers (Arlacchi 1993: 13).

During the 1970s, Sicilian organized crime took on a central, coordinating role in the exploding transnational traffic in drugs, arms, and dirty money. Remarkably, the intensification of this global activity took place with the tacit consent and studied ignorance, if not the outright encouragement, of elements of the Italian establishment. In political analyst Carlo Giuseppe Rossetti's words, the governing class of Italy sustained a 'substantially passive attitude' toward the audacious advances of the narco-trafficking mafia, for a long time offering no 'organic legislative strategy to counter the menace'. Rather, with a few exceptions, the establishment – the governmental regimes, parliaments, mass media and intellectuals of the 1970s and 1980s – 'consented that criminal potentates [would] prosper'. The virtual absence of counter-measures, says Rossetti, 'is an index of the indirect complicity of the political class' in the tolerance for illegality (1994: 84–5).

Below we analyze various aspects of this tolerance: the long-familiar symbiosis between *mafiosi* and politicians of the centrist parties, especially the Christian Democratic Party; the cultivation of a web of associations through which *mafiosi* traditionally 'conditioned' the police and the judiciary; the creation – under Cold War conditions – of a covert structure of power in Italy that furnished mafia potentates with a new range of friends; and the convergence of interests between *mafiosi* and an emergent stratum of rule-bending financiers in the 1970s and 1980s.

In pursuing this analysis, we benefit from the recent emergence of 'pro-transparency' movements in northern and southern Italy – the *Mani Puliti* or 'clean hands' anti-corruption movement of the North and the antimafia movement of Sicily and the South. This latter movement crystallized after the 1982 assassination in Palermo of Carlo Alberto dalla Chiesa, a general of the Carabinieri whom the State had designated to lead the fight against the Sicilian mafia. As we describe elsewhere (see Schneider and Schneider 1994), antimafia activists of the 1980s and 1990s have come, predominantly, from the urban middle and professional classes – groups that have grown disproportionately in Sicily since the 1960s. An important and powerful subset of them consists of magistrates and police officers, who are increasingly committed to exposing and prosecuting the links between mafia and the worlds of finance and politics.

That is dangerous work, as we know from the assassination in the 1980s and 1990s of leading Sicilian magistrates, among the most prominent of whom were Giovanni Falcone and his colleague Paolo Borsellino, who were murdered in the terrible summer of 1992. It is simultaneously full of promise. These two judges, and others in their wake, pioneered a program for encouraging *mafiosi* to turn State's witness, organizing their testimony in courts of law, and protecting them from their inevitably lethal enemies. Ironically dubbed *pentiti* (sing. *pentito*) by the press, there are over 1,200 such 'justice collaborators' today – a rich if controversial source of revelations on complicity (Paoli 1997: 159). In a conclusion, we observe how these revelations, and others like them, frame, and call into question, the epistemological uncertainty that has pervaded social theory over the same arc of time.

Models of Mafia

Thanks to the volume of statements produced by the justice collaborators, and to recent investigative work by the Sicilian judiciary and police, it is possible now to know substantially more about the mafia than it was in even the recent past. The model we outline here also draws on the contributions of a new generation of historians and sociologists of the mafia, in particular the work of Salvatore Lupo (1993), Letizia Paoli (1997), and Paolo Pezzino (1995).

Mafiosi are organized into secret fraternal sodalities called *cosche* (singular *cosca*), evoking the tightly bundled leaves of an artichoke, or more simply, 'families'. The latter term notwithstanding, kinship is not the main principle of recruitment. Most newcomers are chosen to enter the sodality based on their inclinations and a careful assessment of their 'criminal reliability'; unsuitable kin are passed over and some *cosche* even have rules against admitting too many close relatives (see Paoli 1997: 126–8, 226–9; Siebert 1994). And no wonder; some of the most powerful mafia leaders have had at their shoulders a collaborative father, cousin, or brothers (Lupo 1993: 210; Pezzino 1995: 136).

So 'family' as applied to mafia is metaphorical. Like the words 'brotherhood' or 'fraternity', it seeks to import the presumed solidarity of kinship into a fictive kin group. But the solidarity of the *cosca* hinges on more than metaphor, and it is willfully constructed. Although past researchers were skeptical about the existence of initiation ceremonies, according to both the *pentiti* and recent archival research (see Pezzino 1995: 89–119), the initiation was a transformative experience for most members. Marking a clear boundary between inside and outside, between past and future identities, novices held the burning image of a saint, while their 'shooting finger' was pricked and their blood mixed with the ashes of the burned saint, over which they swore an oath of loyalty and silence 'for life'.

The resulting commitment to secrecy means that mafia shares something with other 'secret societies', perhaps especially Freemasonry. Indeed, Pezzino proposes that the earliest *cosche* may have developed out of, or modeled themselves on, the covert Masonic or *Carbonari* lodges that proliferated in Southern Italy and Sicily on the eve of Italian unification (Pezzino 1992: 47–58; 1995: 5–7, 71–2; see also Lupo 1993: 182). At any event, they elaborated the famous code of *omertà* or 'silence before the law' as the first principle of what Paoli (1997) calls their 'normative order'. Demanding sealed lips in relation to all authorities, *omertà* goes hand in hand with the mafia ideology that 'men of honor' (their preferred term for themselves) have the 'courage', 'valor', and capacity to commit acts of violence, rendering the State redundant as a source of dispute settlement and the maintenance of social order.

Most scholars in the past, ourselves included, believed that the first *cosche* originated in the mountainous interior of Western Sicily, the part of the island that was most dominated by vast cereal and livestock *latifundia*. Destabilized in the nineteenth century by the combined expansion of capitalist markets and relations of production on the one hand, and a 'weak' although episodically repressive State incapable of ordering the new economy, on the other hand, this region produced a vibrant array of initiatives: epidemic and then endemic banditry, peasant uprisings, and sodalities claiming to restore 'order', their members referring to themselves as 'men of honor'. Recruitment to the latter was pronounced among persons in the interstices of the latifundist economy – a sort of incipient middle class of carters, merchants, estate guards, bandits and shepherds.

More recent research, however, has uncovered parallel formations in the zones of orchard and vineyard development surrounding Palermo, and in Palermo itself (see Fiume 1991; Lupo 1984; Pezzino 1995). Here, too, a vacuum of State authority in the (broadly understood) 'transition from feudalism to capitalism' was at work, with *mafiosi* characteristically hailing from the realm of private guards and serving as mediators of theft and protection. Significantly, Palermo and other West Sicilian cities (above all, Trapani) experienced to a far greater degree than the cities of Eastern Sicily (and Naples) the unrelenting hegemony of a prepotent baronial class. Indeed, these cities and their hinterlands were the sites, respectively, of the grandest palaces and villas of the very lords who owned the interior latifundia.

Until the end of the Second World War, mafia organization was segmentary. The various families were in communication and resembled one another with regard to values, activities, and ritual performances, but not because they derived from, or belonged to, a corporate centralized translocal organization. After all, their respective members included some of the most mobile Sicilians of the time – men who encountered each other far from home at sheep and cattle fairs, on the road carrying grain, and in the produce markets (and quite possibly the prison) in Palermo. Nevertheless, as Paoli points out, even under segmentary conditions, Palermo and its hinterland, or better, the area between Palermo and nearby Trapani, had a certain weight; this was the center of gravity or 'core' of mafia development (Paoli 1997: 68). Not surprisingly, Palermo families dominated the first attempt, in 1957, to transcend a segmentary structure with the creation of a provincial 'Commission' for Palermo Province. They lost out to others in a power struggle that followed the formation of a 'Regional Commission' for all Sicily in the mid-1970s.

Regarding numbers of affiliates, Paoli summarizes 1994 data from the Central Directorate of the Criminal Police, the 'Criminalpol', which is part of the Italian Ministry of the Interior. As of that date, they knew of 181 mafia families in Sicily with 5,500 adherents. Of these, 59, with 1,500 members, were in Palermo Province. The second 'mafia province', Trapani, had 15 *cosche* with 500 members. Criminalpol cited 42 groups in Agrigento province, but, according to a 1993 estimate of the DIA, the recently created Direzione Italiana Antimafia, only 16 of these belonged to Cosa Nostra, the others being part of an independent criminal organization, the 'star' or *stidda*. The city of Catania on the Eastern Coast became a locale of mafia activity after the Second World War, but otherwise, the (historically less feudal) eastern provinces supported very few *cosche*, although they may have had urban gangs (Paoli 1997: 68).

The mafia does not keep written records of its own activities, but it is most useful to think of it as an institution more or less ordered by certain rules that members agree upon, even if the rules are honored in the breach. One of these is that a family should have at least ten people and that larger families should be broken up into sub-units, called *decine*. It is now known that, through the 1980s, the family of the important rural town of Corleone, set amidst latifundia in the center of Palermo province, had a nucleus of 39 members, including prisoners and fugitives. The *Corso dei Mille* family in central Palermo once counted 65 plus 38 affiliates. In the province as a whole, average family size was 23.8. By contrast, the Catania *cosca* had 44 members plus 170 affiliates, thanks to having collectively 'baptized' all the members of a rival criminal group (Paoli 1997: 162).

Another (frequently violated) rule called for direct democracy, the annual election or re-election of officers from the base. These include, in the 1990s as in the nineteenth century, the *rappresentante* or *capofamiglia*; his *vice-capo*, empowered to fill in during the *capo*'s imprisonment or absence; two or more *capi-decina* where sub-units exist, and a *consigliere* whose role is to advise, and watch over, the *rappresentante* (Paoli 1997: 161–3). At the time of the creation of the Provincial Commission, another layer came into play, the district, or *mandamento*. Grouping about three families into a district, it too had an elected *capo*. There were about 15 such *mandamenti* during the 1980s, each with a representative on the Commission (Paoli 1997: 187).

Mafia families are territorial – so much so that with very few exceptions, each bears the name of a rural town, a small city, or, in the case of the regional capital, Palermo, a suburb or a neighborhood. Each *cosca* assumed the prerogatives of extorting a *pizzo* or tax on business activities in its territory, imposing on the territory's employers requirements that they hire particular mafia dependants, and mediating local conflicts and the return, for a fee, of locally stolen goods. *Mafiosi* from other *cosche* wishing to intrude into these domains had to ask permission of the local *cosca* leader. Even to purchase land or build a house in a zone claimed by a powerful *cosca* sometimes meant supplicating its leader (see Paoli 1997: 223).

Yet from the outset, *mafiosi* also pursued activities that were, by their very nature, geographically deterritorialized: sheep stealing, and the clandestine butchering and sale of stolen meat was a classic example (see Pezzino 1995: 5–6, 60, 206), as were attempts to establish monopolies in particular market sectors, for example fruit or fish. The contraband mediation and sale of tobacco and narcotics, which date from the early twentieth century but flourished after the Second World War, characteristically engaged individual affiliates of several *cosche*, not to mention numerous outsiders from bankers to smugglers to bandits and foreign operatives. Translocal coalitions set up to engage in illicit commerce depended on territorially organized *cosche* for protection and the disciplining of errant dealers – services that could not be garnered from any legally constituted authority. In this respect, the *cosca* and the long-distance network were complementary. Yet they were oriented around competing principles of political economy and were in considerable tension with each other.

Historically, the *cosca* constituted, among other things, a mutual aid society for its members. Building up a common fund, it supported them and their families during times of indictment or imprisonment. The inevitable prison terms rarely interrupted a *mafioso*'s career, not only because corrupt officials made it possible for him to conduct business from jail, but because an incarcerated man also had the assurance that his *cosca* was providing not only lawyers' fees for him, but a lifeline for his wife and children: visiting them, feeding them, even covering the dowries of daughters who were about to wed. Typically, a *cosca* used the common fund to provide support for rank-and-file soldiers who had no other source of income and, operating according to a concept of redistribution, it spread the take from extortion more or less equitably. So much was this the case that one function of the *consigliere* was, precisely, that of watching the money, preventing the *capi* from keeping too much for themselves (Pezzino 1995: 284).

By contrast, the entrepreneurial network follows the logic of accumulation. Participants are recruited from far and wide, but their gain is calibrated to the amount of their investment. Lupo borrows from Alan Block's analysis of organized crime in America the notion that mafia intrinsically embodies two contradictory tendencies, being on the one hand a state-like, territorially organized 'power syndicate'; and also, on the other hand, a source of market-like 'enterprise syndicates' (1980). Different historical moments are marked by the hegemony of one or the other principle, with the contradiction between them eluding resolution, as we will see below in our brief sketch of recent mafia 'wars'.

Apart from its structure, 'rules', values and ceremonial life, questions remain about what mafia meant, historically, and what it means today. Why did it develop? What is it about? Some interpretations are 'functionalist': although not benign in its effects, mafia arose to fulfill some purpose, generally in lieu of a weak or vacuous State. In a recent example of this approach, Diego Gambetta defines mafia as 'a specific economic enterprise, an industry which produces, promotes, and sells private protection', because more conventional sources of protection, above all the police and judiciary, cannot and could not be trusted to fulfill this role (1993). Earlier examples portrayed *mafiosi* as adjudicators of local conflicts, settling disputes of all kinds where agents of the State, the prosecutors and judges, were unable or unwilling to do so. This version, which awards *mafiosi* a positive role in local communities, dovetails with the organization's representation of itself – as composed of 'men of honor' who solve problems (their own and other people's) without resort to the State (see Sabetti 1984).

During our first fieldwork in the mid-1960s, in a rural town of the latifundist interior, a local *mafioso* recommended that we read *I Beati Paoli* if we really wanted to comprehend the 'spirit of mafia'. (A very recent *pentito* has reported reading it in jail.) Authored by a Sicilian, Luigi Natoli, and first published as a serial in the *Giornale di Sicilia*, 1909–1910, this romantic novel tells the tale of a secret fraternal order that met at night in Palermo's subterranean caves and tunnels for the purpose of trying and punishing persons accused of crimes against 'honest citizens'. The novel elaborates on the group's rites of initiation and ideology of solidarity, which, it suggests, molded men from various social backgrounds, some of them extremely modest, into a fraternal whole. What counted was not background but bravura, not social standing in the outside world, but personal honor, sustained if necessary by acts of violence. Paoli argues, and we would agree, that the conceptions of mafia as an organization that fulfilled a necessary function in society are, in the end, too close to this mythology about honor. She suggests, rather, that we think of it as a polyvalent formation with a compelling need to perpetuate itself through time, improving the life circumstances of its members and loyal associates.

The conceptualization of mafia as a persistent institution draws attention to its historically dynamic, predatory nature: its capacity to appropriate resources from a succession of economic activities whose trajectory has followed the transformation of Sicily from a largely agrarian, and pastoral, society to one that is urbanized and, for a while, at the crossroads of the global traffic in heroin. To capture this aspect, one does best, perhaps, with nineteenth-century police reports that represent mafia as '. . . a network of politically protected extortion rings . . . as groups of criminals who terrorized a local community, living off extortion and other illegal gains, and controlling access to jobs and local markets. These groups, however, were always connected to local political parties and factions, whom they supported, and from whom they drew protection' (quoted in

Fentress and Wickham 1992:189). Although individual *mafiosi* settled disputes – among themselves and for third parties – and although they 'sold' protection, their ongoing extortionist projects were most often a disruptive source of the very conflicts and insecurity that people sought mediation for and protection against.

Mafia and State, 1970–1990

Mafia, like the larger society in which it is embedded, has evolved in tandem with the processes of land reform and agrarian transformation, welfare state formation, and the explosive growth of cities that have so characterized Sicily since the end of the Second World War. In 1963, a conflict between rival *cosche* for a foothold in Palermo's lucrative construction boom and expanding fish and produce markets led to the explosion of a car bomb in the Palermo suburb of Ciaculli, in which seven officers of the police and Carabinieri were killed. In a context of growing left political power, peasant mobilization and antimafia pressure on the state, this event provoked mass arrests, a major trial, and the formation of a parliamentary 'Antimafia Commission'. The trial, though, did not result in convictions that were upheld on appeal, and the new Antimafia Commission eventually disappointed its advocates by investigating only small fish (see Chubb 1982). Meanwhile, as Antonino Calderone, brother of an important boss of Catania, has now told the world in a startling 'confession', the mafia was eventually 'saved by drugs'. According to Calderone the arrests of 1962–3, the fact that more than 100 mafia *capi* were under arrest or under strict observation between 1963 and the trial in 1969, and the contingent cost of lawyers undercut the mafia enterprise to the point that many were 'starving' (quoted in Arlacchi 1993: 75). Then, 'we all became millionaires – suddenly, within a couple of years – thanks to drugs' (ibid.: 76).

The shift, though, was neither inclusive nor smooth. The first group to enter the drug traffic was a coalition of Palermo bosses led by Gaetano Badalamenti, whose properties near the city's airport and deep involvement in that facility's construction and operations, and whose close relations with a mobster brother in Detroit, gave him a logistic advantage. Well before the displacement of heroin-refining operations from Marseilles to Palermo and its environs in the late 1970s, Badalamenti and a few of his close associates – Stefano Bontate and Salvatore Inzerillo – had accumulated substantial profits from drug shipments to America. Among those whose ire and envy were thereby provoked was a large and growing contingent of somewhat younger bosses from the provinces, called the

Corleonesi after the rural town of Corleone from which came some of their most audacious leaders. Unable to participate in the narcotics market without first raising money on their own, they staged a series of kidnappings for ransom. But the targets of this activity were not simply rich men. The provincial upstarts sought to kidnap well-heeled construction impresarios who were closely allied to the Badalamenti group – persons who, in fact, depended upon members of this group for protection. To kidnap them was to throw down the gauntlet to what was increasingly being defined as an internal enemy.

Although control over the narcotics traffic was not the only issue, it was an important element in another 'mafia war', which exploded between 1979 and 1983. At that time, a group of *mafiosi* originally identified with Corleone but for some years resident in Palermo and its suburbs, organized a take-over of the city's principal mafia families by assassinating their leaders and those leaders' closest associates. During these 'hot years', the aggressors also killed some 15 police officers, magistrates, and government officials whose involvement in criminal justice or political reform could otherwise have blocked their wholesale movement into drugs (see Chinnici and Santino 1986, 1989).

That Wicked Deal

From their emergence in the latter half of the nineteenth century, *mafiosi* have cultivated ties to officialdom. In this regard the mafia can be defined in part by its historic differentiation from banditry. Bandits operated 'outside the law', more or less supported by the residents of local, rural communities who also opposed State power, whereas *mafiosi* functioned *within* the domain of civil society, anticipating occasional arrests and even convictions as their cost of doing business (Schneider and Schneider 1976). As Pezzino has argued (1995: 46–7), bandits may even have been more radically anti-state than *mafiosi*, having a more conflictual relation with the authorities. Although they certainly had protectors among the powerful, they were considered an embarrassment to their protectors, who often abandoned the bandits at critical moments. Protectors of *mafiosi* tended, on the contrary, to become more deeply involved with them. The historian Renda (1991: 9–10) calls the evolving mafia–State reciprocity 'that wicked deal', because agencies of the newly unified Italian State opted to govern Sicily through rather than against the extortionist groups (in part because these groups proved themselves capable of regulating banditry). *Mafiosi* of course intimidated witnesses; in addition they propagated the ideology of *omertà*, silence before the law. The majority of the charges brought against them were dropped for want of proof or denied on technical grounds at appeal. Yet arrest and incarceration remained a probability, especially for younger members. Indeed, the prison experience played an important role in the socialization/formation of many young mafia recruits. The point was to insure that prison terms would constitute no more than a temporary interruption of the defendant's ongoing business and everyday life. Political leaders and other officials who provided this degree of immunity in turn counted on *mafiosi* to guarantee their local support – a requirement that increasingly took the form of delivering electoral majorities as the suffrage expanded.

According to Calderone, between friends and kin, an average *mafioso* of postwar Sicily could muster at least 40 to 50 votes. With 1,500 to 2,000 men of honor, that would add up to 75,000 to 100,000 'friendly' votes in the province of Palermo alone. Calderone believes the mid-1970s was a turning-point in the political process, after which *mafiosi* began to feel superior to politicians, to feel that the politicians could simply 'not refuse' their requests for favors. Reconstituting the commission that had become defunct after the Ciaculli bombing, mafia leaders even began to indicate which parties to vote for in a coordinated way. Specifically, they endorsed the centrist parties, which, they believed would guarantee a degree of political stasis and compliance that was 'good for mafia'. In Calderone's words, 'we [had] always known that we could not get along with the Left . . . that we have nothing in common with the Communists'. The neo-fascist MSI was also off-limits, although its ranks included a few mafia lawyers. Notwithstanding the new context of expanding narco-traffic, *mafiosi* would continue using their voting power to make politicians of the center into representatives of the mafia (Calderone in Arlacchi 1993: 182–4; Rossetti 1994: 183–4).

Friends, and Friends of Friends

The wicked deal was, however, more than a quid pro quo – a straightforward exchange of protection for votes. It became an organic connection through the self-conscious construction of webs of association that enabled *mafiosi* to rub shoulders with notables in informal settings conducive to amicable mutual enjoyment and casual talk. With a few exceptions, these notables – the mafia's interlocutors – were not *cosca* members. *Mafiosi* referred to them as persons who were contiguous to mafia, and preferred that relation. Belonging to a *cosca* would subject such people to the requirements of a 'dual' structure of power, one official and the other illegal. By not belonging, they could hope to avoid some degree of liability for mafia crimes, and escape, as well, an endless barrage of demands for favors from individual fellow *mafiosi*.

And yet, as interlocutors, 'friendly' lawyers, judges, police officers, bankers, doctors, and public officials, are always potentially useful to the mafia, the more so as they occupy positions of authority in the key institutions of government, law enforcement, health care, banking and so on. The point is to *condition* the interlocutors to make decisions, or non-decisions, that support the mafia enterprise. The targets of the most intense conditioning were, historically, the police, the Carabinieri, and the judiciary. This because, even if every imaginable witness to a crime were silenced by *omertà*, there would still be indictments and convictions to 'adjust'. As noted above, unlike bandits, *mafiosi* lived within a domain regulated by law.

The relation is illustrated in vignettes told by Calderone. Once he and his brother, both *mafiosi* in the East Sicilian city of Catania, were asked to help the wife of a judge whose small property was about to be bisected by the Catania–Enna highway then under construction. Owners of the firm that had won the contract to build this road were already conditioned friends; so the brothers went to them and 'the road was shifted; [the firm] even rearranged the layout of the [judge's wife's] property'. Subsequently, the brothers Calderone became more intimate with the judge; he even paid a visit to the ailing Pippo Calderone when he was in hospital. Here was a judge one could count on to intervene in the sentencing process. The brothers often visited him, taking gifts of fish and black market cigarettes ('Marlboros for him and Muratti Ambassadors for his family': see Calderone in Arlacchi 1993: 156).

Meanwhile, the contracting firm had 'loads of lawyers and judges in their pockets' including a powerful judge, nicknamed Napoleon, who was a supervisor to other judges. The firm did a great deal of work gratis on this judge's property. Other judges lived rent-free in an apartment complex built by the same firm. Having learned through their own connections with a commander of the Carabinieri that one of their cousins was on a list of men to be arrested, the Calderone brothers went to the firm owner, who intervened with the judiciary to have the name struck off the list (ibid.: 156–8). Not surprisingly, Calderone likens the *mafioso* to a spider as he 'builds his web of friends, of acquaintances, of obligations' (ibid.: 20).

During our first fieldwork in Sicily in the mid-1960s, the web of associations that underpinned 'conditioned' relationships was less hidden than it later became, and our understanding of how it worked comes partly from personal observation, as well as from the confessions of the *pentiti*.

Typically, *mafiosi* invited local and regional notables to their major life-cycle celebrations, above all weddings and baptisms. Typically, too, such officials and professionals would be found among the mourners at a *mafioso*'s funeral. To the extent that the *mafioso* had prospered and wanted to exert a claim to higher status, he would seek to include in his retinue of guests the mayor, the local parliamentary deputy, the nearest bishop, a monk or two, a few lawyers, a banker, and owners of land or enterprises in the larger towns and cities. Often, a professional or political notable was asked to become the godparent to a *mafioso*'s child or grandchild, or a witness at the wedding of a *mafioso*'s son or daughter – a mode of establishing a lifetime relation with a potential interlocutor. As a rule, such invitations were not refused. Although they surely elicited varying degrees of apprehension about the *mafioso*'s eventual requests for reciprocity, it was considered flattering and possibly auspicious to be invited.

In addition to the life-cycle celebrations of the 'real' biological families of *mafiosi*, a strategic occasion for nurturing relationships with professional interlocutors was the rustic banquet or *schiddicchia*, held to punctuate a collective event such as the annual sheep-shearings. Here the local priest, veterinarian, and officers of the Carabinieri could be found together with *mafiosi* of the livestock sector and their families, indulging in a feast of roast lamb or goat. Over a five-month period in 1965, Peter Schneider attended a series of banquets organized to seal a peace between butchers and meat dealers from a five-town area. Gathered around the long tables at each successive feast was an expanding number of local and regional dignitaries, impressed and delighted by the multi-course dinners and the hilarious rounds of toasting and mocking, transgressive rituals that followed (Schneider and Schneider 1984).

The reference to rustic banquets should not give the impression that occasions for amicable and entertaining encounters between mafia and other elites excluded the participation of urban notables. As noted above, Palermo, the regional capital, was historically dominated by a quasi-feudal baronage whose constituents owned vast country estates that they visited periodically. Graduates in law from the University of Palermo either descended from this class or mimicked its ways. They too had substantial landholdings and the ability to command respect in one or more rural communities. An older generation of urban magistrates can recollect how taken-for-granted it once was to maintain friendly relations with the *mafiosi* of these locales. Employees of one's estate – the overseers, guards, and shepherds – inevitably belonged to a *cosca*; their children played with your children; they generously welcomed your guests (from Palermo, from mainland Italy, from abroad) when you brought them up to the cheese-processing hut in the mountains for an early morning bowl of fresh ricotta; you graciously attended their baptisms and weddings as a gesture of reciprocal good will.

Following the Second World War, new *cosche* proliferated as Palermo and other cities gobbled up their respective hinterlands, transforming beautiful orchards with nestled villages into an urban sprawl, and rural mafias into urban ones. In 1982, the political scientist Judith Chubb published the results of her prophetic research on mafia involvement in what is now called the 'sack of Palermo' – the runaway real estate speculation and construction blitz that was presided over by several notorious politicians in the Christian Democratic *corrente* or faction eventually headed by long-time prime minister and cabinet member, Giulio Andreotti. Chubb's argument that Salvo Lima and Vito Ciancimino, former mayors and parliamentary deputies, were the protectors and patrons of several *cosche* has now been confirmed by a series of *pentito* statements (see Calabrò 1984). According to Paoli, in the 1960s, the house of one of Lima's personal friends, the mafia boss of the industrial neighborhood of Brancaccio, was considered the 'natural seat' of the Christian Democrats in Palermo (1997: 300, 313).

How did the structure of power that rendered the mafia organic to the State work in this regard? It is our impression, based on the *pentito* reports, that, in addition to participating in celebratory and entertaining occasions staged by *mafiosi*, ties were forged in secluded places that offered an arena for the mutual enjoyment of food, wine, and opportunities to hunt or target shoot. Apparently, *mafiosi* who prospered from the 'sack of Palermo' had pretensions to own such places and often did. Here, however, our knowledge is several steps removed from first-hand experience, dependent almost entirely on the accounts of people we know in Palermo, on journalists and, of course, on the 'confessions' of the *pentiti*. Benedetta Bono, the mistress of a notorious *mafioso* of Ribera in south-central Sicily, Carmelo Colletti, has also provided some revealing details to investigators in the province of Agrigento (Arnone 1988).

Calderone takes note of several convivial occasions when *mafiosi* and their interlocutors hunted rabbits together, making use of the country house or villa of one of them (Calderone in Arlacchi 1993: 116). 'The Costanzos [construction impresarios in Catania] knew that we liked to be in the company of the important, the powerful, from both inside and outside the mafia. And so they would arrange meetings, dinners, and hunting parties to which they would invite the best names in the Cosa Nostra' (Calderone in Arlacchi 1993: 170–1).

It should be noted, however, that such locales were also places where mafia leaders engaged in endless gossip, evaluating their own and other 'families'; where they made weighty decisions to eliminate enemies; where they strategized to gain control of the fragile and contested 'commissions'; and where they hid both armaments and fugitives for extended periods of time (ibid.: 129–30). How intimately their guests from the world of legitimate business and politics knew of these affairs is something every investigating magistrate would like to know.

The rural estate and villa of the boss, Michele Greco, located in the Ciaculli orchards just east of Palermo, is a particularly stunning example of a place that nurtured such encounters. Nicknamed 'the Prince', Greco maintained a shooting range on this property and regularly hosted both *mafiosi* and lay notables. So well did the locale fulfill the functions of an off-stage arena where elite notables and mafia *capi* could enjoy each other's company, that a legend grew up around it evoking the Beati Paoli – the mythic sect noted above, which executed justice in lieu of the State in eighteenth-century Palermo, meeting in subterranean galleries. The initial reports of a police raid on Greco's Ciaculli holding in February 1985 chronicled the discovery of an elaborate underground kitchen, meeting-hall, and network of tunnels, accessible through a trapdoor covered with an oriental carpet in the villa's living-room. The report later turned out to be false. Similarly, the *pentito* Francesco Marino Mannoia reports seeing an opening, 'perhaps one of the tunnels of the *Beati Paoli*', behind the wall of a villa belonging to the Inzerillo family (in Arlacchi 1995: 93).

In addition to a second rifle range and club in Addaura, a seaside resort at the western edge of Palermo owned by other *mafiosi*, a survey of propitious locales for cross-cutting elites to get together would have to include the properties of the super-wealthy *mafioso* cousins Ignazio and Nino Salvo. In their case, exceptionally close ties to the Andreotti current of the Christian Democratic Party helped them monopolize control of the tax-collecting franchise for Sicily during the 1960s and 1970s. In the meanwhile, they joined their own funds with lucrative government and European Community financing to develop agricultural properties for cattle, vineyards, and tourist hotels, most certainly helped by Lima, the Christian Democratic mayor and a regular weekend poker companion of Nino Salvo (Calderone in Arlacchi 1993: 175; Calabrò 1984).

At one of these hotels, the Zagarella, Nino Salvo, the owner, entertained important political personages of both the region and the nation in grand style. Located outside the villa-studded town of Bagheria, a historical watering-place of the old Palermo nobility, in 1995 this hotel became a centerpiece in the dramatic trial of Andreotti when he was accused of having collusive relations with the mafia. Not long after the trial opened in Palermo in October of that year, photographs taken in June 1979 by the press photographer Letizia Battaglia were introduced into evidence showing Andreotti with Nino Salvo at Zagarella, in the company of leaders of the regional Christian Democrats, including Lima. The director of the hotel at the time has testified that Salvo had ordered the 'best possible' buffet and personally conducted Andreotti on a tour of the finest rooms. (Andreotti has denied ever meeting the Salvos, but various *pentiti*, including Francesco Di Carlo in his most recent testimony, claim otherwise. See Arlacchi 1995: 105; Buongiorno 1984; *Il Manifesto*, 11 Oct. 1996.)

That the Salvos were splendid hosts is suggested by Calderone's recollection of them – the 'richest men in Sicily'. Gaetano Badalamente, the precocious boss of narco-trafficking, was 'proud of', and 'guarded', his friendship with them. Meanwhile, a 'parade of people' filled their offices and companies, seeking their favor. The Calderone brothers got Nino Salvo to intervene with Lima in order to arrange the transfer of a troublesome Catania police inspector. 'Outside of Cosa Nostra they were powerful and unreachable. But inside we were all equals . . .'. Dinners at their Palermo apartment were very '. . . refined. African waiters speaking no Italian served the food' (Calderone in Arlacchi 1993: 148).

The meetings in secluded places, including the butchers' banquets, were usually exclusively male. If the owner's wife was present, it was to serve the meal. (Calderone proposes that women took pleasure in serving *mafiosi* 'around big tables' [in Arlacchi 1993: 148], and we have observed the same.) Often men themselves cooked and served the food. In contrast, both men and women participated in weddings, baptisms, and sheep-shearing banquets, with the wives of *mafiosi* and the wives of the professional intermediaries often becoming friends. Should a notable be invited to baptize a *mafioso*'s child or grandchild, his wife would be the godmother.

The Cold War and its Covert Structures of Power

The web of associations outlined above had only a limited potential to cushion the vast expansion of illegal drug-trafficking after 1970. To begin with, the traffic provoked antimafia initiatives on the part of both State and civil society, which, however piecemeal and timid at first, rendered the celebratory occasions and secluded locales less and less comfortable as retreats. For example, a magistrate of our acquaintance remembers his childhood with intense irony. His father, also a magistrate, happened to own a large property outside a notorious mafia town in the Sicilian interior. Relations with the family of the overseer, a *mafioso*, were inevitably close. Their children often played together. Yet, as the elder magistrate's son later pursued his studies, he felt compelled to distance himself from his father's former rural associates. After receiving his law degree, and becoming a magistrate himself, he was eventually approached by the *mafioso* for assistance in dealing with a criminal charge. But since he had not maintained the close ties that had been cultivated by his father, it was relatively easy for him to refuse, even though the elder *mafioso* tried to evoke the young judge's sympathy by reminding him that 'I used to jostle you on my knee.'

This new attitude of diffidence toward mafia on the part of many young officials and professionals moved the structure of associations between mafia and State in a more covert direction. As a report of the Ministry of Interior (1994) claims, in a section entitled 'Mafia and the Social System', 'with the progressive decline of consent from civil society . . . the mafia has reacted by increasing the invisibility of its modus operandi and by ever more taking recourse, when compared to the past, to a network of clandestine relations . . .'. The criminalization of collusion – an uneven and contested process that has nonetheless gone forward in Sicily – in effect propelled such a shift. Even among *mafiosi*, the practice of secrecy increased 'to counterbalance the weakening of . . . popular legitimation' (Paoli 1996: 18; 1997).

At the same time, if mafia potentates were to articulate an illegal and global traffic in heroin, their everyday associations would have to reach higher, indeed to the highest rungs of what Italians call the 'third level' of State and private sector power, and even outside Italy altogether. Organizing and protecting the commoditization of an illegal substance, and accommodating the *sub rosa* arms sales and money laundering that go along with it, necessitated above all the studied ignorance, benign neglect, cover-up, protection, and financial assistance that only this level could offer (see Paoli 1996: 8). How, then, were the collusory relationships forged that made this support a possibility? To cite the Ministry of Interior again, *mafiosi* aligned themselves with covert Masonic lodges, provocateurs, and spies (1994).

A long series of courageous investigations has established that as the mafia, operating from its base in Sicily, was spinning the web of relations that entrapped and conditioned its professional interlocutors, former fascists, secret service operatives, and military personnel were spinning a different, if eventually overlapping, structure of power. This web resembled the covert cliques of army colonels and espionage specialists who staged *coups d'état* in Greece and several Latin American countries during the 1960s and 1970s, claiming to counter the alleged threat of communism. Like these counter-revolutionary cabals, Italian anti-communists felt they had the tacit consent of the American government for the project of blocking a possible electoral victory of the Left in Italy – the country which, after all, had the largest Communist Party in Western Europe (Gilbert 1995: 108–9).

Coups were planned for 1964 and again in 1970. Both failed to materialize, and in the wake of the scandals they generated their respective plotters were made to seem bumbling and incompetent, not a threat to democratic institutions at all (see Paoli 1996: 27, for reference to a further, 1974 plot). The plotters, however, burrowed further underground and are today accused of yet more terrible deeds that occurred in the late 1970s, the end of a decade in which the Christian Democrats tried but failed to improve their electoral margin over the Communists (1976 was both the high point of Communist electoral strength, the party coming within four percentage points of being the strongest in parliament, and the year of the Christian Democrats' most fiercely fought ideological campaign in the name of anti-communism: see Gilbert 1995: 8).

As early as 1984, antimafia investigators like Giovanni Falcone were on the trail of the 'untouchables' – 'third level' persons above suspicion. As one magistrate, Guido Lo Forte, said at the time, such persons are not 'a well-defined supercommission of the mafia', but a mobile structure, 'a collection of power centers, that have relations with mafia *cosche* and make agreements regarding deals, one at a time' (Calabrò 1984: 65ff.). With the fall of the Berlin Wall in 1989, it became possible to pursue new leads about these centers, as illustrated by the reports of various parliamentary commissions on mafia and secret associations, published in the early 1990s. In 1993, for example, Agostino Cordova, investigating magistrate of Palmi in Calabria, soon to be promoted to the more important jurisdiction in Naples, produced a landmark report that concludes that a rash of terrorist acts from 1969 to 1974, as well as the Bologna railroad station bombing of 1980 in which 85 people died and 200 were wounded, had 'germinated in the "humus" of secret associations' (see *Commissione Parlamentare Antimafia* 1993; Paoli 1996: 30–1).

A series of deeper questions are still being pursued: Were the center and right-wing currents of the Christian Democratic Party complicitous in the 1978 assassination of Aldo Moro, the left-wing Christian Democratic prime minister who was kidnapped by terrorists of the extreme Left just as he was about to forge a 'historic compromise' with the Communist Party? Can other terrorist bombings taking place between 1979 and 1981 be attributed to the occult network of coup plotters outlined above? And, did the bombings utilize explosives stolen from secret weapons caches that NATO had 'left behind' in Europe, in case of a Soviet invasion? NATO's 'Project Stay Behind', known as 'Gladio' in Italy, had supposedly been dismantled in 1972, but not all of its arms and munitions could be located when the covert training of militias came to an end (see Gilbert 1995:108–9).

Masonry and 'Adjusting Trials'

Like any complex society, Italy is riddled with 'exclusive' organizations and segments of institutions that are more or less covert. In some cases, their legal status was won – or won and lost and won again – in the course of a historic struggle. For example, the Liberal regimes of the late nineteenth century banned religious fraternities like the Knights of the Holy Sepulchre; but this organization, replete with rites of initiation, is now sanctioned as a prestigious meeting-ground for right-wing Catholics. So is Opus Dei, thought to have 70,000 adherents in Italy and a presence in some 50 countries (*Il Manifesto*, 18 Jan. 1997).

Much of the subsequent discussion focuses on Italian Freemasons, members of an international order defined by a secret rite of initiation. Interdicted by the Church since 1738, when Clement XII declared Masonry to be incompatible with Catholic doctrine, Masons were also later persecuted by Mussolini. Those sympathetic to the fascist regime voluntarily gave up the fraternity for the *fascio,* while others went underground, reconstituting themselves after the war into two divisions: the English-affiliated *Grande Oriente d'Italia*, consisting of some 600 lodges, and the *Gran Loggia d'Italia*, a smaller network of 250 chapters oriented toward France and Belgium (Forgione and Mondani 1994). Renowned for recruiting 'liberal-minded' elites, whether secular or Catholic, the postwar Masons are estimated to number some 15,000. Both during the fascist period and now, Masons have staunchly advocated the right to 'free association', including association of a secret type (Di Bernardo 1987).

Some covert institutions, to wit the secret services, are arms of the State. These throve during the Cold War era, nurtured by the proxy insurgencies and counter-insurgencies of the super-powers, which not only armed and encouraged them, but supported a vast clandestine network of transnational operatives and weapons dealers, some of whose goals were purely commercial (see Arlacchi 1993; De Lutiis 1991; *Il Manifesto*, 5 Feb. 1997; Nicastro 1993; Paoli 1996; Peleg 1990). Apparently, the plotters of the 1960s and 1970s coups in Italy forged their anti-communist alliances by transforming certain branches of Freemasonry into meeting places for a more diverse than usual representation of elites. Their recruitment effort targeted, in particular, like-minded men from the military, the police and the secret services, as well as the usual high personages in government, business and the professions (De Lutiis 1991: 284–7). The transformed Masonic lodge provided a hidden context for this mix of persons, whose powers now included access to the means of violence.

In the language of the Italian press, these branches of transformed Freemasonry were 'covert' or 'deviated'. The model for deviation was the infamous Lodge called Propaganda Due or P2, founded by a former Tuscan fascist and dual citizen of Argentina, Licio Gelli, in the mid-1960s. A police raid on Gelli's Arezzo apartment in March 1981 uncovered evidence that the Lodge had developed a so-called 'strategy of tension' during the 1970s, with the aim of using systematic blackmail, bribes, promises of advancement, and intimidation to displace left-of-center forces from the government. In a 1992 deposition, *pentito* Pino Marchese, nephew of mafia boss Filippo Marchese, named Howard E. Stone, head of the CIA in Italy, as a member of P2 (Nicastro 1993: 166). Carlo Digilio, a more recent *pentito* with CIA connections, is expected to amplify the American role further (*Il Manifesto*, Feb. 5, 1997). Interestingly for our purposes, Freemasonry also reached out to mafia in this period.

The history of Freemasonry in Sicily dates, as in Italy, to the underground movements that helped create the Liberal nation-state over the course of the nineteenth century, (see Poggi 1978: 179ff., 162). In the twentieth century, Masonic lodges recruited the region's professional elites – doctors, lawyers, government officials, and heads of institutions. From the statements of *pentiti*, there was, however, an acknowledged boundary between Masonry and mafia. According to Tomasso Buscetta's deposition of 1984 (among the first and most clamorous 'confessions'), in his day, it was 'absolutely prohibited for a man of honor to be a member of a Masonic order . . . their aims were totally different and in part incompatible' (quoted in Nicastro 1993: 33). Antonino Calderone confirms this, but from a different angle. Many judges were Masons, he reports, which tempted the mafia to want a relationship, yet the Masons considered *mafiosi* 'too cunning to be inducted'. For a *mafioso* to join, moreover, would have meant to serve two masters – a potential betrayal.

And yet, sharing a similar logic of secrecy, initiation, and mutual support and solidarity based on fictive kinship, they apparently got along. Supposedly, the mafia boss, Michele Greco (owner of the Ciaculli estate where notables met for target shooting) in 1946 joined the Garibaldi Lodge in Palermo. His relative, Antonino Cottone, was a member of another lodge, the Lux, from 1948 until 1956, along with the magistrates Giovanni Nasca and Michele Mezzatesta. Other important mafia-Masons of the past included Nino Salvo (holder of the tax-collecting franchise) and his cousin Alberto (Nicastro 1993: 202–3). In 1977, moreover, the boundary was crossed as Palermo boss Stefano Bontate, a pioneer with Badalamente in the expansion of narco-traffic, announced that the Masons wanted a coalition with the mafia's highest members, two or three from each province. Michele Greco and Stefano Bontate were chosen from the Province of Palermo, Pippo Calderone from Catania, Totò Minore from Trapani, and so on (Calderone in Arlacchi 1993: 178–9). According to the former Grand Master of the Grande Oriente, Giuliano Di Bernardo, during the years 1976 to 1980 *mafiosi* competed to become Masons (Di Bernardo 1987, emphasis added; see also Paoli 1996). It was part of their 'strategy' for approaching and infiltrating power (Ministry of Interior 1994).

For Masons to imagine using *mafiosi* was not unprecedented. Calderone reports that in their planning for the attempted coup of 1970 (the so-called Borghese Coup), the nucleus of plotters had approached certain *mafiosi* to engage their participation. At a prearranged time, the mafia was to have accompanied Masons into various prefectures, substituting a Mason for the prefect in each. As an inducement, the plotters offered the reversal of a series of already concluded convictions. The bosses were circumspect about the idea of a right-wing coup, however, having had a bad experience with fascism during the war; and, then, the coup did not materialize. In retrospect, Calderone muses, the mafia only entertained the idea as a bluff, hoping to 'adjust' several trials (Calderone in Arlacchi 1993: 83–6).

That was 1970. Subsequently, in the wake of the coup's failure, Gelli and the inner circle of Propaganda Due had elaborated their 'strategy of tension' through which secret Masonic lodges were formed, recruiting members from an ever-wider array of elites. In 1977, the year that the 'offer' to mafia was made, newspapers began reporting a rift in Masonry between an older faction, loyal to its traditions, and a new, brazen group that 'admitted just anyone'. According to the Palermo press, Masonry had once been restricted to elites in banking, the professions, business and culture, but now, in a squalid degeneration of this tradition, ideologues were joining super-secret lodges almost regardless of their place in society. In the context of this development, opening the door to the mafia was but another step. As Calderone put it, the initiative for an alliance with mafia came from a new secret lodge whose actions were hidden, even from the members of Freemasonry itself (Calderone in Arlacchi 1993: 178–9).

Members of the military secret service appeared on Gelli's list of P2 associates. According to the journalist Franco Nicastro, this is because, by the end of the 1970s, the military secret service, SISMI, had developed close ties to P2, having become a 'sort of super-SISMI', more secret and restricted than before. The Generals Giuseppe Santovito and Pietro Musumeci promoted this transformation, as did the all-purpose *faccendiere* or man of affairs and SISMI informer, Francesco Pazienza. Pazienza was close to Pippo Calò, the Rome-based ally of the 'Corleonesi' – the mafia faction that ascended to dominance after 1979 under the aggressive leadership of Totò Riina (Nicastro 1993: 166–71; De Lutiis 1991).

To confirm these relationships there is the deposition of Marchese, which describes how the Corleonese-allied boss Salvatore Greco, nicknamed 'the Senator', had developed an association with Bruno Contrada, a member of the Secret Services. Pondering how this association might have arisen, Marchese cites Greco's membership in 'some Masonic lodge', where he 'entered into relationships with important persons from a variety of circles' (Nicastro 1993: 166). Early in 1997, after a lengthy and highly controversial trial, Contrada was convicted of having aided the bloody ascendancy of the Corleonesi by, among other favors, tipping them off about pending police actions (see *Il Manifesto*, 17 Oct. 1996).

Thanks to recent investigations, it is now known that Masonic lodges of varying degrees of 'deviation' multiplied in Sicily during the 1980s; indeed, the names of some of them have become familiar watchwords in the press. Readers know, for example, that the sign, '*Centro Sociologico Italiano*', posted on the door of a palazzo in Palermo's Via Roma, is actually a cover for five lodges that hold their meetings inside: Palermo, Lux, Garibaldi, Diaz, and Concordia. The secret lodges in Trapani, the second 'mafia city' of the island, meet under the cover of the Circolo Scontrino in Via Carreca and have names like Iside, Iside 2, Osiride, Cielo D'Alcamo, Hiram, and Cafiero, with the most secret being the 'C Lodge' (Di Bernardo 1987; Ministry of Interior 1993; Nicastro 1993).

How much of this still continues remains an open question. On 26 July 1992, the Collegio of the Gran Maestri of the Sicilian lodges refused to vote a position on mafia, notwithstanding the assassinations of the judges Falcone and Borsellino only a short time before. A year later, Di Bernardo, the Grand Master of the Grande Oriente d'Italia, came under fire for having contributed to the Cordova report. Even though he refrained from supporting the report, claiming that it had gone too far, he was forced to resign. Di Bernardo then went on to found a new network of lodges, the *Gran Loggia Regolare d'Italia*, and to arrange for English, French and German Masonry to break off relations with the GOI, whose new leader,

Armando Corona, is rumored to be close to Gelli and various secret service operatives (Forgione and Mondani 1994).

Masonry and Grand Affairs

If 'deviated' Masonry enmeshed mafia in a covert structure of power during the 1970s, so too did it help *mafiosi* to find appropriate international channels for laundering and investing their considerable sums of liquid capital, accumulated through narco-trafficking. Significantly, P2 held within its orbit a number of financial wizards who represented a new kind of capitalist – let us call them shadow speculators – who rose to prominence in the decades after the Second World War. The participants in this elite were persons of varied national origin whose goals were to accumulate large sums of money through partially hidden speculative activity: prescient real estate investments linked to urbanization; betting on differential stock, futures, and currency values (helped by insider information); evading taxes and regulation; and buying up banks and industries for the purpose of restructuring and reselling them to realize a short-term gain.

To some analysts, the oil crisis and global recession of 1973–4 constituted a huge stimulus to this kind of activity. In Italy, certainly, it led to a soaring public debt and inflation rates of between 17.7 and 21.4 per cent between 1973 and 1977, causing the International Monetary Fund to issue a warning (Galli 1995: 135). In such a context, capital was discouraged from productive investment, at least in large-scale industries of the Fordist type. Italian industries employing more than 500 persons fell from 23.6 per cent to 19.6 per cent of total industries during the 1970s, while industries employing fewer than 100 persons increased from 53.2 to 59.2 per cent (ibid.). At the same time, capital sought relatively greater returns through speculation on interest rate spreads, currency exchange fluctuations, inflationary trends in real estate, stocks, bonds, and a giddy lending boom (from 1973 to 1981) to Third World countries (loans were worth 30 billion in 1973, and 300 billion in 1983: see Moffitt 1983; Spero 1980). The implementation of structural adjustment and deregulation policies in the early 1980s as the profligate loans came due added yet another boost to speculative activity.

Meanwhile, an electronics revolution in information technology permitted round-the-clock banking on a global scale, while ever more prevalent bank secrecy practices furthered the circulation of 'hot' or 'stateless' money in search of short-term liquid assets and tax havens (Naylor 1989). Throughout the 1970s, Switzerland-like enclaves proliferated 'off-shore' on Caribbean and Pacific islands, each competing for the branches and subsidiaries, as well as the blessing, of respectable commercial houses (Blum 1984; Naylor 1989; Permanent Subcommittee 1983). The years from 1964 to 1978 saw international banking expand by 'more than 25 percent per year, much faster than world production and world trade', which grew by only 5.25 per cent and 7.5 per cent, respectively (Moffitt 1983: 217). Opportunities to launder dirty money expanded in tandem. As Canadian economist Thomas Naylor has argued, because the new fiscal paradises are integrated with, and have the support of, legitimate international financial institutions, they work well to hide narco-dollars. Criminal money, to borrow his words, 'joins with and submerges itself into an enormous mass of speculative capital that races around the world . . . at the touch of a computer key' (1989: 62, 69).

During the Cold War, the close connection between traffic in speculative investments, hot money, and drugs was probably facilitated by relations between secret service operatives and offshore banks such as the Nugent Hand Bank of Australia (Kwitny 1987; McCoy 1991). Such institutions supported activities (insurgency and counter-insurgency, arms and drug dealing) that the operatives wanted to hide, whether from legislative bodies that were legally obliged to oversee foreign policy, or from the official makers of foreign policy themselves. The consequence was a triangulation of global markets for hot money, arms, and narcotics whose powerful interactions and potential for accumulation reoriented governments and disrupted societies around the globe (see Arlacchi 1983; Arlacchi and dalla Chiesa 1987; Naylor 1989; Pierre 1982; Sampson 1977).

Among the most important early interlocutors between mafia and this world of shadowy speculators was Michele Sindona, a Sicilian who, at the end of the war, made a small killing in black market grain sales. Having received a law degree from the University of Messina in 1938, he took this money to Milan in 1946, using it to buy up land in zones of urban expansion. By 1950 he had made enough from land deals to buy whole firms; by 1960 he had acquired the set piece of his 'empire' – major shares in the Banca Privata Finanziaria, a small Milan bank. A fortuitous marriage of his cousin to a Vatican Bank insider led to relationships that furthered this meteoric rise (Galli 1995). Renowned for his cleverness and charm, Sindona was soon upstaging another important banker, Enrico Cuccia, the 'Calvinist-style' head of Mediobanca, who was closely allied to the Agnelli interests and other North Italian industrial families, all of whom disapproved of Sindona. Word of this rivalry spread through United States and European financial circles, often to Sindona's favor.

But Sindona did not remain a winner. During the early 1970s, he lost substantial sums betting on currency spreads between the dollar and the lira, and on platinum and silver against gold. Perhaps such losses whetted his appetite for narco-profits, which he allegedly invested in offshore banks on behalf of *mafiosi*, and in United States real estate deals. Grandiose and over-extended, his operations were still destined to crack. As many American readers will know, he purchased the Franklin National Bank in New York in 1973, only to loot some $45 million from its coffers, driving it into bankruptcy by 1974 (*Wall Street Journal*, 7 May 1984; see also Spero 1980).

In the summer of 1979, just prior to his conviction for bank fraud in Italy, he attempted to flee American justice by staging his own false kidnapping, ending up in the arms of Palermo's most potent bosses of the time, the Inzerillos and the Bontates. In 1991, the *pentito* Mannoia revealed how the coalition of narcotics bosses headed by Bontate, Badalamenti, and Inzerillo, having set up their money-laundering channel though Sindona, were sorely destabilized by his troubles. In 1993, another *pentito*, Gaspare Mutolo, made the following claim: that by the end of the 1970s, the Palermo bosses wanted Sindona's head (i.e. they were demanding restitution) and were about to force the extortion of his other depositors (Arlacchi 1995: 40–7).

During that same summer of 1979, Giorgio Ambrosoli was murdered. Ambrosoli was the Italian lawyer presiding over the liquidation of the Banca Privata, which had gone bankrupt along with the Franklin in 1974. Sindona was convicted of ordering this murder and of menacing other bankers (in 1977, Cuccio learned of a threat to kidnap his son) as well as bankruptcy fraud (see Stajano 1991). He committed suicide or was assassinated – there has been no clear determination – in a Milan prison in 1986.

Significantly, Michele Sindona was a 'deviated' Mason. In 1978, Pino Mandalari, a Sicilian accountant who was fiduciary to the leading Corleonese boss Totò Riina and the Grand Master of a Masonic lodge on the Viale Strasburgo in Palermo, told the journalist Nicastro that members of this lodge had recently participated in discussions about the relationship of Italian Masonry to other branches of world Freemasonry, held on a yacht off the island of Ustica. Dr. Miceli Crimi, Sindona's physician, organized the meeting, at which John Connally, United States Treasury Secretary under Nixon, was present (Nicastro 1993: 191). More to the point, Sindona was a close friend of Licio Gelli and a founding member of Propaganda Due. It is widely believed in antimafia circles that affiliates of P2 attempted to obstruct the prosecution of Sindona with the help, possibly, of Giulio Andreotti and other high officials of the Italian State (Arlacchi 1995: 31–40).

In the late 1970s, as Sindona's house of cards was collapsing, Roberto Calvi, another banker friend of Gelli's and member of P2, became engaged with the Corleonesi, rivals of the Inzerillos and Bontates. In the words of the *pentito* Mannoia, 'Salvatore Inzerillo and Stefano Bontate had Sindona, the others (i.e., the Corleonesi) had Calvi' (quoted in Paoli 1996: 21). At first an ally of Sindona, Calvi soon became a rival, competing for, among other things, high-level connections in the Vatican Bank (Piazzesi and Bonsanti 1984). On 18 June 1981 he was found with chunks of cement in his pockets, dangling beneath the Blackfriars Bridge in London (a location freighted with Masonic symbolism). Francesco Di Carlo, a former interlocutor of mafia finance with a base in England who decided to 'confess' in 1996, has implicated Pippo Calò, point person in Rome for the Corleonesi, as the principal organizer of the murder, Calvi having attempted to kite mafia funds to cover the collapse of his 'empire' set piece, the Catholic *Banco Ambrosiano*. According to Di Carlo, Sindona and Gelli were also probable *mandanti*, organizers of the crime (*Il Manifesto* 9, 10 Oct.1996; 10 April 1997).

Summing up both the political and the financial *embrogli* associated with P2, the Cordova report observes that 'deviated' Masonry appears to be 'the connective tissue of the organization of power' in Italy (quoted in Nicastro 1993: 186). The journalist Guido Ruotolo uses the word 'metastasis' to make a similar point (*Il Manifesto*, 16 Apr. 1996). Reports from the Ministry of the Interior refer to 'networks of illicit lobbying', using the English word. All have in mind a capillary formation that extends through virtually the entire national territory, with ties into similar formations worldwide – a sort of 'transversal super-party' for people of all parties occupying high positions of power (Forgione and Mondani 1994; *Commissione Parlamentare Antimafia* 1993: 24). Leonardo Messina, the *pentito*, reminds us that *narco-mafiosi* were players well into the 1980s. Inserting themselves into the 'metastasis', they ended up with 'adjusted' trials and helpful financial contacts. 'Naturally', he adds, 'I am referring to the absolutely secret lodges, for which you would never find membership lists. It is not written anywhere that Riina is affiliated . . .'. According to the 1986 report of the Parliamentary Antimafia Commission, there were '2,441 men of honor whose names appear among the "brothers" distributed among 113 lodges in Sicily'. Of these, 33 were indicted or convicted, and another 335 figured in various police records (see Ministry of Interior 1994). Clearly, Masonry 'opened roads to a certain level' (Nicastro 1993: 187–8).

Conclusion

That we have been able to say anything at all about the increasingly covert structure of power that enabled Sicilian *mafiosi* to commoditize heroin on a global scale in the 1970s is owed entirely to others. To borrow a phrase made famous by the martyred judge, Giovanni Falcone, we 'walk on the legs' of courageous magistrates, journalists, and researchers in Italy and Sicily, some of whom have been killed. This, we believe, raises an epistemological question different from the one that has been debated so intensely in recent social science theory.

There, it is claimed, the truth about 'what has happened in history' is necessarily contingent; the identities that shape consciousness render any claim to 'know' what happened problematic, especially where 'others' are involved. In the face of this epistemological indeterminacy it is common to take refuge in an intensified reflexivity, abandoning empirical inquiry as at best a delusion and at worst an unjustified or arrogant pursuit of power. With all due respect to the postulate of indeterminacy and the 'ultimate' impossibility of knowing what we experience, it would seem that the present case highlights a different problem: how many obstacles to knowing were thrown in our paths by the overt relationships and conspiratorial and collusive practices that flourished in the context of the Cold War – that is, precisely during that epoch when social theory was giving up on 'knowing'.

One might want to pass these relationships and practices off as the surreal and paranoid fiction of writers and film-makers. Certainly, the evidence for them is biased – in this case by the motives and intentions of the *pentiti*, police officers, judges and journalists who constructed it in the first instance, and by us who construct it in the process of historical analysis. Nevertheless, what we are learning now should make us properly humble (perhaps even embarrassed) about how little we knew in the past. And *that* ignorance went well beyond the general condition of cognitive indeterminacy that is characteristic of the human condition. It was the product of structures of power the outlines of which emerge, always imperfectly (by nature imperfectly), in moments of political transparency. The inevitable uncertainty of knowing should not, in other words, be conflated with a blind conviction that there is nothing to be known, even in the realm of deep politics.

Acknowledgements

The research on which this chapter is based was conducted with the generous support of grants from the Harry Frank Guggenheim Foundation and the National Science Foundation, for which the authors are grateful. We also thank Josiah Heyman and the Wenner Gren Foundation for Anthropological Research for organizing a stimulating conference on 'States and Illegal Networks' at which the paper on which the chapter is based was initially presented and discussed.

References

Arlacchi, Pino (1983), *La mafia imprenditrice: L'etica mafiosa e lo spirito del capitalismo*. Bologna: Il Mulino.

—— (1993), *Men of Dishonor: Inside the Sicilian Mafia*. New York: William Morrow.

—— (1995), *Il Processo: Giulio Andreotti Sotto Accusa a Palermo*. Milan: Rizzoli.

—— and Nando dalla Chiesa (1987), *La Palude e la Città: Si Puo Sconfiggere La Mafia*. Milan: Arnaldo Mondadori Editore.

Arnone, Giuseppe (ed.) (1988), *La Mafia di Agrigento: Gli Atti del Processo di Villaseta*. Cosenza: Editrice LPA.

Block, Alan (1980), *East Side – West Side: Organizing Crime in New York, 1930–1950*. New Brunswick, NJ: Transaction Books.

Blum, Richard H. (1984), *Offshore Haven Banks, Trusts, and Companies: The Business of Crime in the Euromarket*. New York: Praeger.

Buongiorno, Pino (1984), 'La piovra con mille facce'. *Panorama* (weekly magazine), 23 July 1984.

Calabrò, Antonio (1984), 'I salvi non si toccano'. *Panorama* (weekly magazine), 14 May 1984.

Chinnici, Giorgio, and Umberto Santino (1986), *L'omicidio a Palermo e Provincia negli Anni 1960–1966 e 1978–1984* (No. 1). (Collana di studi statistico-sociali e demografici, 1.) Palermo: Istituto di Statistica Sociale e Scienze Demografiche e Biometriche, Università di Palermo. (Ricerca svolta dal Centro siciliano di documentazione 'Giuseppe Impastato' e dall'Istituto di statistica sociale dell'Università di Palermo.)

—— and —— (1989), *La Violenza Programmata: Omicidi e Guerra di Mafia a Palermo dagli Anni '60 ad Oggi*. Milan: Franco Angeli.

Chubb, Judith (1982), *Patronage, Power, and Poverty in Southern Italy; A Tale of Two Cities*. Cambridge, MA.: MIT Press.

Commissione Parlamentare Antimafia (1993), 'Il partito trasversale delle logge irregolari'. *Narcomafie* October: 17–24.

De Lutiis, Giuseppe (1991), *Storia dei Servizi Segreti in Italia*. Rome: Editori Riuniti.

Di Bernardo, Giuliano (1987), *Filosofia della Massoneria: L'immagine Massonica dell'Uomo*. Venice: Marsilio Editori.

Fentress, James, and Chris Wickham (1992), *Social Memory*. Oxford: Blackwell.

Fiume, Giovanna (1991), 'Bandits, Violence and the Organization of Power in Sicily in the Early Nineteenth Century', in J. A. Davis and P. Ginsborg (eds), *Society and Politics in the Age of the Risorgimento, Essays in Honor of Denis Mack Smith*. Cambridge: Cambridge University Press, pp. 70–91.

Forgione, Francesco, and Paolo Mondani (1994), *Oltre la Cupola: Massoneria, Mafia, Politica*. Milan: Rizzoli.

Galli, Giancarlo (1995), *Il Padrone dei Padroni: Enrico Cuccia, il Potere di Mediobanca e il Capitalismo Italiano*. Milan: Garzanti.

Gambetta, Diego (1993), *The Sicilian Mafia: The Business of Protection*. Cambridge, MA: Harvard University Press.

Gilbert, Mark (1995), *The Italian Revolution: the End of Politics Italian Style?* Boulder, CO: Westview Press.

Kwitny, Johnathan (1987), *The Crimes of Patriots: A True Tale of Dope, Dirty Money, and the CIA*. New York: W. W. Norton.

Lupo, Salvatore (1984), 'Nei giardini della Conca d'Oro', *Italia Contemporanea* 156: 43–53.

—— (1993), *Storia della Mafia: dalle Origini ai Giorni Nostri*. Rome: Donzelli Editore.

McCoy, Alfred (1991), *The Politics of Heroin*. New York: Lawrence Hill.

Ministry of the Interior (1993), *Rapporto annuale sul fenomeno della criminalità organizzata per il 1992*. May, 1993. Rome: The Ministry.

—— (1994), *Rapporto annuale sul fenomeno della criminalità organizzata per il 1993*. April, 1994. Rome: The Ministry.

Moffitt, Michael (1983), *The World's Money; International Banking from Bretton Woods to the Brink of Insolvency*. New York: Simon and Schuster.

Naylor, R. Thomas (1989), 'Drug Money, Hot Money, and Debt'. *European Journal of International Affairs* 2(3), 55–70.

Nicastro, Franco (1993), *Il Caso Contrada, le Trame di Boss, Poteri Occulti e Servizi Segreti*. Palermo: Edizioni Arbor.

Paoli, Letizia (1996), 'The Integration of the Italian Crime Scene', MS, April.

—— (1997), 'The Pledge to Secrecy: Culture, Structure and Action of Mafia Associations'. Ph.D. Dissertation, European University Institute, Florence.

Peleg, Ilan (1990), 'Models of Arms Transfer in American Foreign Policy: Carter's Restraint and Reagan's Promotion, 1977–1987', Chap. 6, in Robert Higgs (ed.), *Arms, Politics, and the Economy*. New York: Holmes and Meier, pp. 132–54.

Permanent Subcommittee (1983), *Crime and Secrecy: The Use of Offshore Banks and Companies*. (Staff study made by the Permanent Subcommittee on Investigations of the Committee on Governmental Affairs, US Senate, (98th Congress, First Session). Washington, DC: Government Printing Office.

Pezzino, Paolo (1992), *La Congiura dei Pugnalatori: Un Caso Politico-Giudiziario alle Origini della Mafia*. Venice: Marsilio.

—— (ed.) (1995), *Mafia: Industria della Violenza. Scritti e documenti inediti sulla mafia dalle origini ai giorni nostri*. Florence: La Nuova Italia.

Piazzesi, Gianfranco, and Sandra Bonsanti (1984), *La Storia di Roberto Calvi*. Milan: Longanesi.

Pierre, Andrew J. (1982), *The Global Politics of Arms Sales*. Princeton, NJ: Princeton University Press.

Poggi, Gianfranco (1978), *The Development of the Modern State: A Sociological Introduction*. Stanford, CA: Stanford University Press.

Renda, Francesco (1991), 'Prefazione alla seconda edizione'. Preface to F. Renda, *I Beati Paoli: Storia, Letteratura e Leggenda*, 2nd Edition, Palermo: Sellerio Editore (originally published 1988), pp. 7–11.

Rossetti, Carlo (1994), *L'Attaco allo Stato di Diritto, Le Associazioni Segrete e la Costituzione*. Naples: Liguori Editore.

Sabetti, Filippo (1984), *Political Authority in a Sicilian Village*. New Brunswick, NJ: Rutgers University Press.

Sampson, Anthony (1977), *The Arms Bazaar: From Lebanon to Lockheed*. New York: Viking Press.

Schneider, Jane, and Peter Schneider (1976), *Culture and Political Economy in Western Sicily*. New York: Academic Press.

—— and —— (1984), 'Mafia Burlesque: The Profane Mass as a Peace-Making Ritual', in Eric R. Wolf (ed.), *Religion, Power and Protest in Local Communities*. Berlin: Mouton, pp. 114–37.

—— and —— (1994), 'Mafia, Antimafia, and the Question of Sicilian Culture', *Politics and Society* 22: 237–58.

Siebert, Renate (1994), *Le Donne, La Mafia*. Milan: il Saggiatore.
Spero, Joan Edelman (1980), *The Failure of the Franklin National Bank: Challenge to the International Banking System*. New York: Columbia University Press.
Stajano, Corrado (1991), *Un Eroe Borghese: Il Caso dell'Avvocato Giorgio Ambrosoli Assassinato dalla Mafia Politica*. Turin: Einaudi.

–7–

Russian Protection Rackets and the Appropriation of Law and Order

Caroline Humphrey

In Russia, perhaps more than in other countries, people who engage in activities defined by the state as illegal do not necessarily define themselves as criminals. Stalin's harsh legal policies, which defined actions such as tardiness at work, aiding abortions, or accidental loss of secret documents as crimes (Solomon 1996), reinforced the long-standing Russian attitude that divorced community from state notions of law (*zakon*). On the other hand, there were people who joined self-defined bandit gangs. These groups existed, and still exist, both in prisons and camps and in ordinary 'free' life, not accused of any crime. In this chapter I shall attempt an anthropological study of the political-economic logic obtaining in these groups, in particular their discourse and practice of their own 'law' (*zakon*) and the emergence of the protection racket (*reket*) as their central activity.[1]

It will be shown that practices of 'law' within the bandit bands differed significantly from those employed by the Soviet state in the Stalinist period, thus producing a social understanding that there were two worlds. Increasingly, from the 'period of stagnation' of the 1970s to the mid-1980s onwards, the mainstay of the politico-economic practice of the gangs came to be racketeering. What is the protection racket? In simple terms, it is the extortion of regularly paid dues from enterprises in return for 'protection' controlled by a person or group known in Russian slang as the roof (*krysha*). The racket, it will be suggested, was a practice that bridged the two worlds of the criminal gangs and public life. In the current post-Soviet period racketeering has burst the boundaries of the criminal groups, with a variety of 'roofs' found among the police, politicians and private security firms, as well as among the traditional criminal bosses. This is not a situation arising merely by function, but is driven by post-Soviet *anomie* and cultural attitudes to the state. The practices of the racket are dynamic and unstable. They are at once expansive and implosive. At the same time, volatile violence from young street bandits, called 'thawed-outs' in Russian slang, attacks the racket structures but also serves to reproduce them. As with the rackets themselves, the actions here can be seen as the product of particular kinds of persons constructed by the post-Soviet social-cultural environment.

From a theoretical point of view the Russian case is interesting in regard to several questions raised by Smart (1988: 91). In particular, Smart asks how illegal economic activities persist in a situation of regulatory vacuum, that is, without state support for property ownership and the sanctity of contracts. What substitutes for the state? Varese (1994) addresses these questions as regards contemporary Russia. He argues that the post-Soviet spread of property has not been matched by clear property rights legislation, and that the state authorities are ill-equipped to enforce what rules do exist. This situation reduces trust in the state and fosters a demand for protection. Although in principle such a demand might not find a supply, in the Russian case there is a ready flow of individuals trained in the use of arms and without other employment, such as disbanded army soldiers, and former police and KGB officers. This is an argument based on the 'rational choice' of the users of protection and it suggests that protection rackets only emerged after *perestroika* when such a need was established.

Now there is another version of rational choice theory which moves from an economic argument to a more political one. Volkov (1998) argues that if the key to state-formation is the monopolistic control over organized violence and taxation, then the degree of disintegration of the state correlates with the extent to which it relinquishes control over these two monopolies. In Russia, non-state enforcers of rules (such as rackets and mafias) have to a considerable extent displaced the state in the process of post-communist transformation because they have been doing a better job than the state in reducing the transaction costs of exchange and production. Pejovich (1997) suggests that the arbitrary nature of the Russian state is an important reason for its inefficiency: it promotes policies for its own purposes that do not accord with the informal, endogenous heritage of popular rules; such policies are difficult to enforce, and this raises their transaction costs. Non-governmental rule enforcers, on the other hand, are more efficient than the state because they are less arbitrary, closer to ordinary peoples' lives, and, significantly, have incentives (their own profit) to relate the costs of their own activities to the benefits of those to whom the rules are related. Agreeing with this view, Volkov writes that the result is what he calls the 'diffusion' of Russian state functions, including taxation (which people now often chose to pay to the mafias) and rule enforcement. By the late 1990s, the struggle for the control of violence has been largely settled into dispersed spheres of power. Although in principle the state might regain full control, the radical outcome may well be that while the state continues to display its integrity on the international scene and still manages to maintain its symbolic façade, it ceases to dominate in terms of its key domestic functions: protection, taxation, and rule enforcement. Instead, a number of actors will perform these functions, the state being only one of them.

These are valuable contributions with which this chapter concurs; but here I would like to take a slightly different tack. The protection racket is found throughout the world and may well best be seen as an activity with its own independent and systemic characteristics, not a cultural category emerging in each case from a combination of local features. However, to see the problem as only a functional one (the securing of contract and property rights, rule enforcement, etc.) is to neglect the specifically Russian history of criminal culture/society. In other words, it is possible analytically to distinguish the structure of the racket from the values, symbolism and legitimacy attributed to it and from the social production of the kinds of persons who engage in it. Thus rather than seeing racketeers only as agents who happen to have appeared on the scene, this chapter examines the historical dynamic of a criminal culture that has its own momentum and attracts certain people to take part in it. The protection business today includes people from many backgrounds, including the army and the police; but there is evidence that they too are drawn into the ways of thinking, the language and the practices of the gangs that form its backbone.[2]

This culture is the subject of the most diverse imaginings among ordinary people and has given rise to popular genres of thriller (see for example, Berkutov 1996; Koretskii 1996) and cinema, as well as massive newspaper coverage. Clearly we should not confuse what Verdery (1996: 219) calls 'the conceptual mafia' with the 'real thing'. Analysis of the agendas lying behind representations of the Russian mafia would have to be the subject of a different chapter (cf. Pilkington 1994; Ries 1998); and here, acknowledging the diversity of opinions, I have attempted to use a variety of sources to support an argument. This is that the rackets are not only private suppliers of protection, nor simply *ad hoc* usurpers of state functions, but culturally distinctive groupings that use what we might call techniques of predation and patronage evolved from historically earlier Soviet contexts.

When he was asked recently how Russian organized crime differs from other foreign mafias, Konstantinov, Russia's most experienced crime journalist, replied, 'It differs by its strong historical traditions, whose roots go back to the 17th century, by its ideologised character, and further by its intellect and quick-wittedness.'[3] Konstantinov's view of Russian mafias as historically specific, fluid and changing groups that have recently integrated remarkably fast and thoroughly with state structures is similar to Rawlinson's (1997). Both authors point out how racketeering pre-dates *perestroika* and commercialization, while Shelley (1997) draws a parallel between the structures of control of contemporary organized crime and those of the Soviet state. Here I attempt to draw these threads together, focusing in particular on the equivocal legitimacy and dynamics of bandit traditions in the wider context of law in Russia.

That I am not simply making up this idea that we are faced here with different criminal traditions and not just functional solutions to transactional problems can be seen from the following newspaper report. On 11 July 1996 seven people sitting in a cafe in Irkutsk were shot and four of them killed. This was a gangland 'sorting-out' (*razborka*). I quote the report at some length, since it introduces a series of categories to be discussed further.

> The war between these groups started in Spring 1995, when two 'thieves in the law' from Irkutsk were 'crowned' in Moscow. According to police information, one of the main reasons for the coronation of the criminal leaders from Irkutsk was to strengthen the position of the Japonchiks grouping, which was trying to counteract the growing influence of the Georgian criminal clan. The losses in this war were born by only one side: Soloma ('Straw'), Paata and Bakurin, all Georgian 'thieves in the law', were shot.
>
> In the opinion of officials of the Ulan-Ude UOP,[4] the war between the two criminal groupings should not be seen as a conflict along ethnic grounds, since criminal society in general has an international character. The Georgian group includes people of various nationalities, Georgians, Russians, Buryats and Jews. It is two different criminal concepts that are in conflict here, varying perspectives on criminal traditions, and different attitudes to business.
>
> Thus, for example, the Irkutsk 'thief in the law' called Tyurik is the owner of a large packet of shares in the Bratsk aluminium factory and he lives in Spain. On the other hand, the Georgian criminal leaders try not to have close contacts with business and they propound a 'purer' thiefly ideal ('Razborki' 1996).

The Thieves' 'Law'

The internal 'law' of Soviet criminals seems to have been based on much earlier peasant and bandit conventions (Chalidze 1977: 8–9; Rawlinson 1997: 33), a subject which unfortunately cannot be pursued further here.

However, the specific institution of *Vory v Zakone* (literally 'thieves-within-the-law') is known from the late 1920s (Handelman 1994: 26) or early 1930s (Rawlinson 1997: 37; Konstantinov 1996: 85). The situation calls into question several of the dominant stereotypes about the relation between the state and illegal networks. Commonly it is assumed that the state is identified with the law, and illegal networks consist of those people who are beyond either the state or the law. However, such a picture rests on assumptions about the nature of 'the state', as if such a body is to be defined solely within the Western tradition.

In the revolutionary Russia of the 1920s, however, there were two ideological tendencies with regard to the state that reveal its radical difference from Western models. To simplify drastically, these can be noted as follows. First, there was an influential concept of the state whereby it was not conceived as a bounded entity within society, but as ideally coextensive with the whole of the people (*narod*). Although the state in the narrow sense of the organs of government was to be ruled by the dictatorship of the proletariat, nevertheless the concept of the revolutionary state was that it should be inclusive, excluding only the 'enemies of the people', a political rather than a criminal category. In other words, what we are here calling 'illegal networks' were conceived initially not as outside, but as inside the purview of the state. Early revolutionaries borrowed ideas and practices from bandits (folk Russian views of brigands as liberators, traditions of secrecy and nicknames, etc.) and the revolutionary practice of expropriation was recognized at the time to be a version of banditry seen in the rosy light of taking from the rich to give to the poor (Chalidze 1977: 20–3; Rawlinson 1997: 37).[5]

Second, and more remarkable, is the tendency of the Bolsheviks to reject the whole idea of law. Law (*zakon*), in the sense of universally applicable rules and regulations, was seen as a bourgeois invention, devised to protect the alien institution of property rights, and it had no place in socialist society. Instead, misdemeanours were to be judged by tribunals and people's courts in which there would be no professional legal officials but rather judgements according to revolutionary consciousness (Solomon 1996: 21–4).

In fact, private property was never entirely abolished and Lenin almost immediately realised that law was needed in order to accomplish the functions of the new Soviet state. Nevertheless, at the beginning of the1920s there was fierce debate about the need for a code defining specific crimes and punishments – law, like the state, was destined to atrophy, so why not start getting rid of it now? – and anti-law voices were heard even well into the1930s (Solomon 1996: 186). We now know that neither the state itself nor the state's law would wither away in the Soviet Union; indeed, to the contrary. But it must be significant that at more or less the same time that the new Soviet rulers were questioning the value of law and setting up their brutal revolutionary variant, at the start of the 1920s, the criminals were systematizing their own conventions and rules, and that they did this in the idiom of 'law'. The links between the Party and the bandits barely survived the revolution. The bandits' 'law' came to be utterly and strictly hostile to the state.[6] Yet it had a solid internal legitimacy. It was an unwritten law that emerged from inside the society of its own subjects.

The bandits' law applied within the *vorovskoi mir* (the thieves' world),[7] and it is apparent that the term we have been using, 'illegal networks', is not a good description of the organization of this society. Conceived as a separate 'world', its parts also were distinct groups rather than networks. Chalidze's term, *artel*, highlights the importance given to the idea of the collective (1977: 46–7). The bandits themselves came to use the term *bratva* (fraternity). The relations between such base-line groups might be conflictual or alternatively might constitute a patrimonial hierarchy, but in neither case does the idea of a network seem apt.

The criminal *artel* or fraternity had an egalitarian ethos, and it was headed by a chief who was chosen by peers for his leadership qualities. The senior among these achieved the status of *vor v zakone* (thief in the law) and they were crowned (*koronovat'*) at a ritual attended by a large gathering. At least two recommendations were required from other thieves in the law (Handelman 1994: 29). The basic group consisted essentially of the chief's followers, who had sworn to obey 'the law' (*zakon*). Each member had a nickname that superseded his civil name. In other words, a man acquired a new identity on entering and a new way of life. Even today, gangsters meeting one another for the first time ask, 'Are you a *zakonnik*?', are you someone who is subject to the law? These days a common term for the thieves' law is *ponyatiye* (understandings). The idea is that these will govern a person's life, so bandits talk about 'living according to the understandings' (*zhit' po ponyatiem*), and they contrast this with the lives of other criminals, who do not live according to the understandings.

One of the most important of the laws was the injunction not to compromise with the state or the Party. It was forbidden to work for any state organization, to serve in the army, or to have a *propiska* (registration document), and even having worn a Pioneer scarf or a badge of Lenin as a child was enough to disqualify a man from reaching the highest rank and becoming a Thief in the Law. Attachments to the ordinary world in general were not allowed. A thief therefore should not marry. In this highly gendered world, liaisons with women from inside the Thieves' World were common, and women could be members of the bands, but they were held in low esteem and usually badly treated. Forcing a man to take the 'female' role in homosexual acts was an established punishment, or downgrading of status, in the camps. Someone who it was discovered had compromised with the state authorities was punished violently and called a bitch (*suka*).

In general, this was a world that combined in a peculiarly Russian way the egalitarian notion of community (*obshchina*) with a highly authoritarian practice in which the younger *vory* (thieves) had to be subordinate to the older men for years, until they gained their own power. It was expected and virtually required that a thief should be sentenced several times. The 'zone' was a hardening experience, and a well-shouldered sentence was one way to acquire authority. During their time in jail and camps, men accumulated elaborate tattoos that were allegorical signs of their status, hopes, and memories (Baldaev 1989). The tattoos were also proofs of the necessary toughening experience. Thus, when a *vor v zakone* was interviewing his potential successor he might ask him to undress to reveal visual evidence of his suitability for the post (Koretskii 1996: 179).

From the economic point of view, the central institution of the fraternity was the common treasury (*obshchak*). Note the linguistic link with *obshchina*, community. By 'law', the gains from theft, etc. were to be put into the *obshchak*, which was managed by the leader of the gang. The *obshchak* was used to give pensions to widows and families of members, support those in the camps, and set up funds to be used on their release. The members of the fraternity, including the leader, were paid enough to live on from the common treasury, and the *vory v zakone* in particular were expected to lead sober lives, almost like those of bureaucrats, maintaining order, judging violators of the code and administering the *obshchak* (Handelman 1994: 26). They might order a robbery, but privately they had to be examples to the rest, incorruptible, disinterested, and without desire for personal wealth. Likewise, the rank and file thieves could cheat any lay person, but they had to be honest with one another. There were many other quirky rules in the 'law', and these probably varied from place to place, but the main idea was clear. As a contemporary Russian writer has put it, using thieves' jargon which I hope readers are already beginning to understand: 'According to the understandings (*po ponyatiyam*), if you pay (undo, *otstegivat'*) money into the *obshchak* and you are not stuck with any bad deeds that sully your honest name, then you are a "person"'[8] (Berkutov 1996: 141).

The War of the Bitches

I have relatively little information about criminal fraternities in the 1920s and 1930s, and so must fast forward to the period just after the Second World War when the Bitches' War took place inside the camps. This episode is quite well known from the literature (Handelman 1994: 30–1; Rawlinson 1997: 41), so I will mention it only briefly here. The War of the Bitches was a turning-point in the relation between the Thieves' World and the state. After the German invasion of Russia thousands of prisoners answered the call to join the army or munitions factories. Patriotism outweighed the rule against association with the state. The *vory v zakone* were aghast and angered, and when these soldiers returned from the war they were not forgiven. As soon as they found themselves again behind bars, they were set upon as 'bitches' (scabs). Handelman (1994: 30–1) reports that during the1950s hundreds, perhaps thousands, of convicts were beaten or killed in a battle that engulfed the entire Gulag. The 'bitches' who lived long enough to leave the camps cut off their links with the old crime chiefs. Having violated one part of the law, they had little compunction about abandoning the rest of it, especially the prohibitions against going into business and the personal accumulation of wealth. The scene was now set for a close association between the *suchenniye* ('bitchified') groups and state officials and production managers.

This episode shows that for many criminals the thieves' 'law' was not a supreme value, and there were differences of opinion within the thieves' world. Kabo (1993:60) for example, describes how when he was in the camps in the 1950s a period of chaotic violence when the 'bitches' were in power was succeeded by a time of order with the advent of a group of *vory v zakone*. The leaders of the 'bitches' were knifed to death and the next day, Kabo writes, 'the reign of law had dawned. The thieves established a strict and – according to their conceptual system – just order in the zone.' Samoilov (1993: 36), on the other hand, writing of his time in the camps in the 1980s, saw the thieves' law as imposed:

> The *vory* are the enforcers of the 'thieves' law' – that is, the criminal morality that they inculcate and impose on everybody. In that morality, it is not labour but rather thievery, robbery, and pillage that are matters of honour and valour; every murder is a heroic act, drunkenness and debauchery are the supreme pleasures, and a real *kaif* (high) is the subject of fond reminiscences, boasting and envy.

Although it is evident that for Samoilov and many other prisoners the thieves' law was despicable and contrary to general social values, nevertheless he describes it as a morality and indicates that it included a primitive notion of universal justice. For instance, *vory* had the privilege of taking away any packages belonging to lower-status prisoners, except for the bread ration, which was the blood-sustaining *polozhniak* (vital substance) and could not be taken. Any violation of this rule was instantly punished (Samoilov 1993: 36). In this particular aspect, the faint gleam of the notion of justice for all, the thieves' law differed from the principle of the Soviet state law.

The Law of the Soviet State

While it is of course impossible to treat this subject in any depth here, one aspect of Soviet law is particularly relevant to our topic: its instrumentality. Soviet law arose after the revolution as a means of government, in particular for the regulation of the economy. The law explicitly applied differently to different classes of people (Solomon 1996: 33). Although the idea of a separate criminal law was established in the 1920s, largely in order to regulate the New Economic Policy, the law as it developed under Stalin was 'distorted' in several ways according to Solomon (1996: 404) – presumably he is referring to distortions of the law considered as a set of procedures implementing justice. Solomon is not here referring to the Terror, and he argues convincingly that Stalin used two distinct forms, terror and the law, as means of rule. However, even within the sphere of criminal law, instrumentality was primary, tempered only faintly by the scruples of officials administering it.

Soviet law was developed by Stalin in order to strengthen the state's ability to govern, and this characteristic persisted well into the 1980s and still has its reverberations today (see Shelley 1996, 1997). Used as a political resource, new laws required neither the consent of the public nor that of implementing officials. Regulations and edicts issued by specific leaders or branches of government were frequently used to supplement and supersede existing laws, a practice that continued Tsarist traditions of ruling by decree. There was a constant refashioning of law to suit the leaders' immediate needs, with the result that even legal officials often did not know what the law was (Solomon 1996: 415). Furthermore, many decrees were kept secret. The aim here seems to have been to hide regulations whose very existence would have revealed the dictatorial and cruel nature of Soviet rule to the world (e.g. edicts concerning women and children in prison camps, or definitions of 'shirking' as a crime, Solomon 1996: 419). The repeal of laws on shirking, because case-loads were too heavy to be managed by the courts, was also made secret. This time, Solomon argues, Stalin may have been motivated to hide from workers the fact that shirking was no longer a crime (1996: 424–5). In any event, the secrecy of large parts of the law, and its constantly changing content imposed purely by fiat from above, is evidence that it was the embodiment of a general social morality only in a secondary, refracted sense, i.e. a morality that gave precedence to the state as the arbiter of what was lawful.

The Soviet law (*zakon*) was the context within which the bandits' law (*zakon*) evolved. Though some Russian writers have declared that the Soviet Union was a bandit state, or that the zone was a mirror-image of the USSR (Kabo 1993: 63), a closer consideration of the thieves' law indicates that, although there were parallels,[9] it held itself apart from the state's law and preserved some different principles. For a start, one could point to a direct symbolic confrontation of discursive values: gangsters of all types self-identified themselves as thieves (*vor*) at a time when production was the overwhelming Soviet value and theft of state property was an obsession, resulting in constantly changing laws of elaborate cruelty on theft (Solomon 1996: 222–3). Again, the bandits' 'laws' were never edicts or regulations emanating from particular bodies or individuals, however powerful. On the contrary, the bosses, the Thieves in the Law, were expected to follow rather than initiate 'law'. They were supposed to behave in such a way as to deny the merest suspicion that they were bending the 'law' to their own advantage. Of course it is true that the thieves' 'law' was already set up greatly to the benefit of the chiefs; but the point is that individuals could not suddenly change it. Furthermore, the thieves' 'law' was not secret, at least within the *Vorovskoi Mir*. On the contrary, it was open. The 'laws' consisted quite largely of pointless etiquette and taboos that demonstrated, by their observance, a general subordination to the law. It was part of the 'law' that changes to the 'law' could only take place at general assemblies (*skhodnyak*) with the approval of the collectivity (*obshchina*). Finally, the concept of 'the understandings' suggests that the underlying idea of the 'law' was one of legitimacy assured by generalized psychological internalization of the given values. Soviet law, by contrast, being conceived instrumentally rather than normatively, was also responded to by the population instrumentally (this is a simplification that begs many questions, but on the whole is a valid point in this context).

Nevertheless, the ideological status of the thieves' law, which was that it was handed down untouched from previous generations, meant that it came fairly frequently into conflict with practical solutions to problems.[10] Its quirky rules of etiquette and obedience were more easily maintained in the restricted life of the 'zone' than outside. Indeed, one senses in all this that the thieves' 'law' in the outside world was as much a powerful ideological myth as anything else. So far, I have tried to explain that this myth was active in a cultural world that set itself apart from the surrounding context of state-dominated Soviet life. Nevertheless, there were some fundamental similarities in the construction of the politico-economic person in these two spheres. In both cases persons were assigned to ranked categories of power/status. The vast majority of material objects, especially land and buildings, were not owned (products had only a very limited 'social life' as private property: Appadurai 1986), but managed and controlled by corporations at various ranks. The economic person was predominantly one whose initial relation with goods (by theft in the case of the bandits, by production in the case of ordinary people) was that of a temporary holder, for the goods themselves were properly at the disposal of a higher social unity, the *obshchina* (community) and the state respectively. I would now like to look more closely the protection racket, which emerged as a criminal practice from a bridging between these two worlds.

The Principle of the Racket

Chalidze (1977: 33) is of the opinion that there were no organized protection rackets in Soviet Russia, but Varese (1994: 257) points out that the payment of protection money was widespread in the last years of the Soviet regime, when cooperatives were legalized. Estimates suggest that 75 per cent of Moscow's cooperatives and 90 per cent of Leningrad's cooperatives made such payments. Vaksberg (1991), however, sees the origin of the protection racket in much earlier Soviet illegal practices, and it seems to me that with regard to 'techniques of predation' he is right.

The essence of the racket was the payment of a roof (*krysha*) for his political protection of one's source of livelihood. The illegality lay in the acquisition of the payment as private property, removing it from the sphere of state distribution. One of the main functions of the roof was to appear legitimate, to be the public skin over the operation. In this sense, the well-known scandal of Medunov, the Brezhnev-era Party boss of Krasnodar, who stashed away vast amounts of illicit wealth in return for his political patronage, was an example of the protection racket. Medunov's enemies (probably the non-suppliers) had obstacles placed to their careers, while his supporters were promoted. Possible revealers of the scam, like the journalist Vaksberg himself, were threatened with violence. As Vaksberg puts it:

> Economic freedom is the first step towards freedom in general. And that is something a totalitarian government cannot allow. The embezzlement of state property was fine in itself, as was stealing from your neighbour. Neither caused the authorities so much as a blink. There was one indispensable condition, however: that the embezzler should co-opt into his band of accomplices and protectors one or preferably more – and ideally more senior – persons amongst those in power. 'Cut them in', in the language of the underworld (1991: 24).

For this to be understood as a protection racket one only has to make the conceptual shift of seeing career competitors as the potential danger against which protection is required by those paying up. Once the racket was in place, the danger also included the ordinary police. But the technique of predation rested on a prior and more immediate threat from the roof himself, 'Cut me in, or it will be the worse for you.' Such a racket could of course occur without any self-avowed criminals taking part; but if they did, they would take the roles of the embezzler or the protector. In bandit language we have the following scenario:

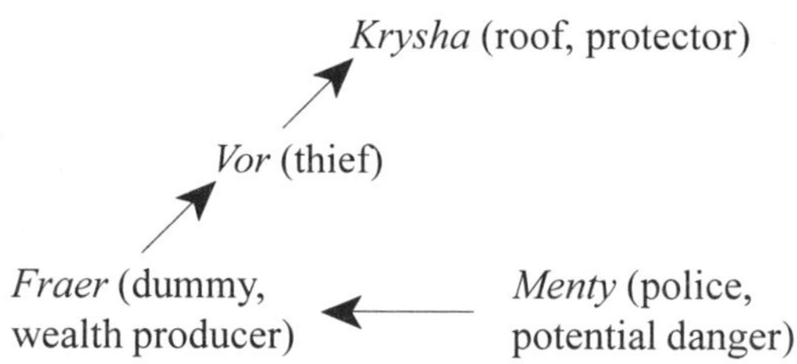

What has made this model so fundamental to current bandit practice is that it has come to apply first and foremost inside the *vorovskoi mir* among the gangsters themselves. A bandit group needs a roof with authority among other criminals to be able to operate regularly, without its source of supplies being attacked by other gangs. Berkutov's novel (1996)[11] of bandit life in St Petersburg in the 1990s is devoted to this theme: it starts with two recently formed bands waiting outside the gates of a distant camp for the emergence of a famous Thief in the Law, each of them eager to engage his protection services as their roof. One of the gangs had for months been feeding him parcels of luxuries paid for from their *obshchak*. By rights they should be the ones he signs up for, but to whom will he in fact offer his patronage?

By the Brezhnev era gangsters realized that the minor rackets they had been engaged in (prostitutes, gambling) could be massively enhanced by moving into the patronage structures of the main shadow economy. A crucial change now took place. Some bosses abandoned the thieves' law to the extent of accepting payments as personal wealth. A leader could still respect the inviolability of the *obshchak*, but accumulate other income on the side.[12] Perhaps, despite the bandit ideology, it was always thus to some extent. Whether this was the case or not in Stalinist times is difficult to tell, but in the period of stagnation, when bureaucrats and managers in the external society became increasingly interested in personal gain, the shift away from the 'modest' *pakhan* (old man) was also certainly taking place (Vaksberg 1991: 27). In other words, racket systems inside the *vorovskoi mir* came to parallel those existing outside, and simultaneously certain of the criminals moved to bridge the gap between the two.

Handelman (1994: 31–2) argues that the important players in this change were the leaders (*avtoritety*) of the groups that had repudiated the hierarchy of the Thieves in the Law, in other words the gangsters known as 'bitches' who had flouted the prohibition on contacts with the state. Once linked into rackets, bureaucrats, factory managers, and the like could themselves become *avtoritety*. By the *perestroika* era in the 1980s the racketeering in the officially protected shadow economy was so lucrative that many younger bandits were attracted to these groups and the authority of the Thieves in the Law diminished. 'In St. Petersburg, when the gangster Authorities sit down to talk with the Thieves-in-Law,' a police colonel told Handelman, 'they are on equal terms. It's like two generals. And the one who wins is the one who is more intelligent, shrewder. And richer' (Handelman 1994: 31–2).

Today, at the street-level the racket works in classic form as follows. A given market-place, let us say, is 'held' by gang X. This means that a rank-and-file member of the gang (a bull, *byk*) is assigned the task of guarding the market stalls at nights from drunks, petty thieves, and so on and charged with extracting a fixed sum from the traders each month. The 'bull's' benefit, apart from the salary he receives, is the opportunity to graze at will on the beers, cigarettes and prostitutes of the market he guards. The gathered money is handed over the chief of the gang, who passes it upwards to the leader who manages the *obshchak*. The 'roof' is paid a generous share.

Although most gangs today also obtain money from other sources (from straight extortion, theft, and so forth at the bottom, through smuggling, the drug trade and financial swindles to investment in casinos, banks, and the like at the highest level) the street protection racket is still the most stable source of income. The ability of subordinate brigades to 'draw up' (*podnimat'*) racket dues is still the source of the bandit leader's authority

(Pogonchenkov 1996). In 1993 in St Petersburg a stable of 60 subject firms was sufficient to support a gang of around 100 members with a little extra income from prostitution.[13] Racketeering determines to a great extent the social organization of the criminal operation. Thus it is the basis for the *geographical organization* of gangs, since it defines the area or the 'points' from which dues are taken (in cities like Moscow these form relatively coherent territories). The protection principle of the racket also implies a *verticalized structure*. The requirement for internal trust generates strictly defined *boundaries* and *entrance requirements*.

It is certainly true that most contemporary gangs have appeared relatively recently, and probably none have a direct history as organizations going back to postwar times. However, their culture and techniques were transmitted, mostly in the camps, through 'generations' of gangsters. Now, there are also new practices and accompanying jargon. The totality becomes almost like a theatrical repertoire of 'acts', which the bandits use both to differentiate amongst themselves and to relate to people in ordinary life. I suggest below that what these acts reveal is that gangs are fundamentally appropriative institutions, rather than firms selling a service of protection. It is in the bandits' interests, however, to purvey the latter impression.

Predation and Selling 'Law'

Quoting the owner of a café who said, 'A roof is when I have bandits to whom I make payments so that other bandits don't disturb me,' Konstantinov (1996: 174) points out that the café owner thereby expressed three misapprehensions: first, a businessman does not have bandits, but bandits have businessmen; second, he does not pay them, but they take money off him; and third, what the bandits offer is not a 'real *krysha*', but the most primitive form of unofficial policing. If Konstantinov is right, the techniques of threat/protection derived from Soviet contexts have evolved towards violence. Protection is no longer a matter of safeguarding of careers but a physical intervention in conflicts over property.

In setting up the arrangement with a businessman, racketeers differentiate between a *probivka* (lit. piercing), which is a polite enquiry ('Are you paying anyone else? If not, you must pay us') and a *nayezd* (raid), which threatens the businessman physically or psychologically. In either case, they 'load' (*zagruzit'*) him with a certain percentage of his monthly profit. The language reveals the predatory orientation. The protection offered is usually no more than a mobile phone number, but may extend to stationing a couple of heavies (who have to be paid for separately from the monthly dues of 20 per cent of the profits, Konstantinov 1996: 174).[14] That contemporary rackets may virtually dispense with protection can be seen from Hohnen's study of the huge Gariunai market in Estonia in 1994. Hohnen (1997: 114–16) found that stall-holders paid the racket large sums two months in advance for tickets for trading-sites, while protection was given only to some traders separately at a much lesser rate.

A 'real roof' is different. In this case, the racketeers become involved in the business, controlling inputs and agreements, recalling debts, obtaining credits, finding orders, sometimes even investing in the business themselves (Konstantinov 1996: 175–6). Such a *krysha* costs from 50 to 70 per cent of the profits each month. This 'full roof' often does not lessen but increases the risks for the businessman. It may draw the firm into illegal activities or 'wars between roofs' that have nothing to do with the business itself and everything to do with bandit rivalries. Firms are sometimes elaborately deceived, for example by being attacked by fearsome thugs hired by the 'protecting' bandits themselves to convince them to pay up. There is also the practice of 'fattening the piglet' (*vyrashivaniya kabanchika*): the firm is cosseted and given full protection over years, while a bank account is opened in its name abroad. When it is judged that no more can be squeezed out, and full protection allows access to the account, the businessman is murdered (Konstantinov 1996: 233).

Konstantinov perhaps gives a too purely predatory description. Rackets must take care to keep the income flowing, though they differ in their tactics in this respect. It is certainly the case that firms and individuals look for roofs as much as having them imposed (Ries 1998). When two firms each have roofs and there is some disagreement, it is the roofs that do the negotiation. What the rackets sell is law, or more correctly, the idea that they are the kind of people who *have law*. I have already described the historical environment of popular Russian ideas of law, and it is worth repeating that in all its variants law is closely identified with control. Hence the mafias' rhetorical cultivation of harsh discipline, which is quite largely directed at the outside world: 'This is what you'll get as our clients,' is the message, 'and this is what we'll mete out to the enemies too.' Thus, curiously, selling legal services is not at odds with predation, since the harsh terms are part of the package of the racketeers' roof. The powerful are expected to dictate their terms and to be jealous and punitive too. Nevertheless, it remains the case that if the firms unwillingly buy into such qualities, the environment allows certain gangs to indulge in predation to an *irrational* extent. This can be seen in what one might call 'over-predation' on the sources of income,[15] not to speak of the internecine beatings and killings.

The 'Thawed-out' Gangsters and Dynamical Systems

Among the many sad facts that have had impact on racketeering is the demoralization of the police and the non-emergence of an independent and incorruptible judiciary. Varese (1994) shows how, taken together, these have created a vast demand for protection from firms, which as an alternative to mafias may create their own strong-arm branches or employ one of the numerous private security firms that have appeared in recent years.[16] However, another dynamic element in these developments is the appearance on the streets of something new, thugs called 'thawed-outs' (*otmorozhenniye* or *otmorozki*).[17]

The idea here is that the Soviet regime froze its people, but now young men have unfrozen, becoming somehow inhuman in the process. *Otmorozhenniye* is slang for people who are cruel, immoral and volatile, unwise and avaricious. The term marks the sense that certain people have appeared who are not simply out-of-work and looking for a way of earning a living, but are caught up in the culture of predation, attracted to it, and prepared to take it beyond its limits. Even other bandits see them as *bespredelnyye*, literally 'limitless', 'out of order'. Crucially, thawed-outs do not live 'according to the understandings', though they may be employed as hit-men and so forth by the *bratva* fraternities. Inside the bandit economy they are contrasted not just with the protection racketeers of longer standing but also with the armed security guards, both of whom are called *profi* (professionals). The distinction is expressed as follows, according to one gangster:

> The amateurs steal from the state. They are not interested in one another's existence and do not think about tomorrow. This is the very lowest racket, when a man is seized by the throat and money is demanded 'from your black eye'. They operate carelessly, beat their victims, attack with knives and pistols, and threaten with words like, 'Shit, give the money or I'll kill you!' In such a situation, the victim should reply, 'Good, I'll get the money tomorrow' and then turn to the police. The *profi*, on the other hand, are far-sighted both in their expressions and their actions. They'll show you your bank account and praise the abilities of your young son. They will on no account ask you for more money than you can afford, in case, as they themselves say, 'the nonsensical idea entered your head of addressing the police' (quoted in Marzeeva 1996).[18]

In other words,'thawed-outs' underlie the protection racket structure with a different type of activity, a dualistic confrontation of direct, violent extraction. I shall return to the relations between the bandit groups, the security firms and the police; but first I address the question of the nature of gangster power relations and the place of 'thawed-outs' in them. It will be suggested that the emergence of 'thawed-outs' is a vital element in the persistence of racketeering and its dynamics.

Some authors have described a hierarchy, variable in its components, for particular cities. For example, Konstantinov (1996: 206) writes that in St Petersburg in 1993–4 there were several powerful, well-organized groups with the following highly vertical structure: brigades (5–10 people), teams (2–5 brigades), groups (2–5 teams), groupings (2–4 groups), and associations (around 5 groupings). The protection racket base seems to construct a stepped series of groups through which resources can move upwards.[19] The most evolved groupings have special sections for banking, counter-intelligence, economic planning, arbitrage and law, and they often also include specialized services, such as counterfeiting workshops. At the beginning of 1994 the main groupings of this type in St Petersburg were the Tambov–Vorkutin, the Azerbaijan, the Chechen, and the Malyshev. At the top of this structure, the criminals may invite the directors of the largest state firms to join in, or they may back pliant politicians for election to office. At the bottom, the lawless 'thawed-outs' are not even counted full members. At all levels, some of the recognized players are in prison or the camps.[20] Dunn (1997: 64) and Pogonchenkov (1996) do not use a hierarchical model, and depict a shifting mass of gangs, of varying sizes and power, operative at the time of their studies (mid-1990s).[21] Dunn (1997: 64) points out that it is essentially meaningless to count the number of gangs, since splits and amalgamations occur.[22] Though there are regional meetings of top leaders, there is no likelihood that one unified structure will appear in Russia.[23]

This is partly because of the persistence of the traditions mentioned at the beginning of this chapter. The *vor* ('thief') tradition is strong in Moscow, while that of sundry *bandity* ('bandits') dominates in St Petersburg. The main distinctions seem to rest on the willingness to enter legitimate business and on treatment of the *obshchak*. In the 'thief' custom, all revenues are paid into the *obshchak* and the gangsters receive shares, while in the 'bandit' tradition only a percentage of the profits are paid into it (Konstantinov 1996: 148). The 'bandits', often known as *sportsmeny*, have a cult of athleticism and physical strength, involving demonstrative abstinence from drink and drugs. The 'thieves' keep stronger ties with bosses in the prisons and camps (where this tradition's authority is still paramount) together with the culture of tattooing, written edicts, observance of 'the law', and so forth. So, although he points out that 'all rules exist to be broken,' Konstantinov (1996: 294) is able to chart significant markers whereby gangs distinguish themselves. For example, he writes that the Kazantsy, even though they operate in bandit-dominated St Petersburg, are oriented to the *vor* tradition, and this can be seen from their use of drink and drugs, their cruelty, and their communitarian treatment of their *obshchak*.

As regards the dynamics of mafiadom, even a well-known grouping such as the Solntsevo gang in Moscow, which has lasted over several 'generations' of leaders (i.e. for about fifteen years) has had changing sources of income over time.[24] The top gangsters are increasingly moving into large-scale financial crime and also into major industries (Pogonchenkov 1996; Investitsionnye 1996: 34; Dunn 1997: 64). The eventual effect on the structure of major gangs of such activities and investments, especially the removal of capital abroad and the acquiring of foreign citizenship by *avtoritety*, is not easy to predict. If we limit ourselves here to the Russian-based gangs operating with a protection racket foundation, it can be seen that the leaders prefer to resolve disputes by peaceful negotiations (*terki*) and to have their subordinate brigades observe territorial boundaries. Nevertheless, the constant advent on to the streets of lawless 'thawed-outs' injects violence from the bottom that can move up through the layers. A brigade is pushed out of one income source, and moves into the territory of another brigade, which is defended by a higher level group, and so on. The more important point is that this direct street violence establishes the need for protection of the businesses on the street, and thereby sets up the conditions of reproduction of the racket.

The predatory logic of the racket entails both intensive and extensive methods: more income from each 'income-spot' (*tochka*) and extension to new 'spots' (Konstantinov 1996: 170). This implies that the metropolitan honey-pots will be constantly at risk of outside attack. Thus gangs from the Caucasus (Azerbaijanis, Georgians, Chechens, Ingushes and Daghestanis), known collectively as the 'wild animals' (*zveri*) by the resident Slav gangs (*slavyanye*), have moved to Moscow, as well as bandits from provincial cities. The outside gangs get a foothold when an established gang is weakened by the death of a leader. If such gang then splits into its lower-level groupings, it may be unable to protect its 'spots', and gangland wars result. In 1996 the external gangs had not succeeded in carving out their own territories in Moscow, but instead preyed in double or even triple rackets on the unfortunate business *tochki*. The Kiev market in Moscow, for example, was controlled by the local Russian Tagan group and also by the Chechen and Azerbaijani gangs (Pogonchenkov 1996).

Two dynamical processes thus occur. When there is over-saturation of an area with protection gangs, the result is what I call *implosion*, the competitive homing in on a single wealth-producing spot by several bands. Berkutov's novel *Krysha* (1996) dramatizes this situation. A successful car-parts dealer is the target for three or four gangs. Each hopes to acquire the horrific video-tape (of the businessman's daughter being raped) that would give them the hold over him to force him to pay up and enter under their 'roof'. The novel ends with all the bandits bar one dead or maimed. Similar real-life cases are documented from Moscow in recent times.[25] This centripetal process co-exists with the process of *expansion*, which is the result of a gang perceiving a wealth-opportunity that seems insufficiently protected. This depends on intelligence, and some gangs are better prepared for lateral extensions of operations than others; but in principle a protection racket structure will expand when there are differences in violence-backed power between groups. However, there seems to be a closure to this process; this occurs when the racket reaches unpropitious ground, either where there is insufficient wealth to be hoovered up[26] or when the ground is effectively dominated by other controllers, such as private protection agencies or the police (see also Note 21).

Recent additions to the 'understandings' thus concern inter-gang conflicts, such as priority given to the band who found the 'spot' first, holding-off while rivals are in prison, prohibition of turning rivals over to the police, compensation for thefts between gangs, and conventions for announcing war. In 'law', unresolved matters should be raised openly at inter-group gatherings, where they are called *pred'yavy* (claims), before battle is engaged (Konstantinov 1996: 168). Of course, unannounced violence in fact occurs at the top as well as at the street level,[27] and gang leaders often ignore the understandings. It is interesting that what certain bosses says about the rules ('We have them just to keep the young ones in order', Konstantinov 1996: 169) accords with the idea that the unwritten ethical code may act as a means of governance.[28] Be this as it may, even if the rules are often ignored, it is certainly wise to know what they are.

A notable feature of the all-Russia pattern is the provincial town or national republic base of many gangs that operate in the metropolitan cities. This centripetal pattern can perhaps be explained by the close relations of trust inside gangs, which contrast with the more predatory relations between them and their clients. The Tambov group, for example, which operated in St Petersburg in the late 1980s to the early 1990s, was started by Vladimir Kumarin, who grew up in the city of Tambov, whence he recruited childhood friends, kin, and other *zemlyaki* (fellow-countrymen). Like several other bandit bosses, Kumarin ostensibly worked as a barman, using the hotel bar as the gang's intimate place. The grouping grew to include hundreds of associates, not all from Tambov; but it is interesting that the home town is not where the band operated. The parents of one of the Tambov bosses in fact worked as respectable officials in that city (Konstantinov 1996: 147-55). All this suggests that many gangs see themselves as raiders on an outside world, avoiding the complications of predation on home ground. The rather closed social worlds of the bosses tend to be short-lived.[29] Nevertheless, they have a certain glamour for those excluded from them.

The Gang Seen in a Shifting Light

The serious criminal groups are hidden from the street. However, the language, dress, and mannerisms of an imagined mafiadom are fascinating for the kids on the block – and this can mean children as young as 10–11. In some cities, certain schools are saturated with rackets (Omel'chenko 1996). If sheer income, as well as outlaw styles, are attractive to youth, nevertheless it is also the case that professional criminalization forces itself downwards and engulfs children who would otherwise have had nothing to do with gangs (Pilkington 1994: 149–54). Street gangs of youths produce 'thawed-outs', who emerge by virtue of their harsh personalities and fighting qualities.[30] Such bands are not normally 'under' (*pod*) regular gangs, but maraud independently. However, individuals may transfer from one status to another. Films and thrillers celebrate this moment: the big move in a young bandit's life is shown when he is accepted into a regular gang 'following the understandings'. Proving oneself in the gang can involve hazing (such as being beaten up for men, and having sex with all the gang members for women), or rites such as the kissing of a dagger.[31] It is difficult to know whether such initiations really happen; but what I would like to touch upon here is the intense swirl of popular suppositions around 'the Mafia', which objectify it in various different guises. One picture is that the bandit has a regular, well-paid occupation.

In a characteristically post-Soviet double vision, the new bandit's occupation may be viewed in the old socialist categories. In Koretskii's *Anti-Killer* (1996), the young bandit's mother is delighted when she hears her son has been taken into a *brigada*, because despite her twenty years of thankless labour,

> . . . contrary to her own experience she thought that the brigade was a second family, her native home. That was how working collectives were depicted in numerous films, books and songs. And the fact that she herself had been

> unlucky – they were drinking all around, swearing, and pressing her to have sex after the shift – did not alter the general impression. . . . Everything depends on the leader.
>
> 'Is your brigadier a good man?' she asked her son.
>
> 'OK,' he stuttered. 'We'll see. The work will show' (Koretskii 1996: 6).

In this mode, the boy himself (not just his mother) is depicted as understanding his activities as 'work' that takes place in 'shifts', and it may even be seen, in bizarrely Soviet terms, as creative (*tvorcheskii*). Here protection is a good, produced like other goods.

However, the post-Soviet perspective in which the *byky* (bulls) can be seen as regular workers can change in an instant to the militia-like frame of the 'profi', where trained and efficient violence is the predominant ideological value. In this case, the *obshchak* no longer has the aura of a beneficial communitarian fund. Instead, paying into it becomes a mark of discipline. As for those who should benefit, equality has long gone: low-ranking thugs are forgotten when they disappear into the camps. The *obshchak* is for the deserving elite. The brigadier's orders are called *razvod*, an army term for the allocation of duties. The social person of the racketeer depicted in this perspective is a hardened, obedient fighter, vigilantly guarding the 'income spots' from raids (*nayezdy*).

This might seem not so very far from seeing the *obshchak* as an army chest and the gang as a patriotic military unit. However, the Chechens are the only ones who may have openly confronted the state in this manner. All three Moscow Chechen gangs pool a common *obshchak*, thought to containing billions of roubles at any one time (Dunn 1997: 66). While Dunn cites traditional uses for the Chechen *obshchak*,[32] Pogonchenko (1996) states that it was used to finance the war against Russia and fill the coffers of the Republic of Ichkeria. If this indeed happened it was unusual: the mafias in general depict themselves as loyal to Russia (if not to the particular government of the day). Some even see a strong state as necessary to their own strength, like two sides honed in war against one another.[33]

Racketeers are often described as providing more than protection, notably practical governance of street business neglected by government officials. For instance, in Koretskii (1996: 250) the brigadier controlling a market turns up and says to his guards:

> 'Four lorries are at the eastern gate with potatoes and they are not being let in.'
>
> 'They have pesticide contamination above the norm,' explained the head guard and drank a gulp of vodka.

> 'What? Have you become a sanitary official?'
>
> 'No. But there must be order (*poryadok*). They want to sell poisoned goods for the same [racket] dues as all the others. I say: let them give 10% for the condition of the potatoes and 30% for their own dues. And even better if they take their shit to the rubbish-dump and don't dirty our market.'

The prevailing relation between racketeer and trader is not threat/resentment, but rather shown as lordly condescension and deferential gratitude. The reason for this is that the trader is usually depicted as engaged in some illicit dealing, which places him in a vulnerable position. When the brigadier mentioned above went to collect dues from an Azerbaijani flower-seller, actually a drug dealer, and found himself initially stopped by the dealers' bouncers, the Azerbaijani soon rushed out, saying:

> 'I am so sorry, my dear friend, they are new people and don't know you yet,' and Hussein met the brigadier with a smile which could have been designed for a beloved brother who had been absent for many years, or for the senior in the clan. 'Now they recognise you, they'll love you like a true friend.' And turning aside to a hovering servant, 'Tea, coffee, fruits, and cognac for my friend! – and make up a bed next-door. If the guest wants, you'll lie with him' (Koretskii 1996: 251).

A slight edginess between the two men never disappears, but the 'guest' avails himself of the cognac and the girl, and then wonders aloud why he has not been offered the *de luxe* room upstairs. Hussein has a secret in this room, as both men know, and preserving it intact is to maintain a boundary, always fragile, between the boss and the client. In such scenarios, 'protection' becomes a most equivocal thing, almost an invention, agreed by both sides to preserve the decencies – for of course the main threat to the Azerbaijani flower/drug-seller is that the brigadier himself will ring up the police and betray him. The underlying message in such novels, it seems to me, is about power, which includes the ability of the gangster to withhold violence – to behave decently, in a civilized manner.

The preoccupation with civilization runs through many accounts. A bandit, for example said to Konstantinov: 'Yes and generally – we are no longer bandits (*bandity*). Perhaps we could be called gangsters (*gangstery*). We are civilized people. We see nothing wrong with the police grabbing various thugs ('untieds', *otvyazannyikh*) and 'thawed-outs', who go round with automatic guns and frighten everyone with their terrible hair-cuts' (1996: 216). In such statements, violence is relegated to a stage in history now left behind, and to the kids on the street who do not know better.

'Roofs' in the Landscape

I move now from discussing the *mores* of gangland to its situation in the wider political economy. Businesses now widely employ their own private security firms as an alternative to, or as well as, paying into the protection rackets (Varese 1994). Some private security firms are former gangs, now legalized by acquiring a license, but most are composed of former policemen and soldiers. However, in Russia these firms cannot be completely separate from the criminal structures. As one director put it: we have to work in 'bandit' territories, the system of the 'roof' is our economic reality, so like it or not we have to deal with the *bratva*. Officially we should have no contacts with the criminal world. But it is not our fault that the criminal organizations have become so powerful (Ivanov 1996). The mayor of St Petersburg, Sobchak, at one point tried to close most of the firms, but he did not succeed (Krom 1996). The situation seems to be that the security firms are like a buffer between the police and the criminal gangs. But they are closer to the latter, both in their rationale, which is frankly commercial in both cases, and in their techniques – indeed they sneer at their former police recruits, who 'hardly know how to hold a gun' (Krom 1996). Nothing is easier than to slip over from the bodyguard to the bandit role in relation to a business you work for each day. 'Frighten them, Vasya, you'll get some money,' as Ivanov (1996) put it.

Meanwhile, according to a recent survey of the Moscow criminal scene:

> The police at some point understood that along with guarding of an abstract public kind, for a very nice money reward they could also guard concrete personalities or commercial structures. Thus the term 'police roof' came into play. In view of the corruption of state powers it is now difficult to say where a given man with epaulettes is 'kept' by the *bratva* or the converse – the 'bandit' is working for the 'patron'. The methods of the guardians of law and order are just the same as those of the bandits (Pogonchenkov 1996).

Hohnen's study of the Gariunai market (1997: 112–17) describes a landscape dominated by a combination of rackets, market managers and police. As mentioned above, their main income is derived from charging large sums for tickets for trading-sites, a task meant to be carried out by the market managers alone. What actually happened was that the managers were left with only a few tickets on the outskirts, which few people wanted to buy, while the rackets commandeered the valuable central places. Soon it appeared that some of these places were also controlled by the police. While some traders said that the police extracted these places as their price for turning a blind eye to the rackets, others maintained that the police had entered the racket themselves and that a 'privatization' had taken place in one of their sections. In fact, all of this divvying up was shrouded in mystery. Though the transaction was in a sense 'legal', since traders were ostensibly paying for places rather than for protection, the owners of the tickets moved into the shadows. Other traders collected the money, and most traders no longer knew to whom they were paying. It was part of the traders' ethics not to enquire, to look away when a neighbouring stall was paid a visit, to communicate in 'half-words' and shared silences (Hohnen 1997: 124).

Such a situation is part of a destructive cycle that has reinforced distrust of the state, and indeed, for vast numbers of people, induced complete alienation from it. One businessman explained how the moment of truth hit him: he started a firm importing computers, and at the end of the first year he paid his tax. A day later, a *brigada* paid a visit. They made it clear that they knew exactly how much tax he had paid, and insisted that an extra 5 per cent of his income was due to them. The businessman was very shaken. He knew that whatever other protection he engaged he would not be able to rid himself of the gang. What was he to do? The only solution, he said, was to count the protection dues against taxes. In fact, why pay taxes at all?

Such calculations – weighing state tax against protection dues as if they were equivalent - is reinforced by prevailing public attitudes, however unjust they may be to those state offices and police departments that work honestly. A journalist writes in the influential paper *Izvestiya*, 'We have no state, only a conglomerate of Mafias. If the police saves me from the bandits, then who will save me from the state?' She continues in a post-Soviet vein dominated by the underlying expectation that the state should be a provider (but no longer is):

> The state quietly takes the lion's share of our salaries, deducting taxes and percentages from our wages, and we also have to pay for light, gas, our apartments and telephones. And we have to pay for so-called communal services. And we have to get that bottle for the plumber, and a box of chocolates for the gynaecologist. And we have to pay 400,000 a month to the English teacher for our child, even though education should be free. No-one puts a knife to our throat taking this money. So this is not called the racket (Marzeeva 1996).

The journalist, who may echo the sentiments of many Russians, continues that she personally would never call providing protection a criminal activity. It is dangerous work, paid at the rate objectively necessary, and 'in any case we have never had much understanding of the people they protect' [i.e. businessmen].

This last point is important, for it hints at the real gap that the gangs first rushed to fill. It does seem to be the case that in the 1980s no one took very seriously the security of the early traders and cooperatives, who were still generally thought of as speculators. The police saw it as fairly unimportant that racketeers were taking money from such people, and this turning a blind eye of course allowed the rackets to grow rich. We may therefore question the idea that it is necessarily a weak state that allows mafias to proliferate (cf. the arguments in Volkov 1998). Rather, it seems that certain actions undertaken by the state, such as prohibition in America in the 1930s or the legalization of cooperatives in Russia, create niches that rackets can exploit. In Russia the government has subsequently hastened to declare war on the mafias, while leaving such niches untouched (for example, the inviolability of deputies has resulted in a new 'deputies' roof' for crime).

The police, for the most part, do battle against crime. But they are involved in many situations, like the market traders' tickets, in which it is difficult to tell what is allowable and what counts as corruption. So they fight identifiable enemies, the bandits who appear on the streets. In the absence of popularly legitimized state law, they may see this battle as a question of each individual officer's calling, or in more abstract terms as a fight of Good against Evil.[34] They are disheartened when their best efforts are undermined by 'bought' or frightened procurators, and even more when the government's laws are unclear or suddenly changed. Konstantinov (1996: 255) cites one policeman's view of the future as follows:

> The question goes back to property (*sobsvennost'*). While the property-owners are still undefined, strictly speaking we police are needed neither by the mafia nor by the state. What is going on is grabbing and division of everything that belongs to no-one. Law will only be needed when the property-owners have sucked it all dry and say: 'Enough!' Then we'll play by the rules.

Gangsters therefore may even have some general sympathy, even among the police, for their own sentiments about the racket, such as:

> I consider that people will require my services a hundred years from now; and a hundred years ago they needed them too. I'll have work and money independent of what political regime is in power. It may be necessary to break some law or other – that is in the blood. But it can be done either on the

> industrial plane (*na plane promyshlennosti*) or on the criminal one. Yes, I receive money from Petya, but Petya will never tell anyone and the police do not know. So on the criminal plane my activities do not exist (Marzeeva 1996).

What is interesting about this is the matter-of-fact slippage from one plane to another, from the criminal to the curiously-expressed idea that the racket is industrial (or productive of a living). This is similar to the switching between discursive planes noted earlier, when the criminal brigade conceptualized in terms of humdrum Soviet labour is alternatively seen as a force of trained and rapacious violence. These planes refer to the variability of attitudes, which is part of the floating cynicism that enables protection to appear as a choice between various equivalent roofs. In fact, the roof itself is a concept that, by its applicability to one and another context, constructs the mental 'stacking up' of homologous socio-political categories. It is not that the security firms, the criminal groups, and the police sections are in fact identical, though they may fulfill some of the same functions; but the wider socio-cultural attitudes to the state, and particular enveloping concepts such as the roof, encourage the view that they are; and this of course promotes their actual likeness.

Conclusion

When a state establishes, or transforms, itself primarily in terms of an economic rationale, before a constitutional or a legal one, it may happen that the law becomes something that is up for definition and appropriation. In this situation, the 'law' of the bandits enters the arena alongside that of the state, and it acquires a greater significance than the familiar notion of 'honour among thieves'. On the one hand, it becomes a technique or an instrument. On the other, it is socially objectified, so it comes to stand for a way of life and an ethical stance; it becomes a 'culture' to which others may be attracted or repelled. As a result, the mafias have something to sell. They sell not only their techniques of order and negotiation, as the rational choice theorists have argued, but also the whole social notion of themselves as the kind of people who are disciplined, orderly and subject to law.

However, given that everyone knows that the bandits' 'law' is not *the* law, why does it nevertheless have such a wide sphere of operation in Russia? Why is the enormous security industry closer in its practices to the gangsters than it is to the police? After all, in America there has also been a huge growth of private police in recent years, but practically all of them operate as approved complements to the police. In this comparison we can perhaps see what an answer for Russia might look like. In the USA arguably the rise of private policing is not the result of rising crime and the failure of the federal police, but of wider changes in society and the growth of 'mass private property', such as shopping malls or gated communities. The state police remain responsible for public space and 'keeping the peace', but private policing has grown to provide crime deterrence for the new mass private properties.[35] In Russia, the legal equivalent of mass private property is much wider. Many people think it amounts to all commercial property, and furthermore that commerce as such is clouded by illegitimacy ('The police should not guard private business! Do tax-payers pay the police so they should guard some stall or other?': Krom 1996). Thus Russian businessmen are placed by the popular imagination in a position resembling less that of the American mall-owner than that of a casino-owner or bookmaker, potentially vulnerable to police raids and hence also to bandit threats and extortions. Recall the Azerbaijani flower-seller: it was because he was also a drug-dealer that the bandit brigadier had such a hold over him. My argument here is in part a historical one. It is because Russian gangsters took hold of 'dubious' activities long ago, because they honed their techniques in the late Soviet ambience of patronage of the illegal shadow-economy, and because ordinary business is still popularly regarded with suspicion, that the private security firms emerging later were forced to compromise in a landscape that was mostly already carved up.

Pejovich (1997: 22–3) is right to see that the security firms and the mafias are essentially similar, in that they are both profit-seekers who have incentives to enforce rules that encourage the production of goods that people want (while the police must make do with enforcing state laws that strengthen the government's political power). However, as I have shown, the mafias paradoxically also have a punitive, predatory aspect to their 'law', deriving from their historical traditions as thieves as well as from requirements of internal control and external conflict. This predation can extend to 'irrationally' denying growth to firms. Gangs differ in this respect, just as they differ in the extent to which they adhere to the old thieves' 'understandings' or whether they have worked out new conventions for themselves. In either case *mafiosi* may (and do) infiltrate the state and elected institutions. But if they are to take part in what Volkov (1998) calls the reconstruction of the state, the regaining by the state of full control over the means of violence, they must acquire a new sense of law. For the bandits' 'law' is really aimed at regulating themselves, and fails utterly in imagination when faced with tasks such as general taxation and state services.[36] When people swear to adhere to the 'understandings' they are swearing to something that is quite limited ethically, but that nevertheless affects their whole life. This is why the gangsters themselves can never be simply vendors of protection. As Marzeeva observes (1996), the bandit ethos taken out into the ordinary world seems in the end to be built on fear, fear that others will treat you as you treat them, that your friends will betray you, women deceive you, your money be stolen. Such fear is very catching. What is so regrettable is that so many people now hold what started as the outlaws' view of life:

> 'I do not want my children to live in a *bespredel'noi* (without order, lawless) country. I myself do not like to break the law. But today in Russia you have to choose: if you try to make some money, you either have to defend yourself or you have to ask someone to protect you. If you are sure you are protected, you can be happy, – but if not, then your life is on borrowed time. Each new day may be your last . . .' (Konstantinov 1996: 282).

Notes

1. Inverted commas have been placed round 'law' when referring to the gangster's *zakon* partly to make the text clear for readers, and partly because the bandits' law did not have the paraphernalia of law as defined by professional lawyers (courts, prosecutors, established procedures, etc.). However, in an anthropological comparative sense this was as much law as any other kind.
2. Thus Konstantinov (1996: 250) writes of what he calls the 'cop's syndome'. According to one officer, this has two phases, the first when the cop sees any person as a potential criminal, and the second when bandits and thieves become more understandable, close and intimate than ordinary law-abiding people. In this second phase the cop begins to feel at home in the world of thieves. And where you feel at home it is easy to change roles, or to take on another role . . .
3. *Komsomol'skaya Pravda*, 9 Dec. 1997, p. 4.
4. UOP (*Upravleniye po bor'be s Organizovannoi Prestupnost'yu*) is the Directorate for fighting Organized Crime.
5. Handelman (1994: 25) notes that the early Bolsheviks made a point of recruiting criminals to their cause, and that the harsh discipline, secrecy and defiance of conventional society of the gangs also characterized the Bolshevik cells and eventually the Communist Party itself.
6. This opposition was strengthened by the waves of anti-revolutionaries, dispossessed factory owners and White sympathizers who joined the bandit ranks after 1919 (Rawlinson 1997: 37).

7. The term 'thief' (*vor*) was used metonymically to refer to all types of self-defined criminals.
8. A 'person' (*chelovek*, pl. 'people' *lyudy*) in criminal slang meant someone who had achieved the highest status category in the camps, namely that of *vor* (thief). Below this status was that of the *muzhiki* (peasants) and below them were the *chushki* (piglets) or *obizhenniye* (the hurt ones). Samoilov notes that within each of the three 'castes' the same triple ranking would occur, so that the *chushki* had their own 'thieves', 'peasants' and 'piglets' (Samoilov 1993: 35–7). Kabo (1993) also notes a triple ranking, though with different names.
9. Kabo (1993: 63–4) points to the tightly knit, disciplined and hierarchical nature of bandit society (similar to that of the Communist Party), the parallel between proceedings against 'bitches' and those against 'enemies of the people', and the fact that low-ranking bandits were expected to labor honestly and pay an income tax.
10. For example, Koretskii (1996: 182) recounts how a Thief in the Law was planning to hand over his ruling position in a camp, but was unable to pass it to the most suitable man, as the latter was disqualified by common knowledge that he had infringed the 'law' in the distant past.
11. The crime novel genre of course has its conventions, and realism is one of them. The wider Russian literary tradition of panoramic inclusiveness and huge casts of characters illustrating every social type is also evident here. Plot structures, hero and villain characteristics, etc. would be an interesting subject for research.
12. In Koretskii's novel *Anti-Killer* (1996: 156) a Thief in Law is attacked by a more traditional bandit for not respecting the law, and he replies, 'I have not broken the law, I have not appropriated the treasury, everyone knows that.'
13. Konstantinov (1996: 278). In some cases the gang may take over the running of the income-source (garages, casinos, prostitutes, etc.) entirely, thus becoming a producer and providing 'protection' to its own sub-section.
14. The cost of such protection with guards in 1993–4 was 20–30 per cent of the profits, and particularly greedy racketeers would demand 40 per cent. The guards are not held responsible in cases of car theft, burglary, or physical attacks, and Konstantinov comments that they really only provide protection against drunks and street hooligans (1996: 175).
15. For example, the St Petersburg Kazantsy were known for their inexplicable cruelty to the businessmen they gave a roof. This

surprised the Tambov gangsters, who said, 'They are completely "thawed-out"; they squeeze their own clients dry and won't let them expand.' But Konstantinov points out (1997: 296–7) that despite all their apparent over-violence, it would be wrong to judge the Kazantsy as lacking in all far-sightedness. It was they of all the gangs who had the strongest position among the law-protection organs of the city.

16. In 1996 in St Petersburg alone there were 468 security organizations and 191 bodyguard services officially registered. These firms employed 11,444 licensed agents, with an additional 1,500 other employees (Ivanov 1996).
17. The 'thawed-outs' have their linguistic place alongside 'cool ones', 'laid-back ones' (*zamorozhennyye*).
18. Varese also points out rightly that estimating a 'sensible', as opposed to a 'predatory' level of appropriation enables the supply of funds to continue regularly (1994: 257).
19. The New York State Organized Crime Force report (1997: 200) makes the interesting observation that Russian *émigré* crime organization in America is different, consisting of 'floating structures on an as-needed basis to enable them to carry out particular crimes'. The difference may well be explainable by the fact that the American Russians do not base their operations on protection rackets, but on crimes of deception, counterfeiting, confidence schemes and insurance fraud (1997: 185–9).
20. In this case, it is forbidden by the thieves' law for other gangs to take over their 'spots', although in practice this does happen, as can be understood from the rash of killings when famous bandits are released (Konstantinov 1996: 152).
21. At the present time (1996) the whole of Moscow and its surroundings is 'under' some fourteen gangs, and practically all businesses pay money to racketeers from the gangs (Pogonchenkov 1996, based on police sources).
22. Dunn (1997: 65) thus provides a different picture of Moscow from Pogonchenkov: there are around 150 gangs, of which 20 are relatively large and well-armed and 6 wield real power. The difference arises mainly from the criteria by which 'a gang' is defined, e.g. Pongonchenkov counts 'the Chechens' as one, while Dunn counts them as three gangs.
23. Handelman (1994: 29) writes that in the early 1990s there were around six hundred city-level bosses in Russia. Formally, these were equal, but some thirty senior leaders set general policy for the country's

entire criminal class at private councils. Within this group, in the late 1980s and early 1990s there was an even smaller core, the *Bratskii Krug* (Circle of Brothers) consisting of around seven leading Thieves in the Law. This seems an overly tidy account, given the evidence of turbulence from other sources. Konstantinov declared at the end of 1997 that although organized crime has grown during the 1990s it is in a state of 'feudal fragmentation', does not have a pyramidal structure for the country as a whole, and is not in fact as 'organized' as is imagined (*Komsomol'skaya Pravda*, 9 Dec. 1997, p. 4).

24. Even some of the currently largest gangs started in late Soviet times with 'protection' of gambling and deceitful games of luck, and moved through prostitution and the cooperatives and supply depots of the Gorbachev era, to commercial businesses in the present ('Investitsionnye' 1996: 34).
25. For example, a similar battle took place in Moscow in 1994 over the Allianz car showroom between a Slav gang and a Chechen gang (Dunn 1997: 68).
26. This can be seen from Hohnen's analysis (1997: 116–17) of the huge Gariunai market. Here only central trading places were judged worth paying for by traders. The racket took from $400 to $2,000 per place, according to the site, but did not bother with distant trading rows where traders made only minuscule profits.
27. The massive Togliatti factory is an example. Bandits have not succeeded in getting places on the board, but they take their toll from all purchasers (one car from each twenty ordered). One man attempted to defy them, the head of the Togliatti finance department, whose father was highly placed in the local procuracy. The bandits left this man alone, but attacked his *krysha* ('roof'): the procurator's car was machine-gunned in the main street of the city, and since then payment of the toll has been universal ('Investitsionnye' 1996: 36).
28. This possibility is discussed by Sacco (1995: 111–12), who suggests that mafia codes of honour have this function because members of gangs are hired on the basis of 'incomplete contracts', i.e. they are people chosen for idiosyncratic abilities to perform unforeseeable tasks for uncertain remuneration.
29. In 1990 Kumarin and around 70 of his confederates were arrested, and in 1993 many of the Tambovtsy still free were murdered when it was rumoured that Kumarin would shortly be set free (Konstantinov 1996: 152–3).
30. These bands may not have defined territories, but they have some notion of common economic resources: for example, it is necessary

to pay a redemption-fee, *vykup*, in order to leave the group (Koretskii 1996: 8–10).

31. Handelman (1994: 22–3) describes several ritualized initiations, for example swearing allegiance before a portrait of the boss in Stavropol, or the respectful visiting of the graves of the elders in Yekaterinburg in 1992.
32. It is used to pay lawyers' fees, bribe officials, and support Chechens serving sentences: Dunn 1997: 66.
33. The bandit 'Gorbatyi' said on his deathbed to Konstantinov, 'A strong criminal world, with harsh discipline and internal laws, is only possible in a strong country. But no-one wants a strong Russia these days . . .' (Konstantinov 1996: 87).
34. Commenting that 'bad and incomplete' law arouses nihilism and the wish to step beyond it, Konstantinov (1996: 272–4) cites a policeman who said that the meaning of his work was the same as the meaning of life. 'And that is the struggle of Good and Evil. This struggle goes on everywhere, including in the soul of each person. I believe in the Good. Evil cannot eternally triumph – life will stop it. In our country much Evil has accumulated. It is difficult to overcome. Difficult, but possible. We must not give in.'
35. *The Economist* 19 April 1997, pp. 25–6.
36. 'Why should I pay all these taxes for pensions?' said one bandit. 'Just give me three *babushki* (old women). I'll look after them. Then let me get on with my own life.'

References

Appadurai, Arjun (1986), *The Social Life of Things*, Cambridge: Cambridge University Press.

Baldaev, D.-D. S. (1989), unpublished drawings of prisoners' tattoos.

Some of Baldaev's drawings of life in the camps are published in the Hungarian journal *Beszélö*, 31 August 1991.

Berkutov, Viktor (1996), *Krysha: Russkiye Razborki*. Moscow: Martin Polina.

Chalidze, Valery (1977), *Criminal Russia: A Study of Crime in the Soviet Union*, trans. R. Falla. New York: Random House.

Dunn, Guy (1997), 'Major Mafia Gangs in Russia,' in Phil Williams (ed.), *Russian Organized Crime: A New Threat?* London: Frank Cass.

Handelman, Stephen (1994), *Comrade Criminal: The Theft of the Second Russian Revolution*. London: Michael Joseph.

Hohnen, Pernille (1997), 'A Market Out of Place? Remaking Economic, Social and Symbolic Boundaries in Post-Communist Lithuania', Ph.D. dissertation, University of Copenhagen.

'Investitsionnye proyekty rossiiskikh banditov', *Kommersant Daily*, 27 August 1996, pp. 34–6.

Ivanov, Andrei (1996), 'Chastnyye okhranniki: svoi sredi chuzhikh, chuzhiye sredi svoikh', *AiF-Peterburg*, no. 51 (174), p. 5.

Kabo, V. R. (1993), 'The Structure of the Camps and Archetypes of Consciousness', *Anthropology and Archaeology of Eurasia*, 1993–4, vol. 32, no. 3, pp. 59–69.

Konstantinov, Andrei (1996), *Banditskii Peterburg*. St Petersburg: Folio Press.

Koretskii, Danil (1996), *Anti-Killer*. Moscow: Eksmo.

Krom, Yelena (1996), 'Profi – eto khorosho trenirovannyi zombi', *Chas Pik*, no. 217 (722), 18 Dec. 1996, p. 10.

Marzeeva, Svetlana (1996), 'Reket zhil, reket zhiv, reket budet zhit', *Izvestiya*, 130, 17 July 1996, p. 5.

New York State Organized Crime Force (1997), 'An Analysis of Russian Emigré Crime in the Tri-State Region', in Phil Williams (ed.), *Russian Organized Crime: A New Threat?* London: Frank Cass.

Omel'chenko, Elena (1996), 'Young Women in Provincial Gang Culture: A Case Study of Ul'ianovsk', in H. Pilkington (ed.),*Gender, Generation and Identity in Contemporary Russia*. London and New York: Routledge.

Pejovich, Svetozar (1997), 'The Transition Process in an Arbitrary State: The Case for the Mafia', *IB Review*, 1, 1.

Pilkington, Hilary (1994), *Russia's Youth and Its Culture: A Nation's Constructors and Constructed*. London and New York: Routledge.

Pogonchenkov, Aleksandr (1996), 'Anatomiya kriminal'nogo mira', *Moskovskii Komsomolets*, 12 August 1996, p. 3.

Rawlinson, Patricia (1997), 'Russian Organized Crime: A Brief History', in Phil Williams (ed.), *Russian Organized Crime: A New Threat?* London: Frank Cass.

'Razborki v Irkutske: Irkutskaya Mafiya svodit schety s gruzinskoi gruppirovki', *Informpolis* No. 30 (174), 25 July 1996.

Ries, Nancy (1998), '"Honest Bandits" and "Warped People": Russian Narratives about Money, Corruption and Moral Decay', MS.

Sacco, Pier Luigi (1995), 'Discussion', in Gianluca Fiorentini and Sam Peltzman (eds), *The Economics of Organised Crime*. Cambridge: Cambridge University Press.

Samoilov, Lev (1993), 'Ethnography of the Camp', *Anthropology and Archaeology of Eurasia*, 1993–4, vol. 32, no. 3, pp. 32–58.

Shelley, Louise (1996), *Policing Soviet Society: The Evolution of State Control*. London and New York: Routledge.

—— (1997), 'Post-Soviet Organized Crime: A New Form of Authoritarianism', in Phil Williams (ed.), *Russian Organized Crime: A New Threat?* London: Frank Cass.

Smart, Alan (1988), 'The Informal Regulation of Illegal Economic Activities: Comparisons between the Squatter Property Market and Organized Crime', *International Journal of the Sociology of Law*, 16, pp. 91–101.

Solomon, Peter H. Jr. (1996), *Soviet Criminal Justice Under Stalin*. Cambridge: Cambridge University Press.

Vaksberg, Arkady (1991), *The Soviet Mafia*. London: Weidenfeld and Nicolson.

Varese, Frederico (1994), 'Is Sicily the Future of Russia? Private Protection and the Rise of the Russia Mafia', *Journal of European Sociology*, XXXV, pp. 224–58.

Verdery, Katherine (1996), *What Was Socialism and What Comes Next?* Princeton, NJ: Princeton University Press.

Volkov, Vadim (1998), 'The Monopoly of Legitimate Violence: Diffusion and Reconstruction of the Russia State, 1987–2001,' MS.

–8–

Neoliberalism, Environmentalism, and Scientific Knowledge: Redefining Use Rights in the Gulf of California Fisheries

Marcela Vásquez-León

Within the past decade, Mexico's traditional ruling party, the PRI (Party of Institutionalized Revolution), has been steadily losing its internal legitimacy *vis-à-vis* the social or 'reform' sector.[1] This is evidenced by such events as the recent Zapatista uprising and the civic rebellion in Chiapas (Harvey 1996) and by the unprecedented number of municipal elections won by the opposition in 1988 and 1994 (Regalado 1996). This crisis of legitimacy on the domestic front is partly a consequence of Mexico's current economic crisis, which extends back to 1982. On the one hand, the economic downturn has been slowly eroding the material capacity of the system required to co-opt different sectors of its population, weakening the party's basis for social control. On the other hand, the economic collapse has driven the state to embrace a neoliberal ideology and to reject many of the postrevolutionary tenets that gave legitimacy to the party since the 1917 Constitution (Powell 1996).

As a prerequisite for gaining acceptance as a fully integrated partner in the global economic order, Mexico has privatized vital sectors of the economy and signed the North American Free Trade Agreement (NAFTA) with the US and Canada (Weintraub 1990). It has also addressed the global environmental crisis by establishing important natural areas as biosphere reserves and furthering the cause of 'conservation and development' through the closure of common property resources such as forests and marine regions (Wexler and Bray 1996). While the state simultaneously appeals to its internal private constituents, the free market, and environmentalism in today's 'rural modernization' strategies, the traditional reform sector is facing a global economy in which it has been, for the first time, left on its own to defend its economic and political interests (Stanford 1994; Harvey 1996).

In this chapter I examine how current global processes of market liberalization, privatization, and environmentalism are impacting state law and how these processes are translated by the state to impact local arenas (Merry 1992). I look at the particular case of the shrimp fishery in the Gulf of California and argue that, through the creation of *bad* laws,[2] the state is manipulating these global themes to renew its forms of social control at the local level. More specifically, by issuing bad laws the state is fomenting the growth of the informal economy, thereby rendering an increasingly large proportion of the population illegal actors, vulnerable to the selective enforcement of regulations and dependent on the benevolence of local bureaucrats.

I further argue that the state is able to justify its adoption of bad laws through the apparently objective knowledge of scientific discourse. By doing this, the state is able to create images of impartiality and disassociate itself from the current problems. What the state is in fact doing is orchestrating a situation of increased inequality in which a small but influential group of private entrepreneurs have acquired the legal right to secure the left-over benefits of a rapidly diminishing resource.

The Mexican fisheries example offers a particularly interesting case where illegality is not the result of state absence, as has been documented for other cases (i.e. Smart 1988; Thoumi 1995; Leeds 1996), but of the state's undue regulatory intervention. Historically, the state has not only designed, implemented, and enforced regulations, but through the illegal use of state power (i.e. corruption through bribery and extortion) state personnel have been able to benefit from the existence of illegal networks. It is also an example of how laws promoted by a power above the state – i.e. international lending institutions and the global forces of environmentalism – that attempt to redefine access to common property resources may actually promote illegal behavior and, at the same time, lead to a vast increase in state and class power.

I begin the chapter by briefly reviewing the literature on the Mexican political system and its links to corruption. I then apply this framework of analysis to the Gulf of California fisheries in an attempt, first to decipher the historical role of the state in fomenting the development of predatory activities; second, to look at the impact of current global processes on the design of laws at the state level; and third, to examine how local bureaucracies interact with rule-breakers and how current global processes affect and change their participation in illegal networks.

The Structure of the Mexican State and its Links to Corruption

The history of development of the shrimp industry in the Gulf of California is a reflection of larger national processes that have occurred within Mexico since the drafting of the Constitution of 1917. From that time on, the state adopted a strong and protectionist role, directing the course of events towards progress and development. It became the owner and ultimate protector of the nation's rich natural resource base, and attempted to control the assignment of rights to natural resources by imposing administrative and territorial hierarchies. Through the creation of state-owned enterprises the state secured control over a large proportion of gains stemming from the exploitation, processing and marketing of commercially valuable resources (L. Lomnitz 1988). It also established a network of public research institutes throughout the country in order to obtain the scientific backing to regulate resource use directly. Not surprisingly, the way natural resources have been administered in Mexico reflects to a substantial degree the changing national interests as well as the general organizational characteristics of the state. A brief analysis of the latter is useful in attempting to understand the role of the state in first fomenting the emergence and persistence of complex illegal networks in the Gulf of California shrimp fishery, and second, in encouraging local enforcement agents and fishery officials, as representatives of the state, to benefit from those networks through the illegal, but informally sanctioned, use of state power.

The first organizational characteristic of the Mexican state is its extreme centralization of political power. Virtually all government and party decisions 'from the most mundane to the most important come out of the executive in Mexico City' (Morris 1991: 25); even local and regional party organizations are practically powerless. Access to state resources at local and regional levels is restricted to a limited number of public institutions that control segments of strategic resources. This has prompted the emergence of informal hierarchical networks consisting of brokers in the effort to capture public and private resources (De La Peña 1989; Greenberg 1990).

A second characteristic of the Mexican state is the corporatist structuring of interest representation. The ruling party has traditionally been formed by sectors that depend on formally sanctioned organizations – until recently, for example, the peasant sector had to be organized in *ejidos* (agrarian reform cooperative and collective farms) in order to acquire collective use rights to the land. By incorporating many of the lower sectors into the formal structure of the revolutionary party through such dependent organizations, the state has been able to control their internal activities. These lower organizations must maintain good relations with state bureaucracies in order to receive support from the corporate structure. Groups external to the official party, such as the private sector, are required to organize in functionally specific organizations sanctioned by the state. Even though the private sector has had more autonomy, it must also conform to the dominant corporatist framework of the system (see L. Lomnitz and Pérez-Lizaur 1987). Given governmental intervention in regulating and providing subsidies to the private sector, maintaining good relations with state bureaucracies has been critical to the success of their business enterprises. Outside this formal structure of control is the informal sector, which includes all those who do not have any political, economic, or legal guarantees within the system. They must rely on social relations based on scarcity and inequality in order to obtain resources. This has allowed both state and private capital to benefit from the informal sector by manipulating the 'marginality' of the latter (L. Lomnitz 1988; Vélez-Ibáñez 1988).

A third characteristic of the Mexican state is the electoral dominance of the PRI, which has controlled national, regional, and local level politics since its formation in 1929. The president of the republic basically appoints and removes public officials at will (Morris 1991: 28). One of the reasons this system has existed successfully for so long is that, as Lomnitz and Adler point out,

> The party encompasses a great diversity of groups and organizations which circle around leaders of different ideologies and interests. The only way to guarantee even the mere hope that each of the groups represented by the PRI finds a place in the government has been through the principle of no re-election in conjunction with an extremely presidentialist system: Mexican presidentialism guarantees that a large number of posts change hands every six-year presidential term (C. Lomnitz and Adler 1990: 47 my translation).

While the PRI has representatives at all levels of government, employees of the government are dependent on their good standing in the party or among upper-level officials for any opportunities of mobility.

The circulation of resources within this very centralized, hierarchical and corporatist structure is largely controlled by vertical patron–client relationships through which corruption and illegality have become an institutionalized component (Morris 1991). Several scholars have used the metaphor of a pyramid to describe Mexican society.[3] Within this pyramid, access to resources is dependent upon brokers and the power of a broker increases as his/her ability to control resources expands. Patron–client relations are a critical linkage of populations to the larger national structure, and representation within the system is the product of negotiation between diverse social groups (Vélez-Ibáñez 1983; Greenberg 1990). In fact, as C. Lomnitz and Adler (1990) note, *negotiations are so critical that they take precedence over both individual sovereignty and the law.* In this system, loyalty is exchanged for access to resources and protection. Needless to say, the exchange is based on relations of dominance and subservience (De La Peña 1989). The system works because, as Carlos and Anderson point out: 'it allows the state to trade off its resources for political obedience' (1981: 185).

Flexibility is introduced into this rigid organization through horizontal class relations. These are symmetrical relationships not based on power, but on mutual trust (Vélez-Ibáñez 1983). Brokers in one sector have friends or relatives who are brokers in another sector (L. Lomnitz 1987: 528), and networks of horizontal elite relationships ensure the maintenance and expansion of elite control. For populations in the informal sector, horizontal networks of exchange offer protection against economic and political uncertainty through, in many cases, the creation of illegal networks.

Integrating Coastal Communities to the National Structure: The Shrimp Industry

Shrimp from the Gulf of California have been one of Mexico's most important foreign exchange earners. In fact, in the 1970s shrimp constituted the third most important export product, after oil and coffee (Hernández Fujigaki 1988). At that time, the Gulf of California was producing more than 50 per cent of Mexico's total exports and was exporting the highest-quality shrimp (*Penaeus stylirostris* or blue shrimp) to the United States. Central government authority played a key role in the development of this valuable industry. The state controlled not only the export market, but also the organization of labor and all matters concerning legislation and the management of the fishery.

Shrimping in the region has traditionally been performed by two sectors. The offshore industrialized sector specializes in the harvesting of shrimp from October to May/June. This sector uses highly mechanized and energy-dependent trawlers that range from sixty-five to eighty feet and use 360 to 649 hp engines. The small-scale sector is characterized by multi-species fishing and by the use of 24-foot fiberglass vessels (*pangas*) with outboard motors of 45 to 75 hp. The shrimp season for this sector lasts from September to December. Some fishermen, however, switch to other fisheries after the peak of the season; others shrimp illegally throughout the year (see Vásquez-León and McGuire 1993).

Because penaeid shrimp can be exploited sequentially at various stages of their life cycle, the fishery lends itself to a great deal of competition between different types of users. Shrimp spawn at sea; once the post-larval stage is reached they migrate inshore to nursery grounds found in estuaries. As shrimp grow and become sub-adults they migrate massively towards the spawning grounds offshore. During this process of migration the resource can be intercepted by the small-scale sector. Once the schools of shrimp reach areas deeper than 10–12 fathoms they can only be captured by offshore trawlers. It is thus assumed that catches for the offshore sector are directly affected by the small-scale sector's fishing capacity. Even though the competition between the two sectors has always been part of the fishery, only recently, with shrimp scarcity and privatization of the industry, has the conflict escalated to the point where the state has resorted to a variety of legislative tactics and even violence to get rid of small-scale fishermen.

There has also been a great deal of competition between private and social interests, fostered largely by contradictory government policies. One of the key contradictions and sources of corruption is a reflection of the state's dominant role and its long-standing dilemma of equity vs. efficiency.[4] In the case of the fisheries the fundamental predicament has been one of commitment to equity under a cooperative structure versus commitment to aggregate national economic growth under a system of private investment. These apparently irreconcilable goals take the form of a central opposition in fisheries policy, which has led to uncertainty as to who actually has rights to the resource. This, as is discussed below, has been another contributing factor to the development of illegal activity as the only way to assert rights and access to the resource.

At some periods, from the 1930s through the 1950s, the state fostered and emphasized the collective use of shrimp resources. It first set up cooperatives and gave them exclusive exploitation rights over the resource. Cooperatives, in turn, were legally required to affiliate to regional federations and were incorporated at a national level through the *Confederación Nacional de Cooperativas* (National Cooperative Federation, or CNC) which belonged to the *Confederación Nacional de Organizaciones Populares* (National Confederation of Popular Organizations, or CNOP).

Through these different organizations the state integrated coastal fishing populations within its corporate structure of interest representation. At the local level this meant that cooperatives would never become autonomous organizations. In addition, since cooperatives provided the only legal avenue to exploit commercially valuable species, the legislation created the first form of illegality in the fishing industry: unaffiliated fishermen, known as *pescadores libres*, became the informal sector.

Up to the 1950s cooperative organization flourished under the tutelage of the state. The industry expanded (Magallón Barajas 1987), public credit institutions were established, and regional federations were allowed to manage state-owned packing and freezing plants. Even though the private sector was excluded from capturing the resource, the state provided major incentives for private capital participation. Through 'contracts of association' *armadores* (individual owners of trawlers and fishing equipment) rented boats, equipment, and processing facilities to cooperatives (Hernández Fujigaki 1988). The state also invested in the development of communication and transportation networks, ports, and fishing infrastructure, which directly benefited private investors.

Through the 1960s, as shrimp became an economically important commodity, the state underscored its commitment to aggregate national economic growth by allowing private investors to increase their share of the profits. At this time the *Cámara Nacional de la Industria Pesquera* (National Chamber of Commerce of the Fishing Industry, or CANAINPES) was formed to represent the interests of *industriales* (industrial investors in the shrimp, sardine and tuna enterprises) at the state level and expand their lobbying power. The desire for export earnings in the international shrimp market prompted continuous support for the private sector (Miller 1990: 87). The 'contracts of association' became increasingly beneficial to private investors (Mexican and foreign), who were obtaining a share of the catch of up to 60 per cent and owned all packaging and freezing operations (Mendoza Martínez 1985). Conflict between *armadores* and cooperative leaders led to the beginning of *guaterismo*, the sale of shrimp in the black market, where cooperatives would surreptitiously sell part of their catch through unofficial channels, thus reducing total official catch and illegally increasing their share of the profits.

By the beginning of the 1970s Mexico's economy started to slow down. The state began to borrow massively in world capital markets as government policies shifted away from the private sector to state intervention and the expansion of public spending.[5] In the shrimp industry government involvement expanded through the consolidation of all state-owned enterprises and participation in marketing through the parastatal Ocean

Garden. The company acquired monopsony control over export shrimp, buying from cooperatives at below market figures. During the 1970s the shrimp industry in the Gulf of California is described by a local analyst as follows: 'This is the period of the official history of the fishery when mismanagement and waste really began; they announced grandiose, extravagant and unrealistic programs that would supposedly turn our country into the world's leading [first] producer of marine resources' (Mendoza Martínez 1985: 43).

Despite a balance-of-payments crisis in 1976 (Lustig 1992), the post-1976 administrations continued the expansion of state intervention in the industry. The *Banco Nacional Pesquero y Portuario* (National Fishing and Harbor Bank, or BANPESCA) was created to provide credit to the private, public, and cooperative sectors; private sector involvement was encouraged through the subsidization of inputs and the relaxation of entry restrictions;[6] and cooperatives increasingly became a source of organized labor: according to a local journalist 'limited to charging 4 to 8 pesos per kilo of shrimp in order to issue the legal papers required for its transportation and marketing . . . the cooperative societies are only providing the legal trademark, while private investors are simply paying production costs and salaries to fishermen' (Cortés Campo 1977).

Shrimp trawler fleets throughout the Gulf and Pacific littoral grew substantially in the 1970s (Fig. 8.1 depicts the sharp growth of the offshore sector in the Gulf's largest port) and the number of small-scale fishermen in the formal and informal sectors more than doubled. The latter brought with them new technologies and the use of outboard motors that allowed them to venture into deeper waters and substantially increase their catches.

Corruption within the cooperative structure became widespread. An elite group of cooperative leaders had already formed. Through *caciquismo*[7] (political-economic bossism) individual politicians, representatives of the PRI, started running cooperatives for personal profit and political gain. The most masterful *caciques* (bosses),[8] who by this time had established themselves firmly in power, were able to maintain control as cooperative leaders by appointing *amigos de confianza* (trusted friends) and relatives as head of cooperatives. They received support not only from the official structure and the PRI, but also from the communities. In exchange for electoral votes, *caciques* used a large proportion of the funds collected from the cooperatives to assist in community development programs. Local *caciques* also received support from high officials from the *Confederacion Nacional de Cooperativas,* who, in exchange for some of the benefits obtained from cooperatives, refused to recognize the legitimacy of democratically elected cooperative leaders.

Guaterismo became more of a problem when fishermen started to use it as a way to protest against corruption within the cooperative structure (Breton and López Estrada 1989). The practice became common. In the words of a local analyst, it was 'almost a law which threatens to ruin the industry . . . the first 500 kilos caught are sold immediately, and the benefits are distributed among the crew . . . the captain that does not participate will have difficulties finding a crew for the following trip' (Mendoza Martínez 1985).

By this time problems stemming from government policies that encouraged the seemingly unrestricted growth of the industry began to surface. The overcapitalization of the fleet led to overexploitation of shrimp stocks and a sharp decline in profits. This prompted the nationalization of the industry in 1981. Through credit from BANPESCA, cooperatives were 'required to purchase virtually everything offered for sale, including trawlers and equipment that were obsolete or in need of expensive maintenance and repair' (Miller 1990: 88).

In an attempt to redistribute benefits from shrimping, shrimp cooperatives were divided. Those having access to interior waters (rivers, estuaries and bays) would not be permitted to fish in the open sea, and those with trawlers were not allowed in interior waters (Miller 1990).

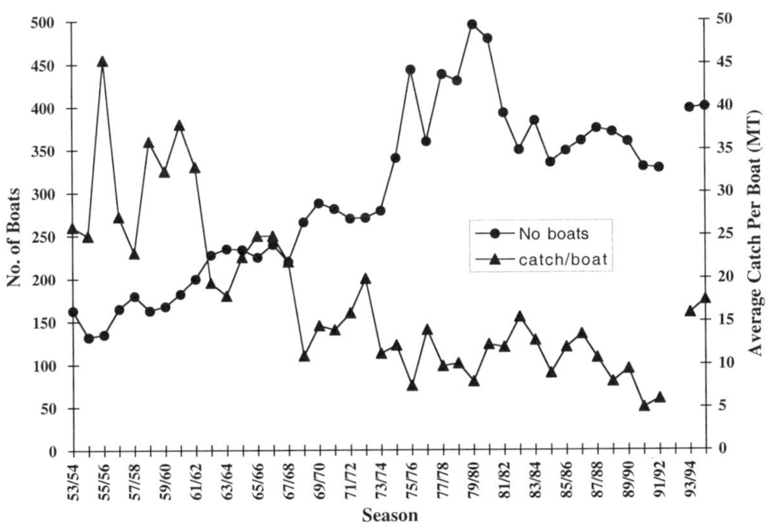

Sources: Magallon-Barajas 1987; CRIP Sonora

Figure 8.1 Number of shrimp trawlers and average catch per boat: Guaymas, 1953–1995

What is significant about this legislation is that it increased the fragmentation of the institutions, protecting offshore cooperatives from competition with their small-scale counterparts. It also increased the possibility of illegal activity. These issues were to become of crucial importance as shrimp resources became scarce.

In 1982 Mexico's economy went into a deep recession and, like most of Latin America, into a debt crisis. Under pressure from international lending institutions, the state started to cut public investment. The fishing industry was particularly hard hit. By the mid-1980s shrimp processing and freezing plants were closed or relocated (Hernández Fujigaki 1988). Cooperatives were forced to turn over their catch to Ocean Garden and future credit became conditional on selling to the parastatal (Miller 1990). In addition, the sale of Mexican shrimp on the international market stagnated, resulting in a significant decline of the industry's relative importance to the economy.[9] This resulted in further economic pressures on cooperatives and, as cooperatives became less and less responsive to fishermen, the volume of shrimp sold in the black market increased. In the small-scale sector the number of fishermen in the informal sector also increased as many preferred to shrimp on their own or under a *guatero* (black market intermediary). The effect of economic decline on local economies also led to the proliferation of illegal estuarine shrimping among non-fisherfolk.

Caciquismo continued to define cooperative organization, and high officials issued credit not on the basis of a cooperative's ability to pay, but depending on the willingness of a cooperative to accept a leader chosen by local *caciques*. Corruption at every level could be sustained while production was good; but when the bad seasons came, the system began to collapse.

By the end of the 1980s cooperatives were on the verge of bankruptcy, BANPESCA ceased operations, and shrimp catches were rapidly declining. The state disassociated itself from the structure of corruption that it had created by allowing formal accusations of mismanagement of funds, extortion, and corruption against regional federations to surface. This provided the opportunity for the re-emergence of the discourse of privatization. Private banks started to confiscate boats and auction them to private investors. By 1992 all the federations of cooperatives throughout the Pacific had been disenfranchised and both the small-scale and offshore fishermen lost political representation and negotiating power *vis-à-vis* financial institutions, the private sector, and the state.

To encourage the privatization of an almost bankrupt industry, the state has had to intervene in significant ways. Private investors have received substantial benefits in the form of subsidies (i.e. a 40 per cent discount in diesel prices), they were able to purchase boats and equipment at below market prices, and, perhaps most importantly, they have been allowed to exert considerable influence in the management of the fishery.[10]

As is discussed below, after 1991 new laws were enacted and enforcement of existing regulations was enhanced with the objectives of allowing the private sector to gain access to enough product to make shrimping an economically viable enterprise, and of limiting the legal access of small-scale fishermen to the fishery. Let us recall that the two sectors operate sequentially at various phases of the life cycle of shrimp. The regulations have affected the small-scale sector, where cooperative organization continues to provide the only legal means of exploiting and marketing shrimp, to such an extent that privatization has meant an open threat to their status as shrimpers. Virtually everything that they do now is considered illegal.

As the process of privatization unfolded in the shrimp industry, and elsewhere in the Mexican economy, NAFTA was being negotiated. Dependent upon the signing of NAFTA was Mexico's need to show that it was a nation concerned about environmental protection. This commitment to environmentalism was demonstrated through the establishment of a series of biosphere reserves around the country. The Gulf of California became a prominent target for conservation, where six protected areas have been established since 1992.[11] The proposal to close several areas to fishing has added an extra source of conflict in coastal communities, as the scope of regulations and of what is defined as illegal have expanded.

Environmentalism has not had much effect on the newly privatized offshore sector. In fact, it may have helped private investors, as it facilitated the passing of NAFTA. As will be discussed below, despite stated concerns with conservation, the Mexican state has failed to respond to environmental degradation in other than a token fashion. The measures to deal with the problems are not only far removed from the local realities of economic uncertainty and need, but are insufficient and arbitrary. As with privatization, small-scale fishermen are also suffering the brunt of conservation efforts.

In the 1990s, illegal activity continues to be an integral part of the shrimp industry, although there are new variants. While the power of local *caciques* has certainly diminished, apparently discontented and unemployed fishermen and perhaps the *caciques* themselves have now turned to a new form of illegal activity, piracy. Every season since 1992 there are accounts of trawlers being raided by *barcos piratas* (pirate ships), which take the shrimp, leaving the crew tied up or, in a few occasions, inside the cold room. In the small-scale sector fishermen have not remained passive. Instead, they have developed and strengthened already existing illegal networks – made up of fishermen, cooperatives, *guateros*, and fishery officials – through which a wide range of illegal activity takes place: a black market, the use of illegal gear, entry violations, infringements of areal and seasonal closures, and open political defiance. Although the nature of these networks has been discussed elsewhere (Vásquez-León 1994), a brief description of one of the activities will illustrate the point. A large number of small-scale fishermen shrimp offshore during the closed season. Since they use an illegal trawling net called *chango*, they are called *changueros. Changueros* can be organized around a specific *guatero*, receiving protection in exchange for their catch. *Guateros*, in turn, have already developed strong ties with enforcement agents. Thus for a certain monthly 'fee', fishery inspectors at various levels will ignore any illegal activity from explicitly organized *changueros*. *Guateros* also cooperate with enforcers to catch independent *changueros*, ironically contributing to the effort to diminish illegal activity.

The Role of Science in the Creation of Bad Laws

Shrimp monitoring and management are an integral component of the fisheries bureaucracy and fall within the state's highly centralized and hierarchical structural organization. Since the shrimp industry started, state policies and regulations have been carefully framed under the endorsement of shrimp scientists. These, as part of the formal fisheries bureaucracy, are involved in a system that requires a certain degree of compliance and agreement with larger government agendas. Thus the basic assumptions under which biologists have issued management recommendations and the recommendations themselves are transformed and translated as they go up what could be called the fisheries pyramid to reflect larger state objectives. These objectives are, in turn, legitimized by scientific discourse.

Shrimp in Mexico, as in most other countries in the world, have been managed under the guidelines of FAO shrimp scientists (McGuire 1991). They have four basic assumptions that frame management recommendations: first, the biotic potential of shrimp is so great that the possibility of overexploitation can be discounted (Chávez and Lluch 1971); second, population recruitment is not affected by changes in adult stock size due to fishing; third, the change in the size of shrimp stocks from year to year is a direct function of environmental conditions and the progressive deterioration of estuarine areas as a result of human activities; and fourth, while fishing effort offshore does not affect the reproductive capacity of a population (spawning adults), fishing effort in the estuarine phase[12] is assumed to have an effect on population recruitment (García and Le Reste 1981).

Based on the above assumptions, which have not gone unchallenged by shrimp scientists (see McGuire 1991; Penn and Caputti 1986), the following basic policies have characterized the management of the fishery. First, there has been no visible attempt to limit fishing effort on adult stocks; instead, shrimp scientists actually endorsed the policy of over-expansion that led to the near-collapse of stocks. Second, nursing grounds have been designated as protected areas where no shrimping is allowed. And third, two *vedas* (closed seasons) have been implemented for each sector. The *veda* for the inshore sector has been designed to regulate age at first capture and protect the growth of juveniles (Rodríguez de la Cruz 1981). The objectives of the *veda* for the offshore sector have changed over the years. At one point, it was designed to protect the resource after it had spawned; now it also aims at protecting spawning adults. In practice, 'the political pressures on managers from an industry as valuable as shrimp have been decisive in the determination of the dates for the *vedas*' (Chapa Saldaña *et al.* 1968: 360). Basically, when shrimp catches decline the *vedas* are manipulated to favor the offshore sector.

These not-so-clear assumptions and management objectives have been used to attribute 'scientifically' the decline in yields for the offshore sector to small-scale shrimpers, who are accused of reducing the reproductive potential of the stock by fishing sub-adults. Science, then, has been instrumental in providing a degree of legitimacy to the privatization process and the resulting proliferation of bad laws that have been issued since the process began. These laws, issued by the Fisheries Ministry in 1991 (Secretaría de Pesca 1991), directly limit the small-scale sector's capacity while allowing the private sector to gain access to enough product to make shrimping an economically viable enterprise.

For example, in the small-scale sector motors with horsepowers (hp) of above 55 can be used only if they have been bought and registered with the *Delegación Federal de Pesca* (Federal Fishing Agency) before 1991; most fishermen use 75 hp motors. The most widely used shrimping net has been banned, and the only nets authorized for shrimping lack selectivity, capture juveniles, and decrease catches considerably. Small-scale fishermen can only shrimp between zero and five fathoms, although they have the capability of fishing at twelve fathoms. If these regulations were to be followed they would increase costs of production, significantly reduce the mobility of fishermen, make travel to distant bays an extremely risky undertaking, increase the capture of sub-adults, and substantially decrease catches and profits. None of these regulations protect the fishery, and their violation is seen as socially legitimate by fishermen and even local bureaucrats and scientists (see Vásquez-León and McGuire 1993).

The offshore sector was also subjected to new regulations. Shrimping is prohibited between zero and five fathoms – apparently revising a previous restriction to over ten fathoms and, thus, actually extending their fishing territory. There were no other regulations that in any way modified trawling practices; instead, it is stated that 'the capacity of shrimp trawlers will not be in any way reduced or modified' (Secretaria de Pesca 1991).

In the areas that have been established as biosphere reserves regulations to limit effort have been ambiguous and the process is still under negotiation. For example, in the apparently final management plan for the Upper Gulf of California and Colorado River Delta Biosphere Reserve (established in 1993), the only restrictions have been placed on the small-scale sector. They cannot fish in what are called nuclear zones. These are zones near the delta that have been defined as fragile, but that have always been important fishing grounds for small-scale fishermen. It is suggested that small-scale fishermen stop fishing commercially and join in the development of eco-tourism as an alternative source of income. The process in the biosphere reserve indicates a pattern similar to that in the shrimp fishery as a whole (see McGuire and Greenberg 1993).

The Fisheries Bureaucracy and the Offenders: On Bad Laws and Good Laws that Turn Bad

To understand how scientific assumptions and recommendations become distorted to serve specific interests as they flow through the system, it is important to look briefly at the fisheries bureaucracy and the role of local-level bureaucrats as sometimes legal and sometimes illegal predators. Fisheries management is characterized by a highly centralized and rigid structure controlled from the top. Prior to 1994 the Fisheries Ministry (SEPESCA) was at the top of what can be considered the pyramid of the government's fisheries bureaucracy.[13] Under SEPESCA is the *Instituto Nacional de la Pesca* (National Fisheries Institute, or INP). The INP, from its central offices in Mexico City, controls all matters concerning research, law, and regulatory enforcement. This is done through regional delegations that implement and enforce national regulations at the local level, and *Centros Regionales de Investigación Pesquera* (Regional Fisheries Research Centers, or CRIPs) located in coastal states. CRIPs are in charge of monitoring particular species, advising central offices as to the need for areal or seasonal closures, and providing the scientific backing for the establishment of legislation. Their main objective, which may differ from larger state objectives, is to determine the equilibrium level of effort that can sustain commercially valuable stocks within the region that they monitor.

Despite its 'democratic' façade, this process leaves little margin for local-level intervention. Legislation and general management of the fishery, regardless of advice provided by local scientists, is done either at the national level or for the entire Pacific coast. At the local level, this has led to a perception of the illegitimacy of the larger system of rule-making and a questioning of the legitimacy of scientific assumptions, the intent of regulations, and the impartiality with which these regulations are implemented. These perceptions, shared by local resource users, and, up to a certain extent, local scientists and enforcement agents, have resulted in open avoidance of regulations, as discussed above, and selective enforcement by local bureaucrats.

The Local Scientists

Fishery biologists are often blamed by their counterparts in the regional fisheries agency and by resource users for the creation of bad laws or the unfair implementation of good laws. For example, fishermen blame local scientists for the manipulation of the closed season:

> scientists have purposely ignored the effect of tides on catchability. The best two ebb tides when all the shrimp come out of the bay going offshore are occurring before the season opens, or just as inspectors from Mexico City happen to visit. We end up having to stay in the bay. And this is no coincidence, they know well what they are doing, they are just being bought by the Fisheries Ministry and the *armadores* (equipment owners) (interview with a fisherman 1992).

Scientists take the blame because it is an implicit component of their jobs – loyalty is exchanged with *armadores* and higher fisheries officials for a sense of security. They have managed to get a job and they know that if they behave they will be able to keep it. Maybe, if they play their cards right, they will even get a promotion, a better salary to keep up with inflation and perhaps they may even one day save enough money to buy a car. But more important than a salary, their job comes with significant benefits. They can become homeowners in one of the government housing complexes, with no down payment and very low mortgage rates. They also get health insurance and the possibility of applying for government grants in order to further their education. In addition, especially among the younger researchers, there is always the belief that their advice, although not always taken, provides the potential for good management. Once in a while they are able to intervene in favor of the resources and the ecosystem that they are monitoring.

Nevertheless they remain in a bind. They do not agree with government policies, yet they have to support them. As one of the shrimp researchers told me, 'I cannot be neutral, nor present real results; I have to support the system.' They are concerned about resources, but they have to yield to the *armadores* and *industriales* (industrial trawler owners) who, after all, provide generous economic contributions that allow investigators to do research.[14]

With privatization CRIP directors are confronted with difficult dilemmas. They have to defend decisions taken in Mexico City that often contradict recommendations made by their group of scientists. When decisions are too controversial at the local level, they must, through the media, provide the necessary scientific justifications. While in the field, I was able to witness one such occasion. At one point, accusations against the private sector were mounting. It was argued that they were endangering sardine stocks by illegally capturing juveniles. Private owners denied the accusations, arguing that what they were doing was capturing a new species of sardine, the *sardina enana* or midget sardine. Thus, the *industriales* claimed, the traditional sardine could now be considered as the *sardina gigante* or giant sardine. The public wanted to know if there were any scientific basis for such allegations, so cameras from Telemundo (a Mexican television network) went to interview the regional CRIP director. He ended up backing the private investors, although he knew that their excuse was preposterous. Through his giving scientific backing to their allegations, the conduct of the private investors was converted from illegal behavior – catching juveniles – to legal behavior – catching a 'new' species of sardine. This particular director resigned soon after. Even though he had an assured future at the fisheries ministry – by the age of 22 he was already regional director of the CRIP – he did not allow himself to be co-opted by the system.

The Enforcement Agents

Local-level administrators and enforcement agents at the delegation of the INP also play an important role within the pyramid. Unlike CRIP researchers, enforcement agents can be looked at as local brokers. They deal directly with resource users, acting in the name of the state, and at the same time are well acquainted with the local socio-economic context in which regulations are to be enforced. Even though one of their main functions is to enforce regulations, they benefit substantially from bending the law and providing the mechanisms *para enderezar lo chueco*, to legalize what is illegal (literally 'to straighten out that which is twisted'). They also promote the interests of the state; it would appear as if one of their mandates was to keep the system of corruption functional under state supervision. In addition, they lend flexibility to an otherwise strict hierarchical structure, allowing communities to make a living from shrimp resources. Unlike CRIP researchers, enforcement agents are also freer to complain about unfair regulations, to recognize the social legitimacy granted to some of the violations, and to dissociate themselves from policy decisions.

Local administrators bend the law partly because of the direct benefits obtained in the form of *mordidas* (literally 'bites', a payment in exchange for overlooking violations), and, in the past, partly as a result of pressure from small-scale cooperatives, which, through the regional federation, had a degree of bargaining power. A salary insufficient to support a family (US $300 per month in 1992) certainly induces inspectors to accept or demand *mordidas* from individual violators. In fact, *mordidas* have been so common that they are simply part of the transaction costs calculated by fishermen, the cooperatives, or the *guateros*. Access to shrimp for small-scale fishermen is largely controlled by vertical networks of exchange where informal arrangements, *arreglos*, among *guateros* and local enforcement agents are always possible.

When the federations of cooperatives were still in operation, *mordidas* in the form of cash or shrimp were often exchanged for 'favors' such as lax enforcement of the law that prohibits small-scale fishermen from shrimping off-shore, informal permits given to cooperatives to start the season early, or the legalization of large quantities of black market shrimp for offshore cooperatives. In exchange, higher officials obtained bribes in the form of gifts, donations, or cash. There is no question that *arreglos* prevailed over any attempt to enforce regulations. *Arreglos* were overlooked by higher levels of authority in Mexico City, and served to placate the cooperatives, the fishermen, and the low-paid officials. In addition, payoffs to authorities outside the fisheries bureaucracy were not uncommon. For example, if a cooperative did not want to pay taxes, it only had to give money to the federation, and the federation would in turn give a *mordida* to state officials so that the taxes would be disregarded.

An additional incentive for inspectors to accept bribes is that they know that they are on the job only temporarily. They openly admit that being an inspector is an opportunity not to be wasted, probably one of the few times in their lives when they will be able to make money. They know that when the regional fisheries delegation changes its executive, at the end of every six-year presidential term, all the inspectors also change. From being legal predators in the eyes of the state, they become private citizens with no more power than that of any fisherman. Being a conscientious and efficient inspector has nothing to do with keeping the job.

The state has basically followed a policy of toleration that allows illegal activity to persist. Black market activity, for example, is widespread, yet there is selective enforcement. Even if the state only made figurative efforts to achieve control, maintaining the illegality of the activities has provided considerable benefits. Strict regulatory enforcement, for instance, would have amounted to substantial costs.[15] The Fisheries Ministry does not have enough financial resources to sustain the high level of enforcement required, nor does it provide enough incentives to officials in charge to avoid instances of corruption. There are only eleven inspection offices throughout the state, which assign from one to four inspectors per community along the entire coast. Inspectors require the cooperation of the local navy, military, and *capitanía de puerto* (harbor master), and of the federal police, none of whom are specifically trained to do the enforcement job. By allowing involvement of local agents in illegal activity the state does not have to increase the budget assigned to regional delegations; instead, salaries can be supplemented through *mordidas*, reducing the need for sophisticated enforcement equipment.

In addition, illegality has allowed the state to manipulate the vulnerability of local actors. A policy of toleration and flexibility gives a sense of control to local actors, yet keeps them under control. In addition, by tolerating illegality the state has also been able to respond to particular interest groups; toleration declines as catches for the private sector drop. Toleration generates a very uncertain situation, with major ramifications for the fishermen.

With the adoption of a neoliberal ideology and the general economic crisis, the state no longer needs, or is able, to appeal to the cooperative sector. Now, more than ever, the usefulness of the status of illegality placed upon small-scale fishermen becomes evident. For example, local arrangements between rule-breakers and bureaucrats started to become increasingly problematic during the 1992–3 season. The private sector, through the CANAINPES, issued a formal complaint to fishery officials calling attention to the illegality of small-scale fishermen shrimping offshore. Since then, visits from Mexico City officials have become frequent and occur during the best tides at the beginning of the season. During these visits, fishermen must remain inshore so as not to jeopardize the 'favor' done by local authorities.

The cost to small-scale fishermen has been high: not only do their catches decline, but they lose access to optimal marketable shrimp sizes. In addition, the private sector has directly brought marines from Mexico City to enforce regulations selectively. These are rotated every year so that they do not become familiar with the system. They are encouraged to resort to violence; several small-scale fishermen have been killed by soldiers, something that had never happened before. For local enforcement agents, especially those at the lower end of the pyramid, privatization has also been costly. But while they have lost many of the opportunities to obtain *mordidas* in the shrimp business, they have gained new opportunities with the creation of biosphere reserves.

At the top of the pyramid the stakes are higher. There are loyalties to be guarded, family assets to be protected, positions of status to be defended, and important horizontal networks of exchange that need to be continuously cultivated. The elites who make the actual decisions regarding fisheries policy must strengthen their alliance with elites in the private sector. This in turn gives support to the system and perpetuates it, since everyone at the top obtains benefits from it. For the director of the *Instituto Nacional de la Pesca* (National Fisheries Institute) at the time privatization was starting, for example, it was important to listen to and execute the requests of the *armadores*; after all, her brother was the president of the CANAINPES for the Sonora chapter.

Even if their position regarding the shrimp industry is indefensible from a biological and economic point of view, people at the top always have a ready argument that justifies their deliberate attempt to eliminate competition from the small-scale sector. Higher officials informally argue, for example, that offshore trawling cannot be banned inside the biosphere reserves. This would, on the one hand, lead to an excess of fishing effort in a smaller area, meaning the rest of the gulf, where the whole fleet would be forced to concentrate. On the other hand, boats are too expensive and the private sector has already invested too much money. 'The easiest thing to do is to get rid of small-scale fishers by making them illegal' (interview with a high-level fisheries official 1993).

The Offenders

From the point of view of offenders, their values, motivations and attitudes toward regulations must be considered in order to assess the effectiveness of the restrictions imposed. Some of these have been examined elsewhere (Vásquez-León 1994). Here, I will briefly note that there are three main problems that preclude fishermen from following regulations: (a) fishermen living at a subsistence level and with little chance of alternative employment on land will remain in the fishery even at the cost of getting punished and even when they perceive a regulation as legitimate; (b) fishermen who do not have the knowledge or equipment to switch fisheries will continue to shrimp even after the season has closed (even though closures are seen as legitimate from the point of view of resource protection, their implementations are perceived as illegitimate); and (c) fishermen, *guateros*, and even whole communities feel that they have as much right to the fishery as the *armadores* and the state. Regulations that favor the latter at the cost of small-scale shrimping are considered illegitimate and are consequently broken by everyone, all of the time.

In the case of the biosphere reserves, while fishermen acknowledge that there is an ecological crisis and an imminent need to reduce effort, they feel that conservation efforts have not directly addressed the major environmental concerns of local communities. For the latter, the problems have to do with the open-access character of management, overcapitalized and ecologically inefficient industrial fleets, and a lack of marketing opportunities for alternative species, issues not directly address by the conservationist agenda.

But what happens when a fishermen decides to follow legal procedures? This is the case of El Neto, a small-scale fisherman who during the process of privatization decided that he would be the first one to take advantage of free trade. He decided to become a legal shrimp dealer. With an export permit he could offer certain guarantees to his clients, 'so that they trust me and don't have to hide when they come to sell here'. He could also pay a higher price than the *guateros* because his costs were going to be lower; he did not have to pay *mordidas*.

For a fee of $100 (US) he was promised a legal export permit for the beginning of the season. While other fishermen were busy repairing nets, he was busy selling fishing equipment. He traded his nets for a couple of scales, hooked up a phone line, bought a car on credit, and started paying cash for shrimp to establish himself as a buyer. The season started; but the permit was delayed. Pretty soon kilos of shrimp started flooding his house. A lack of storage facilities forced him to leave the shrimp at the processing plant, which charged for storage on a daily basis. Three weeks into the season, the shrimp was accumulating along with the charges. He started to delay payments to the fishermen; and the fishermen stopped selling to him.

An export permit good for one season finally arrived three months after the season had started. It was too late: he was in debt, bankrupt, and without fishing equipment. Without direct connections in the regional delegation he was unable to sell his shrimp on the black market for a profit. He was forced to end his career as a shrimp exporter in the same season that he had decided to start.

Conclusions

The case of corruption and illegal networks in the Gulf of California fisheries is a reflection of larger processes occurring within and beyond the Mexican state. Historically, as in the larger system, the structure of the fishing industry in Mexico has been shaped like a pyramid formally organized by sectors differing in power and informally manipulated through vertical and horizontal relationships. In its attempt to control valuable shrimp resources, the state created a complex network of official organizations and private interests. At the same time, it created a structure plagued with contradictions in which corruption and illegal activity became customary.

Everyone benefited from abundant shrimp stocks. The resource bought political power and loyalty from local communities, gave substantial economic benefits to elites in the public, private, and cooperative sectors, and was a significant source of foreign exchange to a modernizing nation. It also created a large informal sector and fomented the emergence and persistence of illegal networks made out of individual fishermen, cooperatives, and even entire communities whose access to shrimp resources was mediated by local brokers, or legal predators representing the state.

Scientific discourse, also under state patronage, promoted the rapid expansion of the industry by justifying the management policies that would eventually lead to the near-collapse of stocks. The system could be maintained as long as catches were high, but when catches dropped the system began to collapse. Corruption within the cooperative structure served as a scapegoating device to explain industry bankruptcy and the problems of overexploitation. It also expedited the elimination of the cooperative sector in the 1990s.

Mexico's transference of the fishery to the private sector was unprecedented. It was, however, one of several efforts to gain legitimacy in the international arena. Along with privatization came a change in the definition of the region, from one of being highly productive to one containing several 'fragile ecosystems' in need of conservation. Since 1991 privatization and environmentalism have led to the proliferation of bad laws that specifically limit legal access of small-scale fishermen to marine resources. Even though, as is rhetorically claimed by the state, the objectives of these laws are to conserve resources for long-term use and increase industry efficiency, the relations of power set in motion point in a different direction. Concealed behind scientific discourse and consistent with the neoliberal worldview, the primary concerns are a perceived need to meet the demands of the influential private sector for exclusive control and rights to increasingly scarce resources, and to conserve resources for a potentially profitable tourist industry. In other words, as resources become scarce, the law is employed directly and instrumentally to define not fishery use, but *who* uses the available stocks. The law defines and defends the dominant class claims upon resources and labor power.

Privatization has also meant that fishermen have lost political representation, and that the state has lost the legitimacy that allowed it to manipulate local actors. New legislation and the use of violence as a new enforcement mechanism are attempts on the part of the state to renew its forms of social control at the local level. Thus the status of illegality imposed on fishermen provides the pretext for the state's forcible intrusion into fishing communities, making them highly vulnerable to structures of power that are external to their immediate realities and even beyond the Mexican state.

There is no question that the global forces of neoliberalism and environmentalism have intruded into the lives of local actors, transforming the relationship between local state bureaucracies and illegal networks. In the past, a policy of toleration, rather than strict regulatory enforcement, characterized the relationship between fishery officials and resource users. Through this policy, the state allowed illegal activity to persist, yet left open the possibility of asserting control or imposing enforcement selectively when it perceived it to be necessary – or when catches dropped too much. Today, local managers are now losing their ability to respond to local circumstances, and resource users have lost the brokers who gave them some power of negotiation with higher officials. There is an increasing impersonality in the mediation of class relations and, as government policies change, even enforcers run the risk of getting punished; as petty predators, they have become an inconvenience to the greater predators, the private sector and higher officials.

Remnants of the old system remain, and even though it is now more costly to break the law, illegal activity has increased. This is a function of an expansion of what is being defined as illegal, of the economic crisis that has left most coastal communities with few employment opportunities, and of the belief among the fishing communities that, regardless of ideological changes at the state level, they have the right to make a living.

Notes

1. In the political literature of Mexico the social or 'reform' sector stands in contrast to the private or the 'modern' sector. The former refers to the collective organization of labor started under the 1917 Constitution and sanctioned by the revolutionary party; the latter refers to private economic interests.
2. De Soto (1986), in his study of the informal economy in Peru, argues that there are good and bad laws that control and regulate economic activities. He defines the informal economy as that part of the illegal economy that results in legitimate economic activities that have to be undertaken illegally because of bad state laws and regulations, which make them too costly if undertaken legally or make legal activity non-viable for many low-income entrepreneurs. An example of a bad law is one that imposes a set of unnecessarily difficult prerequisites on the business of obtaining a permit. A good law would be one that requires the payment of state income taxes. Those who violate bad laws, De Soto argues, generate good illegal benefits, while those who violate good laws generate bad benefits. There is no doubt that when defined in this way the informal economy is very important in Latin America (see Guissarri 1989; Thoumi 1995).
3. The contemporary Mexican political system has been described metaphorically as a pyramid by several scholars (Padgett 1966; Carlos and Anderson 1981; L. Lomnitz 1987). As described by Lomnitz, the Mexican society is a 'set of parallel pyramids inside of which ever smaller multiple pyramids are generated which duplicate themselves hierarchically in a way comparable to the patriarchal family structure' (L. Lomnitz 1987: 522, my translation).
4. For a discussion of contradictory policies in the agricultural sector, see Sanderson 1981.
5. Lustig's observations of the Echeverría administration (1970–1976) reveal the underlying scheme directing further developments in the shrimp industry: 'The belief at the time was that a country in which the state controlled a larger share of investment, owned more "strategic"

sectors . . ., and regulated more of the price-setting mechanism would be more prosperous, more equitable, and less vulnerable to the political pressures of the business sector at home and abroad' (Lustig 1992: 18).

6. Policies in the shrimp industry were only a reflection of what was going on at the national level: 'In the late 1970s, on the mistaken assumption that the rise in world oil prices and the availability of cheap external credit would continue, the Mexican government engaged in a spending spree. The resulting fiscal deficit increased inflation rates and the trade deficit. The fiscal and external gaps were filled with external borrowing' (Lustig 1992: 3).
7. *Caciquismo*, as described by Friedrich (1965), emerged in rural Mexico as a direct result of the struggle for land between different factions. The *cacique* became the leader of a particular faction and maintained power through his skill at being able to organize followers.
8. One of the longest examples of *cacicazgo* (rule by a *cacique*) in the industry was that of Florentino López Tapia. He was the sole officially-recognized leader of all fishing cooperatives in the south of Sonora for over three decades. As part of the administrative council of the federation Sur de Sonora and as intermittent mayor of the city of Guaymas representing the PRI, he would remain the mediator between the cooperative sector and higher levels of authority in the public and private sectors until the beginning of the 1990s.
9. While in 1977 shrimp represented 6.9 per cent of Mexican total exports, this figure declined to less than 2.3 per cent in 1987. Its share in the rapidly expanding US market also dropped from 40 per cent in 1977, to 18 per cent in 1987 and 12 per cent by 1989 (Miller 1990).
10. Top members of the CANAINPES have considerable power within the government structure. They tend to be very diversified businessmen with large investments in the Sonoran economy. For example, one of the largest owners has a chain of supermarkets throughout the state; he is also a producer of beef cattle for export and comes from one of the traditional elite families in Sonora. Several top investors in the shrimp industry also controlled the administrative councils of the private banks that embargoed the cooperatives and have close kinship relations in different sectors or in the government.
11. The Upper Gulf of California and Lower Colorado River Delta Biosphere Reserve, the Islas del Golfo Biosphere Reserve and the Loreto Marine National Park, the Vizcaino Biosphere Reserve, the Cabo Pulmo Marine National Park, and the Cabo San Lucas Submarine Region.

12. García and Le Reste write: 'penaeid shrimps are nearly always heavily exploited, and the size at first capture is below, and often much below, the size at first sexual maturity. This is particularly the case if there is an artisanal or semi-industrial fishery for juveniles. In such cases, the reproduction potential of the stock is greatly reduced and . . . it is possible that the stock declines to a level where great prudence is required' (1981: 137).
13. Recently SEPESCA became part, as a subsecretariat, of the newly created *Secretaria del Medio Ambiente, Recursos Naturales y Pesca* (Ministry of the Environment, Natural Resources, and Fisheries, or SEMARNAP), with the objective of lessening sectoral conflict in the area of natural resource use and protection.
14. The 1993 report on pelagic fisheries issued by the Secretaría de Pesca acknowledges the assistance provided by the CANAINPES: '[with thanks to] the *Cámara Nacional de la Industria Pesquera*, Sonoran Section, especially to the Sector Industrial y *Armadores Sardineros*, for the constant interest in the research agendas developed, and for their valuable economic and equipment related contributions to make the research possible' (Secretaría de Pesca 1993: ii).
15. For a discussion of high enforcement costs in marine environments see Anderson 1986.

References

Anderson, L.G. (1986), *The Economics of Fisheries Management*. Baltimore: The Johns Hopkins University Press.

Breton, Y. and E. López Estrada (1989), *Ciencias Sociales y Desarrollo de las Pesquerías*. Mexico: Colección Divulgación.

Carlos, M. and B. Anderson (1981), 'Political Brokerage and Network Politics in Mexico: the Case of Representative Dominance System', in C. Willier and B. Anderson (eds), *Networks of Exchange and Coercion: The Elementary Theory and Its Application*. New York: Elsevier.

Chapa Saldaña, H., C. Guilbot Taddei and H. Romero Rodríguez (1968), *Ensayo de Interpretación de las Tallas Comerciales de Camarón en los Litorales de Sonora, México*. Sonora: Secretaría de Pesca.

Chávez, E. A. and D. Lluch (1971), 'Estado Actual de la Pesca de Camarón en el Noroeste de México', *Revista de la Sociedad Mexicana de Historia Natural*, 32: 141–56.

Cortés Campo, G. (1977), 'Corrupción General en la Industrial Camaronera', *El Imparcial*, Hermosillo, Sonora, Oct. 3.

De La Peña, J. (1989), 'Local and Regional Power in Mexico', *Pre-publication Working Papers of the Mexican Center Institute of Latin American Studies*. Austin: University of Texas.

De Soto, H. (1986), *El Otro Sendero: La Revolucion Informal*. Lima, Peru: Editorial El Barranco.

Friedrich, P. (1965), 'A Mexican Cacicazgo', *Ethnology*, 4: 190–209.

García, S. and L. Le Reste (1981), 'Life Cycles, Dynamics, Exploitation and Management of Coastal Penaeid Shrimp Stocks', *FAO Fisheries Technical Paper No. 203*. Rome: FAO.

Greenberg, J. (1990), 'Sanctity and Resistance in Closed Corporate Indigenous Communities: Coffee, Money, Violence and Ritual Organization in Chatino Communities in Oaxaca', in L. Stephen and J. Dow (eds), *Class, Politics, and Popular Religion in Mexico and Central America*. Washington: American Anthropological Association.

Guissarri, A. (1989), *La Argentina Informal: Realidad de la Vida Economica.* Buenos Aires, Argentina: Emece Editores.

Harvey, N. (1996), 'Impact of Reforms to Article 27 on Chiapas: Peasant Resistance in the Neoliberal Public Sphere', in L. Randall (ed.), *Reforming Mexico's Agrarian Reform*. New York: M. E. Sharpe, Inc., pp. 151–72.

Hernández Fujigaki, G. (1988), *75 años de Historia de la Pesca, 1912–1987: Avances y Retos*. Mexico: Secretaría de Pesca.

Leeds, E. (1996), 'Cocaine and Parallel Polities in the Brazilian Urban Periphery: Constraints on Local-Level Democratization', *Latin American Research Review*, 31(3): 47–83.

Lomnitz, C. and I. Adler (1990), 'El Fondo de La Forma: La Campaña Presidencial del PRI en 1988', *Nueva Antropología*, XI (38): 45–82.

Lomnitz, L. (1987), 'Las Relaciones Horizontales y Verticales en la Estructura Social Urbana de México', in S. Glantz (ed.), *La Heterodóxia Recuperada. En Torno a Angel Palerm.* Mexico City: Fondo de la Cultura Económica.

—— (1988), 'Informal Exchange Networks in Formal Systems: A Theoretical Model', *American Anthropologist,* 90: 42–55.

—— and M. Pérez-Lizaur (1987), *A Mexican Elite Family 1820–1980*. Princeton, NJ: Princeton University Press.

Lustig, N. (1992), *Mexico: The Remaking of an Economy*. Washington, DC: The Brookings Institution.

McGuire, T. (1991), 'Science and the Destruction of a Shrimp Fleet', *MAST,* 4(1)32: 55.

McGuire, T. and J. Greenberg (1993), *Maritime Community and Biosphere Reserve: Crisis and Response in the Upper Gulf of California*, Occasional

Paper No.2. Tucson: Bureau of Applied Research in Anthropology, University of Arizona.

Magallón Barajas, F. J. (1987), 'The Pacific Shrimp Fishery in Mexico', *CalCofi Rep*, 28: 43–52.

Mendoza Martínez, S. (1985), *Narraciones Críticas y S.O.S. de la Industria Pesquera.* Mexico: Costa Amic Editores, SA.

Merry, S. (1992), 'Anthropology, Law, and Transnational Processes', *Annual Review of Anthropology,* 21: 357–79.

Miller, M. (1990), 'Shrimp Aquaculture in Mexico', *Food Research Institute Studies,* 22(1): 83–107.

Morris, S. D. (1991), *Corruption and Politics in Contemporary Mexico.* Tuscaloosa: The University of Alabama Press.

Padgett, V. L. (1966), *The Mexican Political System.* Boston: Houghton-Mifflin.

Penn, J. W. and N. Caputti (1986), 'Spawning Stock-Recruitment for the Tiger Prawn, *Penaeus esculentus*, Fishery in Exmouth Gulf, Western Australia, and Their Implications for Management', in P. C. Rothlisberg, B. J. Hill, and D. J. Staples (eds), *Second Australian National Prawn Seminar.* Kooralbyn, Qld, Australia: NPS2, pp. 165–73.

Powell, K. (1996), 'Neoliberalism and Nationalism', in R. Aitken, N. Craske, J. Gareth, and D.Stansfield (eds), *Dismantling the Mexican State?* New York: St Martin's Press, pp. 39–57.

Regalado, J. (1996), 'The Opposition and the 1994 Presidential Elections in Mexico', in R. Aitken, N. Craske, J. Gareth, and D. Stansfield (eds), *Dismantling the Mexican State?* New York: St Martin's Press, pp. 152–68.

Rodríguez de la Cruz, M. C. (1981), 'Aspectos Pesqueros del Camarón de Alta Mar en el Pacífico Mexicano', *Ciencia Pesquera,* 1(2): 1–19.

Sanderson, S. E. (1981), *Agrarian Populism and the Mexican State: The Struggle for Land in Sonora.* Berkeley: University of California Press.

Secretaría de Pesca (1991), *Diario Oficial de la Federación*, Mexico City, Sept. 26.

—— (1993), *Pesquería de Pelágicos Menores en el Golfo de California. Temporada 1990/1991.* Guaymas, Sonora: Instituto Nacional de la Pesca, Centro Regional de Investigación Pesquera.

Smart, A. (1988), 'The Informal Regulation of Illegal Economic Activities: Comparisons Between the Squatter Property Market and Organized Crime', *International Journal of the Sociology of Law*, 16: 91–101.

Stanford, L. (1994), 'The Privatization of Mexico's Ejidal Sector: Examining Local Impacts, Strategies, and Ideologies', *Urban Anthropology,* 23(2–3): 97–119.

Thoumi, F. (1995), *Political Economy and Illegal Drugs in Colombia*, Boulder, CO: Lynne Rienner Publishers.

Vásquez-León, M. (1994), 'Avoidance Strategies and Governmental Rigidity: The Case of the Small-Scale Shrimp Fishery in Two Mexican Communities', *Journal of Political Ecology,* 1: 67–82.

—— and T. McGuire (1993), 'La Iniciativa Privada in the Mexican Shrimp Industry: Politics of Efficiency', *MAST,* 6(1/2): 59–73.

Vélez-Ibáñez, C. (1983), *Rituals of Marginality: Politics, Process, and Culture Change in Central Urban Mexico 1969–1974.* Berkeley: University of California Press.

—— (1988), 'Networks of Exchange Among Mexicans in the U.S. and Mexico: Local Level Mediating Responses to National and International Transformations', *UrbanAnthropology,* 17: 27–51.

Weintraub, S. (1990), *A Marriage of Convenience: Relations Between Mexico and the United States.* New York: Oxford University Press.

Wexler, M. B. and D. B. Bray (1996), 'Reforming Forests: From Community Forests to Corporate Forestry in Mexico', in L. Randall (ed.), *Reforming Mexico's Agrarian Reform.* New York: M. E. Sharpe, Inc., pp. 235–45.

–9–

Adolescent Violence, State Processes, and the Local Context of Moral Panic

Mercer L. Sullivan and *Barbara Miller*

Violence, its representations, and its social control are central to the image, hegemony, and legitimacy of the state. Weberian social theory in particular has defined the state in terms of the legitimate monopoly of the means of violence (Giddens 1987; Weber 1978). When this monopoly is challenged, the threat strikes directly at the legitimacy of the state. For this reason, issues of violence and its representation and control provide a direct window into the character and contradictions of a state at a given point in history.

Adolescent violence and societal reactions to it are fundamental problems in the contemporary United States, central to the redefinition of the role of the state at the close of the century. These problems appear paradoxical from cross-cultural and historical perspectives because heightened levels of personal violence are more commonly associated with weak states or areas that are weakly incorporated into state structures (McCoy, this volume, Chapter 5; Wolfgang and Ferracuti 1967). Whether one looks at areas where once-strong state control has diminished (Blok 1974), mountainous or maritime areas where bandits and pirates flourish (Gallant, this volume, Chapter 2; Hobsbawm 1965, 1969), or emergent states (Nugent, this volume, Chapter 3), the absence of strong central state control is often associated with high levels of violence, and strong state control is usually seen as synonymous with the monopolization of the means of violence.

Yet the United States, the strongest state in the contemporary world, has much higher levels of personal violence than other industrialized nations (Zimring and Hawkins, 1997). While this disparity between the United States and other stable, prosperous states has long been evident, trends in violence within the United States have undergone some remarkable fluctuations in recent years. The most notable trend was a sharp spike in adolescent homicide from the middle 1980s through to the early 1990s. We focus in this chapter on relationships between these recent trends in violence, societal reactions to these trends, and consequences for changes in the image and functions of the state.

We argue that recent societal reactions to youth violence can be characterized as a moral panic. As with all moral panics, reactions are disproportionate to the phenomena. This disproportionality, in turn, arises from and may contribute to a wider field of social change (Goode and Ben-Yehuda 1994). In this case, we argue that the current moral panic over youth violence both arises from and has been contributing to a restructuring of the role of the state. This restructuring takes the form of reductions in public investment in social welfare and education and a concomitant transfer of resources to a more repressive apparatus of social control through policing and incarceration.

From this standpoint, high levels of violence in a fully formed state are not necessarily anomalous. State formation is an ongoing process in which the roles of violence and responses to violence remain crucial at the levels of both ideology and practice.

Adolescent Violence and Public Policies at Present

From 1985 to 1992, arrests of adolescents for homicide in the United States more than doubled (Blumstein 1995). This sharp increase in adolescent homicide is all the more disturbing because during this same period arrests of people aged twenty-five and older actually declined substantially (Fox 1996). Societal reaction to this trend has constituted a full-scale moral panic. Responses have included efforts to make juvenile justice systems more punitive, increases in school security, and a host of efforts to prevent youth violence through such means as specialized curricula, conflict mediation programs, and media campaigns (Bernard 1992; Devine 1996; Prothrow-Stith 1991; Zimring 1996). Only recently have data become available showing that juvenile homicide rates seem to have peaked in 1994 (Sickmund, Snyder, and Poe-Yamagata 1997).

As with all moral panics, however, there exists a sharp disjunction between public definitions of the problem and the underlying behaviors giving rise to the panic. A number of researchers have pointed to some of the main dimensions of this disjunction. Contrary to public perceptions that much larger proportions of adolescents are engaged in violent confrontations, what has changed is not so much the proportions of young people engaging in serious violence as the extent to which such confrontations lead to serious injury or death. Lethality, not incidence or prevalence, is the principal vector of change in adolescent violence. Here the evidence points squarely to increases in the possession and use of firearms as the primary causes of the increase in adolescent homicide (Zimring 1996).

In current public policy discourse about adolescent violence in the United States, the policy alternatives have been defined as 'getting tough with juveniles' versus gun control, with the former option appearing to prevail. Juvenile offenders are now increasingly tried in adult courts, with a huge increase since the late 1980s. Although the changes in law that are responsible for this judicial trend were prompted by public fear of violent juveniles, the majority of these removals of juveniles to adult courts are for non-violent offenses (Snyder and Sickmund 1995). Political entrepreneurs appealing to fears of youth violence have passed laws that increasingly punish many adolescents for the violent deeds of a few.

This chapter uses ethnographic material from a study of violence among early adolescents to probe more deeply into the nature of the current moral panic. We argue the following points here:

1. The national moral panic is compounded of many local-level reactions to adolescent violence.
2. At both the national and local levels, moral panics over adolescent violence are connected to a societal withdrawal of public resources from children. Moral panics serve to demonize all adolescents as resources are being withdrawn from them.
3. These processes of demonization and withdrawal of resources are deeply embedded in racial imagery and politics and disproportionately target poor children of color.
4. Moral panic and demonization exacerbate the actual problems, undermining public safety, sense of community, and positive youth development across society.

In developing these arguments, we first review briefly literature on the history and rationale of juvenile justice and on moral panics. Then we present and discuss data on both the moral panic in one community school district in New York City and the actual patterns of adolescent daily life in that community. Throughout the discussion, our emphasis is on the relationship between the state and citizens who are neither children nor adults. This relationship includes both the legal rights and responsibilities of adolescents and the obligations of the state, through its institutions and laws, to provide both social control and education and nurture to adolescents.

Juvenile Justice in American History

The tendency for adults in a society to believe that standards of behavior among young people are deteriorating has been noted as far back as the ancient Greeks. In *The Cycle of Juvenile Justice* (1992), Bernard argues that the current trend towards getting tougher with juveniles is part of recurring cycle in American history over the past two centuries. In his analysis, the belief that the young are dangerous and out of control has been fairly constant throughout that period. Societal responses, however, have cycled back and forth between attempts to provide special treatments for young people and attempts to remove these treatments and impose harsher punishments.

In one phase of this cycle, the state affirms its responsibility for the development of children. In English and American law, this principle has been known as *parens patriae*, meaning literally that the state is 'parent of the country' and thus responsible for all children. This doctrine was first developed in England to deal with orphaned children of the propertied classes, for whom the state assumed responsibility for managing their education and property until they became adults. In Philadelphia in 1838, this principle was applied for the first time to a child whose parents were living but judged unable to give her proper nurture and education, thus putting the child at risk of becoming a pauper and a drain upon the state. On this basis, the child was removed from parental custody and placed in a state-run institution.

The doctrine of *parens patriae* subsequently became the major rationale for the creation of special courts and institutions for dealing with juveniles who break the law. As the parent of the country, the state expressed an obligation to provide both nurture and discipline for children. On this basis, juvenile courts and institutions were charged with providing education and treatment for young offenders in addition to exercising the same functions of social control as adult courts. This exercise of parental authority over juveniles was coupled with a failure to extend them the same rights to due process under the law enjoyed by adults.

In the opposing phase of this historical cycle, policies of *parens patriae* come under attack, for two different kinds of reasons. Some object to the lack of due process under the law in juvenile courts. Others accuse these laws and institutions of being too lenient and allowing youths to flout laws with impunity. In this phase, which characterizes the current period, special protections for youths are stripped away and they are punished more harshly. As punishments become harsher, however, judges and other justice system officials become more reluctant to commit less serious offenders to these harsh treatments. As a result, the options for dealing with a troubled youth become narrower – overly harsh punishment or none at all – and the perceived need for special courts and institutions for young people begins to grow again, pushing the cycle back in the opposite direction.

The laws of New York State, the setting for the ethnographic material to be examined here, include examples of both these opposing moments in public policy in the form of two laws with similar names but contrary intentions. Unlike most states, in which the age of majority is eighteen, citizens of New York State become adults at the age of sixteen. Two separate laws, however, modify the consequences of the age of majority. A youth between the ages of sixteen and eighteen can be sentenced as a Youthful Offender and receive a less harsh sentence than someone nineteen or older. The Youthful Offender law dates from an earlier period during which youths were considered as deserving of special treatment. In a later period, however, the state passed the Juvenile Offender law, allowing youths as young as thirteen to be tried and sentenced as adults for certain heinous crimes. The Juvenile Offender law was passed in 1978 in the wake of an intense moral panic occasioned by the random murders committed by fifteen-year-old Willie Bosket (Butterfield 1995). New York's juvenile offender law was the first in a series of such laws that swept through the states. Since that period, virtually every state has simplified and expanded provisions for treating juveniles as adults.

While Bernard argues that this cycle is two centuries old and shows no signs of abating, the current cycle does contain a notably new element, namely the emphasis on youths as potential agents of lethal violence. In the past, the youthful offenses perceived and feared by adults were overwhelmingly either 'status offenses' (acts illegal for children but not adults, such as running away, sexual activity, drinking, and driving) or property offenses. As Zimring has noted, 'for the first time in modern history, middle adolescent offenders are being identified as a high-risk and high-usage group for firearms' (1996). Moral panics often require new labels to stimulate public fear. The term 'super-predator' has recently been advanced to characterize a new breed of juvenile offender (DiIulio 1996), and has played a conspicuous role in the recent policy debates at Federal and state levels.

Moral panics over juvenile delinquency, then, are not new. What is new is the focus on youths as potential agents of lethal violence. The public perception that 'youths have become more violent', though supported by the evidence of trends in youth homicide, is often mistakenly interpreted to imply that vastly more youths have become violent. In fact, in a nation with several million teenagers, homicides in any given year involve only a tiny proportion of these youths, less than four thousand (Snyder and Sickmund 1995). Yet laws and institutions are being radically restructured as a result of national moral panic over this tiny proportion.

Moral Panics: Societal and Local

First used for an extended analysis of media reaction to youth conflicts in England during the 1960s (Cohen 1972), the concept of moral panic has since been applied to a wide range of phenomena, including reported patterns of drug use, sexual behavior, violence, and invasion by space aliens (Goode and Ben-Yehuda 1994). The concepts elaborated in the moral panic literature provide a useful framework for examining the relationship between recent trends in youth violence in the United States and processes of state restructuring. Two concepts in particular are useful in examining the recent moral panic over youth violence, that of disproportionality between phenomenon and reaction and that of the variety of social actors involved in the social construction of a moral panic.

As elaborated by Goode and Ben-Yehuda (1994), the notion of disproportionality directs attention to the fact that designating a phenomenon as a moral panic does not mean that there is no actual phenomenon being reacted to, but merely that the reaction is out of proportion and thus demands explanation within a wider frame of reference than that defined by the phenomenon itself. This line of reasoning grows directly out of previous sociological theory, particularly labelling theory (Becker 1963) and the wider field of deviance studies more generally. Labelling theory, often wrongly interpreted to imply that all labels are meaningless or harmful, simply insists that attention be directed equally to those being labelled and those doing the labelling. In some cases of moral panic, such as that over reports of widespread satanic ritual abuse of babies (Wright 1993a, b), the phenomenon reacted to appears to be wholly illusory. In other cases, such as the spike in youth homicide beginning in the mid-1980s, an observer may grant the reality of an underlying phenomenon while still arguing that the disproportionate reaction demands other explanations.

The seminal works of Cohen (1972) on scuffles between Mods and Rockers and of Hall *et al.* (1978) on 'mugging', both focused on British media panics, applied this approach to phenomena of youth violence. Both these and subsequent studies of moral panics over youth violence (Chambliss 1994; Hawkins 1995; Tanner 1996; Zatz 1987) emphasize that the disjunction between public imagery and underlying patterns of behavior is not simply a matter of faulty information or random hysteria, but rather a process in which anxiety over social change becomes focused on a specific phenomenon. The causes of the moral panic must thus be traced not just to the specific phenomenon of overt public concern but to these broader patterns of social change. Changes in racial and ethnic composition of communities have been linked to moral panics over youth violence in England, Canada, and the United States. This widening of the analytic frame is a common approach to the analysis of moral panics.

The emphasis in the moral panic literature on the variety of social actors involved in the construction of a panic is particularly helpful for examining the relation of moral panics over youth violence to processes of state restructuring. Cohen (1972), for example, identified six categories of actors in the Mods and Rockers panic: the press, the public, law enforcement, politicians and legislators, action groups, and, finally, 'folk devils', his term for stigmatized youth. Actors representing all these categories played roles in a drama at the level of the state. Extending this line of reasoning to look more closely at state processes, we may note that this dramaturgical perspective moves the analysis away from reductionist notions of the state as a monolithic entity.

Goode and Ben-Yehuda (1994) distinguish three possible loci for the origination of a moral panic: a conspiratorial elite seeking to manipulate a large public, a particular interest group, or a grass-roots social movement. Criticizing previous theorists who have propounded one or another of these as the source of all moral panics, they argue that determination of the origins of a particular panic and of the configuration of social actors in the unfolding drama must be a matter of empirical study.

In the United States, the operation of state processes in relation to issues of youth violence must be studied within the context of hierarchically nested levels of national and local government. Both education and criminal justice are primarily funded and administered at the local level. When the public perceives that young people or their schools are out of control, as Bernard (1992) maintains is the usual state of affairs, then local government is held accountable. For this reason, education and criminal justice are perennially hot issues in local politics. Local-level politicians are continually in need of positions on these issues. At the same time, education and criminal justice have considerable symbolic importance in national politics, and national government provides a small but significant measure of funding for and control over local agencies. The political flows of issues, resources, and interest group alignments between local and national levels over issues of youth violence are thus constant and complex.

The rest of this chapter examines patterns of youth conflict and reactions to conflict in the context of one middle school and its surrounding community in New York City. Despite the fact that a nationwide moral panic over youth violence is evident in recent Congressional legislative processes and has in some sense been going on for quite some time, this particular local panic is very much in process and is also quite specific to its time and place. Our endeavor here is to construct an extended case study (Burawoy 1991; Van Velsen 1967) that connects a local-level moral panic over youth violence to more general trends in the restructuring of state roles in the education, socialization, social control, and protection of youth, with particular attention to the generation and reproduction of inequality.

We argue that moral panics over youth violence both stigmatize young people of color and undercut public safety for everyone. Understanding how this occurs, however, requires attention to the roles played by various social actors in particular local panics and the ways in which these local situations are constituted by and constitutive of national-level state restructuring. The following case is one example.

Youth Conflict and Moral Panic in the Fairhaven Community

The case materials examined here are drawn from a comparative ethnographic study of early adolescents in three different middle schools and communities in New York City. Although serious violent conflicts in the city and elsewhere typically involve people of at least fourteen years of age, the emergence of serious violence is usually preceded by multiple lesser incidents (Elliott 1994). The period of early adolescence (roughly ages eleven through to fourteen, coinciding with junior high/middle school enrollment) is thus a developmental stage of great interest for the study of violence. Middle schools are typically more disorderly than either elementary or high schools, and victimization rates are higher there than in high schools (National Institute of Education 1978). Early adolescence is a particularly stressful stage of development, during which bodily change is rapid, adolescents have much more autonomy in and out of school, and the peer group becomes a salient social context (Hamburg 1986).

Early adolescence is the period leading directly into the developmental stage at which serious violent behavior is most likely to emerge (Elliott 1994). Recent controversies over ‘turning-points’ in careers of crime and violence have hinged on discussions on the relative importance of sociogenic and ontogenetic factors in the unfolding of the life course (Moffitt 1993; Nagin and Paternoster 1991; Sampson and Laub 1993). One of the most enduring patterns known to criminology is the 'age–crime' curve, which shows a rapid peaking of the prevalence within the populations of participation in illegal acts, including violence, during the teenage years and a subsequent sharp decline beginning in the early twenties. It is particularly notable that most people who ever commit illegal acts do so in their teens and do not go on to become adult criminals.

Although early anti-social behavior is a strong predictor of both youthful and adult criminality, it predicts for only a small proportion of those ever so involved. In other words, most people are most likely to get into trouble in their teens if they are ever going to, but, for most people who do get into trouble during this period, this youthful behavior is not connected to anti-social behavior in childhood or criminal behavior in adulthood. The question of the life experiences leading into this high-risk stage of development is thus one of extreme interest. The larger research project from which this chapter is derived is designed to examine the social contexts of early adolescent development, focusing on issues of violence.

This chapter focuses on one of the three school/community sites in the larger study. We refer to the community as 'Fairhaven' and the intermediate school as 'Union'. Although Fairhaven is part of a city, state, and country that can be said to be in the grip of a moral panic over youth violence, Fairhaven is the only one of the three research sites where this panic is salient at the local level. We first describe some of the background and detail of recent events in Fairhaven in order to show the particular local character of moral panic there.

A Changing Community

Fairhaven is a traditional, named local neighborhood within a community school district that contains several such areas. Many residents of Fairhaven are members of white working- and middle-class families that have lived in the area for some time. Fairhaven has been undergoing racial change in recent years. Although much of the housing in Fairhaven consists of modest one- and two-family houses, there is also one large public housing project in the area. Until a few years before our study, that housing project had contained one of the largest concentrations of low-income white families in the city. As a result of a court order, the project began admitting many more families of color. The project is near the middle school and high school of Fairhaven, and many children from the projects attend these schools.

In addition to these residential changes, Fairhaven schools also attract a number of students from the other end of the community school district. That neighborhood area, which is called Hufton, is fairly diverse economically, containing both poor and more middle-class sections, and many of the residents of Hufton are persons of color, both African-Americans and Caribbean immigrants. Since the schools in Hufton have limited space and are severely overcrowded, the school district assigns many middle- and high-school students from the Hufton area to schools in Fairhaven. The city transportation department runs extra buses along the route between the two areas. The combination of changes in racial composition of the local projects and the assignment of Hufton residents to Fairhaven's schools has produced a marked increase in the visibility of teenagers of color on the streets of Fairhaven.

These changes in racial and ethnic patterns of residence and schooling have been accompanied by a number of other changes in the local area. One such change has been in the perceived level of violence. The relationship between these perceptions and the underlying reality is difficult to assess because of the statistical noise associated with year-to-year fluctuations in small-area police statistics. The neighborhood is certainly one of the less dangerous areas in the city, by any measure. There was one shooting in Fairhaven's high school the year before our study, but some local residents now refer in the plural to the 'shootings' in the school. The perception of violence has been linked to a withdrawal of white families from the neighborhood and from the public schools. Although large areas of Fairhaven are still occupied by white, native-born families of moderate- to middle-income levels, some families who have lived in the area for many years have been moving out of the neighborhood, to New Jersey and Long Island. This 'white flight' is closely tied to the age of children. Especially as children get old enough to enter high school, some parents become afraid and move away from the area.

This movement of middle-class white families out of New York City neighborhoods has been going on for years. Many formerly predominantly white neighborhoods have become predominantly African-American, Latino, or Asian. Fairhaven has not yet shifted entirely, but the sense of change is palpable among old-time residents, and fears of people of color and immigrants are frequently invoked in their descriptions of these changes. In many ways, Fairhaven resembles the 'defended neighborhood' typologized by Suttles (1972), in which residents try to hold tightly to existing institutions while also reinforcing their identify by working to exclude those whom they consider 'outsiders'. While some of the expressions of their feeling of community solidarity are positive, this is also the kind of atmosphere in which overt or more subtle racist and xenophobic attitudes can flourish.

Much of our field material describes the workings of a moral panic over youth violence in progress in Fairhaven. The first situation described below shows that panic at full boil, as white residents, merchants, and school officials chafe at the visible presence of minority teenagers. Following that incident, centered at the local high school, we turn to a local middle school, the focal site of our research. We first describe the school's institutional response to problems of real and perceived violence. Then we examine the effects of these community conditions and institutional practices on the lives of young people growing up and going to school in Fairhaven. Following this case material, we offer analyses and interpretations linking this material back to considerations of state processes and the ways in which the state defines and responds to illegal behavior by adolescents.

Local Panic

Many of the fears about youth violence and community change held by Fairhaven's white residents were crystallized in an 'emergency safety meeting' held in Fairhaven HS, in thc aftermath of a highly publicized incident involving black teens, spun as a 'gang war' by the press. A close look at the response to this incident by school officials and other community representatives illustrates the ways in which moral panic over youth violence takes specific form in particular local contexts. The following account, and subsequent field material, are taken from Barbara Miller's field notes.

Field Notes: The seeds for this incident were supposedly planted at a weekend house party, when a boy who attends Fairhaven HS, the school directly across the street from Union Middle School, hit a girl who attends an HS in another part of the city. Monday afternoon, at dismissal time, there was a group of teens waiting outside Fairhaven HS to settle the score. A large group of teens formed, and were chased away from the arca by the team of School Safety Officers and police who patrol the perimeter of the school. The group moved up the avenue and had a confrontation in front of a strip of stores. One of the merchants saw the large congregation of black teens and called the police and a local daily newspaper, who ran a story the next day describing a 'gang war'.

Whether there was actually a fight or not is ambiguous. By some accounts there was no fight, just a big group of teens and a lot of yelling. The police came and took several kids away, though they hadn't broken any laws except possibly someone's idea of 'disorderly conduct'. The most convincing account that no violence took place came from the police themselves. A day or so after the incident, I happened to be in the precinct interviewing a youth officer. At one point, another officer came into the office and asked whether they 'had anything at all, maybe a prior history' on the kids who had been brought in after the alleged brawl. The youth officer said she didn't think so. The other officer commented that he had to find something to charge them on, so that the community could see the police were doing their job to curb youth violence.

While there was nothing extraordinary about a large group of teens getting loud or even physical on a city street, the fact that the press publicized the incident and spun it as a 'gang war' provoked the administration of the middle school and the high school to co-sponsor an emergency 'safety meeting' to be held at the high school. School administrators were particularly bothered by the newspaper article's assertion that 'the school can't control any of their kids'. Both schools are struggling to maintain their reputation as viable institutions for the white residents of the neighborhood, and school officials spend a great deal of energy on institutional impression management.

The safety meeting brought together staff from both schools, their Parents' Association (PA) presidents, youth officers and other police, officers and officials from the division of school safety, and the manager of the local public housing project. Before the meeting began, Union's PA president pressed a youth officer to beef up police presence on the block that is shared by the school and the housing project, a street that provides a hangout for local kids from the projects: 'It's making Union's zoned kids not want to come to Union, all those kids hanging out by the stores, big kids!' The officer responded, 'Legally, we're not allowed to move kids away from the area, only if they're on school grounds.'

The meeting began with Fairhaven's principal stating, 'We called this meeting together because of issues and concerns about what's going on in the community – not necessarily the school building. . . . we're very concerned about the [newspaper] article.' The first to speak was Union's PA president: 'Our problem is the area on Lark Avenue, and it's not necessarily Fairhaven HS students [who are to blame], but our kids are being harassed, and the parents are outraged, we're losing our parents.' Right away, the locus of the problem was placed outside school walls, in 'the community', which is perceived to have fallen prey to a threatening population. Fairhaven HS's PA president responded by defending the high school: 'We're concerned that everyone thinks these kids are from Fairhaven HS, there's no control over these kids . . . [who] congregate in front of the apartment buildings. Our kids get blamed. We can control the inside but we can't always control the outside.' Union's principal added, 'we have to have Lark Avenue cleared continuously. With the projects there, there are more and more kids hanging out.'

From the outset, then, the very presence of local black youth is framed as a problem to be managed by the police. The discussion turned to the fears such youth inspire, and the difference between 'perception' and 'reality'. An officer from the local precinct spoke of the difficulty of moving kids out of an area they are legally allowed to be in, and stated 'Mainly it's a perceptual problem, we're not getting the crime here you may think we are, just big groups of kids.' Fairhaven's principal countered, 'The elderly people here have fears, when they see 60–75 students, it's scary whether they're doing anything or not.' The officer insisted, 'they may just be play fighting, the problem is one of perception.' A housing officer explained to the group that youth-related crime and truancy has declined, 'yet we're providing a great deal of police to the area.' He went on to say that despite low crime rates, they would consider even greater police concentration in the projects.

The discussion continued, with references to 'laws that have to be changed' to discipline kids, ineffective parent control, assignment of special patrols to the area. One high school staff member, who'd been silent through most of the meeting, commented, 'Can we agree that these kids aren't hardened criminals, that the real issue is the number of kids out on Lark Avenue, and the perception that there are mobs?' No one responded directly to his statement.

Despite varying perspectives on whose responsibility it is to control local youth, the consensus was that the problem is how to move youth more quickly out of the vicinity of the two schools. When an officer said there are no longer any loitering laws because of 'civil rights', an assistant principal from the high school suggested making it 'mandatory for them to have to get on the bus instead of having pizza with their friends [on Lark Avenue]. They don't have to know we're not allowed to do this.' The meeting closed with a promise by police to be even more visible in the area, and a suggestion to get the transit authority involved in the effort to make the transport of kids back to Hufton more efficient. *End Field Notes*.

Several points about the above events deserve comment because they point to the complexity of local interactions and social constructions of the problem of youth violence.

First, although these is little explicit reference to race, the youths who were the subject of the community meeting were black and the institutional representatives largely white. In the context of many more explicit references to race in this area, there seems little doubt that the moral panic here was very much motivated by the fear of black teens by whites. The racial issue, however, is complicated because there are in fact many black teens who live in the local area and who do not take the bus out of the neighborhood after school because they live there. We have also documented plenty of fighting on the part of white teens who live in the area. Thus, the effort by school officials to construct this problem as one involving youths who are not 'ours' but rather youths who do not live or attend school in the area flies in the face of reality.

Second, despite the fact that the police representatives attending the meeting were overtly skeptical about the presence of a increased crime problem in the area, the outcome of the meeting appeared to be a commitment on their part to provide an increased presence in the area linked to an increased perception of teens, particularly those of color, as potential criminals.

Institutional Impression Management

The community meeting described above documents the atmosphere of moral panic in Fairhaven and the strong desire of local school officials and merchants to minimize the presence of young people, particularly those of color, on the streets of the neighborhood during the hours after school. Our extensive ethnographic work in one of these schools, Union Middle School, also documents institutional policies for dealing with youth violence and especially with perceptions of youth violence in the local community. In fact, the preponderance of our observations indicate that school policy has been driven above all by the desire to manage the community's impressions about the school in order to preserve an image of the school as a place of safety and order.

This strategy of institutional impression management has been based on fears about the withdrawal of local white and middle-class families from the school, which serves as an important institutional anchor for the community, and from the community itself, through white flight. Interviews and observations with the school's principal and faculty reveal widely shared beliefs that holding on to these families and students is crucial to maintaining the school's standards and reputation. School staff scrutinized districtwide politics and administrative decision-making for evidence of any changes that would bring more minority students into Union Middle

School or move local white students out to other schools through magnet or other special programs.

Curiously, the atmosphere of moral panic around youth violence in the local area led to an institutional impression management strategy of denying and concealing the violent incidents that did take place. Although fully engaged in the moral panic themselves, as seen from their participation in the community meeting described above, Union Middle School's administration was nonetheless committed to minimizing the surrounding community's awareness of any violence within their school. They saw any perception of their school as violent as threatening the ongoing support of the school by the 'good students' (their term, and racially coded) in the immediate community and their families.

The consequences of this public posture of denial by school officials were actually deleterious to conditions of safety inside the school. When pressure from the mayor led to a tightening up of reporting requirements about school incidents, the reaction of school officials here and elsewhere was to decrease their reporting. This led to the widespread practice of 'informal' suspensions, in which students caught fighting and otherwise breaking school rules were told to stay home for a few days without any official records that could be examined by those outside the school. In fact, only a handful of incidents and suspensions were recorded, when hundreds of informal suspensions were being handed out. One consequence of this was to decrease the number of school safety officers (SSOs) assigned to the school. Union should have qualified for at least one additional SSO, but did not because of the low rate of reporting.

Another consequence of this posture of denial was to disavow responsibility for any conflicts that occurred beyond the immediate borders of the school. Any incidents that did occur, even if the disputes had begun inside the school, as they often did, were attributed to the outside. Our field material even indicates that teachers and staff encountering conflicts actively socialized students to carry their fights outside the school boundaries, as in the following incident:

Field Notes: Today I heard that Arnie beat up another kid in his class, Larry, after school yesterday. I waited for Arnie across from the guidance office and asked him about it. I also talked to several other people who had heard about the situation. The stories are a little contradictory, but this seems to be what happened. Larry is a new kid who just moved to the city. He has been getting in a lot of trouble. Besides yesterday's fight with Arnie, he also recently got into a fight with another boy. Arnie told me that he kept hearing that Larry had been bad-mouthing him, saying Arnie is 'retarded', that he is going to beat him up. Arnie then confronted

Larry about it and told him he was going to beat him up if he didn't stop. At this point, Larry said, 'You mean like I did to your mother?', to which Arnie replied,'OK, now I have to kill you.' The next day, Arnie was on the way with his friends Jack and Marcia over to Marcia's apartment in the projects. He saw Larry, ran over to him, knocked him down and punched him a few times. Larry didn't fight back much, and the whole thing ended when a friend of Larry's came over to break it up.

Arnie told me he didn't fight Larry in the schoolyard because he doesn't want to get suspended again. Last year he got suspended twice, once for pushing a girl who had hit him with a bookbag and once because a teacher had confiscated his frisbee and he took it back from the teacher's bag without permission. He says teachers have told him to wait to have a fight until he's off school property. When Ms. Taft talked to Arnie about the fight, he said,'but it didn't happen in school' with a surprised voice, as if he didn't think she would have heard about it.

Later, a teacher told me that she knows Larry's aunt and that she is 'crazy'. She had seen the aunt in front of school the next day trying to organize some older boys to be Larry's 'backup'. *End Field Notes*.

Two points in this story are especially notable. One is the fact that someone like Arnie who gets into fights is actually socialized by school personnel to take his fights away from the school. The other is that one of the responsible adults in Larry's life tries to activate the peer 'backup' system to protect him, rather than expecting that school officials or police should have that responsibility.

Even though Arnie is prone to get into fights, he is still considered a 'good kid' by the school, primarily because he is white and from the immediate local area. Other students, however, those of color and from outside the local area, do not get this benefit of the doubt. In fact, students from outside the local area face many more threats of violence during their daily rounds, because they have to travel farther to school and thus are exposed to challenges from cliques of youths from other neighborhoods and schools who share the buses and travel routes with them. The fact that these students have to travel more and the fact that they tend to be treated differently by school officials when trouble does arise means that they end up both being more exposed to danger and being more tarred by the local moral panic, as the following account illustrates.

Field Notes. I came into school this morning to find Tony, who is prone to being picked on by students and teachers alike, seated on the bench in the main office, crying. His mom, Lisa, was with him. It seems he was beaten up this morning by a boy named Keith as he was getting off the bus, which stops right in front of the projects. Keith lives in the projects across from Union and used to be in Tony's class. He was recently transferred to another school in the district because of his behavior problems.

Tony told me that before Keith was transferred out, he told Tony that he had to find him a gun to help him deal drugs. He threatened to beat him up if he didn't. Tony is kind of an easy target for a tough kid: he's overweight, wears glasses, and has a big mouth. Tony hasn't seen Keith since he was transferred out a few months ago. But this morning as he was getting off the bus, Keith happened to be there. Keith asked about the gun he had requested, and Tony lied and said he had it at home. Keith said he wanted it now, and punched Tony in the mouth. It was still swollen when I saw him.

Tony said there had been a Union teacher at the bus stop when Keith began harassing him who saw what was happening. The teacher just walked away. His mother was upset about the whole thing and wanted the school to do something about it. The school's policy is that since it didn't happen on school grounds, it wasn't their responsibility. Further, the principal and assistant principal (AP) insist they've already transferred the boy out of the school. What else can they do? The assistant principal feels the police should deal with it. Tony's mother wants the school to authorize a transfer, but they don't see the logic in that. The AP confided to me that they try to keep the number of school transfers down – schools with high numbers of transfers look like bad schools.

Meanwhile, the AP becomes stuck on the issue of Tony claiming to Keith that he did, in fact, have a gun at home. She talks to Tony and his mother as they sit on the bench about the consequences of gun possession. Tony's mom sits there looking up at the ceiling, trying to control her anger. They are treating her son, who has just been victimized, like a perpetrator. Tony tries to get out a few 'but I didn't . . .', but the AP never lets him respond. When I spoke to the principal about the incident later, it was clear the AP had told her about Tony's defensive claim to have a gun. She also spoke about him as if he were a criminal, not a victim. *End Field Notes*.

Tony and his mother's inability to communicate with the school administration is clearly problematic here, and it leads to Tony's being doubly victimized, first by Keith and then by the labeling process that stigmatizes him for being associated with possession of a weapon.

The preceding incident suggests that the school deals harshly with students suspected of being dangerous; but that is not always the case. Sometimes the response is swift, as when a boy who brought an unloaded gun to class was quickly transferred; but at other times there is no response at all, as is illustrated by the following incident.

Field Notes: I arrived in school one morning and a school staff member informed me that Danny was arrested late yesterday afternoon in the school for extorting money from two other boys. The extortion, it seemed, had been going on for a number of months, dating almost all the way back to when Danny was transferred mid-year to Union from another school. He and another boy were charged with extorting over $700 from a boy named Neil, and a lesser amount of money from a second boy. Because of the amount of money involved, and the alleged use of threat in extorting it, both boys were being charged with felonies. All of the boys involved are black: the two accused thieves are African-American, the two victims children of West Indian immigrants.

The situation came to the attention of the school when Neil, one of the victims who is also a research participant, admitted to his mother that he had been taking money from her over a period of months, after she confronted him by asking if he had been stealing from her. He complained that a group of boys had been threatening to beat him up if he didn't give them money every day at lunch, and that he had seen these boys beat someone up one day after school and was very afraid of them. He didn't want to tell any adults at school, believing there was really nothing they could do to protect him. Neil's mother immediately called the school and spoke to the 7th grade dean. After speaking to him, she felt very unsatisfied with the degree of concern he showed, and didn't really believe the boys would be punished for what they did. Because of this perception, she decided to report the incident to the police, a step she says she didn't really want to take but was forced into because of the school's relaxed attitude.

The school, in fact, did very little to punish Danny and the other boy. They received standard principal's suspensions, for only three days. When I asked why they hadn't been given superintendent's suspensions, which the chancellor's regulations call for in a case like this, I was told that such suspensions are meted out almost exclusively in cases where weapons are involved.

Danny admits to asking the boys for money, but staunchly denies that it was anywhere near $700. His parents believe this, as do all of the school personnel I've spoken to about this. The general feeling is that the victim and his mother are conspiring to get restitution for more than was actually stolen. Moreover, Danny and his parents, who are divorced but both involved in his life, feel very strongly that Danny has done something wrong and should be punished. But they all feel the whole event has been blown out of proportion, there being no good reason to arrest a kid bothering another kid for what his mom described as 'cookie money'.

The outcome of the court case is still pending, but Danny's mother was sufficiently upset that she has found an apartment in another neighborhood, hoping that Danny can make a fresh start in a new school. *End Field Notes*.

The striking feature of this case is that the school's sanctions against Danny seem so trivial, while the involvement of the juvenile justice system seems also perhaps inappropriate. The emerging theme from all these incidents seems to be the lack of appropriate intermediate sanctions between letting youths who commit serious infractions off with a slap on the wrist and charging them with felonies. All too often, the pattern of response to conflicts among adolescents appears to be too little in the early stages and too much after it is too late and something serious has happened.

While this lack of appropriate intermediate sanctions is a general problem with juvenile justice and a principal source of the historical policy fluctuations between *parens patriae* and getting tough, the school's posture of denial, itself rooted in the local moral panic, greatly exacerbates the problem. If school officials acknowledged the problems in their midst, they presumably would be more able to deal with them. By denying the problems, they contribute to an atmosphere in which adolescents do not trust them or other adults to protect their safety. The first consequence of this is an increase in danger for the entire community.

The second consequence of the posture of denial is that the local moral panic becomes an engine of inequality. Youths from outside the local area, and, indeed, youths of color who live in the immediate area, are far more likely to be labeled, stigmatized, sanctioned or transferred. The moral panic thus contributes to a worsening of the very dangers that are the subject of the panic, while simultaneously increasing inequality.

Engines of Panic: School, Community, and State

Returning to questions of state restructuring, we can distinguish in this case study three categories of social actors involved in the co-production of moral panic: school officials, community representatives, and representatives of the state. Actors from each category contribute to the creation of the panic. While there was some diversity within each category, a separate set of interests was at stake within each. The character and the consequences of the panic derive from the interests of all three categories and from the nature of the interactions among them. Only by identifying the interests and strategies of the various actors and how they interact with those of the others can we arrive a satisfactory analysis of this case that avoids reductionist appeals to images of a conspiratorial elite or a broad-based social movement. (See Heyman, this volume, Chapter 10 for an analysis of a similar problem of attending to different categories of state-level actors with regard to the control of illegal immigration.) Similarly, the relationship of the panic to state restructuring needs to be examined from the vantage points of the actors involved.

Union Middle School is a public institution, funded and administered by the state to provide education and socialization for adolescents. The posture of this school towards problems and images of youth violence is but one of a number of different possible postures. Here, that posture is shaped by the role played by this school in its particular community. As a public institution, this school both denies the existence of problems of youth violence and simultaneously contributes to panic about them. The institutional impression management that leads to denying the problems in order to safeguard the image of school and community goes hand in hand with active participation in a local network of political actors intent upon increasing social controls over minority youths seen as foreign and threatening to the community.

These institutional actions, of course, represent only part of that community, consisting of white, middle-class families who are longtime residents of the immediate local area. Other parts of the school's community, the minority residents of the local housing project and the minority families whose children ride the buses from the far end of the school district, are excluded from the processes of school and community governance leading to these policies. A small group of established white community members also has much greater sway, directly and indirectly, in local government. The attempts of this community faction to increase police surveillance over minority youths in their area can also be linked to their attempts to safeguard resources from the school system, in the form of magnet programs and honors classes that disproportionately serve their children, even as the school's population becomes increasingly drawn from the minority.

Attributing motives of simple personal racism to these community actors, however, misses much of the complexity of their situations and attitudes. This is a community experiencing racial change. Some white families move out to the suburbs, often at the point where their children are becoming adolescents. Those white families that do remain, some as a result of financial inability to move, make the best of what they have. They speak of the virtues of living in a racially diverse community, even as they struggle to control the government resources still being invested there for their immediate benefit. Magnet programs and increased police surveillance are the returns they seek from their political representatives in return for political support. Political entrepreneurship in this environment takes the form of lobbying for a redistribution of public resources toward this community faction within a larger context of shrinking overall public resources.

This local situation is itself embedded in a larger political context of a power shift from cities to suburbs and from the Northeast and Midwest of the United States to the South and West. This power shift is linked to a downsizing of central government and a sharp decrease in the ability of central government to ameliorate the conditions of the urban populations bearing much of the brunt of economic restructuring. In this process, resources are being redistributed from public education and social welfare to an intensified apparatus of social control.

The legitimacy of the state, at both national and local levels, is buttressed and redefined by this shift of resources to intensified internal social control, in a number of ways. The specter of domestic youth violence displaces the Cold War specter of external threat. The reduction of overall social investment in public education, social welfare, and urban development is counterbalanced by the image of the state as guarantor of safety against the enemy within. Within racially and economically mixed communities like Fairhaven, racial tensions thus represent not primordial difference but a squabble over the remaining pieces of a shrinking pie.

Moral panic plays crucial roles in this process, albeit distinctly different roles at local and national levels. At the local level, the panic serves as excuse and vehicle for local-level redistribution of resources, even as it undermines the very fabric of community in the name of which it is justified. At the national level, this local moral panic sustains political entrepreneurs responsible for shifting resources away from some of the very areas and institutional arenas where the local panics rage.

References

Becker, Howard S. (1963), 'Labelling Theory Reconsidered', in Howard S. Becker, *The Outsiders: Studies in the Sociology of Deviance*, New York: The Free Press, pp. 177–212.

Bernard, Thomas J. (1992), *The Cycle of Juvenile Justice*. New York: Oxford University Press.

Blok, Anton (1974), *The Mafia of a Sicilian Village*. Oxford: Basil Blackwell.

Blumstein, Alfred (1995), 'Youth Violence, Guns, and the Illicit-Drug Industry', *The Journal of Criminal Law and Criminology* 86(1): 10–36.

Burawoy, Michael (1991), 'The Extended Case Method', in Michael Burawoy, Alice Burton, Ann Arnett Ferguson, Kathyrn J. Fox, Joshua Gramson, Nadine Gartrell, Leslie Hurst, Charles Kurzman, Leslie Salzinger, Josepha Schiffman, and Shiori Ui, *Ethnography Unbound: Power and Resistance in the Modern Metropolis*. Berkeley: University of California Press.

Butterfield, Fox (1995), *All God's Children: The Bosket Family and the American Tradition of Violence*. New York: Knopf.

Chambliss, William J. (1994), 'Policing the Ghetto Underclass: The Politics of Law and Law Enforcement', *Social Problems* 41(2): 177–94.

Cohen, Stanley (1972), *Folk Devils and Moral Panics: The Creation of the Mods and Rockers*. New York: St Martin's Press.

Devine, John (1996), *Maximum Security: The Culture of Violence in Inner-City Schools*. Chicago: University of Chicago Press.

DiIulio, John J. (1996), 'They're Coming: Florida's Youth Crime Bomb', *Impact*, pp. 25–7.

Elliott, Delbert S. (1994), 'Serious Violent Offenders: Onset, Developmental Course, and Termination – The American Society of Criminology 1993 Presidential Address', *Criminology* 32: 1–21.

Fox, James Alan (1996), *Trends in Juvenile Violence: A Report to the United States Attorney General on Current and Future Rates of Juvenile Offending*. Washington, DC: Bureau of Justice Statistics, United States Department of Justice.

Giddens, Anthony (1987), *The Nation-State and Violence*. Berkeley: University of California Press.

Goode, Erich and Nachman Ben-Yehuda (1994), *Moral Panics: The Social Construction of Deviance*. Malden, MA: Blackwell Publishers.

Hall, Stuart *et al.* (1978), *Policing the Crisis: Mugging, the State and Law and Order*. New York: Holmes & Meier Publishers.

Hamburg, Beatrix (1986), 'Early Adolescence: A Specific and Stressful Stage of Development', in G. Coelho, B. A. Hamburg, and J. E. Adams (eds), *Coping and Adaptation*. New York: Basic Books.

Hawkins, Darnell, F. (ed.) (1995), *Ethnicity, Race, and Crime: Perspectives across Time and Place*. Albany, NY: State University of New York Press.

Hobsbawm, Eric (1965), *Primitive Rebels: Studies in Archaic Forms of Social Movements in the 19th and 20th Centuries*. New York: Norton.

—— (1969), *Bandits*. New York: Pantheon.

Moffitt, T. E. (1993), 'Adolescence-limited and Life-course-persistent Antisocial Behavior: A Developmental Taxonomy', *Psychological Review* 100: 674–701.

Nagin, D. S. and R. Paternoster (1991), 'On the Relationship of Past to Future Participation in Delinquency', *Criminology* 29: 163–89.

National Institute of Education (1978), 'Violent Schools – Safe Schools. The Safe School Study Report to Congress'. Washington, DC: National Institute of Education.

Prothrow-Stith, Deborah (1991), *Deadly Consequences: How Violence is Destroying our Teenage Population and a Plan to Begin Solving the Problem*. New York: Harper-Collins.

Sampson, R. J. and J. H. Laub (1993), *Crime in the Making: Pathways and Turning Points through Life*. Cambridge, MA: Harvard University Press.

Sickmund, Melissa, Howard N. Snyder, and Eileen Poe-Yamagata (1997), *Juvenile Offenders and Victims: 1997 Update of Violence.* Washington, DC : Office of Juvenile Justice and Delinquency Prevention.

Snyder, Howard N. and Melissa Sickmund (1995), *Juvenile Offenders and Victims: A National Report*. Washington, DC: Office of Juvenile Justice and Delinquency Prevention.

Suttles, Gerald (1972), *The Social Construction of Communities*. Chicago: University of Chicago Press.

Tanner, Julian (1996), *Teenage Troubles: Youth and Deviance in Canada*. Toronto, Can.: Nelson.

Van Velsen, Jaap (1967), 'The Extended Case Method and Situational Analysis', in A. L. Epstein (ed.),*The Craft of Social Anthropology*. London: Tavistock, pp. 129–49.

Weber, Max (1978), *Economy and Society*. Berkeley: University of California Press.

Wolfgang, Marvin E. and Franco Ferracuti (1967), *The Subculture of Violence*: *Towards an Integrated Theory in Criminology*. London: Tavistock Publications.

Wright, Lawrence (1993a), 'Remembering Satan: Part I', *The New Yorker*, 17 May, pp. 60–81.

Wright, Lawrence (1993b), 'Remembering Satan: Part II', *The New Yorker*, 24 May, pp. 54–76.

Zatz, Marjorie S. (1987), 'Chicano Youth Gangs and Crime: The Creation of a Moral Panic', *Contemporary Crises* 11(2): 129–58.

Zimring, Franklin E. (1996), 'Kids, Guns, and Homicide: Policy Notes on an Age-Specific Epidemic'. *Law and Contemporary Problems* 59: 25–37.

—— and Gordon Hawkins (1997), *Crime is Not the Problem: Lethal Violence in America*. New York: Oxford University Press.

–10–

State Escalation of Force: A Vietnam/ US–Mexico Border Analogy

Josiah McC. Heyman

Introduction

When attempting to control populations that defy its policies, the United States government gradually adds physical force, reaching massive levels of police or military activity that are described as wars, whether real (Vietnam) or metaphorical ('the war on drugs' and the like). The armed intervention does not necessarily solve the 'problem', while extended conflict and harm to human lives result. This is escalation, defined as adding increments of force to a failing or incomplete system of control. The process of escalation is memorably phrased as 'throwing good money after bad' (Goltz 1997). This pattern of events has occurred in the Vietnam War, the US interdiction policy against narcotics and its border immigration control policy. Why does the US government rely on military and police force to control illegality and defiance? Why maintain such commitments when to escalate is expensive, prone to failure and harmful to human lives? One approach is the critique of flawed policies and approaches specific to a given country or issue. For example, it might involve criticizing US border immigration policy and offering alternatives to that (see Heyman 1998b). The approach in this chapter, and this book generally, differs. It sees the pattern of escalation of force in comparative perspective, as one of several possible interactions of states with illegal or defiant actors. It works from an implicit contrast with non-escalation, for example, a persistent relationship between a state and a tolerated or only moderately prosecuted illegal activity. It characterizes the distinct form and dynamics of the violent, escalatory alternative, and asks why the US state might be prone to such an approach. In this sense, it seeks the systemic causes of specific policy flaws, the repeated 'good money after bad' syndrome.

The evidence of US escalation in Vietnam has been surveyed definitively elsewhere (Kahin 1986), so there is little need to insist that Vietnam was a case of escalation. The reader may be less aware, however, of the escalation of immigration law enforcement on the US–Mexico border. It is a striking example of the 'border effect' about which Thomas Gallant writes in Chapter 2, in which efforts to supress illegal activities along boundaries result in a significant increment to state power. (The reader should know that the INS is the US Immigration and Naturalization Service, and that the Border Patrol is its uniformed police branch.) In 1986, the US had 3,700 Border Patrol officers, mostly stationed on the Mexican border, while in 1996 it had 6,000, with authorization in the 1996 Immigration Act to increase the number to 10,000 (US INS, n.d., files of author; *Migration News* 1996b).[1] Quasi-military policies include the use of the National Guard at the border for all tasks except arrests, the emplacement of a 14-mile steel wall along the San Diego border, an increase in the number of INS helicopters from two in 1980 to 58 in 1992 (within that, the introduction of modern Black Hawk attack helicopters), and the equipping of all Border Patrol sectors with modern electronic motion sensors and night-vision units (Dunn 1996). Narcotics interdiction at the border has grown even more dramatically, including the creation of a large US Customs air force, airborne electronics eavesdropping, air and land radar coverage and the extensive use of military units. Narcotics and immigration law enforcement overlap in the INS (immigration enforcement officers are cross-designated for drug arrests) and the two reinforce each other's escalatory tendencies. My focus here, however, will be on the immigration side, because that has been my fieldwork topic and because surveying two such cases is overwhelmingly complex.

The Vietnam analogy to border policy allows me to start with well-developed understandings about Vietnam, and then to ask parallel questions about the conduct of affairs on the US–Mexico border, where events are still unfolding. Although the analogy facilitates parallel questions, the answers will not necessarily be the same, nor are the two cases are entirely comparable. Vietnam and border immigration and narcotics differ in many ways: the former a shooting war, conducted against a politically organized opponent, outside the soil of the United States; the latter two overlapping police operations, relying on arrests, barriers and some gunplay, to halt market- and network-organized contraband across national boundaries. Many people would not regard guerilla war in Vietnam to be a case of illegality *per se*, but rather struggle between two state orders, while there is no such state-in-the-becoming in border smuggling. However, I have several good reasons for pursuing the analogy.

First, the three cases are not arbitrarily juxtaposed, but are related by direct historical continuity of US state behavior. Vietnam and the two border interdiction policies are a consistent response by the US government to margins that it cannot control. Second, this chapter makes no claim that an opportunistic illegal market is equivalent to a nationalistic struggle embodied in an organized party and military. Once the US government treats disparate cases of defiance as if they are similarly amenable to military control, however, Vietnamese peasants and Mexican smugglers do respond with roughly analogous guerrilla tactics. They operate in small bands, using the land to maneuver and hide, relying on the silence of the local populace for deception and surprise. Such tactical convergences are less important for understanding the people's experience itself (Mexican smugglers do not offer the same ends to peasants as did the National Liberation Front) than for understanding the frustrations and escalatory responses of the US state.

The analogy unfolds as a series of inquiries about different levels in state–illegality interactions. I begin with the inner circles of the dominant state. Like Alan Smart in Chapter 4, I view state elites as power- and revenue-seeking, but confronted by problems with troublesome situations and populations rather than as acting as cloistered manipulators. The next set of inquiries focuses on military and police organizations. These bureaucracies have two faces: upward, as advocates to state elites of bureaucratic interests and doctrines of control; and downward, as working organizations producing arrests and/or deaths. In the latter case, I ask about how ruling politics translate into day-to-day management of policing and warfare, given characteristic evasive interactions with resistant populations. Turning to the opponents of the state, within its limits the analogy raises two topics – the guerrilla-like networks that illegal actors and revolutionary movements partly share; and the surrounding population, the ocean within which the fish of opposition swim (to use a famous metaphor of guerrilla warfare). Finally, the Vietnam analogy suggests that we look not only at the dominant state, but also at secondary states that add to or dampen escalation. Exploring each inquiry in the analogy reveals more about the US state and the border situation than a critique of explicit policy would alone.

By recognizing the pattern of US governmental escalation, I question its tendency to use force to solve all problems on the margins. By speaking to the controversies in immigration and narcotics law enforcement with the experience of Vietnam in mind, I seek a public discussion that might redirect US state rulers – for, as troubled it might be, the US still is a publicly accountable democracy.

Dominant State Elites

Contexts

The US state elites were well-informed about the role of anti-colonialism and nationalism in the Vietnamese communist movement. Yet they ignored the implication of this information, that outside intervention made revolution more, not less viable. This was not just an initial mistake, but a willful error that persisted throughout the war – for instance, Washington failed to recognize the strong appeal of Vietnamese reunification to Buddhists and even some South Vietnamese generals in the post-Diem, pre-Thieu interregnum (Kahin 1986). The scope of US elite vision was narrow because of the Cold War assumption that the US could control all paths of national development in the non-communist world (Schurmann 1974). Military escalation was premised on a bias towards one among several alternative resolutions. Is there an equivalent at the Mexican border?

My argument is that precisely such a bias undergirds escalation. To follow this argument, we have to understand that the US could easily tolerate illegal immigration, for reasons I will explain shortly, but does not rest with this 'empirical' option because of the particular 'ideological' importance of immigration law in the current US (using terms delineated in the book's introduction, Chapter 1). The question is how to explain the particular salience of immigration as a symbol of ideal law and its defense. An argument, which I have developed at length elsewhere (Heyman 1998a, b), is that recent anxiety about immigration derives from anxiety about the domestic public hegemony of the post-Second World War US. Undocumented immigrants form part of a varied set of perceived societal ills, such as increased crime, inadequate education, narcotics use, corporate globalization, insecure jobs and changing labor markets, etc. As outsiders, immigrants are easy to scapegoat, and as an overtly illegal activity, undocumented entry at the Mexican border is a distinctive moral inversion (see Perea 1997, and especially Rodríguez 1997). Recent patterns of US politics support this interpretation of anti-immigrant politics. For example, Patrick Buchanan, a relatively popular right-wing Republican candidate for the US presidency, articulates several anxious responses to fragmenting hegemony: blunt criticisms of US corporations, hostility to the global economy, geopolitical isolationism, belligerent restatements of an idealized moral past, and crude anti-immigrationism. Mainstream, non-Buchananite US politicians encounter this anxious domestic hegemony as a double-edged sword: for their short-term electoral benefit, they incite popular panics, like those against crime described in Sullivan and Miller's Chapter 9; yet domestic distrust and anger is dangerous to the state elites generally. In immigration, for the disatisfied public they offer an apparently decisive solution, escalation of force at the border. I shall detail this shortly. But since my argument is that escalation comes when state elites neglect alternative resolutions, what options are they ignoring?

The US does not effectively enforce the law that makes employment of illegal aliens a crime. First, employers have no effective way to determine who is legally a citizen or a permanent resident and thus eligible for employment. Fraudulent documentation is pervasive, and the language of the law lets the employers off the hook in cases where employees bear fraudulent cards. There is no meaningful politics in favor of a strong national identification card and database system, despite its obvious importance to ending real illegality. Second, the provisions of immigration control are applied to businesses in a thin and intermittent manner, with considerable deference, unlike the mass policing approach taken to the immigrants themselves (Calavita 1990). At the recent peak of anti-immigrant hysteria, the INS and the Department of Labor offered a minimal voluntary, pilot phone-in job control system. In a nutshell, business's illegal practices are managed persistence, to use Smart's term for enduring toleration of law violations (Chapter 4).

In turn, consistently with Smart's market form of illegal persistence, undocumented immigrants persist in moving to illegal labor markets, despite significant chances of being arrested and suffering increasingly harsh penalties. While US businesses get the benefit of managed toleration, the undocumented pay the cost. The bias in enforcing the law against businesses versus undocumented immigrants is vital to the argument that escalation starts when key contexts and options are excised from the view of state elites. There are several reasons to expect that law enforcement will continue to concentrate on immigrants, not employers. As the range of jobs and locations filled by undocumented workers has widened, more labor markets in the US are committed to illegal supplies than ever before (this holds true for legal immigrant labor also). To this is added the US elite's tight association with the ruling Mexican regime and upper classes, and the commitments of both groups to a rapid liberalization of trade that dislocates people and produces migrants. Given the bias against the business control option, and the increasing commitment to migrant labor supplies, US state elites must ignore their most efficacious enforcement options. However, they cannot withdraw from migration control altogether, because illegal immigration publicly threatens ideal law. The response to the gap between ideal law and real illegal practices is escalation along the border.[2] The restorative ideologies that respond to these failures of hegemony, the various wars on drugs, crime and now on illegal immigrants, resemble the Cold War ideology in justifying the ignoring of great, complex realities. Among these realities is the initiative taken by the uncontrolled outsiders themselves.

Dominant State Elites in Traps of their Own Making

The ability of illegal actors to frustrate the enforcement apparatuses of the dominant state adds significantly to an understanding of escalation. Rather than the 'mistaken policy' approach, which focuses exclusively on the state, I utilize both ends of the state–illegality tunnel (to use Smart's metaphor). Given barriers to considering alternatives, when there is an initial commitment of resources, failures induce additional commitments, not withdrawal, for a long period before a culminating crisis.[3] I will discuss later why illegal or defiant networks sometimes frustrate strong states; here I analyze why failures by state organizations induce their masters to advance into quagmires, rather than withdrawing from them.

State elites are deeply concerned with their credibility. After they have propounded a goal to a public (which may be narrow, such as other states, or wide, such as large segments of US society via the media), they have to show that their power, resources, force, and so on can deliver what they promise. Research in foreign policy, specifically the behavior of US state elites in Cold War struggles in Asia, shows the importance of credibility to these people (McMahon 1991a, b, 1994). Credibility is a currency of power for them; if they are not credible, they are less persuasive in dealing with other power actors. Thus, rulers of dominant states will at times make strenuous efforts in minor arenas because they perceive their credibility to be at stake. When non-state networks, which elites barely understand and often willfully ignore, embarrass the dominant state, they put its credibility at risk. A believable response seeks to defeat these opponents, since withdrawal would undermine credibility; but the putative means to victory are mere increments of the same failed tactics. Hence, we have an escalatory cycle.

An important point needs to be made about credibility. It is no more than a proximate variable. Beyond the common thread of credibility, each case differs in the deeper contexts of the interests held, the alternatives ignored and the reputations put at stake. These latter considerations will enable us to link credibility to more systematic analyses of political economy. I sketched a few such points above for immigration, trying to show why the believability of US border control policy has been at stake in the 1980s and 1990s. Despite its limits as a full explanation, however, credibility is important, since it gives us purchase on the motivations of rulers when they recur to brute force as the solution to perplexing issues.

In Vietnam until 1968, and partially thereafter, the failure of existing US policies strengthened commitment to force, not withdrawal or a search for serious alternatives. Let us briefly review one escalatory sequence. In late 1963, South Vietnamese President Ngo Dinh Diem was overthrown; the US was deeply implicated in the coup as it sought to rescue its commitment to a failing government there. The first military junta after Diem was open to reunification negotiations with the North and the internal Buddhist opposition. General Khanh overthrew the first junta in January 1964. The US was also involved in that coup because it feared these negotiations. But Khanh headed an extremely weak government that also hinted at back-door negotiations. The US, trying to reinforce the warlike side of the southern government, began to bomb in the South. The campaign against the National Liberation Front (NLF, the communist guerrilla army in the South) was failing, however, while in civil society the Buddhists emerged as a second opposition. What was the US state elite response in 1964–5? Looking at their internal arguments, we do not find a significant debate over whether to abandon the war, but rather heated discussion about which increases in force would vindicate the failing policy. The record shows various plans and ideological stances, some so extreme that the ultimate choices seem 'reasonable' by contrast. By 1965, the US presidency had settled on bombing North Vietnam and introducing large operational units of ground troops. Specific incidents, such as a guerrilla attack on the US air base at Pleiku and the trumped-up naval incident in the Tonkin Gulf, 'justified' the escalatory steps. However, examination of the historical process shows the predominance of President Johnson and his advisors' fear that political and guerrilla war trends in Vietnam were beyond their control. (Kahin 1986 provides superb evidence on the escalatory process inside the upper US state; a useful summary of the war as a whole is Young 1991.)

Among the lessons of the Vietnam case are that credibility and response must be understood in the context of the social world of state rulers (Halberstam 1972; Kolko 1985). The Cold War era US foreign policy elite were strikingly unified in their worldview, training, networks, and so forth. Members of the inner circle often mistook their personal credibility for that of the nation as a whole. An advisor would perceive that his personal recommendations had failed, and so, in his opinion, it was in the collective interest of the US to revindicate them. The worldview of power elites was central to escalation: they combined an expansive fear of imminent loss with no sense of constraints on the ability to act in response. In a different context, this might be clinically paranoid. One suspects that it is the characteristic worldview of the maximally powerful inside a given social order: they have the most commitments, and are exposed to the widest variety of disruptions and threats, while by past experience they know that their power is substantial and efficacious. The interesting point is that although the Cold War and its peculiar distortions have ended, the US state elite remains with a vast range of commitments and anxieties. Globalization, migration, investment and free trade in Mexico, and so on are to some extent replacing Cold War credibility obsessions for them, opening the possibility of their applying the same mode of thought in these new arenas.

Although for the US–Mexico border we do not have the declassified inside documentation that Kahin obtained for Vietnam, the external pattern of evidence suggests that credibility is again a major concern. However, the credibility at stake on the border is domestic, not geopolitical, as in Vietnam. As was argued above, increasing popular anxiety connects to people's sense that the US government fails to control various illegal or erosive activities. Researchers are beginning to document how fears about illegality on the border are amplified and distorted by the mass media (Chavez 1997), feeding a possessive citizenship ideology that emphasizes the opposition of citizens versus foreigners (Perea 1997; Heyman 1998b). We witness the rise of a restorative movement, often (but not only) associated with Republican right-wing populism, which seeks to repair this torn domestic hegemony. Though it has wide appeal, it does not follow automatically that elite politicians should respond to this politics. Why do they? It does not directly affect their interests – undocumented immigrants supply cheap and malleable labor to numerous sectors within US capitalism; they pay more taxes, in general, than they use services (Fix and Passel 1994). Though I view state elites as generally interested in the well-being of the capitalist economy, domestically and geopolitically, they do need hegemonic trust to get elected and to promote their overt interests, such as capital gains tax cuts. Thus a failure of domestic credibility can induce an elite response not easily explained by economic commitments *per se*. In the 1980s, there was a gradual build-up of incredibility about US immigration policy. For instance, the 1986 Immigration Reform and Control Act, which promised to halt undocumented entry to the US via control of employment, was a visible failure, as explained above. Then, in 1994, anxiety about domestic trust and order exploded in California.

A little background about California will help here. It is politically the most important state in the US, and also the most volatile, media-sensitive one. It had been the epitome of the Cold War US in its combination of imperial military politics, domestic prosperity and citizenship ideology. However, in the early 1990s the state underwent a severe economic shock with the decline of weapons spending. Optimism and prosperity came under question. At this opportune time, Harold Ezell, a former INS regional commissioner and anti-immigrant activist, mobilized prosperous Anglo-Americans[4] behind Proposition 187, a state referendum that sought a law to penalize undocumented immigrants by denying them public schooling, medical care, and so on (Kadetsky 1994; Stefancic 1997). Under pressure because of California's weak economy, Republican Governor Pete Wilson of California, in a heated re-election campaign, seized on the immigration issue. Although he strongly backed Proposition 187, an initiative internal to California, Wilson also federalized the issue by criticizing the US government's control of the Mexican border. Democratic senatorial candidates Diane Feinstein and Barbara Boxer quickly fell in line (all these candidates and the ballot initiative won, incidently). The result was national media attention to the border's lack of credibility.

President Clinton had not had a strong border control agenda until this time; his appointment of Doris Meissner to be INS Commissioner, for example, signaled greater interest in asylum policy than border control. But in these circumstances he reacted dramatically to the sudden loss of domestic credibility. He sent Attorney General Reno to tour the California border, trumpeted past acts of force (for example, the fourteen-mile boundary wall in San Diego county) and initiated new escalation (for instance, a rapid concentration of police and military force in the same area). This key escalatory moment has dominated nearly all immigration politics since 1994. For example, it led directly to the 1996 Illegal Immigration Reform and Immigrant Responsibility Act authorizing doubling the size of the Border Patrol, and it even affected legal immigration and naturalization (more extensive coverage of this period of escalation is provided in Andreas 1997). To summarize these events, the ongoing ability of undocumented immigrants to defeat the border barriers of the US, combined with a tacitly tolerated illegal labor market, surfaced during a politicized moral panic; when embarrassment reached the highest levels of the US government, the response was to escalate force at the border.[5]

An examination of the Jordan Commission, an official policy study group mandated in the 1990 Immigration Act, supports the credibility argument. Their first report to the Congress, issued in 1994, concerned undocumented immigration. Strikingly, their main argument was that undocumented immigration injures US credibility – the report is titled

Restoring Credibility (US Commission on Immigration Reform 1994). After weighing the disputed and ambiguous evidence about benefits and harms of undocumented immigration (for example, employment effects on domestic workers), their strongest case was the simple fact that the US and Mexican publics know undocumented immigration to be illegal yet commonplace, causing a lack of plausibility in US law (1994: iii, v). And what were the recommendations? Not surprisingly, (a) to escalate the border patrol along the Mexican border and (b) to use a national electronic identity registry to control legal access to jobs. Again, not surprisingly, (a) was followed and (b) has been being ignored. The Jordan Commission probably reflects insider politics more than it makes them; but it does corroborate the credibility concerns of US insiders.

Among such insiders, let us examine Harold Ezell, an active member of the Jordan Commission. Ezell, from Orange County, California, the president of a chain of inexpensive restaurants ('Wienerschnitzel'), was a member of Ronald Reagan's inner circle, the so-called 'kitchen cabinet'. He was appointed regional commissioner of the INS Western Region, which includes California, where he was noted for his vocal unhappiness with illegal immigration. From this, he retired to work as an (unsuccessful) immigration consultant for wealthy Asians. Finally, he emerged as a central figure in California's anti-immigrant Proposition 187, while he was 'studying' immigration policy in the Jordan Commission. Ezell is an entrepreneur of border escalation, akin to Maxwell Taylor, McGeorge Bundy and W. W. Rostow in the Vietnam era.

The Ezell case also indicates differences from Vietnam foreign policy elites. The Vietnam era elites came from a well-defined social group, one that collectively ignored or manipulated domestic opinion in favor of geopolitical interests. Ezell is a political insider, but he also works beyond the inner circles as a promoter of anti-immigrant moral panics with a popular base, like the crime panics as described by Sullivan and Miller (see Chavez 1992 on local immigration panics). Immigration politics manifest more complex coalitions than did Cold War foreign policy; in particular, we do not see the high degree of Presidential and presidential advisor initiative – they instead react to fluctuating movements in the domestic sphere. The US foreign policy elite is more strongly committed to free trade with and investment in Mexico, a policy that anti-immigrant sentiments put at risk. Border control is, arguably, a popular symbolic patch hiding this unpopular elite policy. 'Credibility' thus means different things in the two cases, Vietnam and the border. In both instances, however, it derives immediate salience from the ability of guerrilla-like opponents to embarrass the US state.

In late 1994, Mexico's speculative free market boom collapsed, putting many people out of work and badly damaging domestic businesses. Even as the US launched a massive crackdown at key boundary zones, Mexican immigration apparently increased (the evidence is indirect but substantial). Smugglers and migrants moved quickly to new crossing areas – shifting from the highways of southern California to the deserts of Arizona – leaving the INS to react by reallocating its patrols (Bean *et al.*, 1994; *Migration News* 1996a). Although we cannot tell how effective the escalated border control system will be in the future, until now it has been ineffectual, with the undocumented immigrants holding the initiative over the law enforcers. US credibility continues to be at risk.

Control Bureaucracies

Facing Up, as Political Actors

State bureaucracies have separate interests and dynamics from the state rulers above them. It is helpful to think of bureaucracies as facing both up and down. Upward, they face other bureaucracies and the elite circles that direct and mediate among them. Downward, bureaucrats struggle with non-bureaucratic, sometimes guerrilla-like opponents.

When bureaucracies face upward, they seek new authority, resources and endorsement of their ingrained doctrines over critics, usually rival bureaucrats. They often do this by presenting a 'new' approach (or new language for an old approach) to state elites hungry for relief from their gnawing worries. The US elite confidence at the beginning of the Vietnam war derived from new anti-guerrilla doctrines, counterinsurgency and limited war, sold by General Maxwell Taylor (see Gibson 1988: 76). Later in the war, bureaucratic rivalries and self-promoting projects (e.g. Army vs. Airforce; Joint Chiefs of Staff vs. civilian advisors) lead to multiple, escalatory steps (see Kahin 1986 literally *ad nauseam*). Operational units, such as military branches, often push escalation because they ask for more than they can reasonably get, in hopes of getting as much as possible; in so doing, they drive expectations upwards. When we look at the INS, do we find similar or dissimilar behaviors?

From 1920s through to the early 1980s, when undocumented Mexican labor migration was a tolerated illegal market, the INS's tacit doctrine was interception of individual undocumented crossers in open country. In the Border Patrol, this was called 'the game'. Calling it 'the game' suggested that it offered not a solution but a check on the flow (Heyman

1995). In the 1980s and early 1990s, with increasing hostility to undocumented immigrants, the INS obtained clearer mandates to stop illegal immigration at the boundary. But its doctrine remained rather traditional. Inside the INS, reformers were influenced by doctrines from other agencies, mainly anti-narcotics ones (Customs, the DEA, and so forth). Timothy Dunn (1996) shows that narcotics, not immigration, justified most of the INS's build-up in manpower and military technology in the 1980s and early 1990s. He also shows how this anti-narcotics build-up left the INS with an unofficial doctrine of 'low-intensity conflict.' Low-intensity conflict resembles Vietnam era counterinsurgency under a new name and somewhat refined (Dunn 1996; Klare and Kornbluh 1988). It can have several emphases, either anti-guerrilla social and intelligence tactics, or advanced interdiction using surveillance technology. The latter predominates at the border.[6]

Before 1994, the INS anti-narcotics side rivaled immigration control. However, in 1993 at El Paso, Texas, an ambitious Border Patrol Chief Patrol Agent, Silvestre Reyes, launched a series of innovations in immigration policing: massing patrol officers right on the line, withdrawing them from anti-narcotics and interior control, aiming to reduce illegal entry numbers by deterrence rather than arrest. These steps are not the older INS doctrine, nor do they fit the anti-narcotics alternative. Reyes used connections in Congress to survive criticism inside the INS (Brinkley 1994; he eventually left the Border Patrol to run successfully for Congress from El Paso). After 1994, the new Reyes doctrine swept the INS, defeating internal factions that had sought other approaches.[7] The doctrine succeeded because it fitted higher-level politics at that moment, and because it reinforced the favored political status of the Border Patrol in Congress.[8] The Reyes doctrine's success is important because massed Patrol operations, with military support, add significantly to escalation at the border, just as did the anti-narcotics doctrine that preceded it. Bureaucracies perpetually seek to increase their own resources and budgets; but only certain historical situations allow them to be successful in promoting escalation. When they do, escalation arrives with a fanfare, in the form of a justifying doctrine developed by some organizational faction as the policy 'solution' of the moment.

Facing Down: The Bureaucratic Production of 'Control'

Militarized bureaucracies, armies and police forces, contain distinctive work processes (see Heyman 1995). Political contexts shape these organizations into characteristic production goals, techniques and work groups.

Each historical organization – the US military in Vietnam, the Border Patrol – has a characteristic work style. The work process, however, exists not just within the organization itself; active opponents set many terms of the work for militaries and police. Higher-order credibility builds or erodes in this context of day-to-day enforcement work.

Two very different organizations fought in Vietnam, ARVN (South Vietnam's army) and the US armed forces. The manifold failings of ARVN are not particularly relevant here. I focus on the US military, a set of organizations removed in terms of language, national origin and loyalty, local socio-political knowledge and mode of operations from the populations they were to penetrate and control. I denominate their work situation 'alienated militarized bureaucracy', a term that characterizes US interventions both in third world wars and law-enforcement operations.

James William Gibson (1988) analyzes the US military approach to Vietnam as a mass production model: war turned from a complex social-political struggle to a single, simple measure of success. The main measure was the body count (dead bodies attributed, accurately or not, to the enemy). A secondary measure was villages controlled (again, based on flawed data). Technical means of production (firepower, air mobility and top-down bureaucratic organization) sought to increase the simple measure. Perhaps large bureaucracies always favor simple systems of production measurement and control; if so, this has significant implications for the escalation of violence.

Because of flawed assumptions about the war, described above, and the fact that the US military were functioning as outsiders, the Americans had little call on the loyalty of most of the Vietnamese population (see below for evidence). They were unable to deliver control night and day in the countryside. In response, the US military concentrated the Vietnamese population in physically controlled areas, while designating the remaining areas 'free fire zones.' In concentration zones, the ostensibly civilian status of the populace somewhat constrained the behavior of US forces; but in the free fire zones, anyone, NLF military or not, could be bombed, shelled, shot at, and so on.

The mass production structure of war had two 'mis-behavioral' consequences. First, the US military was consistently unable to accomplish its mission. I am not arguing who won or lost thc 'war', ultimately the result of politics in Vietnam and US; but, looking at on-the-ground dynamics, the US military lagged behind its opponents. The NLF, not the US, consistently had the initiative to engage or withdraw from engagement; a Pentagon study in 1966, for example, found that the NLF initiated three-fourths of all combat engagements (Gibson 1988: 108–9). Still, production pressures mounted to achieve 'victorious measures', especially body counts. This led to a complex fabric of official lying and self-deception – fake body counts protected the careers of field officers; then higher levels of the military aggregated phoney data and added deceptive interpretations (Gibson 1988: 124–5; Sheehan 1988). Ultimately, the disparity between the official production of false knowledge and the real failures of the campaign reinforced the incredibility of the war.

The direct contact with the populace required to kill opponents and control civilians was delegated to alienated US soldiers. The US command had 'rules of engagement', i.e. a card with guidelines on treatment of civilians and the enemy. But this veneered over the reality of the war: that US soldiers had a very difficult time distinguishing between the NLF and the general populace. Hence, they sometimes violated the rules of engagement protecting civilians and even enemy soldiers. Features of the work process leading to these violations included the facts that: (1) US soldiers were under the duress of production pressures; (2) they worked in strong cliques, with little meaningful managerial control over small-group behavior; and (3) the small groups often experienced frustration, exhaustion, fright and a populace that betrayed the US and helped the NLF. As a result, (4) work groups rationalized the behavior of their members, constructing false compliance with the formal rules while fulfilling the real military mandates of creating refugees and body counts (Gibson 1988: 129–205).

In following up the analogy, we must keep in mind the great differences between Vietnam and the border. The former was a war with deadly weapons, whose main objective was killing the enemy; the border is not (yet) a war zone, the main objective is arrest and removal of undocumented immigrants, and weapons, if used at all, are used in incidental violent situations, often drug-related (most Border Patrol officers carry 9 mm. automatic pistols and many have automatic assault rifles). Another difference is that boundary interdiction of infiltration was only a small element of the Vietnam war, whereas that precisely describes the US–Mexico border case. Thus, the purpose of this section of the analogy is not to claim that the border is a 'war zone', but to ask questions about alienated militarized bureaucrats, the preferred instrument of US government policies in both cases, to see if this casts light on enforcement behavior and human rights issues.

At the border, as in Vietnam, a complex political task (increasing compliance with migration laws by employers, immigrants, their kin, and others, usually far from the border) is reduced to a simple-minded mass production model. The INS uses numbers of arrests at the Mexican boundary, termed 'apprehension statistics'. (In fact, because most arrested undocumented Mexican immigrants depart voluntarily and return to the US very quickly, sheer numbers of arrests add little to compliance [Heyman 1998a].)[9] One incident reminiscent of falsified body counts,[10] when Border Patrol agents in San Diego county accused management of deliberately manipulating apprehension numbers (*New York Times* 1996), shows the importance of this statistic in the organization work process.

Is the Border Patrol alienated from the people and places where it works? In general, yes, though not as completely or obviously as the US military in Vietnam. The Border Patrol operates in border towns where the majority population is Latino, sometimes overwhelmingly. My 1991–2 Border Patrol interviewees were 64 per cent Anglo-American and 36 per cent Latino. So the Patrol is more Anglo than the border populace, but not overwhelmingly so. The self-conceptions of the Latino officers and the Anglo officers were similar, however – in both cases they felt separate from the local populace. For example, I had open-ended discussions with all the officers about the local community. Most felt it was unsupportive and expressed great frustration with people's passive non-cooperation. They were suspicious about border-town compromises with the traffic in undocumented immigrants. Even though a large minority of officers were raised in border towns, the Patrol assigns officers to communities other than the ones they grew up in. The Patrol also actively socializes its members through the Patrol academy, resulting in a quasi-military *esprit de corps*. Latino and Anglo officers alike proudly emphasized their US citizenship; in particular, Latino INS officers who identify as citizens reject ethnicized identification with Mexican-origin immigrants.[11]

The border does not have free fire zones, but the INS increasingly has 'non-accountable zones' where it operates unwatched and with few legal constraints. This development began in the late 1980s in the lower Rio Grande, where Central American entrants, many of whom were potential asylum seekers, were arrested and put in camps or trapped between Mexico and the US interior by strict highway inspection, discouraging them from making asylum claims (Koulish 1992; Kahn 1996). This approach has shifted from Central American refugees to undocumented Mexicans and Central Americans generally. To understand this, we can think of the US side of the border as having two basic tactical settings. In urban downtown and neighborhood areas where undocumented immigrants cross or wait for rides north, the Patrol is relatively constrained by the presence of witnesses. Many 'Mexican-looking' people there are US citizens, legal permanent residents (legal immigrants), or have border-crossing (shopping and visiting) cards, thus requiring of INS officers a modicum of attention to legal process in questioning and arrest. On the other hand, in non-urban areas (ranch, hill and desert country), and at night in towns, the Patrol has fewer such encounters and is little watched. Furthermore, most arrested undocumented Mexicans and Central Americans sign away their right to a deportation trial in exchange for a quick return to their home country (termed 'voluntary departure'); hence, they do not enter a legal process where they have counsel or even contact with a judge that would constrain Patrol behavior.

Given the non-accountability of routine operations on the border, what do Patrol officers do with their discretion? Managerial control over officers in the field is weak, a degree of autonomy that is accepted as long as they produce arrest numbers; for example, my participant observation showed that officers function only in radio contact with supervisors. Officers form small cliques that support, help and protect each other. Their ethic is to 'work hard' – that is, to contribute hard physical effort and support each other when making arrests – a perspective largely determined by the organizational mandate to 'get the numbers'. Their attitude to formal regulations and procedures, including rules governing physical force in arrest, is superficial compliance, but actual disdain. This is not to say that officers routinely abusively deploy physical force, but that they resent formal rules for getting in the way of their job effectiveness. For this reason, they tend to close ranks and support each other, even when one officer behaves in a troublesome fashion (see the Michael Elmer case, discussed in *Americas Watch* 1995). I have characterized their working philosophy as 'negative *esprit de corps*' (Heyman 1995); it resembles other police cultures (Skolnick 1966). An additional factor of considerable importance is the overlap between narcotics and immigration interdiction: Patrol officers anticipate the violence that sometimes characterizes narcotics smuggling arrests. This reinforces a shared perception of threat in the border environment and preparedness for an armed response.

This work pattern has two troublesome consequences, though each is less marked than in the Vietnam War situation. The first concerns the contest between the state and its opponents, and the second the treatment of immigrants and bystanders along the border.

We do not know how effective the Border Patrol is in stopping undocumented entrants, since we only know of failed entries (arrests) and not successful covert entries. But the work process suggests problems similar to those of the US military in Vietnam. The immigrants have the initiative not just in the simple sense of choosing to cross the border, but in the more important sense of changing favored crossing points, times and tactics, while the Patrol lags until it detects, figures out and responds to the new tactics. Smugglers lead the process by maneuvering around US interdiction, while independent crossers follow their example.[12] The Patrol, with its bureaucratic production approach and small work groups in the field, succeeds at arrest but not at controlling the dynamic flow. For example, smugglers counteracted escalation in western San Diego county, California, the preferred immigration corridor of the 1980s, by shifting to Arizona and the mountains of eastern San Diego county. In their ability to move and open new crossing points, smugglers control the border right now. By way of proof, the Mexican economic decline of 1994–6 increased successful illegal entries (measured indirectly) despite significantly higher INS hours devoted to arrests (Singer and Massey 1997: 22–5).

Since the border is not a free fire zone, straightforward violence by the US state is not tolerated. Rather, it is sporadic, rooted in the conduct of individuals and small work groups. Documented criticisms of the Border Patrol include violations of both legal and physical human rights, including some shootings (American Friends Service Committee 1990, 1992; Americas Watch 1992, 1993, 1995; Nagengast, Stavenhagen and Kearney 1992; 'Petition' 1992). Unlike the situation in the Vietnam War, arrest is supposed to be peaceful for violators as well as for bystanders. Also unlike what happens in the Vietnam and narcotics cases, the device of voluntary departure reduces the reasons for violence in the arrest situation – there is little to be gained for the undocumented immigrant in resisting arrest. However, certain aspects of Border Patrol work do create potentials for violence. These include the ideological and political mandate to stop undocumented immigration, the incomplete fulfillment of which frustrates Patrol officers; the fact that smugglers and immigrants, not officers, have the initiative, which is also frustrating; the presence of unaccountable zones near the border; production pressures for numbers; the relative autonomy of officers and superficial regard for restrictive guidelines; and the increase in armaments caused by anti-narcotics interdiction in the same area. Timothy Dunn's most recent work (1997) demonstrates that these factors in the recent immigration build-up are indeed causing human rights harms.

If we are careful about the limits of the analogy, the well-documented patterns of Vietnam do usefully suggest questions about the emerging situation on the Mexican border. In particular, we find in both cases that alienated militarized bureaucracies do not apply effective physical control over more flexible state opponents; and that enforcement workers sometimes violate rights of bystanders and opponents. These observations bring into question the preferred US model for control: mass production of enforcement and the creation of zones outside the rule of law.

State Opponents

We must be cautious about associating undocumented immigrants and smugglers with the NLF and North Vietnamese armies; this implies that all four are equivalent 'enemies at war' with the United States. This element of the analogy is misleading, considering that undocumented labor migration is a tacitly managed illegal market in the US, not a challenge to US geopolitical domination. (Significantly, this deceptive part of the analogy is most heavily used in media imagery about 'wars', drug and immigration, which encourage escalation on the border [Chavez 1997].) A nationalistically charged war directed by a cohesive, top-down Leninist party differs greatly from an illegal market loosely coordinated by smugglers and migrant networks enjoying only a tacit legitimacy among common Mexicans. Importantly, the US state treats such disparate phenomena as parallel forms of resistance or defiance amenable to armed enforcement, as it also does with narcotics. A useful move in the analogy is to ask if this consistent US action induces some guerrilla-like responses in parallel.

The opponents of the US, especially the NLF, the guerrilla and popular front arm that conducted most of the fighting in Vietnam through the Tet offensive of 1968, when it was badly depleted, operated with several distinctive tactical advantages over the US and the Army of the Republic of [South] Vietnam (ARVN): (1) knowledge of the country, terrain and people; (2) trust – the ability to move among the people without betrayal; (3) some direct assistance (for example, intelligence) from the people; (4) flexibility and autonomy for local units, though the ultimate strategy was top-down, not local, as seen in the Tet offensive; (5) dispersion; and (6) surprise, because the NLF usually had the initiative. The NLF was notable in the annals of guerrilla war, but hardly unique; these advantages are widespread, especially when there is tacit popular support (Asprey 1975). The question is, can we usefully encompass certain behaviors of illegal networks in this category of tactics?

Before advancing to this question, however, characterizing 'popular support' in Vietnam will inform such questions about the border. A US study found that Vietnamese peasants would help the NLF when there was not too much risk and what is more important, felt it was unthinkable to betray the NLF to the enemy (Kolko 1985: 136, 134–5, 201–7). Kolko explores how threats to the peasant household economy – ARVN drafting of sons and US bombing of home villages – account for the rejection of the US, even in the face of massive coercion. Uprooted and opportunistic persons increased as the war went on, which was a serious problem for the NLF and sometimes gave the appearance of (purely instrumental) support for the US/South Vietnam. While opportunism was a resource for the dominant state, it was not sufficient to exclude the defiant organization from the populace. Is 'popular support' for undocumented immigration similar?

I suggested above that a vast set of small migrant networks are loosely led and coordinated by smugglers. Unfortunately, there is no thorough study of present-day smuggling at the US–Mexico border; my impression from two periods of fieldwork there (not focused on smuggling *per se*) is that migrant smuggling cliques are small in scale, localized and have members on both sides of the border. Migrants have a good deal of autonomy, since they often cross on their own or with the help of kin, or because they hire the services of smugglers in the first place. Thus, undocumented immigration has elements that promote connectedness and responsiveness to local contexts.

The consensus of INS Patrol officers when I interviewed them in 1991–2 was that undocumented immigrants generally, and smugglers especially, tactically surpassed the INS for the following reasons: (1) use of the terrain and the night (INS electronic night-vision and motion detection devices equalize the contest only until smugglers and migrants move to new paths); (2) surprise and deception (one such tactic is for large numbers of persons to cross; when Patrol officers are occupied arresting the first few, larger groups enter unobstructed); (3) holding the initiative, as explained above; and (4) dispersion and flexibility. I witnessed the role of flexibility in outrunning bureaucratized planning during my observation with the Border Patrol in southern Arizona in 1992. A Patrol station had a checkpoint on the main highway running north from the border (itself a response to an earlier migrant initiative, hiring taxi-cabs as smuggling vehicles on a regular run on this highway). The checkpoint was having its intended effect – slowing down the use of cars for transportation away from the border. However, the undocumented immigrants shifted to a railroad line, where they hitched rides north on the tops and sides of freight cars, or walked the line the fifteen or so miles required to bypass the checkpoint, whereupon a vehicle could pick them up. An officer I accompanied stopped one train, but as it halted the migrants clinging to it escaped into the dense brush alongside the track; there they lurked until the train moved again, when at risk of life and limb they dashed out, leapt on the cars and headed north, triumphant over the Border Patrol.

Besides flexible tactics, the Vietnam analogy (also Leeds 1996) also suggests that two levels of popular support, active help and passive non-betrayal, might play a role on the border. This analogical inquiry requires that we examine the presence of support, if any, among several populations on both sides of the international boundary. First, the boundary and the interior of Mexico offer a haven to smugglers and undocumented immigrants – they can run back, securely regroup and move in search of a new entry point. Undocumented migration to the US is not illegal in Mexico; smuggling for profit is, but when I lived in the border city of Agua Prieta, Sonora, Mexico (1984–6) it was not held to be a reprehensible crime that ought to be reported to the authorities. Rather, Mexicans regarded smugglers as exploitative and tricky (they call them *coyotes*, which refers to the same skulking animal as in English, or *polleros*, pluckers of chickens [immigrants]) but also as necessary adjuncts to illegal immigration, which in turn has considerable legitimacy. Inside Mexico, there is a deep well of sympathy for defying the US immigration laws (see Herrera-Sobek's collection of migrant ballads [1993]). It is an extremely common experience, it is central to the economic survival of many households and Mexicans share widely an interpretative framework of resenting unilaterally imposed US power. For example, my friend Tomás Durazo (a pseudonym), who had spent many years working illegally in the US, and who bore decent personal memories of these times, even to his arrest by the INS, nevertheless burst forth in enthusiastic critique of the US when he and I perused a newspaper article about a mass Border Patrol round-up of undocumented aliens in Texas. This popular lack of sympathy for US policies, together with corruption tolerated by Mexican police and border officials, offers the tactical advantage to smugglers and migrants of using Mexico as a secure base of operations.

Cross-border smuggling requires operations in both nations. Among the Mexican-origin populace in US border cities, who are usually the local majority, there are both toleration and resentment of undocumented migration. Pablo Vila (1997) identifies a strain of Mexican American discourse in El Paso that divides the US self from Mexican immigrant others, who are associated with poverty, welfare and backwardness. This is consistent with my experience in Douglas, Arizona in 1984–6. Interestingly, however, when I witnessed an actual case in Douglas where opinions could have affected the struggle between smugglers and the Border Patrol, the Patrol lost. My close friends Ray and Ginny Rodríguez (pseudonyms) lived next door to a safe house, a place where smuggled migrants, after successful border crossing, wait for rides north. They commented with some annoyance, even resentment, about the large number of men housed there, the constant movement in and out of the house, the backyard cooking, and so on, but they made no move to report it to the police or the Border Patrol. (This might be explained by fear of the smugglers, though I had no indication from them of such concerns.) The Patrol had a superficial, drive-through presence in their dense Mexican-origin *barrio*;[13] they could not have uncovered such houses without intelligence from people like the Rodríguezes. The broader picture is complex. There is some support for INS operations in Latino areas of the border; likewise, in my 1991–2 fieldwork with the INS I listened to officers cultivating local opportunists and informants. But my assessment of the whole situation is that while Mexican-origin persons do not identify with undocumented immigrants, they generally do not betray migrants to the government.

Vila's (1997) research with Anglo-Americans shows greater distance from undocumented immigrants. There have even been demonstrations of Anglo folk militarism directed against undocumented immigrants. While significant at the political level of escalation, at the tactical level this does not greatly affect the border, because Anglo-Americans dominate only a few sections of the boundary, notably some beach neighborhoods in south San Diego county and some ranch areas. Border rural settlements, Anglo, Latino and Indian, are highly varied, and we know little about their role in smuggling, even though their terrain is central to guerrilla-like tactics in this region. Border Patrol officers, according to my interviews, live mostly in outlying suburban developments in border towns, which simply reinforces their alienation from the places and people, *barrio* and ranch, who make undocumented migration possible.

Review of the border suggests weakness in dominant state power. The flexible and non-bureaucratic conduct of state opponents trumps clumsy bureaucratic enforcers. Meanwhile, a general reluctance of the populace to help the dominant state hobbles its intelligence. These guerrilla-like advantages of the state opponents undermine US governmental credibility and exacerbate the escalatory cycle, since they are strong and persistent. Thus, the Vietnam analogy to the border offers more than just two failed/failing policies put side-by-side; it suggests that a state-centered policy critique is not enough, that understanding the state opposition is essential.

Secondary States

The state–illegality problematic often involves more than one state and more than one legal ideology. Although not a case of crime, in Vietnam the US political and legal order was exported on to Vietnamese soil in the form of the Republic of Vietnam (South Vietnam), while the nationalist and communist alternative was embodied in the Democratic Republic of Vietnam, aided by the external states of the Soviet Union and China. Given the focus on US immigration policy in this chapter, I will not launch on an extended discussion of Mexico as a secondary state; but it is worth essaying a few observations. First, popular legitimacy in Mexico makes possible the smuggling market and border-crossing tactics. A secondary state is thus necessary for the persistent illegality in the primary state. Unlike South Vietnam, second, Mexico's government has true national legitimacy, a form of legitimacy that is most salient in relation to the US, while weakest on issues of economic and political order inside Mexico. As I mentioned, Mexicans are particularly critical of US immigration control. Yet, third, Mexico is economically dependent on the US, and what is more important, US state elites underwrite the internal projects of Mexico's state elites. A good example is the Clinton administration's struggles to pass NAFTA and calm domestic US criticism of Mexico's narcotics control in order to underwrite the Mexican project of neo-liberalism (the latter described in Vásquez-León's Chapter 8). Yet recently, as part of its desperate attempt to capture the initiative on the border, the US has pressured Mexico to enforce laws against immigrant smuggling and to let the INS conduct more extensive operations inside Mexico (it already gathers significant intelligence there). Mexico's state elite, therefore, faces a real contradiction between the corrosive, delegitimizing pressures of the US and their nationalist imperative to preserve autonomy (Toro 1995 is an excellent source on this contradiction in the case of narcotics). The credibility of the Mexican state, not especially strong anyway, is put at considerable risk.

Concluding Observations

The favored US response to political defiance and illegality, in selected cases, is to crush it by force. The intentions of the US state are frustrated, however, because of guerrilla-like tactics with popular underpinnings. This loss of credibility leads to escalation, in which force follows failure that follows force. One danger of the US model is that it puts alienated, militarized bureaucracies into the field, seemingly advanced and professional but in fact clumsy and ineffectual and worse yet, intermittently harming the rights of bystanders and opponents. As frustrating as such escalatory cycles may seem, one might suppose them necessary to defend order and law. But behind such escalations there are important contexts misunderstood, illegalities and alliances accepted and alternatives ignored. This is the actual lesson of Vietnam for the border: not that the border is a 'quagmire' like Vietnam (each case has its own historical dynamics), but that the US model of militarized control is deeply flawed. Escalation is not inevitable, though; in a democracy it should be subject to public debate and choice. We can gain more rational control over our future through democratic accountability for state elites.

An important question emerging from this chapter is why the US engages in this type of response to political defiance and certain oppositional types of illegality. Looking at the chapters in this book, we can (as a first-order model) draw a continuum of state ruler responses to persistent illegalities, from alliance, through toleration, to escalation of suppressive force. For example, Vásquez-León's Chapter 8 describes the Mexican government's shift from tolerance of informal arrangements in shrimping toward outright illegalization and prosecution; interestingly, this change is taking place in the same political and economic context of North American free trade and social polarization as Mexico–US immigration. I start my approach to the continuum topic with the assertion that states, like their opponents, are no more than organized systems of violence and revenue (see Tilly 1985). But states *are* different, because in taking the state form, their elites lay claim to particular crystallizations of political and legal legitimacy. Some legitimacies are very superficial, like South Vietnam. Other states inherit quite powerful legitimacy from important political moments of the past, as the Mexican state has with anti-US nationalism. The credibility of state elites means that they must guard the appearance of ruling legitimacy, although other objectives, such as revenue and geopolitical power, may cause state rulers to ally with illegal networks. For example, US state rulers go covertly to illegal networks to get loose money, guns, etc. whose public acquisition would require flaunting an illegitimate goal, such as support for heroin smuggling (see McCoy 1991). Because visible geopolitical and domestic credibility is an important resource to state elites, they deeply fear its loss. On such occasions they may turn against their own contacts with and toleration of illegality. My argument has been that domestic US anxiety forced somewhat reluctant US central government actors to turn against tolerated illegal markets in migrant labor. Inability to truly effect this reversal, however, resulted in an escalatory cycle. We still have to ask why some illegal or defiant actors threaten credibility and others do not. I have no good answer for that. There is still much to be learned about why particular historical state–illegal practice combinations come to rest at different points on the continuum.

Finally, it is worth contemplating the consequences of the US government's treating all these people, Vietnamese peasants and revolutionaries, drug and immigrant smugglers, Andean coca growers and Mexican undocumented workers, as if they are 'resisting' the US military/political machine. By listing all these cases, I express skepticism that all 'resist' the US state in the same way, or even at all; undocumented immigrants in a tolerated illegal labor market, for example, contribute measurably to US state revenues (Fix and Passel 1994). The other studies in this book similarly do not support a simple equation of illegality and resistance. Yet that is how the US state treats all these cases. In the instance of the Mexican border, for example, escalating US enforcement creates a tactical alliance between undocumented immigrants and alien smugglers, despite the collective Mexican distrust of such persons, seen in terms such as *coyote* and *pollero*. As a result, immigrants are thrust into a covert underworld, where they are sometimes exploited, vulnerable to both the US immigration police and their erstwhile allies, the smugglers (Heyman 1998). Once we go beyond simply seeing illegality as a separated anti-state or immoral margin (Nugent, this book, Chapter 3), we can understand and seek to change the actual historical situations that do place people, often poor and peaceful, beyond the pale.

Notes

1 Interestingly, the number of apprehensions at the border, showing very indirectly the trends in numbers of undocumented entrants, has not increased in the last ten years; it peaked in 1986 at 1.7 million, then dipped to about one million, and in Fiscal Year 1997 looks to be about 1.3 million (*Migration News* 1997). Thus, the escalation of force is not simply a proportionate response to increases in the size of the 'problem'.

2. This brief passage summarizes many arguments and sources about current US immigration policy. Justification and documentation for my arguments can be found in Heyman (1995, 1998a, b), while an independent but parallel line of analysis can be found in Calavita (1994).

3. This pattern of action broadly fits Roy Rappaport's (1993) criticism of 'problem-solving', in which problems are isolated from their contexts, and inappropriately large amounts of effort are directed at their solution, often exacerbating the underlying contextual causes.

4. 'Anglo-Americans' or 'Anglos' is a quasi-ethnic label used in the western US for persons who are not immigrants, not Latino or Asian, and also not Black. It does not refer only to persons of English ancestry.
5. Certainly, this is not to ignore other measures, such as increasing the legal vulnerability of undocumented and even legal immigrants once inside the US by cutting off the rights to legal appeals against deportation, by denying them social services, etc.
6. The INS operations at the border rarely fit low-intensity doctrine; for example, except in some anti-narcotics work, they do not involve close work with local people, informers, etc. Truthfully, nearly all patrolling against undocumented immigrants, including alien smugglers, and most against narcotics smugglers, is barrier-based interdiction (see the descriptions in Heyman 1995). But Vietnam, with its reliance on airmobility, firepower, and anonymous killing, did not resemble Maxwell Taylor's doctrine of counterinsurgency either. Dunn's important book (1996) shows that the importance of low-intensity conflict doctrine is instead its ideological power inside the US government, a magic talisman in a world of complex social processes, in this case border migration, which justifies the manpower and equipment used in cruder modes of forceful interdiction.
7. Doris Meissner, the INS commissioner throughout this period, was associated inside the INS with de-emphasis of the border in favor of non-border immigration policing (e.g., apprehending persons who overstay visas), employment control and asylum policy reform; other factions in the INS favored anti-narcotics.
8. Congress traditionally favors the Border Patrol because of its tough image as the guardian of the US's boundaries, by contrast with the more complex, less romantic immigration-processing tasks of other INS branches (Juffras 1991).
9. The political use of apprehension numbers has changed in interesting ways, but this number as a (misguided) measure of US immigration policy remains pre-eminent. Before the Reyes doctrine, more apprehensions were seen as good by the INS, since it showed their greater effort, and also greater need (incorrectly implying that more arrests meant more persons trying to enter the US). The Reyes doctrine emphasized deterrence, so now the emphasis is on reducing the number of arrests, both in local sectors and border-wide. In the latter sense, apprehension statistics have shown some 'successes' (El Paso) and some 'failures' (San Diego county); but overall arrests at the border were up from 1994 to 1996.

10. Arrests are a more reliable figure than body counts, however – less prone to outright fakery because each arrest is physically recorded and signed for.
11. The Border Patrol can be contrasted with INS Inspectors, the officers who regulate admission of persons at legal ports of entry on the border. In my 1991–2 interviews, inspectors were more Latino than any other branch. They are commonly hired and assigned in their home border town. There is less branch *esprit de corps*, and more local port identification. Because inspectors wave people through the border as easily as they arrest them, they can become enmeshed in complex, localistic webs of gossip, favoritism, tolerated illegal markets, etc.
12. About half of undocumented Mexican immigrants use smugglers (Chavez, Flores and López-Garza 1990), a figure that appears to have increased because of the intensification of enforcement in the 1990s.
13. *Barrio*, the Spanish word for neighborhood, is used in the US southwest for concentrated, often long-established Mexican American neighborhoods. In this sense, it is a distinctive social space for US immigration law enforcement.

Acknowledgements

The research for this chapter was supported by grants from the Harry Frank Guggenheim Foundation and the Wenner-Gren Foundation for Anthropological Research. It was presented first at a conference on States and Illegal Networks sponsored by the Wenner-Gren Foundation, and second at the American Anthropological Association 1997 meetings. I thank the participants at both sessions for their comments and for assisting me with sources. I also thank the foundations for their support. All responsibility for errors of fact and interpretation remains my own.

References

American Friends Service Committee (1990), *Human Rights at the Mexico–U.S. Border*. Second Annual Report, Immigration Law Enforcement Monitoring Project, Philadelphia: American Friends Service Committee.

—— (1992), *Sealing Our Borders: The Human Toll*. Third Annual Report, Immigration Law Enforcement Monitoring Project. Philadelphia: American Friends Service Committee.

Americas Watch (1992), *Brutality Unchecked: Human Rights Abuses*

Along the U.S. Border with Mexico. New York: Human Rights Watch.
—— (1993), *Frontier Injustice: Human Rights Abuses Along the U.S. Border with Mexico Persist Amid Climate of Impunity*. New York: Human Rights Watch.
—— (1995), *Crossing the Line: Human Rights Abuses Along the U.S. Border with Mexico Persist Amid Climate of Impunity.* New York: Human Rights Watch.
Andreas, Peter (1997), 'Changing Border Games: The Escalation of U.S. Immigration Control in the Post-NAFTA Era', a paper presented at the 1997 meeting of the American Political Science Association, Washington, DC.
Asprey, Robert B. (1975), *War in the Shadows: The Guerrilla in History*, Vols. 1 & 2. New York: Doubleday.
Bean, Frank, *et al.* (1994), 'Illegal Mexican Migration and the United States/Mexico Border: The Effects of Operation Hold-the-Line on El Paso/Juarez', unpublished MS from the Population Research Center, University of Texas at Austin, 15 July 1994, cited in *Migration News* vol. 1(2) and 1(8), located on the internet at the University of California, Davis (http: //migration.ucdavis.edu/archive/mn_94/).
Brinkley, Joel (1994), 'A Rare Success at the Border Brought Scant Official Praise', *New York Times* 14 Sept. 1995, p. 1.
Calavita, Kitty (1990), 'Employer Sanctions Violations: Toward a Dialectical Model of White-Collar Crime', *Law and Society Review* 24: 1041–69.
—— (1994), 'U.S. Immigration and Policy Responses: The Limits of Legislation', in Wayne A. Cornelius, Philip L. Martin, and James F. Hollifield (eds), *Controlling Immigration: A Global Perspective*. Stanford, CA: Stanford University Press, pp. 55–82.
Chavez, Leo R. (1992), *Shadowed Lives: Undocumented Immigrants in American Society*. Ft. Worth: Harcourt, Brace, Jovanovich College Publishers.
—— (1997), 'The Construction of an Anti-Mexican Discourse: An Analysis of Popular Magazine Images', a paper presented at the 1997 annual meeting of the American Anthropological Association, Washington, DC.
——, Estevan T. Flores and Marta López-Garza (1990), 'Here Today, Gone Tomorrow? Undocumented Settlers and Immigration Reform', *Human Organization* 49: 193–205.
Dunn, Timothy (1996), *The Militarization of the U.S.–Mexico Border 1978–1992: Low-Intensity Doctrine Conflict Comes Home.* Austin: Center for Mexican American Studies, University of Texas at Austin.

—— (1997), 'Border Enforcement and Human Rights Violations in the Southwest', in Chris Ellison and W. Alan Maritin (eds), *Race and Ethnic Relations in the United States: Readings for the Twenty-First Century*. Los Angeles: Roxbury.

Fix, Michael, and Jeffrey S. Passel (1994), *Immigration and Immigrants: Setting the Record Straight*. Washington, DC: The Urban Institute.

Gibson, James William (1988), *The Perfect War: The War We Couldn't Lose and How We Did*. New York: Random House.

Goltz, Sonia M. (1997), 'Escalation Research: Providing New Frontiers for Reciprocal Influences of Organizational Behavior and Behavior Analysis', a paper presented at the 1997 Association for Behavior Analysis conference, Chicago, IL.

Halberstam, David (1972), *The Best and the Brightest*. New York: Random House.

Herrera-Sobek, María (1993), *Northward Bound: The Mexican Migrant Experience in Ballad and Song*. Bloomington, IN: Indiana University Press.

Heyman, Josiah McC. (1995), 'Putting Power in the Anthropology of Bureaucracy: The Immigration and Naturalization Service at the Mexico–United States Border', *Current Anthropology* 36: 261–87.

—— (1998a), 'Immigration Law Enforcement and the Superexploitation of Undocumented Aliens: The Mexico–United States Border Case', *Critique of Anthropology* 18: 157–80.

—— (1998b), *Finding a Moral Heart for U.S. Immigration Policy: An Anthropological Perspective*. American Ethnological Society Monograph No. 7. Washington, DC: American Anthropological Association.

Juffras, Jason (1991), *Impact of the Immigration Reform and Control Act on the Immigration and Naturalization Service*, The Rand Corporation Report JR-09; The Urban Institute Report 91-08. Santa Monica and Washington, DC: The Rand Corporation and The Urban Institute.

Kadetsky, Elizabeth (1994), '"Save Our State" Initiative: Bashing Illegals in California', *The Nation* 259: 416–22.

Kahin, George McT. (1986), *Intervention: How America Became Involved in Vietnam*. New York: Alfred Knopf.

Kahn, Robert S. (1996), *Other People's Blood: U.S. Immigration Prisons in the Reagan Decade*. Boulder, CO: Westview.

Klare, Michael T., and Peter Kornbluh (eds) (1988), *Low Intensity Warfare: Counterinsurgency, Proinsurgency, and Antiterrorism in the Eighties*. New York: Pantheon.

Kolko, Gabriel (1985), *Anatomy of a War: Vietnam, The United States, and Modern Historical Experience.* New York: Pantheon.

Koulish, Robert E. (1992), 'Systematic Deterrence Against Prospective Asylum Seekers: A Study of the South Texas Immigration District', *New York University Review of Law and Social Change* 19: 529–70.

Leeds, Elizabeth (1996), 'Cocaine and Parallel Polities in the Brazilian Urban Periphery: Constraints on Local-Level Democratization', *Latin American Research Review* 31(3): 47–84.

McCoy, Alfred (1991), *The Politics of Heroin: CIA Complicity in the Global Drug Trade.* Brooklyn: Lawrence and Hill.

McMahon, Robert J. (1991a), 'Interpreting America's Failures in the Third World', *Diplomatic History* 15: 131–6.

—— (1991b), 'Credibility and World Power: Exploring the Psychological Dimension in Postwar American Diplomacy', *Diplomatic History* 15: 455–72.

—— (1994), *The Cold War on the Periphery: The United States, India, and Pakistan.* New York: Columbia University Press.

Migration News (1996a), 'INS: Sanctions, Apprehensions, Immigration, and Naturalizations' *Migration News* (April 1996), http://migration.ucdavis.edu/By-Month/MN-Vol-3-96/MN_Apr_96.html.

—— (1996b), 'Immigration Overhaul' *Migration News* (October 1996), http://migration.ucdavis.edu/By-Month/MN-Vol-3-96/MN_Oct_96.html.

—— (1997), 'INS: Enforcement, Deportations, Sponsorship: Border Enforcement' *Migration News* (November 1997), http://migration.ucdavis.edu/archive/mn_97/nov_97-02.html

Nagengast, Carole, Rodolfo Stavenhagen, and Michael Kearney (1992), *Human Rights and Indigenous Workers: The Mixtecs in Mexico and the United States*, Current Issue Brief No. 4. La Jolla, CA: Center for U.S.–Mexican Studies, University of California, San Diego.

New York Times (1996), 'Border Patrol Accused of Falsifying Files on Illegal Immigration Crackdown', *New York Times* 14 July 1996, p. 12.

Perea, Juan F. (ed.) (1997), *Immigrants Out! The New Nativism and the Anti-Immigrant Impulse in the United States*. New York: New York University Press.

'Petition' (1992), Petition to the Inter-American Commission on Human Rights of the Organization of American States. Los Angeles: Peter A. Schey, Designated Attorney of Record.

Rappaport, Roy A. (1993), 'Distinguished Lecture in General Anthropology: The Anthropology of Trouble', *American Anthropologist* 95: 295–303.

Rodríguez, Néstor P. (1997), 'The Social Construction of the U.S.–Mexico Border', in Juan F. Perea (ed.) *Immigrants Out! The New Nativism and the Anti-Immigrant Impulse in the United States*. New York: New York University Press, pp. 223–43.

Schurmann, Franz (1974), *The Logic of World Power: An Inquiry into the Origins, Currents, and Contradictions of World Politics*. New York: Pantheon.

Sheehan, Neil (1988), *A Bright Shining Lie: John Paul Vann and America in Vietnam*. New York: Random House.

Singer, Audrey, and Douglas S. Massey (1997), 'The Social Process of Undocumented Border Crossing', a paper presented at the 1997 meetings of the Latin American Studies Association, Guadalajara, Mexico.

Skolnick, Jerome H. (1966), *Justice Without Trial: Law Enforcement in Democratic Society.* New York: Wiley.

Stefancic, Jean (1997), 'Funding the Nativist Agenda', in Juan F. Perea (ed.) *Immigrants Out! The New Nativism and the Anti-Immigrant Impulse in the United States.* New York: New York University Press, pp. 119–35.

Tilly, Charles (1985), 'War Making and State Making as Organized Crime', in Peter Evans, Dietrich Rueschemeyer, and Theda Skocpol (eds), *Bringing the State Back In*. Cambridge, UK: Cambridge University Press, pp. 169–91.

Toro, María Celia (1995), *Mexico's "War" on Drugs: Causes and Consequences.* Boulder, CO: Lynne Reinner.

US Commission on Immigration Reform (1994), *U.S. Immigration Policy: Restoring Credibility*. Washington, DC: US GPO.

US Immigration and Naturalization Service (n.d. [1992]), 1986–1991 Summary of Resources by Program. MS, files of author.

Vila, Pablo (1997), 'Narrative Identities: The Employment of the Mexican on the U.S.–Mexican Border', *The Sociological Quarterly* 38: 147–83.

Young, Marilyn B. (1991), *The Vietnam Wars, 1945–1990*. New York: Harper and Row.

List of Contributors

Thomas W. Gallant (Ph.D. Cambridge) teaches history and anthropology in the Department of History at the University of Florida. He has published a book *(Risk and Survival in Ancient Greece: Reconstructing the Rural Domestic Economy*) and numerous articles on the social history and historical anthropology of southern Europe and the Mediterranean, with particular emphasis on the themes of peasant economics, imperialism and law, gender and identity, and honor and violence.

Josiah McC. Heyman (Ph.D., City University of New York) is associate professor of anthropology at Michigan Technological University. He is the author of *Life and Labor on the Border: Working People of Northeastern Sonora, Mexico, 1886–1986* and *Giving a Moral Heart to U.S. Immigration Policy: An Anthropological Perspective*, as well as articles in *Current Anthropology, American Ethnologist, Journal of the Royal Anthropological Institute, Research in Economic Anthropology, Journal of Political Ecology,* and *Critique of Anthropology*. In addition to his work on states, immigration, borders and bureaucracy seen here, he has also written about working classes, consumption and material culture.

Caroline Humphrey obtained a BA in Social Anthropology from the University of Cambridge in 1965, an MA in Mongolian Studies from the University of Leeds in 1971, and a Ph.D. in Social Anthropology from the University of Cambridge in 1973. She is currently a Fellow of King's College and Reader in Asian Anthropology at the University of Cambridge. She has carried out anthropological research in the USSR / Russia, Mongolia, Nepal, India and Inner Mongolia (China). She is author of books on Inner Asian pastoralism, collective farms in Russia, theories of ritual, and Mongolian shamanism. She has also published articles on gender, kinship, economic exchange and barter, Jainism, Buddhism, and Post-Socialist transformations. Her book *Karl Marx Collective* , newly updated as *Marx Went Away – But Karl Stayed Behind*, won the J. I. Staley prize for outstanding work in anthropology.

Alfred W. McCoy is professor of Southeast Asian History at the University of Wisconsin–Madison. Educated at Columbia (BA), the University of California–Berkeley (MA), and Yale (Ph.D.), he has spent the past quarter-century writing about modern Southeast Asian history, focusing on two topics – modern Philippine history and the political economy of opium in the Golden Triangle. He is the author of several books on Philippine history, two of which have won that country's National Book Award – *Philippine Cartoons* (Manila, 1985) and *Anarchy of Families* (Manila, 1994). His book *The Politics of Heroin in Southeast Asia* (New York, 1972) aroused considerable controversy at the time of its publication. Now regarded as a standard work on the subject, it has remained in print for a quarter-century and has been translated into eight languages.

Barbara A. Miller is an Ethnographer at the Vera Institute of Justice. She is completing her Ph.D. in Cultural Anthropology at New York University. She has published two books for teenage readers on contemporary social issues.

David Nugent received his Ph.D. from Columbia University in 1988, and is currently Associate Professor of Anthropology at Colby College. He is the author of *Modernity at the Edge of Empire: State, Individual, and Nation in the Northern Peruvian Andes, 1885–1935* (Stanford University Press, 1997). He has also published in *American Anthropologist, American Ethnologist* and *Man*. His 1993 article, 'Property Relations, Production Relations and Inequality: Anthropology, Political Economy, and the Blackfeet', published in *American Ethnologist,* 20(2) 1993, won the 1994 Robert F. Heizer Prize of the American Society for Ethnohistory.

Jane Schneider (Ph.D., University of Michigan) teaches anthropology at the Graduate School of the City University of New York and is co-author, with Peter Schneider, of two books: *Culture and Political Economy in Western Sicily* (1976), and *Festival of the Poor: Fertility Decline and the Ideology of Class in Sicily* (1996). She is editor of *Italy's 'Southern Question': Orientalism in One Country* (Berg, 1998), and co-editor (with Annette B. Weiner) of *Cloth and Human Experience* (1987). Her current research focus is the Antimafia Movement in Palermo.

Peter Schneider (Ph.D., University of Michigan), Professor of Sociology at Fordham University, has been engaged, with the collaboration of Jane Schneider, in a series of research projects dating from the 1960s that have charted Sicily's transformation from a predominantly agrarian society to one that is both urban and urbane. Having co-authored two books on this transformation (see entry for Jane Schneider), he is currently completing research on the changing relationship of the mafia and 'antimafia' in Sicily, in preparation for a forthcoming book.

Alan Smart (Ph.D. University of Toronto) is an associate professor and Head at the Department of Anthropology, University of Calgary, and has been conducting field research in Hong Kong and China since 1982. He is the author of *Making Room: Squatter Clearance in Hong Kong* (Hong Kong: Centre of Asian Studies) and articles in journals such as *Cultural Anthropology, Critique of Anthropology, International Journal of Urban and Regional Research, Society and Space,* and a variety of edited volumes.

Mercer L. Sullivan (Ph.D., Columbia) is Senior Research Fellow at the Vera Institute of Justice in New York, and Associate Professor at the School of Criminal Justice at Rutgers University. He is the author of *Getting Paid: Youth Crime and Work in the Inner City*, published by Cornell University Press.

Marcela Vásquez-León (Ph.D., University of Arizona) is anAdjunct Research Scientist at the Bureau of Applied Research in Anthropology, University of Arizona. She has engaged in research on the political ecology of fishing communities and on the analyses of fisheries management strategies in the Gulf of California, Mexico. She has also done research on land use change in Sonora, Mexico as part of a larger effort that attempts to understand the human dimensions of global environmental change. She has published articles in *Journal of Political Ecology* (1994) and *Maritime Anthropological Studies* (1994, with Thomas McGuire), and authored several chapters in T. McGuire and J. Greenberg (eds), *Maritime Community and Biosphere Reserve: Crisis and Response in the Upper Gulf of California*, Occasional Paper No.2, Bureau of Applied Research in Anthropology, University of Arizona.

Index